THE
100
BEST
STOCKS
TO BUY IN
2015

PETER SANDER
AND
SCOTT BOBO

AVON, MASSACHUSETTS

Published by
Adams Media, a division of F+W Media, Inc.
57 Littlefield Street, Avon, MA 02322. U.S.A.
www.adamsmedia.com

ISBN 10: 1-4405-8005-7
ISBN 13: 978-1-4405-8005-5
eISBN 10: 1-4405-8006-5
eISBN 13: 978-1-4405-8006-2

Printed in the United States of America.

10 9 8 7 6 5 4 3 2 1

Cover design by Elisabeth Lariviere.

This book is available at quantity discounts for bulk purchases.
For information, please call 1-800-289-0963.

Contents

I. THE ART AND SCIENCE OF INVESTING IN STOCKS / 5

II. THE 100 BEST STOCKS TO BUY / 53

Dedication

We continue to dedicate this book to all of you active investors who have the sense of purpose and independence of thought to make your own investing decisions—or at least to ask the right questions. You continue to be wise enough—and inquisitive enough—to realize that not all the answers can be found in one place and smart enough to seek the convenience of a good place to start.

Acknowledgments

Peter would like to again recognize his coauthor, research partner, and life friend Scott Bobo, who continually brings his insight and humor to help make complex matters simple, interesting, and fun. He also recognizes—and endorses—the good work of Value Line, Inc. and their Investment Survey, which does more than any other known source to turn piles of facts and figures into a simple readable page. Next, no book happens without the added value of exercise to keep a body in shape and a mind clear, and to that end he offers his thanks to his exercise companions. And of course his boys Julian and Jonathan and life partner Marjorie inspire him to do this book year after year.

Scott would like to acknowledge the tireless efforts of his friend and coauthor Peter Sander in setting and keeping a high standard in the research and writing of this series. His diligence is what makes these books and our readers successful. Scott's wife Lorie continues to train Scott in the fine art of dissecting financial statements and has yet to complain about the bread crumbs on the keyboard. Scott's brother and sister, in spite of everything, still pick up the phone when he calls. Finally, Scott would like to acknowledge his mother's fearless spirit as a source of inspiration.

PART I

THE ART AND SCIENCE OF INVESTING IN STOCKS

By Peter Sander

The Art and Science of Investing in Stocks

It isn't news to most of you. The stock markets were up more than 20 percent in 2013–2014.

And boy, were we worried. We were worried that for the first time in our five-year history tending the helm of *The 100 Best Stocks to Buy*, all the work we did and all the reading you did to climb on board with our thinking would lead you to a poorer performance than if you simply bought an S&P 500 index fund. All that work—all that work for naught.

We reviewed our performance in early March, and we were a couple of percentage points behind the benchmark S&P 500 index. Up almost 18 percent, but behind. Ugh.

And we weren't the only ones who fretted about this. Warren Buffett, the indisputable master of the art, was also trailing the S&P by a similar margin with his Berkshire Hathaway portfolio.

Misery loves company, and who could want more than the company of the likes of Mr. Buffett? But what we really want is happy readers . . . and happy investors.

Alas, the story has a happy ending.

Turns out, our *100 Best Stocks* performance had faltered due to a short-term pullback in our generally favored form of investment: dividend-paying stocks. The reins at the Fed had just been turned over to Janet Yellen, and uncertainty around that, plus the gradual and ongoing reduction of "quantitative easing" led to an uptick in interest rates, which made our dividend-paying stocks look relatively less attractive. For about three years the average S&P dividend yield has exceeded average ten-year Treasury yields, but with these changes, would that continue to be the case? Investors, large and small, began to sell dividend payers in favor of (1) less risky Treasury securities or (2) more "growth"-oriented issues, such as Facebook, Amazon, and others in the Internet, biotech, and other more "energetic" spaces in the market.

That left us holding the bag, kind of—at least for a moment. We still felt our dividend-seeking strategy was right, especially because we not only seek yield but also *growth* in the dividend. As you'll see later, almost two-thirds of our picks have raised their dividends for at least eight of the past ten years (perhaps taking a couple off for the Great Recession), and 45 of our *100 Best Stocks* have raised consistently for ten years, hell or high water notwithstanding.

So at the end of the day, we're about growth, too—just a different kind of growth.

In the end, the markets came back our way. The high flyers began to sell off, and the steadier market performers resumed their upward march once more. By April 1, 2014, our *100 Best* list gained 23.85 percent for the measurement period, including dividends, compared to 22.4 percent for the S&P, also including dividends.

Whew. We made it. Did we think our list would ever return almost 24 percent in one year? In last year's edition of this book, we sounded a very defensive note; we didn't think even last year's 19.2 percent gain was sustainable, let alone something to improve upon, for 2014. We continued to "ride our horses," changing only eight picks going into 2014, despite complaints from some of our detracting readers that we "offer nothing new" from year to year.

That complaint notwithstanding, our approach remains "sell when there's something better to buy." So we didn't "sell" much going into 2014. We remain defensive and quite convinced that 24 percent won't happen in again 2015; in fact, we'd be happy with anything in the 5–10 percent range (and of course, beating the S&P 500). However, albeit while making us a little nervous, we did rotate 13 new picks into our 2015 *100 Best Stocks* list. We abandoned some paper stocks, utility stocks, and what we felt were a few too many "consumer staples" issues in favor of a bit greater embrace of world change, sprinkled with a few traditional branding standbys like Ralph Lauren and Allstate. Oops, we usually don't talk about specific picks this early in the narrative but thought you might be curious. Sticking to our investing guns, though, even these new, more growth-oriented picks all pay steady, worthwhile, and growing dividends and are generally leaders in their marketplaces while keeping the interests of their shareholders in mind.

Back to the other "theme" of this opening narrative: what you, as a reader, get from the 2015 edition of *The 100 Best Stocks to Buy* as you hold this copy in your hands (or on your e-reader, as the case may be). Many of you read our book every year to get our latest "take" on the market and 100 "takes" on what we think are the best individual investments for individual investors. Once again, we'd like to acknowledge—that is, we'd like to *thank you directly* for—your loyalty. Without that loyalty, especially in today's publishing environment, neither this nor any future editions of this book would likely happen.

We do listen. We listened to an ongoing complaint that our picks and our narrative weren't "fresh" enough, having been constructed in the early spring of the previous year without even the benefit of a single earnings report for the year prior to the picked year under our belt. For our 2014 list, many of our picks were taken before even the first 2013 earnings release was out, and a few of them hadn't even provided their final financials for the year 2012.

We respond to that by reminding you that the attractive (and detractive) features of our picks don't normally change quarter to quarter or even year to year. That's on purpose. Too, despite technology's latest, it still takes time to publish a book, and because of that, we've always recommended this book as a place to *start*—not finish—your research.

But we also responded by moving the publishing schedule back a bit so our narratives and numbers are fresher. What you see here is largely based on April–June, not February–May information. We hope you notice a difference, but we don't think it will be a *huge* difference.

Another "change" we made for last year was the unveiling of my (Peter's) personal e-mail address, mainly to receive inquiries and get feedback. Although any author does this with a bit of trepidation, we were delighted with the result. We got excellent inquiries and useful feedback from a number of you. So here goes—we'll do it again—my email address is *ginsander@hotmail.com*. Keep the feedback coming.

A couple of you asked how well our picks had done in the long term. It's a great question, and we, being engineering-minded long-term investors, dedicated to the proposition of measured performance, decided to find out. So we did a little analysis, presented later in this section (in Table 0.2), and we think you'll be pleased with the results. We were.

Those of you who have been with us for a while may note that we've cut out a few "traditional" pieces of this narrative covering strategic investing and some of the principles of value investing. We did that for three reasons. First, many of you loyal readers have read (or not read) the same material over and over—that's not a good thing. Second, the length of our individual stock narratives has been increasing, and we thought you'd rather have more information there, and less up front. Third, many if not most of these principles are available in my other books for those of you new (or not so new) to the game, most specifically my *The 25 Habits of Highly Successful Investors*, also from this publisher, and *All About Low Volatility Investing*, which McGraw-Hill released in early 2014.

Needless to say, technique and philosophy are important, and we won't abandon their discussion in this book. However, our purpose here is to give you some investing ideas and to share some rationale for how we came up with them, and we remain faithful to both purposes in the ever more complex and rapidly changing investment environment we find ourselves in as we enter 2015.

As we like to say: *"Invest long and prosper."* Our sole objective is to do whatever we can do to help you do that. Thanks for being one of our readers, and for many of you, thanks again for being a loyal reader through the years.

Beating the Averages—Most of Them, Anyhow

Last year we did so well against most of the major market sectors that we decided, as sort of an experiment, to do a little more formal analysis of where our horse finished among all the others running the race. So we created a "Table 0.1" comparing the performance of the *100 Best Stocks* list against major sector benchmarks as measured by Lipper, a division of Thomson Reuters and major supplier of quality financial information and analytics especially for the mutual fund sector.

Last year, we came in second, beaten out *only* by the Health/Biotech sector. We'll take that. This year, a resurgent European market, a strong tech sector, and surprising strength in the financial sector beat us out; we came in number five in a field of 40. Not bad, we'll take that, too. Especially given the volatility in the Health/Biotech and Science/Technology sectors, and with our long-held skepticism of the Financial sector (we continue to carry only three stocks from that sector).

▼ **Table 0.1: Performance Compared to Major Benchmarks**

100 BEST STOCKS 2014 COMPARED TO LIPPER MUTUAL FUND INDEX BENCHMARKS
ONE-YEAR PERFORMANCE, APRIL 1, 2013–APRIL 1, 2014

Fund Benchmark	1-year return	Fund Benchmark	1-year return
Health/Biotech	37.0%	International Multicap Growth	14.8%
Science and Technology	29.9%	Utility	14.1%
European Region	26.5%	International Large Cap Growth	13.2%
Financial Services	24.2%	Japan Region	8.9%
100 BEST STOCKS TO BUY 2014	23.9%	China Region	8.5%
International Small/Mid Cap Value	22.4%	High Yield Bond	6.7%
International Small/Mid Cap Core	20.4%	Real Estate	3.7%
International Small/Mid Cap Growth	20.3%	Multisector Income	2.7%
International Multicap Value	20.2%	Pacific Ex-Japan	2.6%
Telecommunications	19.2%	Pacific Region	1.7%
Global Large Cap Value	19.2%	General Bond	1.0%
Global Multicap Growth	19.0%	Emerging Markets	0.7%
Global Multicap Value	18.9%	Short U.S. Government	−0.3%
Global Large Cap Core	18.7%	Short/Intermediate U.S. Government	−1.0%
Global Large Cap Growth	17.4%	General U.S. Government	−1.8%
Natural Resources	17.0%	General U.S. Treasury	−3.0%
Global Multicap Core	16.7%	Intermediate Municipal Debt	−3.8%
International Large Cap Value	16.3%	Inflation Protected Bond	−5.8%
International Multicap Core	15.7%	Latin American	−15.1%
International Large Cap Core	15.5%	Precious Metals Equity	−31.0%

Source: Lipper/Thomson Reuters, Barron's Weekly

A Five-Year Stretch Run

We recently realized that it's been five years since we took over the publication of the *100 Best Stocks to Buy* series from John Slatter, the previous author. That, and a couple of poignant reader queries got us to ask ourselves: "So how well did we do?" How well did we achieve the goals of applying solid, value-based, marketplace-based investing techniques and philosophies to picking great companies, the 100 Best of them for you to invest in? More simply stated, would you have been better off to not buy our book, not take the time to pursue individual stock investing, and throw it over the wall to a low-cost S&P 500 index fund?

Although we've beaten the S&P every year, sometimes by a lot, sometimes by not so much, we approached this analysis nervously, wondering if what we did was really worthwhile. Wondering whether it really produced value for you, the individual investor.

We don't have a lot of fancy Wall Street–style analytical tools at our disposal, ones that can do deep analysis of things like "risk-adjusted" returns. But we did examine our results for the past five years, starting with The *100 Best Stocks to Buy* 2010 list, and compared that to our S&P 500 benchmark. We compounded the return to show what would have happened, say, if you had started with $100,000 with us in 2010 and invested in our portfolio to the present. We made some changes to how we calculate performance—mostly in including dividends—so were careful to pick matching comparative benchmarks for each year. What we came up with is the following:

▼ **Table 0.2: Performance Compared to Major Benchmarks**

FIVE-YEAR PERFORMANCE COMPARISON: *100 Best Stocks* versus **S&P 500**

ANNUAL PERFORMANCE OF EACH *100 BEST* LIST AND COMPOUNDED CUMULATIVE PERFORMANCE

		2010	2011	2012	2013	2014
100 Best Stocks	Gain, percent	**62.5%**	**20.0%**	**5.5%**	**19.2%**	**23.8%**
	Compounded	62.5%	94.9%	105.6%	145.1%	203.5%
	$100,000 invested in 2010	$162,500	$194,919	$205,639	$245,122	$303,461
S&P 500	Gain, percent	**44.6%**	**13.1%**	**5.4%**	**15.6%**	**22.4%**
	Compounded	44.6%	63.5%	72.4%	99.3%	143.9%
	$100,000 invested in 2010	$144,600	$163,543	$172,374	$199,264	$243,899
Net advantage, $100K invested, *100 Best Stocks*		$17,900	$31,376	$33,265	$45,858	$59,562

* For 12-month periods beginning April 1 of previous year, dividends included after 2011

As you can see, over this five-year period, both lists did quite well, but the *100 Best Stocks* list, when compounded, did almost 25 percent better through the five-year period. We did not include dividends in our 2010 and 2011 analysis, but especially then, they pretty much tracked the S&P in terms of return yield, so they don't affect the comparison much. Note also the power of "winning big" in the first year or two of a measurement period. The "beat" was significant in 2010; the *100 Best* performance then never really looked back—a significant illustration of the power of compounding and how much timing can make a difference in long-term portfolio performance.

Individual Investor: This Book Is for You

If you bought this book, you're probably an astute and experienced individual investor who invests in individual stocks in individual companies. Are you alone? Heck no. In fact, shoved along a bit by the hits most people took in the Great Recession, more and more investors are putting themselves in the driver's seat. Why? It's simple, and easily explained by the old adage: "Nobody cares about your money more than you do."

The trend toward self-directed investing was highlighted in an April 2013 *Wall Street Journal* article entitled "A New Era for Do-It-Yourself Investing." In the study central to the article, they asked mostly middle-tier investors whether they were relying more or relying less on advisors since the 2008–09 financial crisis. Some 50 percent of respondents said "less"; only 21 percent said "more." (The rest said "no change.") They cited a trend toward "investors wanting to be more involved" and toward brokerages offering do-it-yourself services with only occasional help from professional advisors when requested.

Does this mean that everyone is picking their own stocks? No, not necessarily, and not entirely. They may still be using any of among 14,000 mutual funds or 1,500 exchange-traded fund (ETF) "products" (or hedge funds, if they're wealthy enough) that do the driving for them. But more and more investors are making informed choices themselves; fewer are leaving the choice of those products—or individual stocks, for that matter—to someone else. What's really emerging is more of a hybrid model, where investors are making their own decisions, but sprinkling in some help in the form of professional advice, or professional management given by mutual fund managers, and automatic diversification as given by index funds, ETFs, and other kinds of instruments. Individually picked investments—with some help along the way.

Every edition of *The 100 Best Stocks to Buy* is intended as a core tool for the individual investor. Sure, it's hardly the only tool available. Today's explosion of Internet-based investing tools has made this book one of hundreds of choices for acquiring investing information. With the speed of cyberspace, our book will hardly be the most current source. In fact, we know, despite recent changes, that we're still at least six months out of date. If you check our research, you'll be able to come up with two to three quarters of more current financial information, news releases, and so forth.

So does the delay built into the publishing cycle make our book a poor information source? Not at all. As we previously said, it works because the companies we choose don't change so much and because they avoid the temptation to manage short-term, quarter-to-quarter performance. We chose these companies *because* they have sustainable performance, so who cares if the latest details or news releases are included? In *The 100 Best Stocks to Buy in 2015*, as with all of our previous editions, we focus on the *story*—the story of each company—not just the latest facts and figures.

To that same point, *100 Best Stocks* goes well beyond just being a stock screen or a study of stocks to invest in. Analysis forms the base of *100 Best Stocks*, but it isn't the rigid, strictly numbers-based selection and analysis so often found in published "best stocks" lists. Sure, we look at earnings, cash flow, balance sheet strength, and so forth, but we'll also look far beyond those things. We'll look at the intangible and often subtle factors that make truly great businesses—that is, companies—great. That is, once again, the *story.*

Great companies have good business fundamentals, but what makes them really great is the presence of intangibles and subtleties—the brands, the marketplace successes, the management style, the competitive advantages—that will *keep* them great or make them greater in the future. In our view, good intangibles today lead to better business fundamentals down the road.

100 Best Stocks is not a simple numbers-based stock screen like many found on the Internet and elsewhere today. It is a selection and analysis of really good businesses you would want to buy and own, not just for past results, but for future outcomes. Does "future" mean "forever"? No, not anymore. While the *100 Best Stocks* list correlates well with the notion of "blue chip" stocks, the harsh reality is that "blue chip" no longer means "forever."

We feel that the 100 companies listed and analyzed in the pages that follow are the best companies to own for 2015. That said, the word "own" has become a more active concept these days. Gone are the days of "own forever," like the halcyon days when Peter's parents, Jerry and Betty Sander, bought their 35 shares of General Motors, lovingly placed the stock certificate in their safety deposit box, and henceforth bought nothing but GM cars. Today, there is no forever; the economy, technology, and consumer tastes simply change too fast, and the businesses that participate in the economy by necessity change with it. Ownership is a more active concept than it was even 10 or 20 years ago.

So going forward, we offer the *100 Best* companies to own now and for 2015, those that have the best chances of not only surviving but evolving with— or even ahead of—the economy based on their current market position and approach to doing business. We think these are the best companies to (1) stay with or perhaps stay slightly ahead of business change, (2) provide short- and long-term returns in the form of cash and modest appreciation, and (3) do so with a measure of safety or at least reduced volatility so that you can burn your energy doing other things besides staring at stock quotes day and night.

Bottom line: Our intent is simple and straightforward. We provide a list and a set of facts and stories. You take the information as it's presented, do your own assessment, reach your own conclusions, and take your own actions. Anything more, anything less, won't work. You're in charge. And we suspect that you like it that way.

What's New for 2015

For those of you who've stayed with us over the years, this edition will take the same approach as before. For those of you reading for the first time, here are some guidelines and ideas we follow.

First and once again: no changes to the author team of Scott and Peter (we'll introduce ourselves in a minute). No significant changes to the structure or format of our presentation. Continuing forward is our emphasis on sustainable value, strong market position and other intangibles, and sustainable and growing cash returns to investors, in the form of dividends and share buybacks as well as share appreciation. We continue to take interest in the persistence of dividend increases above and beyond the yield itself, and we continue to stay focused on total shareholder returns. For the most part, we are playing the hand that got us here.

However, although we say every year that our investing style and presentation has remained essentially the same, the style of the best artists, writers, or even software programmers evolves over time; as with any blend of science and art, investing most certainly included, the approach evolves; the style acquires a little of this and a little of that and loses a little of something else as time goes on. Experience matters and is taken into account. Changes in the world investing context and environment factor in. And heck—we're getting older and perhaps a bit wiser. Maybe we see things a little differently than we did five years ago . . . and certainly 35 years ago. All of these factors influence the mix; here are a few directions we've taken recently and with this edition:

■ *Low-volatility bias.* We continue to think it's important to get good returns but also to sleep at night. *Steady* growth, *steady* returns, *steady* dividend increases—that's what we prefer. While we present "beta" as a measure of market correlation, we look deeper into the actual patterns and history of earnings, dividends, cash flow, and yes, share price. If it's a wild ride (or if there *are* no earnings, cash flows, etc.), we don't get on; we prefer to watch instead. You'll never find the likes of Facebook on our list.

■ *Still playing defense.* We took a more defensive stance for 2014 and almost wound up with some explainin' to do as the markets forged ahead. That list, while providing enough growth opportunity to beat the market as it turned out, was really constructed to beat the market in a down market, that is, to be down only 5 percent if the market dropped 10 percent. We continue to take that position. A number of our *100 Best Stocks* seem fully valued at this juncture. We were nervous about riding them any further. We evaluated each carefully using our "sell if there's something better to buy" philosophy and tried to visualize how they would do "on a sloppy track." We trimmed the list, as will be described later on, to reduce some of this exposure and to get out of industries like paper and coal-fired electric utilities that feel as if they've run their course. We rotated in 13 new stocks, a few of which, as technology stocks, might be considered a bit more aggressive. We also added two new small-cap stocks ("market cap," or total market value less than $1 billion) and two mid-caps (to $5 billion) to our list. But we consider them good values at the price, and all of them pay a decent dividend yield, giving us some additional downside protection. Bottom line: We're still playing defense, maybe just a bit more aggressively.

■ *Our second investment product.* Last year we tiptoed into the "invest-ment product" space, adding a real estate investment trust (REIT) rather unimaginatively called "Health Care REIT, Inc." Our goal was to gain the diversification, yield, and defensiveness of a managed portfolio, in this case a portfolio of senior housing and health facilities. Our approach was to find not just a real estate investment but a *good business* that just happened to own real estate. Although Health Care REIT suffered along with other REIT investments for the rest of 2013, it's working out well in 2014 and we believe our thesis is supported. So we did it again, this time picking out Public Storage (PSA), another good business built on a foun-dation of self-storage facilities. We considered adding another investment product—perhaps an ETF to give us some exposure to the cloud computing and networking space, but found nothing that really floated our boats (as you'll hear in our later discussion of ETFs, you get the bad stuff with the good, most not focused enough for our purposes). Upshot: We will consider investment products—REITs, other types of investment trusts, funds ETFs, and others from time to time, but we won't add them unless we (1) understand them, (2) have a specific rationale, and (3) feel that they provide a *"100 Best"* opportunity to deploy your hard-earned cash.

■ *Looking across the pond(s).* A number of you have asked over the years, "Why no foreign stocks?" Our reply has consistently been that we don't understand them as well—their markets, their accounting, their business structure—and we feel the best way to play international strength is to buy U.S. companies that export to a lot of overseas markets. So far, with the modest exception of 2013 where European turmoil and a China slowdown bit into this thesis, it has largely worked and we stick by it. But the recent stimulus efforts in Japan, which made excellent slow-moving Japanese firms more competitive and attractive on the world stage, and solid business performance and dividend yields from the likes of Toyota, Panasonic, Kyocera, Vodafone, and others, induced us to take another look. We did. We looked hard at a short list of about six companies and came away with the same feeling: We just don't understand their businesses and their numbers well enough. Many, like Toyota, just seem "too big to manage"—very difficult to manage effectively in a changing global context. While we looked at Japan and struck out, for this year, anyway, we did make another venture into Philips N.V., which seemed to be in a lot of the right places—LED lighting, energy management technologies, and strong in Europe, which now might be a good thing. It has a good yield, and we think, the opportunity for steady growth, so we picked it. It isn't our first foreign company; we've had Total S.A., Teva, Perrigo, and a few others. But, it's the first time we've *looked* for a foreign company and found one. We'll see where this goes next year.

In addition to these changes in our thought process(es), as a more practical matter and as we mentioned earlier, we pushed our deadline for completing this manuscript back far enough to include a more significant chunk of 2014 performance in our 2015 picks. We hope you'll notice the difference—such as there is.

About Your Authors

If you're a regular reader of the *100 Best Stocks* series you've probably seen the following before. It's about us, and not much has changed about us, so feel free to skip this section if it's altogether too familiar—or if it doesn't matter much to begin with.

Peter Sander

Peter is an independent professional researcher, writer, and journalist specializing in personal finance, investing, and location reference, as well as other general business topics. He has written 41 books on these topics, as well as numerous financial columns, and performed independent, privately contracted research and studies. He came from a background in the corporate world, having experienced a 21-year career with a major West Coast technology firm.

He is, most emphatically, an individual investor, and has been since the age of 12 (okay, so Warren Buffett started when he was 11), when his curiosity at the family breakfast table got the better of him. He started reading the stock pages with his parents. He had an opportunity during a "project week" in the seventh grade to read and learn about the stock market. He read Louis Engel's *How to Buy Stocks*, then the pre-eminent—and one of the only—books about investing available at the time. He picked stocks, and made graphs of their performance by hand with colored pens on graph paper. He put his hard-earned savings into buying five shares of each of three different companies. He watched those stocks like a hawk and salted away the meager dividends to reinvest. He's been investing ever since. (Incidentally, Warren Buffett bought Cities Service preferred shares, Peter bought Burlington Northern preferred shares following much the same principles, and how ironic that Mr. Buffett came to own all of Burlington Northern. Perhaps Peter will come to own a big oil company someday.)

Yes, Peter has an MBA from Indiana University in Bloomington, but it isn't an MBA in finance. He also took the coursework and certification exam to become a certified financial planner (CFP). By design and choice, he has never held a job in the financial profession. His goal has always been to share his knowledge and experience in an educational way, a way helpful for the individual as an investor and a personal financier to make his or her own decisions.

He has never earned a living giving direct investment advice or managing money for others, nor does he intend to.

A few years ago, it dawned on Peter that he has really made his living finding value, and helping or teaching others to find value. Not just in stocks, but other things in business and in life. What does he mean by value? Simply, the current and potential *worth* of something as compared to its price or cost. As it turns out, he's made a career out of assessing the value of people (for marketers), places (as places to live), and companies (for investors).

Scott Bobo

Peter and Scott have been friends and colleagues since, roughly, tenth grade (a long time!). Scott has been part of the team for four years and has been huge not only in identifying the *100 Best Stocks*, but also analyzing them and explaining their pros and cons crisply and in plain English so that you can make the best use of the list. Having Scott on the team allows you to get the combined wisdom and observations of two people, not just one, in an arena where one plus one almost always equals something greater than two.

Scott has been an investor since age 14, when he made the switch from analyzing baseball box scores to looking at the numbers and charts in the business section. In his 20-plus years in engineering and technology management, he's learned that a unique product value proposition is important to the success of any company. He has also learned (the hard way) that proper financial fundamentals are critical. From a development manager's perspective, comprehending a new product's risk/reward proposition is one of the keys to a company's success. From an investor's perspective, it's also one of the keys to successful value investing in a dynamic, innovation-driven market.

Scott adds a strong analytical touch. But he is most at home as an applications engineer, explaining how a company's products work and how they apply to a customer's needs. Consequently, and in addition to analytical legwork, Scott really adds an extraordinary and very real-world sense of how a company's products "fit" in the marketplace. Determining whether a company's products are relevant, best-in-class, and have a competitive advantage over others is an oft-overlooked core skill for a value investor. Scott brings this skill to the table in a big way.

Scott is the co-creator and the driving force behind our *100 Best Aggressive Stocks* and *100 Best Technology Stocks* books, published for 2012.

How do these diverse experiences of Peter and Scott translate into picking stocks? Just like customers or places to live, we want companies that produce the greatest return, the highest value, *per dollar invested*. And *for the amount of risk taken*. The amount of risk taken translates into additional dollars that an investment might cost, analogous to living in a great place rampant with crime or with questionable schools that might cost you more in the long term. The companies we will identify as among the *100 Best* have, in our assessment, the greatest long-term *value*, and if you can buy these companies at a *reasonable price* (a factor that we largely leave out of this analysis because this is a book and prices can change considerably), then these investments deliver the best prospects.

Later we'll come back to describe some of the attributes of value that we look for.

A "Low-Volatility" Investing Book

You've heard about—and just read about—the new trend toward low-volatility investing. This term means investing to minimize risk and volatility—to be able to sleep at night and count on your otherwise unpredictable retirement—and achieve decent investing returns all the same. That's the subject of Peter's new book *All About Low Volatility Investing* (McGraw-Hill, 2014), and some of the "DNA" from that book has leaked into this one. But that's not what this subsection is about.

What we're getting at here is the low-volatility nature of the sequential editions of this book. We try to keep the analysis the same, and for the most part we keep the presentation the same. Each year we make a few adjustments, pruning away a few stocks and adding a few others. We do that adhering to our core principles without having any particular number of changes in mind.

When we first took over this series from John Slatter for the 2010 edition, we made 26 changes, not a revolution but perhaps a strong evolution of the philosophy toward core value principles, strong competitive advantages and intangibles, and healthy cash returns. After that first year we went back to more of a fine-tuning mode, changing 14 stocks for the 2011 list, 12 for 2012, and back to 14 for 2013. In 2014 we held the line in a measure of defense and the simple inability to find "better horses," and changed only eight stocks. This year, we feel that a few more of our horses might be ready to fade and have brought in 13 fresh ones for this year's ride. As described earlier, the methodology used for analysis and selection of the *100 Best Stocks* remains largely unchanged. We continue to focus on fundamentals that really count, like cash flow; profit margins and balance sheet strength; and those intangibles such as brand, market share, channel and supply-chain excellence, and management quality that really determine success *going forward*. We continue to place more focus on dividends. More and more, especially in today's volatile markets, we feel that investors should get paid something to commit their precious capital to a company; it's a sign of good faith to investors and provides at least some return while waiting for a larger return in the future—or if things go south later on. So once again, 98 of this year's *100 Best* pay at least some dividends. The two "culprits" that don't remain CarMax and Itron. These stocks are included because of other prospects; we can turn our heads the other way on the dividend for a while but would expect some dividends eventually as the business models mature. Additionally, for dividend-paying stocks, we continue our preference for companies with a track record for regular dividend *increases*. A couple of years ago we started tracking, for each company, the number of dividend increases or *raises* (yes, you can think of them as comparable to a raise in your own wage or salary) in the past ten years. We are proud to report that of the 98 *100 Best* stocks paying dividends, fully *89* of them *raised* their dividend from 2013 to 2014. Of the 89, *45* of them have raised their dividends in each of the past ten years, and 18 more have raised them each of the past eight or nine years (most took a year or two off during the Great Recession), adding up to 63 or almost two-thirds of our stocks able and willing to give you annual raises. Pretty good stuff, in our view.

As in all editions, we review the performance of our 2014 picks in some detail, and continue with our "stars" lists identifying the best stocks in six different categories:

1. Yield Stars (stocks with solid dividend yields—Table 6)
2. Dividend Aggressors (companies with strong and persistent records and policies toward dividend *growth*—Table 6.1)
3. Safety Stars (solid performers in any market—Table 7)
4. Growth Stars (companies positioned for above-average growth— Table 8)
5. Prosperity Stars (formerly Recovery Stars—companies poised to do particularly well in a strong economy—Table 9)
6. Moat Stars (companies with significant sustainable competitive advantage—Table 10)

So, if you're an investor partial to any of these factors, such as safety, these lists are for you.

2013–2014: The Beat Goes On

Now comes the part of this narrative where we diagnose what went on in the year gone by and attempt to turn that into a prognosis for the coming year. Always a challenge.

Frankly, the strong market performance in 2013 and especially the early months of 2014 surprised us. A lot of things went right, some of which are sustainable and point toward a continuously improved future—and some of which leave us in doubt.

Impressively, the markets, as measured by our benchmark S&P 500, rose 22.4 percent during our measurement year, April 1, 2013, through April 1, 2014. We see several factors that contributed to this:

■ *Continuing accommodative Fed policy.* Mostly through bond purchases under the "QE" (quantitative easing) program, the Fed continued to pump billions into the economy, keeping interest rates down, fostering commerce and business investment, and, oh by the way, depressing the value of the dollar, stimulating export demand. The Fed has finally started easing up on this policy, and we think the gradual nature of the so-called "tapering," with no surprises, is probably the right way to do it, although it shocked our higher-yielding picks a bit when it first started. We read this accommodation as moving from a positive in the past to a neutral effect going forward.

■ *Recovery in Europe.* The more precarious parts of the European region have stopped giving us nerve-wracking headlines for the moment (though the situation in the Ukraine still bears watching, but for political more than economic reasons). As well, and at last, Europe has become a positive factor in world demand for things such as cars, machinery, consumer staples, and other products—a mild tailwind instead of a headwind. The resulting strength in the value of the euro will also help many companies in our list sell more to this market, which had been in the doldrums for years.

■ *Strength in U.S. manufacturing.* Much to our pleasure (and according to our prediction) we see a continued steady, if not ground-shaking, reshoring of manufacturing to American soil. Companies are finally getting the memo that it isn't just about labor costs—long inflexible supply chains and the inability to control quality negate the savings, sometimes in a big way; Chinese labor costs are going up; and improved availability and declining costs of U.S. energy resources, especially natural gas, have helped. True, some supply chains, especially for electronics products, simply aren't deep enough to support U.S. manufacturing. But it's good to see companies like Whirlpool once again building small appliances in Ohio, and it's good to see that some 21 percent of U.S. manufacturers, according to a recent poll, are moving some production back to the U.S. We tend to be invested in lots of companies that benefit from this, like W.W. Grainger and Illinois Tool Works, as well as several companies that benefit from strong U.S. exports to global markets, such as Procter & Gamble, IBM, and others.

■ *Persistence of share buybacks.* Companies have accumulated huge hoards of cash, as they have learned how to manage expenses and leverage their infrastructure to produce more for less. Although a big chunk of that cash is parked overseas for tax reasons, companies continue to actively buy back shares, producing rather silent but persistent returns to existing shareholders. We see no signs of that abating. S&P's Howard Silverblatt estimates that S&P 500 companies bought back an estimated $160 billion in the first quarter of 2014, lagging only the $172 billion in the third quarter of 2007, suggesting a significant outrunning of the near-record $445 billion that was repurchased during all of 2013. More than half of the companies on our *100 Best Stocks* list could be classified as "buyback aggressors," retiring 10–20 percent and sometimes more of their outstanding shares since 2004—which, of course, serves to increase returns, both to the shareholders who sell and those who remain to enjoy a higher rate of return on the remaining shares.

- *Moderating commodity prices.* We tend to like companies that add value to raw commodities, turning them into high-quality finished products for the global marketplace. As such, our *100 Best* list tends to be sensitive to commodity prices, although we have a few key plays in companies that *provide* such commodities, like Mosaic and our energy picks. When commodity prices attenuate, which is the case now and will continue into 2015 in our view, our companies do well. When they creep or spike upward as they did in 2012–2013 with the U.S. drought and other factors, it puts a pinch on some of our plays—though we try to pick companies with enough brand strength and market presence to raise their prices at least somewhat in tandem. We expect commodity prices to generally support our list this year.

- *Continued nervousness about the financial system.* Although we've moved on from the pre-crash days when financial companies produced some 20–25 percent of GDP simply by moving money around, we still fret over debt levels, greed and corruption in the banking sector, and the persistent lack of value add in much of that sector. Some of these chickens are coming home to roost as big investment banking houses and others have thrown in the towel on declining trading and transaction-based revenues and have started laying off workers. We still think there's a long way to go; moving money around has its place in capitalism, but too much is too much. We still have only three financial sector companies on our list, companies we feel are the best of the breed: Allstate, State Street, and Wells Fargo. With these crosscurrents in mind as a backdrop, we note that as of mid-2014, we see relatively few "headline" issues that are giving stocks indigestion. The positive factors continue to hold the day, and the markets rise gradually higher anticipating a gradually improving U.S. and world economy. Notably, the "VIX" volatility index just reached a five-year low. We look for the year to fall far short of last year's 22 plus percent gains, but without a resurgence in headlines, we could see another 10–15 percent as companies do what they do and continue to get better at doing what they do. Bring in a few headlines, and all bets are off for the market. We feel—and there's a little hope mixed in with that—that our companies, while many are at all-time highs, will fare better than most if things get jumpy. Stay tuned.

Report Card: Recapping Our 2014 Picks

If you had told us that the S&P 500 was to rise 22.4 percent during our measurement period, we would have said, "That's nice," and braced ourselves to do a bit worse than that. Our picks tend to be more the "steady-Eddies" and dividend producers (our average yield is about 2.5 percent compared to 2.2 percent for the S&P).

As mentioned earlier, it wasn't looking too good going into the stretch. Our dividend payers were being pushed to the far outside by the specter of increasing interest rates. But we finished strong and eked out the 23.85 percent gain we already crowed about.

At this juncture, we'll do a short refresher on how we evaluate our gains. There are many ways to evaluate the performance of a group of stocks over time. Some are simplistic, such as simply averaging the percent gain in each share price. But such a method may not weight a portfolio very realistically, for it assumes you buy the same number of shares of Apple at $550 (before the recent split) as you would Southwest Airlines at $22. We continue to feel it's better to take the approach of an investor with $100,000 to invest—who invested $1,000 in each of the *100 Best Stocks* across the board, regardless of share price. Sure, you end up with some weird quantities of shares in your portfolio, but the portfolio, and thus the performance metrics, isn't weighted in favor of more expensive stocks.

The Bottom Line

If you had invested $100,000 in our *100 Best Stocks 2014* list on April 1, 2013—$1,000 in each of the 100 stocks—you would have ended up with $121,337 on April 1, 2014, not including dividends paid during that period. That's a 21.3 percent gain. Including dividends of some $2,513, you would have ended up with $123,850. The S&P, as measured by the buyable SPDR S&P 500 ETF Trust, was ahead just 22.4 percent, including dividends ($122,400) during that period—a clear victory for us but maybe only by a length or two.

BUT, DID WE BET THE FARM?

So you'd be justified to ask: Did we roll the dice? Did we take a lot of risk to exceed our S&P 500 benchmark? Some investors and investing professionals these days might be inclined to; however we think we did the opposite. With our low-volatility conscience peering over our shoulder as a witness, we approximated portfolio risk by averaging the "beta" figures, reported in our narratives, for all *100 Best* stocks. Beta represents the correlation between an investment and the market: A beta greater than one is considered more volatile and thus more risky than the market; a beta less than one is considered less risky than the market as a whole. Our "composite" beta was just over 0.94, suggesting that our picks, in total, were 6 percent less volatile, and thus less risky, than the market. Bottom line: We beat the market with less risk. More gain, less pain—not a bad place to be.

Winners and Losers

The full list of the *100 Best Stocks* 2014 and how they did through the comparison period can be found in Appendix A. At this point, we'll give a short overview of what really worked and what didn't within the list. First, the winners:

▼ **Table 1: Performance Analysis:** *100 Best Stocks* **2014**

TOP WINNERS, 1-YEAR GAIN/LOSS, APRIL 1, 2013–APRIL 1, 2014; * = NEW FOR 2014

Company	Symbol	Price 4/1/2013	Price 4/1/2014	% change	Dollar gain per $1,000 invested
Harman International	HAR	$44.01	$111.58	153.5%	$1535.33
Southwest Airlines	LUV	$13.35	$23.94	79.3%	$793.26
St. Jude Medical	STJ	$39.70	$66.63	67.8%	$678.34
McKesson	MCK	$107.25	$176.04	64.1%	$641.40
Seagate Technology	STX	$35.25	$57.00	61.7%	$617.00
Corning (*)	GLW	$13.01	$20.97	61.2%	$611.84
Stryker Corporation	SYK	$54.21	$81.88	51.0%	$510.42
Aetna	AET	$50.47	$75.05	48.7%	$487.00
Total S.A.	TOT	$45.40	$66.00	45.4%	$453.74
UnitedHealth Group	UNH	$56.33	$81.81	45.3%	$452.87
Macy's	M	$41.02	$59.51	45.1%	$450.76

Top WINNERS, 1-Year Gain/Loss, April 1, 2013–April 1, 2014 (continued)

DuPont	DD	$47.71	$67.76	42.0%	$420.25
Johnson Controls	JCI	$34.42	$48.21	40.1%	$400.64
Illinois Tool Works	ITW	$59.65	$82.20	37.8%	$378.00
FedEx	FDX	$97.70	$134.11	37.3%	$372.67
CVS Caremark	CVS	$54.14	$74.29	37.2%	$372.18
FMC Corporation	FMC	$56.58	$77.32	36.7%	$366.56
Valero	VLO	$40.71	$55.51	36.4%	$363.55
Tractor Supply	TSCO	$53.15	$71.72	34.9%	$349.39
Union Pacific	UNP	$139.68	$188.44	34.9%	$349.10

Our overall winning percentage was better than ever as mentioned earlier, with some 89 of our *100 Best* picks finishing ahead of last year even before dividends (last year it was 87). The good were good and the better were better: We didn't get as much leverage from "new" picks—only Corning made the Top 20 list; we had four "newbies" on last year's list. Okay, we only had eight newbies in all; maybe that's part of why.

Our biggest winners may be there because of their involvement with megatrends—and in some cases, like last year, overdue recognition of latent value. Harman International tops our list with a gain over two-and-a-half-times our starting value, our biggest winner in a while (we had a couple of bigger ones in 2011 as beaten-down companies like International Paper rose from the ashes). But Harman was square in the center of the "megatrend" of the digital automotive cockpit, and their leadership didn't go unrecognized. Among others, five of our top ten are in the health-care sector and two make key components supporting the rapidly evolving digital age: Corning and Seagate. The rest are a mix of beneficiaries from improved domestic manufacturing, a stronger Europe, health-care reform, less expensive supply inputs, and overall economic wellness.

Now, for the losers:

▼ **Table 2: Performance Analysis: *100 Best Stocks* 2014**

TOP LOSERS, 1-YEAR GAIN/LOSS, APRIL 1, 2013–APRIL 1, 2014; * = NEW FOR 2014

Company	Symbol	Price 4/1/2013	Price 4/1/2014	% change	Dollar gain/loss per $1,000 invested
Itron	ITRI	$46.40	$35.82	-22.8%	$(228.02)
Iron Mountain	IRM	$34.85	$27.84	-20.1%	$(201.15)
Mosaic	MOS	$58.48	$49.80	-14.8%	$(148.43)
Target Corporation	TGT	$66.73	$60.57	-9.2%	$(92.31)
Health Care REIT	HCN	$64.69	$59.72	-7.7%	$(76.83)
IBM	IBM	$208.97	$194.50	-6.9%	$(69.24)
Valmont Industries	VMI	$156.19	$150.90	-3.4%	$(33.87)
Southern Company	SO	$44.78	$43.50	-2.9%	$(28.58)
Coca-Cola	KO	$39.28	$38.41	-2.2%	$(22.15)
McCormick & Co.	MKC	$72.07	$71.62	-0.6%	$(6.24)
Kellogg	K	$62.65	$62.62	0.0%	$(0.48)
J.M. Smucker	SJM	$97.03	$97.14	0.1%	$1.13
Campbell Soup	CPB	$44.40	$44.56	0.4%	$3.60
AT&T	T	$34.86	$35.09	0.7%	$6.60
Bemis	BMS	$39.32	$39.72	1.0%	$10.17
International Paper	IP	$45.31	$45.86	1.2%	$12.14
Verizon	VZ	$47.10	$47.75	1.4%	$13.80
Aqua America	WTR	$24.79	$25.14	1.4%	$14.12
McDonald's	MCD	$96.49	$97.90	1.5%	$14.61
Suburban Propane	SPH	$41.32	$42.01	1.7%	$16.70

While we would have liked to have all *100 Best Stocks* turn out to be winners, the odds are stacked pretty highly against that. That said, only 11 losers out of 100 ain't bad.

This year, we didn't do well with stocks that started with the letter "I"; our top two losers and another one of the top 20 met that criterion. Of course, that's not the reason, and we fully continue to embrace any company for our *100 Best* list regardless of its first letter.

Our losers were a mishmash of companies that confused the markets (like Iron Mountain), got caught in the vice of negative headlines (Target, Mosaic), suffered from the malaise of key customer groups (like Itron and Valmont and their utility and public sector customers), suffered from interest-rate jitters (Health Care REIT, Southern), had high input costs (J.M. Smucker, Campbell, and others), or simply are at the wrong end of long-term trends (Iron Mountain again, International Paper and the demise of business moving at the speed of paper). There was no *one* trend apparent here, and no *one* lesson that shifted our investment perspective. When you pick a hundred companies, some will fall off; there will be losers.

Value—Now More Than Ever

We remain steadfast in the principles of value investing.

For intelligent investors, chasing the latest fad doesn't work; buying something and locking it away forever doesn't work anymore, either. Investors must make intelligent choices based on true value and follow those choices through time and change. It all points to taking a value-oriented approach to investing and to staying modestly active with your investments.

The next obvious task is to define what we mean by a "value" approach. Essentially, it is to think of buying shares in a company as buying the company itself; it is about putting yourself in an entrepreneurial frame of mind, not just an investment frame of mind. Would you want to own that business? Why or why not?

Fundamentally, whether or not you want to own the business depends on two factors: first, the returns you expect to receive on your investment in the near- and long-term future, and second, the risk you'll take in generating those returns. Fortunately, the third factor the prospective entrepreneur must consider—"Do I have the time for this?"—is less of an issue for the investor.

You are looking for tangible value—tangible worth—for your precious, scarce, and hard-earned investment capital. That return can come in the form of immediate cash returns (dividends), longer-term cash returns (dividends and especially growing dividends), or as growth in the value of assets longer term. If you realize your return in the form of owning a share of a larger company eventually, that's still a legitimate return. Cash flow received later in the form of a higher share price or a takeover is still cash return; it is just less certain because of the forces of change that may take place in the interim. It is also theoretically worth less because of the nature of discounting—a dollar received tomorrow is worth more than a dollar received 20 years in the future.

The point: Many investment experts distinguish between "value" and "growth" investing; in fact, mutual funds are often classified as being one or the other. We dismiss this separation; growth can be an essential component of a firm's value. That growth can come either in the form of asset values or cash returns—i.e., growing dividends.

Value also implies safety. The safety comes in three forms. First is the fundamental quality and soundness of the firm's financial fundamentals—that is, income, cash flow, and the balance sheet. Value companies have plenty of reserves, a large enough *margin of safety*, to weather downturns and unforeseen events in the marketplace. Second, they have strong enough intangibles (brands, market position, supply-chain strength, etc.) to *maintain* their position in that marketplace and generate future returns. When we say this year, as we did last year, that our list should fare better in a *down* market than the S&P 500 as a whole, it's these safety factors, and particularly the intangibles, that support our premise.

Third, if you're really practicing value-investing principles, you buy these companies at reduced prices, when the markets are down, when the company is out of favor. You're looking for situations where the price is less than what you perceive to be the value, although calculating the value that precisely is elusive. When you "buy cheap" you provide another margin of safety; that margin makes it less likely that the stock will drop further. It gives you room for error if you turn out to be wrong about a choice. Again, it's much like buying a business of your own—you want to pay as little as possible in case things don't turn out as you'd expect. In today's markets, admittedly it's hard to buy cheap, but many of the 13 new adds for 2015 for the moment at least, appear to be bargains relative to the market. Sell when there's something better to buy.

Stay Active

What do we mean by "stay active"? Staying active means that you should remain abreast of your investment and, like any business you own, keep an eye on its performance. Periodically review it as you would your own finances to see if it is making money and generally doing what you think it should be doing. You should keep an eye on company-related news, financials, earnings reports, and so forth—it's all part of being an individual investor and owner of companies.

Beyond that, time permitting, you should listen in on investor conference calls (usually at earnings announcements) to see what management has to say about the business. In addition, you should watch your business in the marketplace. See how many people are going to your local Starbucks and whether they are enjoying the experience, and look for other signs of excellence. We're not talking about constantly monitoring the stock price. Instead, we're suggesting an oversight of the business as though it were one you happen to own that, while professionally managed, requires an occasional glance to make sure everything is still acting according to your best interests. We also recommend a periodic review—at least annually—of whether your investments are still your best investments. Evaluate each investment against its alternatives. If you still perceive it to be the best value out there, keep it. If not, consider a swap for something new. Sell if there's something better to buy.

The *100 Best Stocks* for 2015: A Few Comments

For 2015, barring unforeseen events, we anticipate a continued gradual recovery for the U.S. and global economy. Tailwinds include continued accommodative monetary policy even with the gradual taper, a stronger and less expensive domestic energy base (oil imports are down 20 percent from two years ago), and an expanding reality and mentality that U.S.-based manufacturing can and does work. Exports, particularly to Europe, should recover, although the stronger economy also means more imports. We're approaching a presidential election year and that usually means good things, although with today's Washington gridlock it's more of a wait-and-see. Although we'd like to see this happen faster, we still see a continued semi-subconscious adjustment away from low value–add industries toward a back-to-basics, make-things-that-people-need mentality; with capital allocated to things like research labs and factories, not housing and real estate.

Still of concern is the rapid and still-uncontrolled rise in health-care costs. Recent data showed that almost half the jobs created since the trough of the Great Recession are in health care–related fields. Health-care businesses should prosper, but health care also acts like a tax for the rest of us—unless we start exporting health care in a meaningful way (many of the companies we choose in the sector do export health care in the form of pharmaceutical products or health-care technologies). At a personal level, although the numbers don't show it so much, we're seeing signs of inflation as demand picks up for food products, airfares and other transportation costs, and a number of services.

America is the great nation of consumers; with some 72 percent of economic activity arising from consumption, this country is far and away the leader in that department. We wonder if that is sustainable. (China is 34 percent, Japan is 60 percent, Germany is 57 percent—you get the idea.) We also fret about the growing income gap; clearly the rich are getting richer at the expense of everyone else; that the second-largest category of job increases was in food service, retail, and hospitality suggests that the benefits of economic recovery aren't as helpful to some as others.

Where does this all take us? We, as usual, stick to companies with great business models, that have brand, marketplace, and financial strength sufficient to master the crosscurrents of change and the emergence of megatrends. We do factor such megatrends as the cloud, the demise of paper in the workplace, the "always-on" nature of personal connectivity (and the prospect of marketers taking advantage of it), and availability of health care for everyone. We've wanted to see a megatrend toward more energy wisdom; that one's been put on hold by new domestic energy supplies although we're still betting on it for the longer term. We continue to see a "national" economy, where large national brands gradually usurp local favorites, providing extra lift for big brands and big names like Coke and Deere and Tiffany. (The beer industry, where local microbrews have gained significant share, is an exception; we wonder if such localization might hit a few other industries. That's a wait-and-see.)

For 2015, as always, we look for companies with good business models, which produce high-value-add things that people (or companies) need, do it efficiently, and generate a lot of cash. Good businesses. Not just companies that make a lot of money, but good businesses with a sustainable future. We think our "core" list is still pretty good regardless of what the market does; this year we've made 13 changes taking in some of the themes we've mentioned above, or simply switching horses where we felt it made sense. Sell when there's something better to buy. As is our custom, we'll start with the companies removed from the 2014 list:

▼ **Table 3: Companies Removed from 2014 List**

Company	Symbol	Category	Sector
Abbott	ABT	Growth and Income	Health Care
Amgen	AMGN	Conservative Growth	Health Care
Automatic Data Processing	ADP	Conservative Growth	Information Technology
Baxter	BAX	Aggressive Growth	Health Care
Church & Dwight	CHD	Aggressive Growth	Consumer Staples
Cincinnati Financial	CINF	Income	Financials
Dominion Resources	D	Growth and Income	Utilities
Duke Energy	DUK	Income	Utilities
International Paper	IP	Conservative Growth	Materials
Iron Mountain	IRM	Aggressive Growth	Information Technology
Molex Inc.	MOLX	Conservative Growth	Industrials
Suburban Propane	SPH	Income	Energy
Tractor Supply	TSCO	Aggressive Growth	Retail

As usual, only one cut was "easy"—it has become a tradition to see one of our companies acquired by someone else (it's happened the past three years). This year, it was Molex Inc.

From there, our cuts come from a mixed bag of reasons, with "sell when there's something better to buy" winding through all of them. First, two mega-trends came into our thinking. As mentioned, we see the gradual migration of business (and personal) activity away from paper; we took the scissors to International Paper, which makes it, and Iron Mountain, which stores it. Second, new environmental regulations are making it tough for coal-fired electric utilities, particularly those with large unregulated wholesale "merchant" power operations that can't recover their costs through rate increases—we cut Duke Energy and Dominion from the list. We were a bit overweight in utilities anyway; the three remaining (Southern, NextEra, and Otter Tail) have significant alternative energy investments and thus should do better in our view.

We cut Abbott and Baxter, for the time being anyway; both are splitting their research pharma and medical supply businesses in the interest of focus. We're not sure this is the right strategy, as the supply businesses are steady and balance the ups and downs of research pharma. Such a split doesn't work out so well for Abbott, and Baxter is doing the same thing. When the dust settles, we may get back in—or into parts of—these businesses.

We've struggled to really understand Amgen's business and don't see where the growth will come from, especially as the market gets more skeptical of biotechs. We had a nice run with Cincinnati Financial, took our "gains," and replaced it with Allstate, which is in the same business but on much more solid brand and financial footing. We felt too loaded down with Consumer Staples stocks, thought one had to go. Church & Dwight got the arm and hammer. Too, we felt we didn't need two payroll processors, so we cut ADP and stayed with Paychex, which is more oriented to small and medium-sized businesses, the growth vector for payrolls. Although Suburban Propane still pays a nice yield, it didn't do much in a year where propane supply/demand economics could have produced more; its generous dividend is still not very well covered. Finally, we got off the Tractor Supply after a really nice run through the fields; we feel they're starting to saturate and run out of new fields to plow; the whole idea may be getting a little long in the tooth as well.

Sell when there's something better to buy. So we did that in 13 cases, and here they are:

▼ Table 4: New Companies for 2015

Company	Symbol	Category	Sector
Allstate	ALL	Conservative Growth	Financials
Daktronics	DAKT	Aggressive Growth	Technology
Devon Energy	DVN	Conservative Growth	Energy
General Electric	GE	Growth and Income	Industrials
Microchip Technology	MCHP	Aggressive Growth	Technology
Oracle	ORCL	Aggressive Growth	Information Technology
Philips N.V.	PHG	Growth and Income	Industrials
Public Storage	PSA	Growth and Income	Real Estate
Ralph Lauren	RL	Aggressive Growth	Consumer Discretionary
ResMed	RMD	Aggressive Growth	Health Care
Schnitzer Steel	SCHN	Aggressive Growth	Industrials
Scotts Miracle-Gro	SMG	Growth and Income	Materials
Steelcase	SCS	Aggressive Growth	Industrials

We just explained Allstate. Daktronics, one of our two small cap picks, is our play in the megatrend that real-time digital marketing will hit you (almost) everywhere, whether you want it to or not. We wanted to get some play in the domestic energy and especially the "fracking" boom, so Devon is our pick. We think General Electric is back, having repositioned themselves as a manufacturing, not a financial company. Microchip Technology makes the sort of intelligent electronics that will allow your smartphone to talk to your refrigerator, thus addressing our megatrend of digital everything, everywhere, the so-called "Internet of things." Oracle, in our view, will benefit more than others from the "cloud"; we still have IBM and Seagate as plays in this area, too. Philips N.V. plays the international space and especially Europe and is into things we like such as LED lighting. Public Storage is a great business based on a solid REIT. Ralph Lauren is a pure brand play; best in breed in the clothing space. ResMed is a focused play on the megatrends of aging and mega-body size, and should do well as more accept their much easier-to-use solutions for sleep disorders. Schnitzer Steel, our other new small cap, is a particularly well-run recycler of metals that knows how to collect stuff and market it as scrap to Asian producers. Scotts Miracle-Gro (one of our two new mid-caps) is another brand play that should do well as they brand more services—not just products—for value-conscious homeowners. Finally, Steelcase, our other new mid-cap, is a dark horse in the megatrend of the digital workplace; we think the traditional cubicle farms of the 1970s and 1980s are overdue for a refresh.

All of these companies pay a decent dividend, have relatively attractive entry points (as of mid-2015), and offer ways to play new trends in addition. We can hardly contain our excitement as we think we've found a few "something better to buys" in a difficult, likely overpriced market.

To give a bit of a big-picture view of our changes, Table 5 gives our annual summary of what changed by sector. You can see our modest shift away from Utilities and Health Care (the two pharma companies, Abbott and Baxter) and toward Industrials (GE, Philips, Schnitzer, Steelcase). Most of the rest are adjustments and replacements.

▼ **Table 5: Sector Analysis and 2015 Change by Sector**
NUMBER OF COMPANIES:

Sector	On 2014 list	Added for 2015	Cut from 2015	On 2015 list
Business Services	2			2
Consumer Discretionary	4		1	5
Consumer Staples	14	-1		13
Consumer Durables	1			1
Energy	7	-1	1	7
Entertainment	1			1
Financials	4	-1	1	4
Health Care	16	-3	1	14
Heavy Construction	1			1
Industrials	12	-1	4	15
Information Technology	7	-2	3	8
Materials	6	-1	1	6
Real Estate	0		1	1
Restaurant	2			2
Retail	10	-1		9
Telecommunications Services	3			3
Transportation	5			5
Utilities	5	-2		3

A TRIP TO THE "5 AND 10" STORE

As we performed our analysis for the 2015 edition of *The 100 Best Stocks to Buy*, we started to notice something about our picks. A lot of our companies have a regular, fairly predictable top-line (revenue) growth in the 5 percent range, and a bottom-line growth (earnings per share) of 10 percent or thereabouts.

Now that, when you think about it for a large, stable, established company, is a solid achievement. Shouldn't 5 percent on the top line normally lead to 5 percent on the bottom line? Yes, unless you're a particularly well-managed company.

Our "5 and 10" picks (we recognize 27 of them in Table 5.1) do more than most. They reduce costs, increase efficiency, and buy back shares consistently.

Shouldn't there really be more such companies our on list? Well, yes, maybe there would be, except that some deliver *more* top-line growth in the 10s and bottom lines in the 15s and 20s. These do even better, but that said, we don't think you can go wrong with a visit to the neighborhood "5 and 10s," either.

▼ Table 5.1 "5 and 10" List, 2015

COMPANIES WITH REGULAR 5% TOP-LINE, 10% BOTTOM-LINE GROWTH

Company	Symbol	Company	Symbol
3M Company	MMM	Paychex	PAYX
Allstate	ALL	Philips N.V.	PHG
Becton, Dickinson	BDX	Praxair	PX
Clorox Company	CLX	Ross Stores	ROST
Comcast	CMCSA	St. Jude Medical	STJ
ConocoPhillips	COP	Stryker Corporation	SYK
Devon Energy	DVN	Target Corporation	TGT
DuPont	DD	Time Warner	TWX
Eastman Chemical	EMN	United Parcel Service	UPS
Honeywell	HON	United Technologies	UTX
Macy's	M	Valmont Industries	VMI
McCormick & Co.	MKC	Wal-Mart	WMT
Norfolk Southern	NSC	Waste Management	WM
Otter Tail Corporation	OTTR		

Yield Signs

We continue to like dividend-paying stocks. We like stocks that pay meaningful dividends, and stocks that have a tendency to raise their dividends over time.

With dividend-paying stocks, especially those inclined to raise their dividends, you get an attractive yield from the day you buy the stock, but you'll also get handsome raises over time. As we reported earlier, 89 of the 98 dividend-paying stocks on the 2014 *100 Best* list raised their dividends in 2013, and 43 of those have raised their dividends in each of the past ten years. We like this a lot. A company that raises its dividend 10 percent will roughly double the payout in just seven years. (Calculation? Rule of 72—divide the percent increase into 72 and you'll get the number of years it takes to double: 72/10 equals 7.2 years.) You could end up with twice the income in addition to any gains or growth in the price of the stock.

We continue to focus on those healthy companies willing to not only share a portion of their profits but also to give you, the investor, a periodic raise to recognize the value of your commitment of precious investment capital. In that spirit, in our presentation format we show the number of dividend increases in the past ten years in the header right after Current Yield. We also present the Dividend Aggressors list in our "stars" lists, which you'll see shortly. Dividend aggressors are companies with substantial payouts that are also growing those payouts at a persistent and substantial rate. There are lists of "dividend achievers" floating around on the Internet, and there are even a few funds constructed around a dividend achievers index. Our Aggressors are—well—a bit more aggressive.

The climate for dividend growth continues to be favorable. Standard & Poor's estimates that dividends for its "500" will rise some 9.9 percent in 2014 to a record $38.98 for all shares in the 500 (a yield of 2.0 percent, slightly down due to the ever-increasing denominator). Companies are swimming in cash ($1.1 trillion for the "500"), and rather than commit to expensive wages or business investments that might not pan out, they are simply returning cash to previously starved shareholders. Lower commodity input prices will help further. Finally, companies whipped themselves into shape during the Great Recession and continue to do so, now having enough to invest in their businesses *and* return cash to shareholders. The risks in the bond markets and the persistence of favorable dividend tax treatment for investments (not as good as before, but still good) continue to contribute to this story.

The growing-dividend-plus-growing-stock scenario continues to be one of our favored retirement-planning and retirement-investing scenarios. While we do expect markets overall, and our selected stocks in particular, to appreciate over time as good businesses capture more markets, become more efficient, and get better in general, stock price growth has become less dependable than in the past. The decades-long record of 10–11 percent annual growth, we think, will become more difficult to match. As a result, we think the more solid play is to invest for dividends, and particularly for dividend growth—and hey, if the stock price happens to grow, too, so much the better.

Appendix B shows dividend yields for all *100 Best Stocks* for 2015. Appendix C shows all *100 Best* companies, sorted by percentage yield.

Dancing with the Stars

We continue developing and sharing our "star" categories—groups of stocks, essentially the "best of the best" in categories we chose to highlight—yield stars, dividend aggressors, safety and stability stars, growth stars, prosperity stars, and moat stars.

▼ **Table 6: Top 20 Dividend-Paying Stocks**

COMPANY	Symbol	Projected 2014 dividend	Yield %	Dividend raises, past 10 years
Health Care REIT	HCN	$3.20	5.4%	10
AT&T	T	$1.84	5.2%	10
Total S.A.	TOT	$3.35	4.8%	7
Southern Company	SO	$2.10	4.7%	10
Verizon	VZ	$2.12	4.5%	8
Otter Tail Corporation	OTTR	$1.20	4.1%	5
ConocoPhillips	COP	$2.76	3.6%	10
PepsiCo	PEP	$2.60	3.6%	10
Waste Management	WM	$1.92	3.6%	10
Philips N.V. (*)	PHG	$0.93	3.5%	6
Clorox Company	CLX	$0.74	3.4%	10
McDonald's	MCD	$3.24	3.4%	10
Chevron	CVX	$4.28	3.3%	10
General Electric (*)	GE	$0.88	3.3%	0
Paychex	PAYX	$1.40	3.3%	8
Public Storage (*)	PSA	$5.60	3.3%	8
Seagate Technology	STX	$1.72	3.3%	8
Procter & Gamble	PG	$2.56	3.2%	10
Sysco	SYY	$1.16	3.2%	10
Daktronics (*)	DAKT	$0.40	3.1%	6

* – New this year

▼ **Table 6.1: Companies with Strong Dividend Track Records**

Company	Symbol	Dividend	Yield %	Dividend raises, past 10 years
3M Company	MMM	$3.44	2.5%	10
Apple	AAPL	$13.16	2.3%	3
Chevron	CVX	$4.28	3.3%	10
Clorox Company	CLX	$2.74	3.4%	10
Coca-Cola	KO	$1.24	3.0%	10
General Mills	GIS	$1.64	3.1%	9
Health Care REIT	HCN	$3.20	5.4%	10
J.M. Smucker	SJM	$2.32	2.4%	10
Johnson & Johnson	JNJ	$2.80	2.8%	10
Kimberly-Clark	KMB	$3.36	3.0%	10
McDonald's	MCD	$3.24	3.4%	10
NextEra Energy	NEE	$2.92	3.1%	10
Norfolk Southern	NSC	$2.00	2.6%	10
PepsiCo	PEP	$2.16	2.3%	10
Procter & Gamble	PG	$2.56	3.2%	10
Seagate Technology	STX	$1.72	3.3%	8
Southern Company	SO	$2.10	4.7%	10
United Parcel Service	UPS	$2.68	2.8%	10
Waste Management	WM	$1.92	3.6%	10
Wells Fargo	WFC	$1.40	2.4%	7

REMEMBER, THERE ARE NO GUARANTEES

While dividends and especially high yields are attractive, remember that corporations are under no legal obligation to pay them! Interest payments on time deposits and bonds are much more clearly defined, and failure to pay can represent default. With dividends, there is no such safety net. Companies can—and do—reduce or eliminate dividends in bad times. Keep an eye out for changes in a company's business prospects and don't put too many eggs in a single high-yielding basket.

Safety Stars

Safety stars are companies we think will hold up well in volatile and negative stock markets as well as recessionary economies. They have stable products and customer bases, and long traditions of being able to manage well in downturns. This list is unchanged from last year.

▼ **Table 7: Top 10 Stocks for Safety and Stability**

Company	Symbol	Company	Symbol
Aqua America	WTR	J.M. Smucker	SJM
Becton, Dickinson	BDX	Johnson & Johnson	JNJ
Campbell Soup	CPB	Kimberly-Clark	KMB
Clorox Company	CLX	McCormick & Co.	MKC
General Mills	GIS	Sysco	SYY

Growth Stars

Looking at the other side of the coin, we picked ten stocks we feel are especially well positioned to grow, even in a negative economy and especially in a positive one. We made more changes here than any other "stars" list, removing Itron, Mosaic, Perrigo, and Tractor Supply and adding Daktronics, ResMed, Starbucks, and Corning.

▼ **Table 8: Growth Stars: Top 10 Stocks for Growth**

Company	Symbol	Company	Symbol
Apple	AAPL	Nike	NKE
CarMax	KMX	ResMed	RMD
Corning	GLW	Seagate Technology	STX
Daktronics	DAKT	Starbucks	SBUX
Harman International	HAR	Visa	V

Last year we shifted into post–Great Recession gear, replacing our "recovery stars" list with a "prosperity stars" selection. For this year we removed Johnson Controls, although it's still a good pick, and replaced it with Steelcase, as we think that companies flush with cash will increasingly embrace the digital office.

▼ **Table 9: Prosperity Stars: Top 10 Stocks for a Growing Economy**

Company	Symbol	Company	Symbol
Allergan	AGN	Southwest Airlines	LUV
CarMax	KMX	Steelcase	SCS
Dupont	DD	Tiffany	TIF
Fluor Corporation	FLR	Whirlpool	WHR
Illinois Tool Works	ITW	W.W. Grainger	GWW

Moat Stars

Finally, we get back to one of the basic tenets of value investing—the ability of a company to build a sustainable and unassailable competitive advantage. Value investing aficionados call such an advantage a "moat," for it represents a barrier to entry for competitors that will likely preserve that advantage for some time. The moat can come in the form of technology, the use of technology, a brand, enduring customer relationships, channel relationships, size or scale, or simply a really big head start into a business that makes it hard or even impossible for competitors to catch up. The appraisal of a moat is hardly an exact science; here we give our top ten picks based on the size and strength (width?) of the moat. For this year, we removed Iron Mountain (and from the *100 Best* list entirely; it was yesterday's, not today's, moat) and added the venerable brand champ Ralph Lauren.

▼ **Table 10: Moat Stars: Top 10 Stocks for Sustainable Competitive Advantage**

Company	Symbol	Company	Symbol
Apple	AAPL	Starbucks	SBUX
Coca-Cola	KO	Sysco	SYY
Monsanto	MON	Tiffany	TIF
Pall Corporation	PLL	Visa	V
Ralph Lauren	RL	W.W. Grainger	GWW

What Makes a *Best Stock* Best?

Now we get down to brass tacks. What is it that defines excellence—sustainable excellence—among companies? That's been a topic of considerable debate for years, and with all the study that's gone into it, it's amazing that nobody has hit upon a single formula for deciphering undeniable excellence in a company.

That's largely because it isn't as scientific as most of us would like or expect it to be. It defies mathematical formulation. Fundamentals such as profitability, productivity, and asset efficiency tell us how well a company has done and, by proxy, how well it is managed and how well it has done in the marketplace. Fundamentals are about what the company has already achieved and where it stands right now, and if a company's current fundamentals are a mess, stop right now—there isn't much point in going any further.

In most cases, what really separates the great from the good are the intangibles, the "soft" factors of market position, market acceptance, customer "love" of a company's products, its management, its aura. These features create competitive advantage, or "distinctive competence," as an economist would put it, that cannot be valued. Furthermore, and most importantly, they are more about what a company is set up to achieve in the future.

To paraphrase Buffett at his best: Give me $100 billion, and I could start a company; but I could never create another Coca-Cola.

What does that mean? It means that Coca-Cola has already established a worldwide brand cachet; the distribution channels, customer knowledge, and product development expertise cannot be duplicated at any cost. When companies have competitive advantages that cannot be duplicated at any cost, they have an enduring grip on their markets. They can charge more for their products. They have a moat that insulates them from competition, or makes it much more expensive for competitors to participate. They're perceived by loyal customers as having top-line products worth paying more for.

Strategic Fundamentals

Let's examine a list of strategic fundamentals that define, or keep score of, a company's success. This list can be used as a checklist, although it's hard to find a company that shows excellence in all of these areas.

Are Gross and Operating Profit Margins Growing?

We like profitable companies; who doesn't? But what really counts is the size of the margin and especially the growth. If a company has a gross margin (sales minus costs of goods sold) exceeding that of its competitors, that shows that it's doing something right, probably with its customers and/or with its costs. But competitive analysis is elusive; there is no dependable source of "industry" gross margins, and comparing competitors can be difficult because no two companies are exactly alike; it's easy to mix apples and oranges.

We like to see what direction gross margin is moving in—up or down. A growing gross margin also signals that the company is doing something right. That isn't perfect, either; as the economy moved from boom to bust, many excellent companies reported declines in gross and especially operating margins (sales minus cost of goods sold minus operating expenses) as they laid off workers and used less capacity. Still, in a steady-state environment, it makes sense to favor companies with growing margins. In a declining market, companies that can protect their margins will come out ahead.

Does a Company Produce More Capital Than It Consumes?

Make no mistake about it—we like cash. Pure and simple, we also like it when a company produces more cash than it consumes.

At the end of the day, cash generation is the simplest measure of whether a company is being successful, especially over the long term. Sure, if a company buys an airplane or opens a factory or a bunch of stores in a given quarter, it will be cash-flow negative. But that should be a temporary thing; over the long haul, it should produce, not consume, cash. Companies that continually have to borrow or sell shares to raise enough cash to stay in business are on the wrong track.

So how do you determine this? You'll have to become familiar with the Statement of Cash Flows or equivalent in a company's financial reports. "Cash flow from operations" is usually positive and represents cash booked from sales less cost of goods sold, with adjustments for noncash items like depreciation and for increases or decreases in working capital. In simple terms, is the cash going into the cash register from the business?

"Cash used for investing purposes" or similar is a bit of a misnomer and represents net cash used to "invest" in the business—usually for capital expenditures, but also for short-term noncash investments like securities and a few other smaller items usually beyond scope. This figure is typically negative unless the company sells some part of its infrastructure. Over the long haul, cash generated from operations should well exceed cash used to invest in the business.

Companies in expansion mode may not show this surplus, and that's where "cash from financing activities" comes in. That's the cash generated from issuing debt or selling securities—or paying off debt or repurchasing shares, if things are going well—and dividends are included here as well. Again, a successful company will produce more cash—capital—from the business than it consumes, just as a successful household does the same, or else it goes into debt. Smart investors track this surplus over time.

Are Expenses under Control?

Just like your household, company expenses should be under control, and anything else, especially without explanation, is a yellow flag.

The best way to test this is to check whether the "Selling, General, and Administrative" expenses (SG&A) are rising, and more to the point, rising faster than sales. If so, that's a yellow, not necessarily a red, flag, but if it continues, it suggests that something is out of control, and it will catch up with the company sooner or later. In the recent downturn, companies that were able to reduce their expenses to match revenue declines scored more points, too.

Is Noncash Working Capital under Control?

Working capital is a hard concept to grasp—even for small entrepreneurs who live with its ups and downs on a daily basis. Insufficient working capital is one of the biggest causes of death for small businesses, and working capital and especially changes in working capital can signal success or trouble.

Using a simple analogy, working capital is the circulatory lifeblood of the business. Money comes in and money goes out, and working capital is what circulates in the veins in between. In its purest sense, it is cash, receivables, and inventory, less short-term debts. It's what you own less what you owe aside from fixed assets like plant, stores, and equipment.

If receivables are increasing, that sounds like a good thing—more people owe you more money. But if receivables are rising and sales aren't, that suggests that people aren't paying their bills, or worse, the business has to finance more to achieve the same level of sales. Similarly, a rise in inventory without a rise in sales means that it costs the business more money—more working capital—to do the same amount of business. That costs twice, because unless the firm is lucky, more inventory means more obsolescence and potentially more deep-discount sales or more write-offs down the road.

A sharp investor will check to see that major working capital items— receivables and inventory—aren't growing faster than sales; indeed, a company that generates more sales with a decrease in working capital is becoming more productive.

Is Debt in Line with Business Growth?

Like many other "fundamentals" items, you can tear your hair out looking at debt figures and trying to decide whether they're in line with asset levels, equity levels, and industry norms. A simpler test is to check and see whether long-term debt is increasing or decreasing, and in particular, whether it is increasing faster than business growth. Gold stars go to companies with little to no debt, and to companies able to grow without issuing mountains of long-term debt.

Is Earnings Growth Steady?

We enter the danger zone here, because the management of many companies have learned to "manage" earnings to provide a steady improvement, always "beating the street" by a penny or two. Stability is a good thing for all investors, and companies that can manage toward stability get extra points. It's worth checking for, but with the proverbial grain of salt.

Still, a company that is able to manage its sales, earnings, cash flow, and debt levels more consistently than competitors, and perhaps more consistently than what would be suggested by the ups and downs of the economy, is desirable—or at least more desirable than the alternatives.

Is Return on Equity Steady or Growing?

Return on equity (ROE) is another of those hard-to-grasp concepts, and another subjective measure when valuing assets and earnings. But at the end of the day, it's what all investors really seek: a return on their capital investments.

Like many other figures pulled from income statements and balance sheets, a ROE number, without any context, is hard to interpret. Does a 26.7 percent ROE mean, in itself, that a company is excellent? The figure sounds healthy, to be sure—it's a heck of a lot better than investing your money in a CD or T-bill. But because earnings and asset values are subjective, it may not represent true success. In fact, a company can increase ROE simply by borrowing money (yes!) and investing it into the business, even if it isn't invested as productively as other previous funds were invested. The math is complicated; we won't go into it here.

So the true test of ROE success is to check whether it is steady or increasing. Increasing—that makes sense. Why *steady?* Because if a company makes profits in a previous period and reinvests them in the business, that amount of money becomes part of equity (retained earnings). If the company reinvests productively, it will produce more returns, and ROE will at least keep up. If the company can't reinvest those earnings productively, ROE will drop—and perhaps it should be paying the earnings to you as dividends instead of investing them unproductively in the business. So if ROE is steady, the company still has good investments to make, and management is probably doing the right thing.

We should note that many investment analysts today prefer return on invested capital (ROIC) as a metric over ROE. ROIC is return, or profit, divided by total equity *plus* debt. This gets you past the distortions that adding debt to the balance sheet might cause. Since the traditional balance sheet equation holds that assets = liabilities + capital, you can simply use total assets as the denominator—essentially the measure is "return on assets." Some analysts prefer to go farther by removing the cash balance from the asset denominator, to reflect the assets deployed and in use to generate returns and to get around the distortions of large reserve capital infusions often found at startup companies.

Does the Company Pay a Dividend?

Different people feel differently about dividends, and as shown earlier, we're placing greater emphasis on dividend-paying stocks and especially those that *grow* their dividends. After all, save for the eventual sale of the company to someone else, a dividend is the only true cash that an investor will realize from buying a stock in a corporation, other than by selling the stock. At least in theory, investors should receive some compensation for their investments once in a while.

Yet, many companies don't pay dividends or don't pay dividends that compete very effectively with fixed-income yields. Why do investors put up with this? Because, in theory anyway, a company in a good business should be able to reinvest profits more effectively than the investor can (or else why would the investor have bought the company in the first place?). Investors trust that reinvested profits will eventually bring the growth in company value that will be reflected in the share price, or eventual takeover, or an eventual payment of a dividend or, better yet, growth in that dividend.

That's the theory, anyway, but there are still lots of companies that get away with paying no dividend at all. Can we tolerate this? Yes, if a company is really doing a great job with their retained profits, like Apple before they started paying dividends two years ago, or CarMax. But we favor companies that offer at least something to their investors in the short term, some return on their hard-earned and faithfully committed capital. If nothing else, it keeps management teams honest and shows that management understands that shareholder interests are up there somewhere on the list of priorities. And getting an ever-*increasing* dividend—and owning a stock that has most likely appreciated because the dividend has increased—is like having your cake and eating it, too: a true favorite among investors.

Strategic Intangibles

When you look at any company, perhaps the bottom-line question follows the Buffett wisdom: If you had $100 billion in cool cash to spend (and we'll assume the genius intellect to spend it *well*), could you re-create that company?

If the answer is yes, it may still be a great company, but it may not be great enough to fend off competition and keep its customers forever. If the answer is no, the company truly has something unique to offer in the marketplace, difficult to duplicate at any cost. That distinctive competence, that sustainable competitive edge—whatever it is, a brand, a trade secret, a lock on distribution or supply channels—may be worth more than all the factories and high-rise office buildings and cash in the bank a company could ever have.

What we're talking about are the intangibles, the "soft" factors that make companies unique and that add up to more than the sum of their parts, the factors that ultimately drive future revenues. Intangibles not only define excellence, they define the future, while fundamentals mainly define the past. Seven key intangibles follow, although you'll think of more, and some industries may have some unique ones, like intellectual property in the technology sector.

DOES THE COMPANY HAVE A MOAT?

A business moat performs much the same role as its medieval castle equivalent—it protects the business from competition. Moats are usually a combination of brand, product technology, design, marketing and distribution channels, and customer loyalty all working together to protect a company. A moat doesn't just protect the existence of a company, it helps it command higher prices and earn higher profits.

Whether a company has a narrow moat, a wide moat, or none at all is a subjective assessment for you to make. You can get some help at Morningstar (*www.morningstar.com*), whose stock ratings include an assessment of the moat.

Coca-Cola has a moat because of the sheer impossibility of surpassing its brand and brand recognition worldwide. Tiffany has a moat because of its immediately recognized brand and elegantly simple, stylish brand image and the enduring and timeless panache around that. The Moat Stars list presented earlier identifies the top ten stocks with a solid and sustainable competitive advantage.

DOES THE COMPANY HAVE AN EXCELLENT BRAND?

It's hard to say enough about brand, especially in today's fast-moving, highly packaged, highly national and international marketplace. A strong brand means consistency and a promise to consumers, and consumers sold on a brand will prefer it over any other, almost regardless of price. People still buy Tide; Starbucks is still synonymous with high quality and ambience. Good brands command higher prices and foster loyalty, identity, and even customer "love."

Ask yourself if a company has a sought-after brand, a brand customers would pay extra to buy or align with, a brand that would be difficult to duplicate at any cost. Would customers rather fight than switch? Think about Starbucks, Coca-Cola, Allstate, Tiffany, Smucker's, Ralph Lauren, Scotts, or Nike, or the brands within a house, like Frito-Lay (Pepsi), Tide (P&G), Mark Levinson (Harman International), KitchenAid (Whirlpool), or Teflon (DuPont).

IS THE COMPANY A MARKET LEADER?

Market leadership usually—but not always—goes hand in hand with brand. The trick is to decide whether a company really leads in its industry. Often—but not always—that's a factor of size. The market leader usually has the highest market share, and the important point is that it calls the shots with regard to price, technology, marketing message, and so forth—other companies must play catch-up and often discount their prices to keep up. Apple is a market leader in digital music, Nike in sports apparel, and Starbucks in beverages—and so forth.

However, sometimes the nimble but smaller competitor is the excellent company and *headed for* market leadership. Examples like CarMax, Perrigo, Valero, and Southwest Airlines can be found on our list.

Does the Company Have Channel Excellence?

"Channels" in business parlance means a chain of players to sell and distribute a company's products. It might be stores, it might be other industrial companies, it might be direct to the consumer. If a company is considered a top supplier in a particular channel, or a company has great relations with its channel, that's a plus.

Companies such as Patterson, Deere, Fair Isaac, McCormick, Nike, Pepsi, Procter & Gamble, Scotts Miracle-Gro, Sysco, and Whirlpool all have excellent relationships with the channels through which they sell their product.

Does the Company Have Supply-Chain Excellence?

Like distribution channels, excellent companies develop excellent and low-cost supply channels. They are seldom caught off guard by supply shortages and tend to get favorable and stable prices for whatever they buy. This is often not an easy assessment unless you know something about a particular industry. Nike and Target, or Procter & Gamble again, are examples of companies that have done a good job managing their supply chains.

Does the Company Have Excellent Management?

If a company *doesn't* have good management, performance fails and few inside or outside the company respect the company. It's not easy for an investor to determine if a management team does a good job or acts in shareholder interests. Clues can include candor and honesty and the ability of company management to speak in accessible, easily understood terms about the company (it's worth listening to conference calls as a resource). A management team that admits errors and eschews other forms of arrogance and entitlement (i.e., luxury perks, office suites, aircraft) is probably tilting its interests toward shareholders, as is the management team that can cough up some return to shareholders once in a while in the form of a dividend.

This may be the most subjective and elusive assessment of all, as few investors work with these folks on a daily basis. Still, over time, you can garner a strong hunch about whether a management team is effective and on your side.

Are There Signs of Innovation Excellence?

This question seems pretty obvious, but it's not just about the products that a company sells. "First to market" definitely offers business advantages.

The less obvious part of this question is whether the company makes the best *use* of technology to make operations and customer interfaces as efficient and effective as possible. Southwest Airlines may have missed our list in the past because of the difficulty of achieving excellence in an industry where players can't control prices or costs. But it does make our list today. Why? Simply because, after all of these years, amazingly, it still has the best, simplest, easiest-to-use flight booking and check-in in the industry. Sometimes these sorts of innovations mean a lot more than bringing new, fancy products and bells and whistles to the market. You can also look to Apple, CarMax, Daktronics, FedEx, Itron, Philips, ResMed, Steelcase, UPS, and Visa for more examples of companies that have deployed technology and innovative customer interfaces to achieve sustainable competitive advantage.

Choosing the *100 Best*

With all this in mind, just how was this year's *100 Best Stocks* list actually chosen?

SIGNS OF VALUE

Following are a few signs of value to look for in any company.

 » Gaining market share
 » Can control price
 » Loyal customers
 » Growing margins
 » Producing, not consuming, capital (free cash flow)
 » Steady or increasing ROE
 » Management forthcoming, honest, understandable

SIGNS OF UNVALUE

. . . and signs of trouble, or "unvalue":

 » Declining margins
 » No brand or who-cares brand
 » Commodity producer, must compete on price
 » Losing market dominance or market share
 » Can't control costs
 » Must acquire other companies to grow
 » Management in hiding, off message, making excuses, difficult to understand, or in the news for all the wrong reasons

While we didn't apply a specific formula or screener to the universe of stocks, we did take a few measurable factors into account to narrow the list from thousands to a few hundred issues. Those factors came from several sources, but at this point we must tip our cap to Value Line and the excellent research and database work they do as part of the Value Line Investment Survey. If you aren't familiar with Value Line, it's worth a look for any savvy individual investor, either online at *www.valueline.com* or, in many cases, at your local library.

When to Buy? Consider When to Sell

We've said it over and over: Sell when there's something better to buy.

Selling is hard. So is removing something from our *100 Best* list (unless it became part of a takeover transaction). If it's hard to figure out when to buy a stock, it's even harder to figure out when to sell. People tend to get married to their investment decisions, feeling somehow that if it isn't right, maybe time will help and things will get better. It's human nature.

Or they're just too arrogant to admit that they made a mistake. That's also human nature.

There are lots of reasons why people hold on to investments for too long a time. Here's the fundamental truth: Buying and selling should be much the same process. Let's look at it from the point of view of selling. When should you sell? Simply, as we've said repeatedly, when there's *something else better to buy*. Something else better for future returns, something else better for safety, something else better for timeliness or fit with today's go-forward worldview; a *megatrend* as we've referred to it. That something else can be another stock, a futures contract, or a house, or any kind of investment. It can also be cash—sell that stock when . . . when what? When cash is a better investment. Or when you need the money, which is another way of saying that cash is a better investment—at least it's safer for the time being.

Similarly, if you think of a buy decision as a best possible deployment of capital because there's no better way to invest your money, you'll also come out ahead. It really isn't that hard, especially if you've done your homework. And it's also made easier if you avoid rash overcommitments; that is, you avoid buying all at once in case you've made a mistake or in case better prices come later down the road.

ETFs: Different Route, Same Destination (Almost)

The *100 Best Stocks to Buy* series continues to be about—well—the 100 best individual companies in which you can buy shares to build into your investment portfolio. The objective is to use these selections as a starting point to build a customized portfolio of your very own, a portfolio that earns decent, better-than-market, long-term returns from excellent companies while—because they're excellent companies—taking less risk than you would with most investments. Because you're doing it yourself, you save money on fees and expenses and come away with the pride of ownership of doing it yourself.

That said, not everyone has the time or inclination to do this. Not everyone wants to sail through the treacherous channels of company financial information and the foggy mysteries of intangibles and marketplace performance to figure out which companies are really best to own and to keep a finger on the pulse to make sure they stay that way. You may want to own individual stocks. But just as buying a kit makes many aspects of building a new outdoor deck easier, so does buying a stock "kit": a product or package of stocks to do what you might otherwise have to struggle through on your own. If you could get such a kit product cheap enough and aligned to your needs, then why wouldn't you? It will save time, and you'll be firing up the barbecue and enjoying those outdoor parties with your friends a lot sooner. Or, perhaps at the risk of more tiring analogies, buying individual stocks is like ordering à la carte from a menu. You're not sure if what you're getting works together, so why not do a *prix fixe* to let the chef do some of the driving? Okay, enough . . .

Such is the impulse to find investment products—packages, a *prix fixe* menu—that mimic the performance of the *100 Best* stocks. Honestly, we would love it if some fund company would come to us and "buy" our index to build a fund you could buy, but that hasn't happened yet. But in that spirit—and because we've written a lot about the merits of individual stock versus fund investing before—we'd like to offer this special section about using exchange-traded funds (ETFs) as a path to own portfolios crafted with many of the *100 Best Stocks* principles in mind.

WHAT ABOUT AN ETF AS A *100 BEST STOCK*?

As we noted at the beginning of this narrative, we were tempted this year to find a "product" solution to investing in some of the more opportunistic but murky sectors of the economy, notably cloud computing in this year's example. In "doing the driving for us," we thought we could gain some exposure to this key sector without having to really understand the nuts and bolts of individual companies within it. However, after some analysis, we didn't find a good fit, and those that were close carried with them the illness of many, if not most, funds, especially ETFs which are constructed around an index—we get the bad and ugly with the good, the mediocre, and in this case, outdated companies with the leaders. So we dropped the idea for this year, but may pick up the idea of adding some ETFs to our *100 Best* list in future editions.

The ETF Universe

We're talking about ETFs here, not traditional mutual funds. Although total traditional mutual fund assets still outweigh ETF-held assets by a factor of eight to one, traditional mutual funds are more expensive and haven't performed as well as ETFs—or the market benchmarks—over time. So we will limit this discussion to ETFs, but if you're working with a professional advisor or are limited to traditional funds through your 401(k) or some other investment platform, the discussion can apply to traditional funds, too.

ETFs are packaged single securities trading on stock exchanges (rather than directly through a mutual fund company), which create a basket of securities that track the composition of specially designed indexes. With most ETFs (excluding "actively managed" ETFs) there are no fund managers making individual stock purchase or sale decisions. The fund follows the index.

These indexes started out as broad, bland, and obvious—the first ETF, the SPDR S&P 500 ETF Trust, has tracked the S&P 500 index since 1993. Since that inception, hundreds of new indexes have been created to track everything from broad baskets of stocks to the price of certain commodities in Australian dollars. Last year we made an attempt to identify the indexes—and the funds built around them—that mimic *100 Best Stocks* principles.

As of early 2014, there are some 1,578 exchange-traded products, of which 1,375 are ETFs and 203 are so-called "exchange-traded notes," or ETNs, which are actually fixed-income securities adjusted in value to track an index without actually owning the components of the index. The ETF space is growing by more than 100 funds every year and has amassed about $1.76 trillion in assets. There are generalized and specialized ETFs covering stocks, bonds, fixed-income investments, commodities, real estate, currencies, and the so-called "leveraged and inverse" funds designed to achieve specialized investing objectives. Within each of those groups, the segments available divisions by market cap, style (growth versus value), industry, sector, strategy, country, and region.

ETF Advantages

There are numerous advantages of ETFs over traditional funds—reasons why they are "where the puck is going" in packaged investments:

- *Easy to research.* ETFs are relatively easy to understand and easy to screen using commonly found screening tools at online brokers.

■ *Transparency.* It's easy to learn what individual stocks an ETF owns and what comprises the underlying index, both through the online portals and through the index providers' websites.

■ *Low fees, low cost.* Fees typically range from 0.1 percent for the most generic index funds to 0.2–0.8 percent for more specialized funds— about half of the typical figures found in traditional mutual funds.

■ *Easy to buy and sell.* It's like buying and selling an ordinary stock.

■ *Easy to match your objectives and style.* New funds are showing up every day, and many match a quality, low-volatility, value-oriented style we're aligned with.

Dining with the 100 Best: A Special ETF Menu

Our *100 Best Stocks* list doesn't really follow any investment style. It isn't just growth or value. It isn't just large cap, it isn't just high yield, nor is it just tied to certain industries or sectors of the economy. It is a blend of excellent companies in the right businesses, doing well in those businesses, with a potential for strong, steady, and growing investor returns. There is no index or any other screenable classification to select those companies. If there were, there'd be little reason to publish this book.

So as we search for ETFs that run with the same tailwinds as our *100 Best* list, we start with the name of the fund and the index that the fund follows. "Dividend Achievers" or "Buyback Achievers" tells us we're looking on the right part of the menu. Then we dig in and look at the actual portfolio composition (again, most investing portals and brokerage sites let you do this—we use Fidelity, *www.fidelity.com*). If we see lots of *100 Best* stocks on the list, it confirms that we're on the right track.

As we mentioned, last year we selected eight ETFs that we thought most closely followed our *100 Best* style and principles, and could be used to build or supplement parts of your portfolio. This year, we attempted to find others to add without success. We share the list in the table below, and in the typical spirit of our presentations, we show the performance of these eight funds during our measurement period. As you can see, two of the eight outperformed our *100 Best Stocks* list, exceeding the 23.85 percent annual gain, with the PowerShares Buyback Achievers Portfolio leading the way (we've been telling you all along that share buybacks are a good thing!). Aside from these two, most failed—rather dramatically—to keep up. The lessons from this table should be self-evident; we will revisit this list again next year.

▼ *100 Best Stocks—ETF "Imitators"*

ETFS WITH STRONG 100 BEST COMPOSITION AND STRATEGIES

ETF	Symbol	Sponsor	Total Assets	Expense Ratio	Price 4.1.2013	Price 4.1.2014	% gain	Share value	Yield %	Total return	What attracted us:
Powershares Buyback Achievers Portfolio	PKW	Invesco	$2.9B	0.71%	$34.65	$43.97	26.9%	$0.27	0.8%	27.7%	Compelling strategy, strong long-term results
Market Vectors Wide Moat ETF	MOAT	Van Eck	$680.2M	0.49%	$23.95	$29.44	22.9%	$0.23	1.0%	23.9%	Compelling strategy, new fund, low cost
100 Best Stocks 2014 Portfolio										23.85%	
Powershares S&P 500 High Quality Portfolio	SPHQ	Invesco	$365.7M	0.29%	$17.89	$20.79	16.2%	$0.37	2.1%	18.3%	Growth and stability of dividends, lots of *100 Best*
iShares Dow Jones Select Dividend Index Fund	DVY	Black-rock	$13.6B	0.40%	$65.47	$73.38	12.1%	$2.22	3.4%	15.5%	Growth plus income, lots of *100 Best Stocks*
SPDR S&P Dividend ETF	SDY	State Street	$12.6B	0.35%	$67.25	$73.77	9.7%	$2.90	4.3%	14.0%	Diverse portfolio, "Dividend Aristocrats" index
iShares MSCI USA Minimum Volatility Index Fund	USMV	Black-rock	$2.5B	0.15%	$33.67	$36.08	7.2%	$0.83	2.5%	9.6%	Low-volatility focus, lots of *100 Best Stocks*, low cost
Powershares S&P 500 Low Volatility Portfolio	SPLV	Invesco	$3.9B	0.25%	$32.19	$34.02	5.7%	$0.86	2.7%	8.4%	Low-volatility focus, lots of *100 Best Stocks*, low cost
First Trust Morningside Dividend Leaders	FDL	First Trust	$712.1M	0.45%	$21.49	$22.50	4.7%	$0.70	3.2%	7.9%	Lots of *100 Best Stocks*

Selecting ETFs is an art in itself and was covered in an earlier book we did in this series called *The 100 Best Exchange-Traded Funds You Can Buy 2012*. Unfortunately that book didn't find a large enough market to be updated each year, but it is still useful in its original form. There are many other ETF resources, again at your online broker or through a specialized ETF portal called ETFdb (*www.etfdb.com*). This portal and its classification page (*www.etfdb.com/type*) can be helpful in finding individual ETFs that suit your taste.

We'll leave the ETF discussion here for this year; the good news is that at least you can invest in ETFs and still follow the *100 Best* style. Now we invite you to accompany us into the real matter at hand: *The 100 Best Stocks to Buy in 2015*.

PART II

THE 100 BEST STOCKS TO BUY

The 100 Best Stocks to Buy

Index of Stocks by Company Name (*New for 2015)

Company	Symbol	Category	Sector
—A—			
3M Company	MMM	Conservative Growth	Industrials
Aetna	AET	Conservative Growth	Health Care
Allergan	AGN	Aggressive Growth	Health Care
Allstate*	ALL	Conservative Growth	Financials
Apple	AAPL	Aggressive Growth	Consumer Discretionary
Aqua America	WTR	Growth and Income	Utilities
Archer Daniels Midland	ADM	Conservative Growth	Consumer Staples
AT&T	T	Growth and Income	Telecommunications Services
—B—			
Becton, Dickinson	BDX	Conservative Growth	Health Care
Bemis	BMS	Conservative Growth	Consumer Staples
—C—			
Campbell Soup	CPB	Conservative Growth	Consumer Staples
CarMax	KMX	Aggressive Growth	Retail
Chevron	CVX	Growth and Income	Energy
Clorox Company	CLX	Conservative Growth	Consumer Staples
Coca-Cola	KO	Conservative Growth	Consumer Staples
Colgate-Palmolive	CL	Conservative Growth	Consumer Staples
Comcast	CMCSA	Aggressive Growth	Telecommunications Services
ConocoPhillips	COP	Growth and Income	Energy
Corning	GLW	Aggressive Growth	Information Technology
Costco Wholesale	COST	Aggressive Growth	Retail
CVS Caremark	CVS	Conservative Growth	Retail
—D—			
Daktronics*	DAKT	Aggressive Growth	Technology
Deere	DE	Aggressive Growth	Industrials
Devon Energy*	DVN	Conservative Growth	Energy
DuPont	DD	Growth and Income	Materials
—E—			
Eastman Chemical	EMN	Conservative Growth	Materials
—F—			
Fair Isaac	FICO	Aggressive Growth	Business Services
FedEx	FDX	Aggressive Growth	Transportation
Fluor Corporation	FLR	Aggressive Growth	Heavy Construction
FMC Corporation	FMC	Aggressive Growth	Materials

Company	Symbol	Category	Sector
—G—			
General Electric*	GE	Growth and Income	Industrials
General Mills	GIS	Growth and Income	Consumer Staples
—H—			
Harman International	HAR	Aggressive Growth	Consumer Discretionary
Health Care REIT	HCN	Growth and Income	Health Care
Honeywell	HON	Aggressive Growth	Industrials
—I—			
Illinois Tool Works	ITW	Conservative Growth	Industrials
IBM	IBM	Conservative Growth	Information Technology
Itron	ITRI	Aggressive Growth	Information Technology
—J—			
J.M. Smucker	SJM	Growth and Income	Consumer Staples
Johnson & Johnson	JNJ	Growth and Income	Health Care
Johnson Controls	JCI	Conservative Growth	Industrials
—K—			
Kellogg	K	Growth and Income	Consumer Staples
Kimberly-Clark	KMB	Growth and Income	Consumer Staples
Kroger	KR	Conservative Growth	Retail
—M—			
Macy's	M	Aggressive Growth	Retail
McCormick & Co.	MKC	Conservative Growth	Consumer Staples
McDonald's	MCD	Aggressive Growth	Restaurants
McKesson	MCK	Conservative Growth	Health Care
Medtronic	MDT	Aggressive Growth	Health Care
Microchip Technology*	MCHP	Aggressive Growth	Technology
Monsanto	MON	Aggressive Growth	Industrials
Mosaic	MOS	Aggressive Growth	Materials
—N—			
NextEra Energy	NEE	Growth and Income	Utilities
Nike	NKE	Aggressive Growth	Consumer Discretionary
Norfolk Southern	NSC	Conservative Growth	Transportation
—O—			
Oracle*	ORCL	Aggressive Growth	Information Technology
Otter Tail Corporation	OTTR	Growth and Income	Utilities/Industrial
—P—			
Pall Corporation	PLL	Aggressive Growth	Industrials
Patterson Companies	PDCO	Aggressive Growth	Health Care
Paychex	PAYX	Aggressive Growth	Information Technology
PepsiCo	PEP	Conservative Growth	Consumer Staples
Perrigo	PRGO	Aggressive Growth	Health Care
Philips N.V.*	PHG	Growth and Income	Industrials
Praxair	PX	Conservative Growth	Materials

Company	Symbol	Category	Sector
Procter & Gamble	PG	Conservative Growth	Consumer Staples
Public Storage*	PSA	Growth and Income	Real Estate
—Q—			
Quest Diagnostics	DGX	Aggressive Growth	Health Care
—R—			
Ralph Lauren*	RL	Aggressive Growth	Consumer Discretionary
ResMed*	RMD	Aggressive Growth	Health Care
Ross Stores	ROST	Aggressive Growth	Retail
—S—			
Schlumberger	SLB	Aggressive Growth	Energy
Schnitzer Steel*	SCHN	Aggressive Growth	Industrials
Scotts Miracle-Gro*	SMG	Growth and Income	Materials
Seagate Technology	STX	Aggressive Growth	Information Technology
Sigma-Aldrich	SIAL	Aggressive Growth	Industrials
Southern Company	SO	Growth and Income	Utilities
Southwest Airlines	LUV	Aggressive Growth	Transportation
St. Jude Medical	STJ	Aggressive Growth	Health Care
Starbucks	SBUX	Aggressive Growth	Restaurants
State Street Corp	STT	Conservative Growth	Financials
Steelcase*	SCS	Aggressive Growth	Industrials
Stryker Corporation	SYK	Aggressive Growth	Health Care
Sysco	SYY	Conservative Growth	Consumer Staples
—T—			
Target Corporation	TGT	Aggressive Growth	Retail
Tiffany	TIF	Aggressive Growth	Retail
Time Warner	TWX	Conservative Growth	Entertainment
Total S.A.	TOT	Growth and Income	Energy
—U—			
Union Pacific	UNP	Conservative Growth	Transportation
UnitedHealth Group	UNH	Aggressive Growth	Healthcare
United Parcel Service	UPS	Conservative Growth	Transportation
United Technologies	UTX	Conservative Growth	Industrials
—V—			
Valero	VLO	Aggressive Growth	Energy
Valmont Industries	VMI	Aggressive Growth	Industrials
Verizon	VZ	Growth and Income	Telecommunications Services
Visa	V	Aggressive Growth	Financials
—W—			
Wal-Mart	WMT	Conservative Growth	Retail
Waste Management	WM	Growth and Income	Business Services
Wells Fargo	WFC	Growth and Income	Financials
Whirlpool	WHR	Conservative Growth	Consumer Durables
W.W. Grainger	GWW	Conservative Growth	Industrials

CONSERVATIVE GROWTH

3M Company

Ticker symbol: MMM (NYSE) □ S&P rating: AA– □ Value Line financial strength rating: A++
Current yield: 2.5% □ Dividend raises, past 10 years: 10

Company Profile

The 3M Company, originally known as the Minnesota Mining and Manufacturing Co., is now a $30 billion diversified manufacturing technology company with leading positions in industrial, consumer and office, health care, safety, electronics, telecommunications, and other markets. The company has operations in more than 70 countries and serves customers in nearly 200 countries. Due to the breadth of their product line and the global reach of their distribution, the company has long been viewed as a bellwether for the overall health of the world economy.

3M's operations are divided into five business segments (approximate revenue percentages in parentheses):

■ The Industrial business (34 percent) serves a variety of vertical markets, including automotive, automotive aftermarket, electronics, paper and packaging, appliance, food and beverage, and construction. Products include industrial tapes, a wide variety of abrasives, adhesives, specialty materials, filtration products, closures, advanced ceramics, automotive insulation, filler and paint system

components, and products for the separation of fluids and gases.

■ The Safety and Graphics business (18 percent) serves a broad range of markets that increase the safety, security, and productivity of workers, facilities, and systems. Major product offerings include personal protection, like respirators and filtering systems, safety and security products such as reflectorized fabrics and tapes, energy control products, traffic control products including sheeting for highway signs, building cleaning and protection products, track and trace solutions, and roofing granules for asphalt shingles.

■ The Health Care business (17 percent) serves markets that include medical clinics and hospitals, pharmaceuticals, dental and orthodontic practitioners, and health information systems. Products and services include medical and surgical supplies, skin health and infection prevention products, drug delivery systems, dental and orthodontic products, health information systems, and antimicrobial solutions.

- The Electronics and Energy segment (17 percent) serves the electrical, electronics, communications, and renewable energy industries, including electric utilities. Products include electronic and interconnect solutions, microinterconnect systems, high-performance fluids and abrasives for semiconductor and disk drive manufacture, high-temperature and display tapes, telecommunications products, electrical products, and optical film materials that support LCD displays and touch screens for monitors, tablets, mobile phones, and other products.
- The Consumer segment (14 percent) serves markets that include retail, home improvement, building maintenance, office, and other markets. Products in this segment include office supply products such as the familiar Scotch tapes and Post-it notes, stationery products, construction and home improvement products, home-care products, protective material products, and consumer health-care products. This segment grew considerably with the 2012 acquisition of the Avery Dennison office products line.

Financial Highlights, Fiscal Year 2013

After a flat FY2012, stronger domestic manufacturing activity and a balanced strength across all product lines led to a moderate 3.2 percent advance in the top line. A 1.6 percent currency headwind was offset by a 1.4 percent increase due to acquisitions. Some operating efficiencies from a new IT system and some organizational realignments brought a slightly improved net profit margin, advancing the bottom line 4.8 percent; a 3.5 percent share count reduction hiked per-share earnings 6.3 percent, while the dividend rose almost 8 percent. For FY2014 and FY2015, the company expects more of the same and then some—steady sales, margin, profit, per-share earnings, and dividend growth with moderate share buybacks behind the scenes. Sales growth is expected in the 5 percent range with per-share earnings growth in the 10 percent range during the period—one of a notable bunch of such "5 and 10" companies we have on our list.

Reasons to Buy

We like the steady "5 and 10" approach to long-term business and investment success; 3M appears to be a classic case. We also like the steady to improving markets—the company makes many steady-selling products essential to manufacturing and day-to-day operations of other companies and organizations and seemingly essential to most of us, e.g., Post-it notes and Scotch tape. The company appears to do better than the markets during strong periods and also holds value better than most during downturns. There is a persistent focus on innovation here, both in its products and in its internal operations and marketing—and it's more the slow, steady than a flash-in-the-pan variety. Cash flows are strong and shared with shareholders. Finally—we don't make this comment often but are starting to look at it more closely these days—3M's rather large $20 billion pension plan is almost fully funded; we don't see that very often but it reflects the sound financial management exhibited by the rest of the company.

Reasons for Caution

3M is, and always will be, vulnerable to economic cycles, although as we pointed out, the business holds up pretty well in down cycles. The markets have recently seen more in the company's success, which has driven the share price up to new highs and also increased the "beta" from a placid .80 to 1.16, signaling the potential for more volatility. We still think there's value here, but it comes with a bit more risk than in past years.

SECTOR: **Industrials**
BETA COEFFICIENT: **1.16**
10-YEAR COMPOUND EARNINGS PER-SHARE GROWTH: **10.0%**
10-YEAR COMPOUND DIVIDENDS PER-SHARE GROWTH: **6.5%**

	2006	2007	2008	2009	2010	2011	2012	2013
Revenues (mil)	22,293	24,462	25,269	23,123	26,662	29,611	29,904	30,871
Net income (mil)	3,851	4,096	3,460	3,193	4,169	4,283	4,445	4,659
Earnings per share	5.06	5.60	4.89	4.52	5.75	5.96	6.32	6.72
Dividends per share	1.84	1.92	2.00	2.04	2.10	2.20	2.36	2.54
Cash flow per share	6.71	7.29	6.65	6.15	7.43	7.85	8.35	9.09
Price: high	88.4	97.0	84.8	84.3	91.5	98.2	95.5	140.4
low	67.0	72.9	50.0	40.9	68.0	68.6	82.0	94.0

3M Company
3M Center
St. Paul, MN 55144–1000
(651) 733-1110
Website: *www.3m.com*

E GROWTH

Aetna Inc.

Ticker symbol: AET (NYSE) ❑ S&P rating: A+ ❑ Value Line financial strength rating: A ❑ Current yield: 1.2% ❑ Dividend raises, past 10 years: 3

Company Profile

Founded in 1853, Aetna is one of the nation's longest-lived insurers. Longevity, though a point of pride (and marketing value) among insurers, is not by itself a qualifying criterion for inclusion in our *100 Best Stocks* list. Today's Aetna, a product of a 1996 merger between Aetna Life & Casualty and U.S. Healthcare, is also one of the largest and most important diversified health-care, insurance, and benefits companies in the United States.

The company's three distinct businesses are operated in three divisions. Health Care provides a full assortment of health benefit plans for corporate, small business, and individual customers, including PPO, HMO, point-of-service, vision care, dental, behavioral health, Medicare/Medicaid, and pharmacy benefits plans. The Group Insurance business provides group term life, disability, and accidental death and dismemberment insurance products primarily to the same sort of businesses that might sign up for its health plans. The Large Case Pensions business administers pension plans for certain existing customers.

The health-care business is by far the largest segment and the focal point

of our selection of this company. The business touches some 44 million individuals. Obviously, the company is a big player in the Affordable Care Act and its related reforms. While future outcomes are uncertain, much of its majority base in providing employer coverage is left relatively intact. Prior to the ACA as now, Aetna has proven itself to be a pacesetter among insurance providers, mainly through its support and innovations in the area of consumer-directed health care.

For example, with Aetna's consumer-directed HealthFund plans, subscribers become responsible for a portion of their own health-care costs and are given the tools to shop for health-care alternatives and maximize preventive care. Aetna originally led the way with some of the first health savings account–compatible products in 2001. Since then the company has led the industry in developing tools, such as the Aetna Navigator price transparency tool, designed to help patients evaluate the cost and outcomes of procedures in different geographies. The company also has championed patient- and doctor-accessible medical records and other techniques for making health-care delivery more efficient—as they put it, "Industry-leading use of patient data and new connections [to help] you play a greater, more informed role in your own health." Aetna is a big believer in the use of analytics—using a "big data" approach to predict the types of medical conditions their covered clients are likely to encounter in the coming years based on correlations among contributing factors in their large data pool. More generally, the company follows an industry trend to focus less on "episodic" care at a medical facility toward more long-term wellness—a "health plus health care" model. Obviously, being able to tell a particular patient how to avoid a predicted condition is a big win for both parties. Predictability permits the company to assemble coverages appropriate to the patient's needs, saving money for both the company and the client.

Over the years, the company has made several, mostly small acquisitions on the international front and in health administration; a larger one in 2013 with Coventry Health prescription management service took place.

Financial Highlights, Fiscal Year 2013

Despite ongoing uncertainties with the Affordable Care Act and increased scrutiny of payer obligations and profits across the industry, FY2013 was an excellent year for Aetna. Helped along by the Coventry acquisition, revenues charged ahead some 29 percent over FY2012, with earnings ahead just over 16 percent. Per-share earnings did not keep pace as the company issued about 35 million shares in the acquisition, breaking a long trend of buying back shares. FY2014 and forward should return to a steadier EPS growth path, and improving margins and a recently approved $750 million (10 million shares, or 3 percent) will drive per-share earnings ahead to $6.27–$6.35, or 8 percent in FY2014, and a heftier 13 percent in FY2015, again on robust revenue growth.

Reasons to Buy

We feel that Aetna continues to pace the pack in terms of both business and technology innovation, and as such will not only adapt faster to the new ACA environment but will also lead the way more generally in information-driven health care and health-care utilization. The company's financials remain solid, with strong earnings and cash flow levels and trends and significant cash reserves. The recent focus on dividend increases (obvious from the following chart) and continued aggressive share buybacks also bode well. Even with the 2013 issuance of shares, the company will have retired some 30 percent of its float from 2007 through 2013.

Reasons for Caution

The complete effects of health-care reform have yet to become fully visible, and it could turn out that ACA and other initiatives leave the company with a more expensive base of insured—with a lag in ability to recover that cost. That said, the company is well positioned to draw on its analytics to make relatively quick adjustments. Public and governmental scrutiny of health insurers has never been higher, and burgeoning health-care costs can be difficult for even a company of Aetna's capability and influence to manage. These factors could produce some negative surprises, and the aggressive rise in the stock price since mid-2012 makes it important to seek good entry points.

SECTOR: Health Care
BETA COEFFICIENT: 0.92

10-YEAR COMPOUND EARNINGS PER-SHARE GROWTH: 41.5%
10-YEAR COMPOUND DIVIDENDS PER-SHARE GROWTH: 20.0%

	2006	2007	2008	2009	2010	2011	2012	2013
Revenues (mil)	25,146	27,600	30,951	34,765	34,246	33,700	36,596	47,295
Net income (mil)	1,602	1,842	1,922	1,236	1,555.5	1,850	1,658	2,058.4
Earnings per share	2.82	3.49	3.93	2.75	3.68	5.15	5.14	5.86
Dividends per share	0.04	0.04	0.04	0.04	0.04	0.45	0.73	.80
Cash flow per share	3.63	4.36	5.07	3.83	5.20	6.25	6.43	7.24
Price: high	52.5	60.0	59.8	34.9	36.0	46.0	51.1	69.5
low	30.9	40.3	14.2	16.7	25.0	30.6	34.6	44.4

Aetna Inc.
151 Farmington Avenue
Hartford, CT 06156
(860) 273-0123
Website: *www.aetna.com*

AGGRESSIVE GROWTH

Allergan, Inc.

Ticker symbol: AGN (NASDAQ) ▫ S&P rating: A+ ▫ Value Line financial strength rating: A+
Current yield: 0.2% ▫ Dividend raises, past 10 years: 1

Company Profile

Allergan is a health-care products company making pharmaceutical, over-the-counter, and medical device items for the ophthalmic, neurological, and dermatological fields as well as for use in an assortment of cosmetic medical procedures such as breast and facial aesthetics, and other specialty medical markets. The company was founded in 1977 and originally exclusively marketed ophthalmic products for contact lens wearers and other products for eye inflammation and other disorders; over the years it has diversified into a variety of medical and medical cosmetic products.

The company operates in two segments. The Specialty Pharmaceuticals segment markets the long-line ophthalmic products, including contact lens products, glaucoma therapy, artificial tears, and allergy- and infection-fighting products. Brand names include Restasis, Lumigan, Refresh, Alphagan, and Acuvail among others.

Specialty Pharmaceuticals also sells Botox for a variety of medical conditions and for cosmetic use. Botox is used not only for the familiar skin wrinkle therapies but also for neuromuscular disorders; recently it has been approved for use in treating chronic migraines, a new market with substantial potential. It has also been approved for an overactive bladder condition. In total, with these approvals, the "therapeutic" side of the Botox business (in contrast to the "cosmetic") is quite healthy. Botox treatments have now been approved for about 80 percent of Medicare and commercial patients. With more uses by more people and a recent price increase, not surprisingly, Botox-related revenues advanced some 12 percent in FY2013. The segment also offers a number of popular skin-care and acne medications for both acute care and aesthetic use, including acne care, psoriasis, and eyelash enhancement. Brand names include Aczone and Tazorac for acne and psoriasis, Vivite for aging skin care, and Latisse for eyelashes.

The Medical Devices segment makes and markets breast implants for augmentation, revision, and reconstructive surgery. The segment also markets other skin and tissue regenerative products for aesthetic and reconstructive purposes for burn treatment and other traumas, mostly for facial applications.

The approximate FY2013 business breakdown by revenue is 49 percent eye care (versus 47 percent in FY2012), 32 percent neuromuscular including Botox (versus 30 percent), and the rest breast and facial treatments and implants. The company sold a division that produced obesity intervention products—lap bands—and we think that was a good move. Foreign sales continue to account for about 39 percent of the total, and R&D expenditures are 17 percent of sales.

In mid 2014, the company was in the midst of evaluating, rejecting, and reevaluating a takeover offer from Valeant Pharmaceuticals that would value the company in the $160–$170 per share range including cash, Valeant shares, and valued R&D rights. The fundamentals of the company are unchanged by the offer, but prospective investors should read up on the latest information.

Financial Highlights, Fiscal Year 2013

Regulatory approvals and more mainstream acceptance of the company's neuromuscular and facial products continues to take the wrinkles out of the top line; FY2013 revenues advanced a healthy 8.5 percent, while stronger pricing and operating leverage increased margins and thus per-share earnings almost 14 percent. Momentum is gaining into FY2014 and FY2015, with revenues even absent the obesity intervention products projected forward by 10 percent each year, with earnings up in the 15 percent range each year. Cash flows are strong but have not for the most part been shared with shareholders yet, as the company continues to invest heavily in R&D and approvals for new applications of Botox.

Reasons to Buy

Allergan tends to be more economically sensitive and cyclical than other pharmaceutical and medical products companies because much of what they sell supports cosmetic, thus elective, and thus cash-paid (in contrast to insurance-paid) procedures. Allergan's share price moves with the broader economic trends, which are in its favor right now. That said, the steady eye-care products segment tends to buffer the company somewhat against down cycles.

We find a lot of interest in the steady increase for the uses for Botox and, most importantly, the acceptance of those uses; Botox appears to be a stronger growth vector than many pharmaceutical companies have at this juncture; the company is also learning how to capitalize on the opportunity. We also like the prospects in overseas markets as treatments become available for a growing (and aging) middle class.

Reasons for Caution

Obviously, today the biggest opportunity but also the biggest risk lies in the Valeant takeover offer; this could fall through before 2015 even gets started.

Despite their thorough approval processes, pharmaceutical and medical device products come with an inherent risk of short- and long-term failure with painful financial and brand-image consequences. Cosmetic devices are particularly sensitive—witness what happened to Dow Corning with breast implants in the 1970s. The company is more economically sensitive than many in this industry. Naturally, we'd like to see more cash returns to shareholders, but this may require some patience.

We continue to carefully watch Allergan to make sure the story is still working and, more importantly, justifies the stock price. We stayed with the company—and again we were proved right. This year we're still cautious even though the company is well positioned with in-demand products and broader applications in good demographics. Allergan continues to trade at a 32 P/E multiple and is a dividend payer in name only. This makes it unique in this book. It may not be the right stock for everyone, and may require some patience to find the right buying opportunity.

SECTOR: **Health Care**
BETA COEFFICIENT: **0.69**
10-YEAR COMPOUND EARNINGS PER-SHARE GROWTH: **15.0%**
10-YEAR COMPOUND DIVIDENDS PER-SHARE GROWTH: **1.0%**

	2006	2007	2008	2009	2010	2011	2012	2013
Revenues (mil)	3,063	3,939	4,403	4,503	4,883	5,347	5,710	6,196
Net income (mil)	452	575	786	850	975	1,057	1,172	1,332
Earnings per share	1.51	1.86	2.57	2.78	3.16	3.41	3.84	4.42
Dividends per share	0.20	0.20	0.20	0.20	0.20	0.20	0.20	0.20
Cash flow per share	1.98	2.58	3.46	3.65	4.03	4.29	4.76	5.33
Price: high	61.5	68.1	70.4	64.1	74.9	89.3	97.1	116.4
low	46.3	52.5	29.0	35.4	56.3	68.0	81.3	81.3

Allergan, Inc.
2525 Dupont Drive
Irvine, CA 92612
(714) 246-4500
Website: *www.allergan.com*

CONSERVATIVE GROWTH

Allstate Corporation

Ticker symbol: ALL (NASDAQ) ❑ S&P rating: AA- ❑ Value Line financial strength rating: A+
Current yield: 1.9% ❑ Dividend increases, past 10 years: 6

Company Profile

For the past three years we've had one lone horse in the *100 Best* insurance race, and now we've decided to switch horses. After an exciting run in 2013, where "dark horse" Cincinnati Financial rang up a 37 percent gain, pretty exciting for a stock picked almost exclusively for its 5 percent dividend, that horse pretty much ran with the pack in 2014. "Sell when there's something better to buy" is our mantra, and we decided to switch to a company with a bit more open track in front of it. We decided we'd be in good hands with Allstate.

While Cincinnati Financial occupied a solid niche position primarily selling property and casualty lines to business clients through agencies, Allstate broadens the offering considerably into the branded consumer and retail insurance space. The primary business is property/casualty (auto and home, mainly) and some commercial lines, but the company also sells life insurance, annuities, and accident and health insurance.

The company prides itself on its four-tiered brand and channel strategy for delivering choice and advice to customers where, when, and how they want it. The company sells its own Allstate product through 9,300 exclusive agencies and its "Encompass" subbrand through independent agencies. The company owns and operates the e-commerce insurance portal Esurance and also sells its product direct, along with other insurance brands, through its "Answer Financial" phone portal for self-directed consumers looking for choices. That said, the lion's share of premiums ($25.2 billion, or 92 percent) is earned through the Allstate brand, while Encompass and Esurance contribute about $1.2 billion, or 4 percent each. By product line, auto leads the way with about two-thirds of premium dollars, homeowners with 24 percent, with the rest coming from life, commercial, and other business lines.

Financial Highlights, Fiscal Year 2013

Allstate rode a higher market share, a strong pricing environment, and a favorable loss environment to a strong year in FY2013 and a stronger and more stable business footprint going forward. Premiums written increased 4.2 percent in FY2013. After years of erratic performance, underwriting income per share appears to be stabilizing in the $4–$5 range, while investment income has also ticked up into the $8–$9 per-share range. These figures precede expenses; hence the bottom line winds up also in the $5–$6 range. At day's end, Allstate is earning more income on both major fronts, underwriting and investing, and is doing it in more stable fashion with decent gains projected going forward. Property/casualty premiums are guided 5–6 percent higher for both FY2014 and FY2015; earnings should at least maintain current levels assuming "normal" accident and catastrophe rates (FY2013 was unusually low in the company's view) with solid double-digit gains over time if current underwriting trends prevail and interest rates rise to boost investment income—although such rises could hurt initially as about 75 percent of the company's investments is in fixed income securities.

Cash payouts to shareholders look to stabilize and increase steadily, and the company has been aggressive in reducing share counts—about 6 percent retired in each of the past two years and more than a third since 2004.

Reasons to Buy

We like the market position, channel strategy, increased stability, and upside potential both in underwriting and in investment performance. The company has sold some underperforming operations (including Lincoln Benefit Life) and has gained a solid strategic foothold on its reputation, brand, and channel strategy. Esurance and other "direct" models are gaining traction (Esurance grew policies in force some 26.7 percent in 2013), while the company is also offering a better product mix and better cross-selling opportunities through its traditional agencies. The Allstate brand is turning from a slight negative to a positive through stronger advertising, product offering, and general branding initiatives. One example is the new "Package" policy, combining auto and homeowners into a single policy sold under the Encompass brand. While improving the top line through such initiatives, there is also clearer focus on expenses, the bottom line, stability, and overall shareholder returns going forward; in our view Allstate has become a solid blue-chip performer in a difficult industry with a pretty decent upside going forward.

Reasons for Caution

Competition is stiff and another hurricane-infested year like 2005 could also hurt, although Allstate is more geographically diverse than some of its competitors. Interest rates on the industry's traditional investment instruments may continue to be weak for some time. For years, the brand suffered from a reputation for poor claims performance and a salesy approach. Although the company is more aware of its relatively erratic past and seems to be doing something about it, the prior volatility of its results in revenues, earnings, and dividends paid is hard to ignore.

SECTOR: **Financials**
BETA COEFFICIENT: **1.02**
10-YEAR COMPOUND EARNINGS PER-SHARE GROWTH: **1.5%**
10-YEAR COMPOUND DIVIDENDS PER-SHARE GROWTH: **2.0%**

	2006	2007	2008	2009	2010	2011	2012	2013
Property/Casualty premiums (mil)	27,369	27,233	26,967	26,194	25,957	25,942	26,737	27,618
Net income (mil)	4,993	4,636	1,445	1,976	1,535	699	2,143	2,559
Earnings per share	7.67	6.47	3.22	3.47	2.83	1.34	4.34	5.70
Dividends per share	1.37	1.49	1.64	1.01	0.80	0.83	1.09	0.75
Underwriting income per share	(0.99)	3.12	(1.96)	(0.58)	(0.58)	(4.19)	2.49	4.95
Price: high	66.1	65.9	52.9	33.5	35.5	34.4	42.8	54.8
low	50.2	48.9	17.7	13.8	26.9	22.3	27.0	40.7

Allstate Corporation
2775 Sanders Road
Northbrook, IL 60062
(847) 402-5000
Website: *www.allstate.com*

AGGRESSIVE GROWTH

Apple Inc.

Ticker symbol: AAPL (NASDAQ) ❏ S&P rating: NR ❏ Value Line financial strength rating: A++
Current yield: 2.3% ❏ Dividend raises, past 10 years: 2

Company Profile

Apple has traditionally been one of the more interesting and controversial analyses we do each year, and this year is no exception. Commentary from investors large and small and supporters and pundits deep and wide continues almost unabated on whether the company is still a superhero among modern enterprises or has lost its edge and is headed to the boring ranks of other greying technology firms. At the end of the day, the decision is whether the rapid transformation of this company into a cash-bearing value stock makes up for a slowdown in innovation and its previous power to not only lead but define markets. If you take the view that cash is king, this company has a lot to offer—as much if not more than ever.

Apple has gone from being a niche supplier of high-end gadgets to a familiar bellwether of consumer technology and industrial design, and their products have become and continue to be bellwethers in all major consumer segments from preteen to seniors. The company designs, manufactures, and markets personal computers, tablet computers, portable music players, cell phones, and related software, peripherals, downloadable content, and services. It sells these products through its own retail stores, online stores, and third-party and value-added resellers. The company also sells digital content through its iTunes store.

The company's products have become household names: The iPhone, iPod, iPad, and MacBook are just some of the company's hardware products. While the software may be less well-known, iTunes, QuickTime, OSX, and the emerging iCloud are important segments of the business, each with its own revenue stream.

It's hard to imagine the current consumer tech landscape without Apple's presence at the top of the heap. Their product line, while comparatively narrow, is focused on areas where the user interface is highly valued. Apple has leveraged this focus on the user experience into a business that is far and away the most profitable in the industry.

Apple has become a case study in creating extraordinary value through innovation, innovative leadership, and marketing excellence. But while wildly successful, the company came upon a test anticipated for some time: the passing of Steve Jobs in October 2011. Steve was clearly the driving and leading force in Apple's innovation, style, and success (for more on this leadership style, we refer you to coauthor Peter Sander's recent book *What Would Steve Jobs Do?*). There are some considerable doubts the momentum can be maintained in the absence of this unique guiding light and under the current CEO Tim Cook, but Mr. Cook does bring some other wisdom and a strong operational focus to the table. The question will continue to be whether this operational focus will stifle innovation and growth as it has in so many big-tech brethren.

Financial Highlights, Fiscal Year 2013

Whew, that was a lot to say for the strategy, position, and health of any company—let's get down to the numbers, which remain the envy of the corporate world. Reflecting a maturity in current markets and the failure to create any new ones (a mild scold for Apple and business as usual for others), Apple turned in a 9.2 percent revenue gain to almost $171 billion. Only 9.2 percent higher after a 44 percent gain in 2012? Shame, you say. But that's still almost $16 billion in new business. Yes, growth rates will slow—projections call for another $10 billion increase over each of the next few years. Ten billion? That's the value of a good-sized company or two. However, on the earnings front there was a bit more uncertainty as competitive pricing pressures came into play,

dropping the net profit margin 5 percent to 21.7 percent. (Again, lots of takers in the rest of the business world for a 21.7 percent net margin, no?) Total net profit declined some 11.3 percent to just over $37 billion (again, with a "b"). But some of the net profit increase was due to increased depreciation, and as such, cash flows, and especially cash flow per share, was up almost 2 percent to $48.70. By 2015, the company expects that per-share cash flow to hit $60 and earnings to rise once again to about $51 per share, 7 percent ahead of today's level. But the real increase is in shareholder payback—dividends, started in 2012, rose to $12.20 per share in FY2013 and are projected to rise to $20 in five years—and share buybacks will consume 100 million shares by that same five-year period. This is a big deal when the shares are trading in the $500 range.

Reasons to Buy

Apple's most well-known product, the iPhone, seems ubiquitous. You probably have one. Everyone you know has one. They're everywhere, and you can be forgiven for thinking that the market for this product is saturated. The truth, however, is this: The iPhone has less than 20 percent market share. We think Apple slipped by not having lower-priced products ready when Android-based phones flooded the market, but the good news is that Apple still has 50 percent of the market's earnings with its lower volumes and the number one models in the market based on market share. The introduction of the iPhone 5S and some lower-priced models in the fall of 2013 improved volumes and maintained market share while taking a small toll on earnings; we expect the market to hit the sweet spot in price, performance, and profitability not too far from the 5S price point. The market still recognizes the iPhone as a strong industry standard and if not the leader, certainly a gorilla niche in the market, and we feel much of this advantage will carry over to emerging markets and particularly China.

Thanks to Carl Icahn and others, Apple has taken some steps to address the vocal critics of their massive cash hoard. Shareholders have already ben-efitted as described and will continue to do so as the company places new emphasis on returning cash.

We haven't given up on innova-tion, either, and feel that Apple still has room to create some blockbusters in the "wearable" technology space— smartphone technology integrated into clothing, for example, and in flex-ible display technologies (see Corning, another *100 Best* pick). We see other major "vertical" applications of iPhone form and technology in cars (check out "CarPlay") and in the health-care space for remote patient monitoring and such. Breakthrough technolo-gies in the TV space have been talked about for some time; while not gain-ing much traction to date, we could

still tune in to some upside in that lucrative space.

The company split its shares seven for one in mid-2014. That in itself cre-ates no change in real share value, but the effects on the stock price remain to be seen as the shares appear more affordable and a better fit for smaller investor accounts.

Reasons for Caution

Phones, in our view, will never be as profitable on a per-unit basis for Apple as they were through 2012. Apple deliv-ered a user experience that no one else could touch initially, but the Android platform, led by Samsung hardware offerings, have caught up in many major markets. Revolutionary year-to-year advances—at least in the traditional hand-held part of the category—seem unlikely. In other categories, there is some concern about competition and price erosion in the tablet space, but production efficiencies and scale should help offset at least some of this.

In the main, we're pretty happy about Apple's ability to generate income, and now, to distribute it to shareholders. The franchise is the world's most valuable in market capi-talization—at the moment, deservedly so. But nobody can sit on their laurels, especially when their laurels are this high off the ground and in plain sight of every competitor. Apple will need to restart the innovation machine with something besides lower-cost versions of existing products.

SECTOR: **Consumer Discretionary**
BETA COEFFICIENT: **1.00**
10-YEAR COMPOUND EARNINGS PER-SHARE GROWTH: **96.5%**
10-YEAR COMPOUND DIVIDENDS PER-SHARE GROWTH: **NM**

	2006	2007	2008	2009	2010	2011	2012	2013
Revenues (mil)	19,315	24,006	32,479	36,537	65,225	108,249	156,508	170,910
Net income (mil)	1,989	3,496	4,834	5,704	14,013	25,922	41,733	37,037
Earnings per share	2.27	3.93	5.36	6.29	15.15	27.89	44.15	39.75
Dividends per share	—	—	—	—	—	—	2.65	11.40
Cash flow per share	2.59	4.37	5.97	7.12	16.42	29.85	47.92	48.70
Price: high	93.2	203.0	200.3	214.0	326.7	426.7	705.1	575.1
low	50.2	81.9	79.1	78.2	190.3	310.5	409.0	385.1

Apple Inc.
1 Infinite Loop
Cupertino, CA 95014
(408) 996-1010
Website: *www.apple.com*

GROWTH AND INCOME

Aqua America, Inc.

Ticker symbol: WTR (NYSE) □ S&P rating: A+ □ Value Line financial strength rating: B++
Current yield: 2.0% □ Dividend raises, past 10 years: 10

Company Profile

If you're like most people, by the time you landed on Water Works as you circled the Monopoly board, you had already deployed your investment capital elsewhere and weren't so excited about its modest growth and yield prospects. You can't build houses or hotels on Water Works, and the monopoly power for owning it in tandem with the Electric Company doesn't seem as powerful as other investments on the board. So you may have passed it up.

Well, times have changed since Monopoly was created. The strategic importance of water, the efficiencies of operating water utilities across a wide geography, and their stability as investments (we didn't care so much about that in Monopoly), have made water utilities a more desirable investment, one for which you might just have plunked down $150 as you circled the board.

"Water Works," in this case, is Aqua America, Inc., a U.S.-based publicly traded water and wastewater utility, serving approximately 3 million customers in nine states: Pennsylvania, Ohio, North Carolina, Illinois, Texas, New York, New Jersey, Indiana, and Virginia, operating 1,447 public

water and 187 wastewater treatment systems. Like many modern utilities, the company also owns a nonregulated subsidiary supplying industrial water and services with a new and special emphasis on the Pennsylvania, Texas, and Ohio shale industries. As an example, in mid-2012, the company and a partner deployed a new water pipeline specifically to serve Marcellus shale operators, eliminating some 4,000 water truck trips every two months.

The company has pursued growth aggressively through acquisitions, bringing in nearly 200 acquisitions and growth ventures in the past ten years, including 15 acquisitions during 2013. Recently, the company announced acquisitions in Pennsylvania, New York, and Virginia and the divestiture of most of its portfolio in northern Florida, Maine, and Georgia. Normally we're not too thrilled with growth-by-acquisition strategies, but in this case it makes sense because a lot of local public jurisdictions and private operators see the logic in turning smaller plants over to a larger company, where economies of scale and management can take effect. That, in essence, is Aqua America's strategy, and we like it.

Financial Highlights, Fiscal Year 2013

Acquisitions and a few divestitures make true revenue and earnings trends hard to capture, but in FY2013 Aqua America grew revenues a modest 1.4 percent overall. Earnings, aided by some one-time tax benefits as well as new unregulated sales to the shale energy industry, jumped some 34 percent; without these benefits they would have grown in the low double-digit range. Projections for both top- and bottom-line growth through FY2015 are in the mid–single-digit range from this point with no retracement of earnings back to the previous year's levels despite the one-time tax benefit. The company has raised its dividend for 22 straight years.

Reasons to Buy

In the midst of a raging-bull market, we make this choice in defense against the next pullback—we'd like to have a few choices that will likely be relatively immune from such an event. That, plus an interest in steadily growing cash returns, fuels our interest in Aqua America. The company is a relatively small and simple business compared to a lot we look at. It occupies a strategic position in a key utility area, especially as more water works become available as public sector operations are trimmed. The company is earning the maximum return on equity allowed by regulators, suggesting a "best in class" operating effectiveness; it is also beginning to expand the use and strength of its brand. The stock has a low beta of 0.26, indicating stability and persistently growing earnings and dividends. The payout percentage—dividends as a percent of net profits—has trended downward, and that, along with strong cash flow, suggests a pickup in the size of dividend increases into the 8–10 percent range annually.

Reasons for Caution

Water distribution requires a lot of expensive infrastructure, and a lot of the current infrastructure is old: In fact, the need to replace infrastructure is one reason some smaller utilities are selling out to Aqua America. Such replacement costs could be high and a drag on earnings in the short term, but the company has managed them well as evidenced by a decline in long-term debt as a portion of total capitalization despite these capital expenditures. We chose this investment in part due to its relatively inelastic demand and steady earnings and cash flow into the future even in bad economic times; however, Aqua may participate less in economic growth and rising equity markets than other stocks we choose. This isn't necessarily a negative; it's just good to know the temperature of the water you're getting into.

SECTOR: Utilities
BETA COEFFICIENT: 0.26
10-YEAR COMPOUND EARNINGS PER-SHARE GROWTH: 8.5%
10-YEAR COMPOUND DIVIDENDS PER-SHARE GROWTH: 7.5%

	2006	2007	2008	2009	2010	2011	2012	2013
Revenues (mil)	533.5	602.5	627.0	670.5	728.1	712.0	757.8	768.6
Net income (mil)	92.0	95.0	97.9	104.4	124.0	144.8	153.1	205.1
Earnings per share	.56	.57	.58	.62	.72	.83	.87	1.16*
Dividends per share	0.35	.038	0.41	0.44	0.47	0.50	0.54	0.58
Cash flow per share	1.01	1.10	1.14	1.29	1.42	1.45	1.51	1.82
Price: high	23.8	21.3	17.6	17.2	18.4	19.0	21.5	28.1
low	16.1	15.1	9.8	12.3	13.2	15.4	16.8	20.6

Aqua America, Inc.
762 West Lancaster Ave.
Bryn Mawr, PA 19010-3489
(610) 525-1400
Website: *www.aquaamerica.com*

These figures were adjusted for 5-for-4 stock split

Archer Daniels Midland Company

Ticker symbol: ADM (NYSE) ❑ S&P rating: A ❑ Value Line financial strength rating: A+
Current yield: 2.2% ❑ Dividend raises, past 10 years: 10

Company Profile

ADM is one of the largest food processors in the world. It buys corn, wheat, cocoa, oilseeds, and other agricultural products and processes them into food, food ingredients, animal feed, and biofuels. It also resells grains on the open market. Rather than the finished consumer products most food processors are known for, ADM produces and distributes intermediate components for food product manufacture and is the largest publicly traded company in this business. Among the more important products are vegetable oils, protein meal and components, corn sweeteners, flour, biodiesel, ethanol, and other food and animal feed ingredients. Foreign sales make up about 48 percent of total revenue and apparently will continue in that range as an intended acquisition of Australia's GrainCorp—a play to reach that market and more broadly, China and the rest of Asia—was rejected by the Australian government in late 2013. The company retains a 19.8 percent interest in that enterprise.

The company is highly vertically integrated and owns and maintains facilities used throughout the production process. It sources, transports, stores, and processes agricultural materials in more than 75 countries on six continents, with 270 processing plants and an extensive sea/rail/road network.

The company operates in four business segments: Oilseeds Processing (39 percent of FY2013 sales), Corn Processing (15 percent), Agricultural Services (46 percent), and Other (less than 1 percent). The Oilseeds Processing unit processes soybeans, cottonseed, sunflower, canola, peanuts, and flaxseed into vegetable oils and protein meals for the food and feed industries. Crude vegetable oils are sold as is or are further refined into consumer products, while partially refined oils are sold for use in paints, chemicals, and other industrial products. The solids remaining from this processing are sold for edible soy protein, animal feed, pharmaceuticals, chemicals, and paper.

The Corn Processing segment milling operations (primarily in the United States) produce food products too numerous to list, but include syrup, starch, glucose, dextrose, and other sweeteners. Markets served include animal feeds and the vegetable oil market. Fermentation of the dextrose yields ethanol, amino acids, and other specialty food and feed products. The ethanol is processed for beverage stock or industrial use as the base for ethanol-blended gasoline and other fuels.

The Agricultural Services segment is the company's storage and transportation network. This business is primarily engaged in buying, storing, cleaning, and transporting grains to/from ADM facilities and for export. It also resells raw materials into the animal feed and agricultural processing industries.

The Other segment engages in financial activities, including commodity futures and merchant activities.

Financial Highlights, Fiscal Year 2013

The end of FY2013 saw ADM finally emerge from a down cycle in many of its businesses, but too late to substantially affect yearly results. The weak harvest from drought-ridden 2012 drove commodity prices for most of ADM's key inputs substantially higher, holding operating margins in the low to mid 3 percent versus 4–5 percent in years prior. At the same time, prices of most of its products were flat, and lower for key products like ethanol. As such, the company reported a 10 percent decrease in per-share earnings on essentially flat revenues.

The story reverses in FY2014 and beyond. Commodity prices have dropped both in the U.S. and major producing regions in Latin America. Ethanol and biofuel prices have risen. Prices for most of the company's oilseed products have held. Operational efficiencies, particularly in Latin America, have taken hold. All factors together point to greater margins, profits, and cash flows, even on relatively stagnant top-line figures. Profits are expected

to rise almost 50 percent from FY2013 levels, and strong cash flows will also turn into significant share buybacks—resulting in a forecasted per-share earnings gain of 50–55 percent for FY2014. For FY2015 and beyond, progress slows to a more typical 6 percent earnings growth rate, which could rise if in-progress operational efficiencies improve margins. Investors patient with the weak period were rewarded—the dividend was raised almost 45 percent at the end of FY2013.

Reasons to Buy

Agriculture is still a key strategic business on a global basis, and increased demand for food and especially middle-class Western diets from emerging market customers bodes well. The company is and has been a strong player in the biofuels industry. While uncertainties continue in the ethanol and biofuels segment, the company's experience and scale in ethanol and biodiesel are strong positives, and the company should win as other smaller players exit the market.

There are four major suppliers that dominate the world market for commodity foodstuffs: Archer, Bunge, Cargill, and Dreyfus—the "ABCD" of world foods. Growth through selective acquisitions is an important factor to success in this business—if you miss an attractive opportunity, you can be reasonably certain one of your competitors will not. ADM continues to grow its presence in the emerging markets of Asia, South America, and Eastern Europe. Sales growth outside the United States has far outpaced domestic growth, and ADM's presence and extensive transportation capability give it a decided advantage over its smaller competitors, many of which are focused only in certain markets or certain industries. We like the solid track record for growth in dividends and overall shareholder value, and recently the share price has caught up with some of this progress.

Reasons for Caution

We saw how agricultural cycles and production can negatively impact this company, but we expect that the worst is over. Still, there's a cyclical—even a volatile—component that's hard to ignore (that said, the beta of 0.70 suggests some safety, even though that changed from 0.47 last year). The stock price has woken from its doldrums, a sign that the markets have recognized its steady progress and niche strength, but that makes new investments more vulnerable to poor conditions like those seen in 2012 and 2013. Entry points should be picked carefully.

ADM is heavily invested in the corn-ethanol-fuel processing chain. Ethanol exists at the margins of the transportation fuels market, and continued softness in demand for gasoline will have a disproportionate effect on its profitability. Federal government policy toward ethanol subsidies and ethanol imports (primarily sugar-based ethanol from Brazil) both bear watching. Finally, the company does produce that nasty-sounding but relatively benign high fructose corn syrup; a pickup in nutritional health sentiment in the food and especially the beverage industry won't help.

SECTOR: **Consumer Staples**
BETA COEFFICIENT: **0.70**
10-YEAR COMPOUND EARNINGS PER-SHARE GROWTH: **14.0%**
10-YEAR COMPOUND DIVIDENDS PER-SHARE GROWTH: **14.0%**

	2006	2007	2008	2009	2010	2011	2012	2013
Revenues (mil)	36,596	44,018	69,816	69,207	61,692	80,676	89,038	89,804
Net income (mil)	744	1,561	1,834	1,970	1,959	2,036	1,496	1,342
Earnings per share	2.00	2.38	2.84	3.06	3.06	3.13	2.26	2.02
Dividends per share	0.37	0.43	0.49	0.54	0.58	0.62	0.69	1.00
Cash flow per share	3.00	3.51	3.97	4.21	4.49	4.54	3.56	3.42
Price: high	46.7	47.3	48.9	33.0	34.0	38.0	34.0	44.0
low	24.0	30.2	13.5	23.1	24.2	23.7	34.3	27.8

Archer Daniels Midland Company
4666 Faries Parkway, Box 1470
Decatur, IL 62526
(217) 424-5200
Website: *www.adm.com*

GROWTH AND INCOME

AT&T Inc.

Ticker symbol: T (NYSE) □ S&P rating: A- □ Value Line financial strength rating: A++
Current yield: 5.2% □ Dividend raises, past 10 years: 10

Company Profile

Measured by revenue, AT&T continues to be the largest telecommunications holding company in the U.S. Although known for years as the center of the wireline local and long-distance telecom service, it has evolved to be the largest provider of wireless, commercial broadband, and wi-fi services in the United States and has become a large player in consumer broadband services with its ISP service and U-verse bundle product.

At 54 percent of total revenues, the AT&T Wireless subsidiary has emerged as the largest business segment, providing voice, data, and text through its familiar wireless service. In particular, wireless data grew 18.7 percent in FY2013, and why not—as more and more of us, especially under the age of 40, consume ever larger chunks of data on our smartphones and as people of all groups sign up for data-everywhere plans for their tablets. The company's wireless strategy centers on the idea of migrating its customer base to smartphones and providing the best and most reliable experience on those smartphones and related devices.

That said, in total, the wireless percentage of the total revenue mix has dropped from 56 percent.

Why? Because in the next segment, the Wireline Data/Managed IT Services—whose servers and trunk lines account for a major part of the global Internet—now account for 29 percent of the sales mix.

The traditional wireline voice subsidiaries—the part that descended from the old "Ma Bell" of decades ago, now account for only 17 percent of revenues and offer services in 13 states, and the wireless business provides voice coverage primarily for traveling U.S. customers and U.S. businesses in 220 countries.

The company has long been focused on offering one-stop-shopping services—with one price on one bill. These efforts have had varying success, but the U-verse product, an IP-based bundling of TV, data, and voice services turning the TV, the PC, and the cell phone into integrated display and transaction devices, is a particularly important development. In mid-2014 the company made an unsolicited $48.5 billion offer ($67.1 billion including assumed debt) for satellite TV provider DirectTV in a play to expand TV, content, and bundled offerings. The jury is still out on whether this will happen and whether it will pan out strategically for AT&T.

Financial Highlights, Fiscal Year 2013

Although the wireless data subsegment is promising, overall this type of company will never experience double-digit growth, and FY2013 and beyond are no exception. But even slow, steady, single-digit growth makes for good business when you're this big and you generate this much cash. For FY2013, the company recorded a modest 1 percent increase, while earnings actually dropped slightly, reflecting continued network development costs and some softness in new subscriber acquisition (which we feel is less important now than profiting more on current subscribers). Some headwinds in the form of price competition (mainly from T-Mobile) started an attenuation in wireless contract prices including a new flat $160 family offering up to 10mb of data; this trend was also thought to soften the immediate near term. But longer term the future looks bright as revenues advance and at a slightly higher pace than costs. FY2014 revenues are guided ahead in the 2–3 percent range; earnings are guided ahead about 2.4 percent in FY2014 and a firmer 6.5 percent in FY2015 as the current trends gain momentum. In early 2014 the company authorized the repurchase of some 300 million shares, or 6 percent of the float, which if carried out, could drive per-share earnings some 11 percent higher. The company is projecting to retire roughly a billion shares (16 percent of float) over the ten-year period starting in 2007.

Reasons to Buy

We think all core businesses are healthy. Beyond that, we think wireless data consumption is on an unstoppable rise—almost as addictive as caffeine is to our Starbucks customer base (another *100 Best* stock) and destined to grow as text evolves to Instagram picture transmissions among teenagers, as people watch more movies on their phones (admittedly, we still don't get this), and so forth. As we mentioned, this part of the business is growing 16–20 percent per year, and aside from capital investments, many of which have been already made, much of this drops to the bottom line. The company continues to grow (and aggressively market) the U-verse product bundle and has overcome some technology barriers giving it more reach, and increasing volumes offer operating leverage over the longer run. More conceptually, we are evolving to a 24/7 connected, always-on world, where, for instance, real-time health monitoring can be done from everywhere, and AT&T will play a big part of that.

Likewise, shareholder cash returns will continue to be above average, with a strong dividend payout, regular increases, and steady share buybacks.

Reasons for Caution

Aside from the DirectTV acquisition and its related risks and dilution of management bandwidth, competition is the main worry. Markets, market analysts, and company analysts continue to fret about subscriber growth, but as suggested earlier, the company now views "better" as better than "more," and we like that approach.

Still, competition also can hurt revenues and profits from existing customers, and we've seen some mild signs of increased price competition that bear watching. While the company has successfully built out a quality set of networks, capital expenditures in this sort of business continue to be a factor and could interrupt cash flow growth.

SECTOR: **Telecommunications Services**
BETA COEFFICIENT: **0.46**
10-YEAR COMPOUND EARNINGS PER-SHARE GROWTH: **1.5%**
10-YEAR COMPOUND DIVIDENDS PER-SHARE GROWTH: **4.5%**

	2006	2007	2008	2009	2010	2011	2012	2013
Revenues (mil)	63,055	118,928	124,028	123,018	124,399	126,723	127,434	158,752
Net income (mil)	9,014	16,950	12,867	12,535	13,612	13,103	13,698	13,463
Earnings per share	2.34	2.76	2.16	2.12	2.29	2.20	2.33	2.50
Dividends per share	1.22	1.42	1.60	1.64	1.68	1.72	1.76	1.80
Cash flow per share	4.63	5.36	5.56	5.46	5.60	5.31	5.70	6.10
Price: high	36.2	43.0	41.9	29.5	29.6	31.9	38.6	39.0
low	24.2	32.7	20.9	21.4	23.8	27.2	29.0	32.8

AT&T Inc.
208 S. Akard Street
Dallas, TX 75202
(210) 821-4105
Website: *www.att.com*

CONSERVATIVE GROWTH

Becton, Dickinson and Company

Ticker symbol: BDX (NYSE) ◻ S&P rating: A+ ◻ Value Line financial strength rating: A++ Current yield: 1.9% ◻ Dividend raises, past 10 years: 10

Company Profile

Becton, Dickinson is a global medical technology company focused on improving drug delivery, enhancing the diagnosis of infectious diseases and cancers, and advancing medical lab work and drug discovery. The company develops, manufactures, and sells medical supplies, devices, laboratory instruments, antibodies, reagents, and diagnostic products through its three segments: BD Medical, BD Diagnostics, and BD Biosciences. These products are sold to health-care institutions, life science researchers, clinical laboratories, the pharmaceutical industry, and the general public. International sales account for about 56 percent of the total. BD is a familiar brand both for observant patients in clinics, medical offices, and hospitals and for the nursing and medical community.

The company operates in three worldwide business segments: Medical (53 percent of FY2013 sales), Biosciences (14 percent), and Diagnostics (33 percent).

The BD Medical segment produces a variety of drug-delivery devices and supplies, including hypodermic needles and syringes, infusion therapy devices, intravenous catheters, insulin injection systems, regional anesthesia needles, and prefillable drug-delivery systems for pharmaceutical companies.

BD Diagnostics offers system solutions for collecting, identifying, and transporting blood and other specimens, as well as instrumentation for analyzing these specimens. Testing systems include those for sexually transmitted diseases, microorganism identification and drug susceptibility, and certain types of cancer screening. The business also provides customer training and business management services.

BD Biosciences provides research tools and reagents to accelerate the pace of biomedical discovery. Clinicians and researchers use BD Biosciences' tools to study genes, proteins, and cells to understand disease, improve technologies for diagnosis and disease management, and facilitate the discovery and development of new therapeutics.

Financial Highlights, Fiscal Year 2013

Coming off a fairly lackluster FY2012, Becton, Dickinson had a solid FY2013, with top-line revenues advancing 6 percent—which may not sound stellar but in light of currency headwinds it's not a bad performance. To underscore this point, per-share earnings advanced only 2 percent, but without the aforementioned currency effects, they would have advanced 8 percent.

For FY2014, strong diabetes care, emerging market growth, and a recovery on the surgical front all point to a strong performance especially in the Medical business and low to mid-single-digit growth in the other two businesses. In all, management is going for a 4.7 percent increase in the top line and a 7.2 percent increase in per-share earnings in FY2014 and a stronger 9.2 percent increase in per-share earnings in FY2015. Both figures are helped along by a 3 million share (1.5 percent) decrease in the number of shares outstanding.

Reasons to Buy

Becton, Dickinson continues to be a classic "blue chip" company, as recession-proof as any stock on our list, while also offering decent growth potential, especially in earnings, cash flow, and dividends. The company has achieved double-digit growth in earnings, cash flow, dividends, and book value for the past ten years, and revenue growth has only slightly missed that mark. Operating margins are consistently strong in the high 20 percent range.

The company is well branded and well established in all of its markets, and it offers a solid way to play the long-term "health" of the healthcare industry. BDX has reduced share count almost 22 percent since the end of 2006 and has more than doubled its dividend over that period. Share count reductions of 1–2 percent per year look to continue for the next few years; the company recently authorized another $450 million for this purpose. There appears to be little to get in the way of continued dividend increases and share reductions.

Reasons for Caution

One has to always be wary of the possible distortions on demand, supply, pricing, and quantity of health care consumed, given the Affordable Care Act and the adaptation of the health-care community to that legislation. Too, this sector has been growing and profitable for a long time; that attracts competition, and cost-conscious health-care providers may back off a bit on purchases. Recently the stock has been on an accelerating run to a new all-time high; it might be prudent to look for a better entry point.

SECTOR: **Health Care**
BETA COEFFICIENT: **0.68**
10-YEAR COMPOUND EARNINGS PER-SHARE GROWTH: **12.5%**
10-YEAR COMPOUND DIVIDENDS PER-SHARE GROWTH: **15.5%**

	2006	2007	2008	2009	2010	2011	2012	2013
Revenues (mil)	5,835	6,560	7,156	7,160	7,372	7,828	7,708	8,054
Net income (mil)	841	978	1,128	1,220	1,185	1,272	1,123	1,159
Earnings per share	3.28	3.84	4.46	4.95	4.94	5.61	5.36	5.81
Dividends per share	0.86	0.98	1.14	1.32	1.48	1.64	1.80	1.98
Cash flow per share	5.08	5.82	6.60	7.13	7.25	8.27	8.30	8.79
Price: high	74.2	85.9	93.2	80.0	80.6	89.4	80.6	110.9
low	58.1	69.3	58.1	60.4	66.5	72.5	71.6	78.7

Becton, Dickinson and Company
1 Becton Drive
Franklin Lakes, NJ 07417–1880
(201) 847-6800
Website: *www.bd.com*

CONSERVATIVE GROWTH

Bemis Company, Inc.

Ticker symbol: BMS (NYSE) □ S&P rating: A □ Value Line financial strength rating: A
Current yield: 2.7% □ Dividend raises, past 10 years: 10

Company Profile

You open a stick of string cheese. You pull the little tab at the end and out pops the stick of cheese, which had been happily stored in its little plastic sack through thousands of miles of trucks, warehouses, more trucks, a stockroom or two, the store, your refrigerator, and now maybe your lunch bucket or bag. You enjoy the string cheese with a sandwich made from lunchmeat packaged in a little zippered plastic bag. Afterward, you take your regular dose of allergy medication, packed up in one of those 12-tablet plastic trays with a metal foil backing to tear through.

Who makes this stuff? Did you ever stop to think about it? How it makes our lives easier, as well as those of manufacturers and distributors of these products? Neither had we, until our search for strategic and vital niche holders led us to one of the other companies in Kimberly-Clark's quiet and productive original hometown of Neenah, WI.

"Freshness," "Convenience," and "Sterility" are the three buzzwords that adorn the top of the company's home page, and they go a long way to explain their value add in the food chain. Bemis makes all kinds of packaging, mainly for the food and pharmaceutical industries. Flexible Packaging products include bags, wraps, and containers, many with a pressure-sensitive or zipper closure, and all labeled for the client's products, rolling out of 71 facilities to the end of packing lines in 12 countries. The Pressure Sensitive product group makes a line of pressure-sensitive materials, clearly for use in their own packaging, but also for the printing, graphic design, and technology markets. Those custom-designed graphics on the sides of large vans and other vehicles start out as a Bemis pressure-sensitive film. About 30 percent of sales are international.

The company recently sold four paper-packaging plants to Hood Packaging Company—plants that make items like paper bags for pet foods—in a continued attempt to adjust the business mix toward higher margin businesses.

Financial Highlights, Fiscal Year 2013

FY2013 was another mixed year for Bemis. The ongoing strategy to optimize profitability brought some small divestitures including a bulk shrink film business, and currency headwinds particularly in Latin America led to a 2 percent decline in revenues—however, an increase in operating margin from 11.7 percent to 12.1 percent brought a 5 percent increase in net income; that and a 2 percent share buyback led to a 6 percent increase in per-share earnings. The strategy seems to be working, and, with a guided 3.4 percent increase in FY2014 revenues (and 2.9 percent in FY2015) combined with continued similar increments in margin, should drive healthy annual earnings increases approaching 10 percent.

Reasons to Buy

This is not an exciting company, but it is a strong niche player providing critical packaging technologies to the industries it serves. New and innovative food packaging designs are becoming more desired as convenience and quality outweigh cost as a priority; the new packaged salads are a good example of packaging for a product not packaged before; new zip-top containers for lunchmeats, cheeses, etc., show how the package is moving up the value-add scale. The company has a significant beachhead in growing Latin American markets, China, and Australia and is investing in new technologies and applications such as package design enhancements for microwaving, easy-open packages for elderly customers (we continue to applaud this one!), and new technologies and delivery systems for the health-care and pharmaceutical industries. We like the strategy of fine-tuning the business mix toward more profitable, higher value-add packages, and the company seems to be executing it well and getting the desired results from it. Cash flow and cash returns to shareholders are steady and increasing; the issue has appealingly low volatility and is generally a good defensive play. The fact that the stock did little until 2013 makes us think the market is waking up to the contents of this package.

Reasons for Caution

To a degree, Bemis is exposed to price volatility in both food and energy and to the economy in general. When food prices rise, consumers get more sensitive to price and may hesitate to pay for convenience packaging—I'll choose and boil my own Brussels sprouts, thank you; no boiling bags for me. When energy prices go up, that does bad things to plastic resin prices, and this company makes almost everything it sells out of plastic. Aside from those two downsides, which are partially offset by niche strength (price wars in their product space aren't much of a concern), Bemis is a safe and steady—if not exciting—business. It certainly hasn't been an exciting stock, at least over the past ten years, and while cash returns and increases in those returns have been slow and steady, we do see room to pick up the pace. Maybe this will happen as margin expansion strategies take effect; ultimately this might put a little oomph in the stock price.

SECTOR: **Consumer Staples**
BETA COEFFICIENT: **0.70**
10-YEAR COMPOUND EARNINGS PER-SHARE GROWTH: **4.0%**
10-YEAR COMPOUND DIVIDENDS PER-SHARE GROWTH: **6.5%**

	2006	2007	2008	2009	2010	2011	2012	2013
Revenues (mil)	3,639	3,649	3,779	3,515	4,835	5,323	5,139	5,030
Net income (mil)	195.6	181.6	166.2	147.2	203.3	212.4	225.3	237.0
Earnings per share	1.83	1.74	1.65	1.38	1.83	1.99	2.15	2.28
Dividends per share	0.76	0.84	0.88	0.90	0.92	0.96	1.00	1.04
Cash flow per share	3.32	3.38	3.29	2.81	3.84	3.87	3.66	4.19
Price: high	35.0	36.5	29.7	31.4	34.3	34.4	33.9	42.3
low	27.8	25.5	20.8	16.8	25.5	2.2	29.5	33.7

Bemis Company, Inc.
One Neenah Center, 4th Floor
Neenah, WI 54957-0669
(920) 727-4100
Website: *www.bemis.com*

CONSERVATIVE GROWTH

Campbell Soup Company

Ticker symbol: CPB (NYSE) ❑ S&P rating: A- ❑ Value Line financial strength rating: B++
Current yield: 2.8% ❑ Dividend raises, past 10 years: 9

Company Profile

Campbell Soup Company is the world's largest, as they like to say, "maker of convenience foods." To most of the free world, that still translates to soup and the ubiquitous pop-culture-iconic Campbell's Soup can. But there is a lot more to this story.

While there are 17 such brands under the Campbell's North American roof, the original Campbell's Soup is still far and away the most important. The company owns 60 percent of the prepared soup market. Their three top soups are three of the top ten grocery products sold in the United States every week. Approximately 80 percent of U.S. households purchase the soup, and the average inventory on hand is six cans. Few brands have enjoyed such penetration and loyalty.

The company has five reporting segments. To highlight the company's own vision of breadth beyond soup, the former U.S. Soup division (including U.S. Sauces), is now referred to as Simple Meals division and accounts for 35 percent of sales with a stronger targeting and message around the concept of convenience. Other divisions include U.S. Beverages (9 percent), Global Baking and Snacking (28 percent), International

Simple Meals and Beverages (11 percent), and North America Foodservice (17 percent). Within each segment reside the many familiar brands that constitute the business: Swanson, Prego, Goldfish, SpaghettiOs, Pace, V8, Pepperidge Farm, Bolthouse Farms, Arnott's, Wolfgang Puck, and, of course, Campbell's, which still accounts for 26 percent of total company sales.

Campbell's products are distributed to 120 countries worldwide and are sold through its own sales force and through distributors. U.S.-based operations accounted for 77 percent of revenue in FY2013. Products are manufactured in 18 principal facilities within the United States and in 13 facilities outside the country. The vast majority of these facilities are company owned.

Campbell's product strategy continues to center on three large, global categories—simple meals, baked snacks, and healthy beverages—which they feel are well aligned with broad consumer trends. The company's growth strategy has evolved toward greater innovation in product marketing and brand recognition and new packaging designed to broaden use in today's fast-paced economy, as well as a healthy dose of internationalization. New store displays and branding advertise soups in four easily recognized categories: Classic Favorites, Healthy & Delicious, Taste Sensations, and Healthy Kids. The company has stepped up R&D through its new Pepperidge Farm Innovation Center, where all baked goods R&D takes place, and has introduced new "Skillet Sauces" and "Slow Cooking Sauces." We think these will play well in the evolving market for convenience cooking. Together, these activities will move the brand forward while maintaining core values and the core customer base—a sound strategy. Furthermore, "Nourishing Peoples' Lives Every Day" should play well in the international space, a frontier on which the company is just beginning to capitalize.

Campbell's $1.55 billion cash purchase of Bolthouse Farms in 2012 gave the company a strong presence in the important and growing "super premium" healthy beverage and dressings segment. Bolthouse, based in Bakersfield, CA, is best known for its line of natural carrot snacks and vegetable and fruit juice matching offerings by Odwalla and others—and often beating them on price. Bolthouse gives the company better exposure to millennials, a market not well addressed by Campbell's traditional brands. In 2013, the company also acquired Plum Organics, a maker of organic foods for infants and young children, and the Kelsen Group, an international producer of gourmet cookies, including those tins of Danish butter cookies, one of our favorites—which, incidentally, also gives the company an expanded sales channel for its Pepperidge Farm and Arnott's brands.

Financial Highlights, Fiscal Year 2013

The addition of Bolthouse Farms and stronger sales of soup (especially Campbell's Chunky) in the U.S., in turn a result of new products and sharpened marketing, drove sales about 12 percent higher with 4 per cent "organic" growth. Reported earnings were flat, but excluding special items, rose about 7 percent. Through FY2014, the company expects a 5–6 percent sales growth and 3–5 percent earnings growth from continuing operations. A resumption of fairly aggressive share buybacks and continued business progress leads to a 5–6 percent per-share earnings growth projection on a 4 percent sales increase in FY2015, with slightly accelerating sales, earnings, share buyback, and dividend growth beyond that.

Reasons to Buy

Brand strength is a key reason to stock a few shares of Campbell in your investment pantry. Campbell owns the number one or number two position in each of the product categories in which it participates. It dominates the $4 billion

U.S. soup market and is making headway in key foreign markets too.

Beyond that, we see FY2011 through FY2014 as investment years. We like the new focus on innovation (the company was named to *Forbes*'s "100 Most Innovative Companies" list) and think this company could kickstart growth with a few product category and packaging winners, not to mention its still largely untapped international opportunity. The company estimates that some 12 percent of sales will be from new products in 2014, compared to 8 percent in 2011.

Campbell isn't trying to capture the remaining 40 percent of the soup market that it doesn't own; it's trying to grow the overall size of the market and letting its 60 percent share do the talking. The strategy, well known in the food industry, is to maintain and slowly grow its core brands while generating new growth, leveraging distribution and sales channels, and increasing brand presence through new products often not directly associated with the Campbell brand. The strategy sounds pretty tasty to us.

Reasons for Caution

Even with the recent emphasis on innovation, the company's brands and core customer base are aging, and adoption of new products may prove slow, especially among the younger set. As others, like Coca-Cola, have found out over the years, there are risks inherent with tinkering with a long-established brand. We would hope that Campbell succeeds with its new ventures without pulling the rug out from under the old ones.

SECTOR: **Consumer Staples**
BETA COEFFICIENT: **0.33**
10-YEAR COMPOUND EARNINGS PER-SHARE GROWTH: **5.5%**
10-YEAR COMPOUND DIVIDENDS PER-SHARE GROWTH: **5.0%**

	2006	2007	2008	2009	2010	2011	2012	2013
Revenues (mil)	7,343	7,867	7,998	7,586	7,676	7,715	7,707	8,052
Net income (mil)	681	771	798	771	842	846	783	786
Earnings per share	1.66	1.95	2.09	2.15	2.45	2.54	2.44	2.48
Dividends per share	0.74	0.82	0.88	1.00	1.05	1.15	1.16	1.16
Cash flow per share	2.41	2.78	3.07	2.87	3.25	3.48	3.35	3.82
Price: high	40.0	42.7	40.8	35.8	37.6	35.7	37.2	45.8
low	28.9	34.2	27.3	24.8	24.6	29.7	31.2	34.8

Campbell Soup Company
1 Campbell Place
Camden, NJ 08103–1799
(856) 342-4800
Website: *www.campbellsoup.com*

AGGRESSIVE GROWTH

CarMax, Inc.

Ticker symbol: KMX (NYSE) ❑ S&P rating: NR ❑ Value Line financial strength rating: B+
Current yield: Nil ❑ Dividend raises, past 10 years: NA

Company Profile

"The Way Car Buying Should Be." That's the slogan used by this clean-cut chain of used vehicle stores and superstores and its new big-box, retail-like model for selling cars. CarMax buys, reconditions, and sells cars and light trucks at 131 retail centers in 64 metropolitan markets, mainly in the Southeast, Midwest, and California, but gradually moving to a more nationwide footprint. The company specializes in selling cars that are under six years old with less than 60,000 miles and in excellent condition; the cars are sold at a competitive price for their condition in a no-haggle environment. The price is the price; the emphasis is on the condition of the vehicles and on a helpful and friendly sales and transaction process. Sales representatives are compensated for cars they sell, but not in such a way that drives them to push the wrong car on a customer. The company sold some 526,929 used vehicles in 2013, up 17.7 percent from 447,728 in 2012 and 29 percent beyond the 408,080 sold in 2011. The average selling price is $19,408; average gross margins are $2,171 per vehicle.

CarMax is gaining footholds in new markets such as Philadelphia, Denver, and the D.C. area, and most reports suggest they are gaining market share in the markets they serve with a high degree of customer satisfaction. CarMax opened 13 new superstores in all in 2013; in 2014 they plan to open stores in Portland; Reno; Spokane; Cleveland; and Madison, Wisconsin—all new markets—and they still have some biggies like Seattle and Minneapolis–St. Paul to go. The company is also testing small-format stores in markets like Harrisonburg, VA, and Jackson, TN.

The health of the economy and consumer spending have swung car buying into a higher gear, but with newfound consumer prudence. Many of these purchases are heading to the one- to six-year-old used car sector of the business, where prices are 40–60 percent lower than comparable new cars. In addition to "retail" used car sales, CarMax is a big player in auto wholesaling, having moved about 342,000 units mostly taken in trade; the company is the world's largest used car buyer. The company also earns income through its financing unit, known as CarMax Auto Finance, or CAF.

CarMax also has service operations and sells extended warranties and other products related to car ownership. The company has state-of-the-art web-based and mobile tools as well as other aids designed to make the car selection, buying, and ownership experience easier. As CarMax puts it, customers request four things when they buy a car:

1. Don't play games
2. Don't waste my time
3. Provide security
4. Make car buying fun

The company's offering is aimed at reducing these concerns and providing the right experience. The offering continues to be unique in the industry, and competitors would have a long way to go to catch up.

Financial Highlights, Fiscal Year 2013

For the year ending February 28, 2014, which the company calls FY2014 but we will refer to as "2013" because most activity occurred in that year, unit volume was 17 percent higher, revenues were 15 percent higher, and same-store sales growth was 12 percent—a new record for the company. Contributing to the success: CarMax reported a significant 32 percent growth in online and mobile vehicle shopping activity, and higher conversion rates in the store with an assortment of physical and process tweaks.

The gross margin per used vehicle increased 1.4 percent from $2,141 to $2,171, but some contraction in wholesale vehicle sales and financing margins resulted in a slight downtick in overall gross margins. Taken together, and even with high store-opening expenses, net profit rose more than 17 percent from 2012, and with the newly initiated share buybacks, per-share earnings rose almost 20 percent.

The company announced a $300 million share repurchase plan in late 2012, the first of its kind and a sign of increased returns to shareholders. With that program, the company repurchased 6.9 million shares for $306 million, fully fulfilling that commitment. In early 2014, the company added another $500 million to that repurchase authorization, with an end date of December 31, 2014. That's enough to buy back approximately 5 percent of its shares.

Reasons to Buy

Quite simply, CarMax continues to be a buy if you believe the traditional dealer model is broken and if you believe people will continue to see value in late-model used vehicles.

Additionally, CarMax brings the latest in business intelligence and analytic models to the car-marketing process, in procurement, merchandising, pricing, and selling the vehicles. Do green Jeep Cherokees sell well in Southern California? Then let's find some, put them on the lot there, and set a market-based price. KMX is well ahead of the industry in making analysis-based supply and selling decisions and has quite successfully deployed analytic tools to adjust prices and inventories quickly to market conditions, a competency that bodes well for the future.

While the auto industry has recovered, selling some 17 million new cars this year, the used car business is also strong—and much larger—at 39 million used cars sold annually. CarMax is increasingly a big player, taking market share from traditional used car dealers, but there's fertile ground to capture more. The company estimates that it has only 5 percent of the current market for zero-to-ten-year-old used vehicles in markets in which they operate, and only 3 percent of the total nationwide—all while being the largest player and twice the size of the nearest competitor.

The company is positioned well both for organic growth through market share and for geographic growth; there is still plenty of fertile ground for new growth especially in the Northeast and Northwest and smaller metro areas. The footprint is slowly but surely becoming a nationwide one, which will not only help volumes but also brand recognition, pricing power, buying power, and cost absorption.

The small-format store test, if successful, could add to this.

Finally, we like the repurchase program, which is stronger than most both in volume and in specificity; we don't always see concrete time commitments for a repurchase plan, nor exact execution against those commitments. When done this way, more shareholder value is created because it's dependable. So far, at least, CarMax has said what it's going to do, and done what it's said in this area.

Reasons for Caution

CarMax will always be somewhat vulnerable to economic cycles, the availability of credit, and the availability of quality used vehicles to resell. We should note that vehicle availability is less of a concern for the moment, as the Great Recession recedes into the past and vehicle leasing has come on strong again—a great source of late-model used cars. Rising interest rates could be a particular concern, as they hurt car buying and reduce financing margins. As this company is still in the growth phase, and new dealerships involve putting lots of new cars on the ground, working capital needs are extensive, long-term debt has risen, and cash returns to shareholders have not met our norms; however, the new share repurchase program takes a big step toward fixing that.

SECTOR: Retail
BETA COEFFICIENT: 1.60
10-YEAR COMPOUND EARNINGS PER-SHARE GROWTH: 17.5%
10-YEAR COMPOUND DIVIDENDS PER-SHARE GROWTH: NA

	2006	2007	2008	2009	2010	2011	2012	2013
Revenues (mil)	7,466	8,200	6,974	7,400	8,975	10,004	10,963	12,574
Net income (mil)	198.6	182.0	59.2	281.7	380.9	413.8	425.0	510.0
Earnings per share	0.92	0.83	0.27	1.26	1.67	1.79	1.87	2.24
Dividends per share	—	—	—	—	—	—	—	—
Cash flow per share	1.08	1.05	0.52	1.52	1.95	2.19	2.0	2.70
Price: high	27.6	29.4	23.0	24.8	30.0	37.0	38.2	53.1
low	13.8	18.6	5.8	6.9	18.6	22.8	24.8	38.0

CarMax, Inc.
12800 Tuckahoe Creek Parkway
Richmond, VA 23238
(804) 747-0422
Website: www.carmax.com

GROWTH AND INCOME

Chevron Corporation

Ticker symbol: CVX (NYSE) ◻ S&P rating: AA ◻ Value Line financial strength rating: A++
Current yield: 3.5% ◻ Dividend raises, past 10 years: 10

Company Profile

Chevron is the world's fourth-largest publicly traded, integrated energy company based on oil-equivalent reserves and production. It is engaged in every aspect of the oil and gas industry, including exploration and production, refining, marketing and transportation, chemicals manufacturing and sales, and power generation.

Active in more than 180 countries, Chevron (formerly Chevron-Texaco via the 2001 merger) has reserves of 7.1 billion barrels of oil and 24.1 trillion cubic feet of gas, with a daily production capacity of 2.6 million barrels of oil equivalent and 4 billion cubic feet of gas per day. In addition, it has global refining capacity of more than 2 million barrels per day (bpd) and operates more than 22,000 retail outlets (including 8,060 company owned) around the world. The company also has interests in 30 power projects now operating or being developed. The upstream capacity is concentrated in North America, Africa, Asia, and the Caspian Sea region, with less exposure to the Middle East than some competitors. The company is more concentrated in oil (less in gas) than

some of its competitors, although it has invested in new shale gas developments. The company is a player in new technologies in exploration and production, including "ultra-deep water" and other difficult environments, and, not surprisingly, in the current "fracking" boom in both the typical North American venues and other less obvious places, like Argentina and Lithuania. The emphasis on oil continues to be a strength recently as oil prices have climbed, while gas prices have generally fallen, although the company is currently benefitting from a current turnaround in natural gas prices as well.

Its downstream (refining/retailing) businesses include four refining and marketing units operating in North America, Europe, West Africa, Latin America, Asia, the Middle East, and southern Africa. Downstream also has active global businesses in manufactured products including lubricants, specialty chemicals and additives, specialty refining units for aviation and maritime markets, and various logistics activities, including pipelines, shipping, and a global trading unit.

The company's global refining network comprises 23 wholly owned and joint-venture facilities that process about 2 million barrels of oil per day. Gasoline and diesel fuel are sold through more than 22,000 retail outlets under three well-known consumer brands: Chevron in North America; Texaco in Latin America, Europe, and West Africa; and Caltex in Asia, the Middle East, and southern Africa.

Chevron is the number one jet fuel marketer in the United States and third worldwide, marketing 550,000 barrels per day in 80 countries. The company's fuel and marine marketing business is a leading global supplier and marketer of fuels, lubricants, and coolants to the marine and power markets, with about 500,000 barrels of sales per day.

Financial Highlights, Fiscal Year 2013

High exploration and production expenses, relatively flat crude oil prices, and some softness in refining margins led to a rather lackluster FY2013 performance—if you can call earning $21.4 billion in net profit "lackluster." The good news comes in the form of firming natural gas prices (although the future is far from certain) and the payoff from large exploration projects, as well as the boom in new resources available through fracking and other new "high tech" recovery methods. Exploration investments will soon start to pay off, and with firming prices the company is

projecting a 5 percent gain in top-line revenue and bottom-line profits for FY2014. While these numbers won't excite particularly in light of FY2012's performance, the company also sports one of the lowest debt-to-equity ratios in the industry, strong cash flow, and a rock-solid balance sheet.

Reasons to Buy

For exploration and production strength and geographic and technological diversity, few companies exceed Chevron's strengths. The company is most exposed to some of the best sectors and geographies in the business and has established a good brand and track record for discovery, production, and downstream operations. Like many in the industry, the company has cut back its refining base a bit, but will likely remain in the refining business for the long term—we think that is the best strategy. The company has a solid record of earnings, cash generation, and cash distribution, with dividend growth to outpace earnings growth currently and in the foreseeable future. With a payout ratio (dividends as a percent of earnings) of just 35 percent dividends have plenty of room to grow. We think shareholders will be well rewarded with growing cash returns in the long term.

Reasons for Caution

While recent exploration and production activities have been promising, like many other "big oil" players Chevron has struggled to increase reserves faster than they deplete them to support annual demand. Some of the softness in reserves, it should be noted, has come from exiting joint ventures and selling off some assets, but investors should be wary of long-term reserve erosion, as has plagued Royal Dutch Shell, ExxonMobil, and others. Too, the cost of recovering oil and gas with ever-increasing use of technology is rising—although current production from "fracking" and other new methods is starting to pay off. The company is always vulnerable to oil and gas price declines, which could occur as more producers and competitors bring more "fracking" and other new assets online. Closer to home for shareholders, while there is a modest share buyback program, we think the company could hit the buyback button a little more often.

SECTOR: **Energy**
BETA COEFFICIENT: **0.96**
10-YEAR COMPOUND EARNINGS PER-SHARE GROWTH: **19.5%**
10-YEAR COMPOUND DIVIDENDS PER-SHARE GROWTH: **9.0%**

	2006	2007	2008	2009	2010	2011	2012	2013
Revenues (bil)	210.1	220.9	273.0	172.6	204.9	253.7	241.9	228.8
Net income (bil)	17.1	18.7	23.9	10.5	19.0	26.9	26.2	21.4
Earnings per share	7.80	8.77	11.67	5.24	8.48	13.44	13.32	11.09
Dividends per share	2.01	2.32	2.53	2.66	2.84	3.09	3.51	3.90
Cash flow per share	10.09	12.11	16.69	10.95	15.99	19.98	20.05	18.43
Price: high	76.2	95.5	104.6	79.8	92.4	111.0	118.5	127.8
low	53.8	65.0	55.5	56.1	66.8	102.1	95.7	108.7

Chevron Corporation
6001 Bollinger Canyon Road
San Ramon, CA 94583–2324
(925) 842-1000
Website: *www.chevron.com*

CONSERVATIVE GROWTH

The Clorox Company

Ticker symbol: CLX (NYSE) ❑ S&P rating: BBB+ ❑ Value Line financial strength rating: B++
Current yield: 3.4% ❑ Dividend raises, past 10 years: 10

Company Profile

A leading manufacturer and marketer of consumer cleaning and other household products, Clorox markets a broad line of highly trusted and recognized brand names, including its namesake bleach, Green Works natural cleaners, Formula 409, Liquid Plumr, and Pine-Sol cleaning products; Fresh Step and Scoop Away cat litter; Kingsford charcoal; Hidden Valley, KC Masterpiece, and Soy Vey dressings and sauces; Brita water-filtration systems; Glad bags, wraps, and containers; and Burt's Bees natural personal care products. In the U.S., Clorox owns the number one or number two market share position with 90 percent of its products, and that continues to be a key part of its long-term strategy.

The company is divided into four segments:

- Cleaning Products (30 percent of FY2013 sales) includes laundry (10 percent), home-care (17 percent), and professional (5 percent) cleaning products. Home-care products include disinfecting sprays and wipes, toilet bowl cleaners, carpet cleaners, drain openers, floor-mopping systems, toilet and bath cleaning tools, and premoistened towelettes. Professional products are for institutional, janitorial, and foodservice markets and include bleaches, disinfectants, food-storage bags, and bathroom cleaners.

- Lifestyle (16 percent) offers Dressings and Sauces (Hidden Valley, Soy Vey, and others), Water Filtration products (Brita), Natural Personal Care (mainly Burt's Bees).

- Household Products (30 percent) includes Bags & Wraps (Glad and others, 14 percent), Charcoal (Kingsford and MatchLight brands, 9 percent), and Litter (7 percent).

- International (22 percent) is set up as a separate entity to market and distribute an assortment of U.S.-made and locally made brands from 39 manufacturing facilities to markets in over 100 countries.

To give an idea how far Clorox has come as a consumer company, it was founded in 1913 as the Electro-Alkaline Company. It has been known as the Clorox Company since 1957, although it was owned by archrival Procter & Gamble from 1957 until 1969 when the FTC forced divestiture to promote competition. The company positions itself not only as a brand leader but also a leader in environmental responsibility and in responding to changing demographics, as exemplified by new formulations and packages specifically targeted to the Hispanic market.

Financial Highlights, Fiscal Year 2013

Clorox rode several crosscurrents of currency fluctuations, especially in key Latin American markets and strong generic competition in some of its markets offset by new product innovations, new packagings, and targeted product launches (like Fraganzia bleach for the Latin market) to a 3 percent overall revenue gain, which the company estimates at something closer to 6 percent without the currency effects. Per-share earnings, helped along by cost reduction strategies, eked out a 5 percent gain with zero effect from share buybacks (which should resume again in FY2014).

Going forward, the company projects a 3–5 percent overall organic top-line growth, which could drop to 1–3 percent with currency effects. Per-share earnings are projected to rise about 1 percent in FY2014 and a healthier 10 percent in FY2015, as currency effects moderate and cost

reduction and supply-chain improvement programs gain effect. The company places special emphasis on free cash flow growth, which it projects in the 10–12 percent range annually.

Reasons to Buy

Even in a slowing consumer market, Clorox, due to its strong brand position and market share, has proven in the past that it's able to increase prices. As a personal preference, we especially like the Green Works products, which, unlike many "green" products, seem to actually work and to have become a standard on store shelves.

That said, many consumers have switched away from name-brand products; just how many remains to be seen. Clorox has proven itself to be a strong, well-managed, cash flow and shareholder-oriented defensive player. Dividend raises have been strong and persistent—12.5 percent most recently—and the company has reduced share count almost 40 percent since 2004. The stock has tended to trade in a very tight range even with negative news; with a beta of 0.43 for our *100 Best* portfolio it remains mostly a safety and stability play.

Reasons for Caution

We've seen the lessons of high commodity prices and of dipping too far into the acquisition pool, as was the case in the Burt's Bees acquisition, which resulted in an enormous 2011 write-off. We remain concerned that the company could be tempted again into poor acquisitions to spur growth, as it's pretty challenging to grow demand and market share for bleach, trash bags, and charcoal. Finally, the stock has posted some strong gains in past years, which have finally moderated, but current share prices leave little room for error.

SECTOR: Consumer Staples
BETA COEFFICIENT: 0.43
10-YEAR COMPOUND EARNINGS PER-SHARE GROWTH: 7.0%
10-YEAR COMPOUND DIVIDENDS PER-SHARE GROWTH: 11.0%

	2006	2007	2008	2009	2010	2011	2012	2013
Revenues (mil)	4,644	4,847	5,273	5,450	5,534	5,231	5,468	5,623
Net income (mil)	443	496	461	537	603	258	543	541
Earnings per share	2.89	3.23	3.24	3.81	4.24	2.07	4.10	4.31
Dividends per share	1.14	1.31	1.66	1.88	2.05	2.25	2.44	2.63
Cash flow per share	4.17	4.55	4.82	5.22	5.68	3.51	5.56	5.80
Price: high	66.0	69.4	65.3	65.2	69.0	75.4	76.7	96.8
low	56.2	56.2	47.5	59.0	59.0	60.6	66.4	73.5

The Clorox Company
1221 Broadway
Oakland, CA 94612
(510) 271-7000
Website: *www.clorox.com*

CONSERVATIVE GROWTH

The Coca-Cola Company

Ticker symbol: KO (NYSE) ❑ S&P rating: A+ ❑ Value Line financial strength rating: A++
Current yield: 3.0% ❑ Dividend raises, past 10 years: 10

Company Profile

The Coca-Cola Company is the world's largest beverage company. For more than 100 years, the company has mainly produced concentrates and syrups, which it then bottles or cans itself or sells to independent bottlers worldwide. These bottlers add water (still or carbonated, depending on the product), sugar, and other (often local) ingredients, then bottle and distribute the products to restaurants, retailers, and other distributors. The company owns the brand and is responsible for consumer brand marketing initiatives, while the distributors handle all downstream merchandising. The company operates in more than 200 countries and markets nearly 500 brands of concentrate and finished beverages. These concentrates are used to produce more than 3,500 different branded products, including Coca-Cola.

In 2010, the company took a big step toward full integration of its supply chain with the purchase of the North American operations of Coca-Cola Enterprises (CCE), the largest of its network of bottlers, in order to streamline distribution and marketing, give greater control of pricing, and cut about $350 million in redundant costs. At the same time, Coke sold distribution in Norway, Sweden, and a future in Germany back to CCE, reaffirming the third-party bottler model in international, or at least European, markets. The company continues to acquire some of its smaller bottling franchises.

The company continues to strive to expand its beverage offerings beyond the traditional carbonated soda drinks. Major brands besides Coke include Minute Maid juices, Dasani and Evian bottled waters, Powerade and Full Throttle sports beverages, Nestea iced teas, and major brands such as Ayataka Green Tea and I Lohas water in Japan and others similarly local to their markets.

The total numbers are staggering: 3,500 products, 500 brands, 17 of which have reached $1 billion in sales, 28.2 billion cases worldwide, which equates to 637 billion servings per year, 1.9 billion beverages consumed per day, and 21,990 servings per second, all processed through more than 250 bottlers serving 200 countries, and all handled through the world's largest beverage distribution system. In terms of unit case volume, 79 percent of all sales are overseas—29 percent in Latin America, 15 percent in Eurasia/Africa, 21 percent in the Pacific, and 14 percent in Europe. In revenue terms, the company counts about 58 percent as overseas sales.

Financial Highlights, Fiscal Year 2013

For FY2013, worldwide total unit volumes grew 2 percent, down from the 4 percent growth rate reported in FY2012. While North American unit sales were flat (no pun intended), and Europe again showed a slight 1 percent drop, sales advanced 3 percent in the Pacific region, 1 percent in Latin America, and 7 percent in the much smaller "Eurasia" region (which doesn't include Europe). The heavy international exposure came home to roost in the top line when converted to dollars, however, with a 4 percent currency headwind, which resulted in a 2.4 percent revenue decline. Earnings, however, backed by an increase in margins, grew at a moderate 3.3 percent. Going forward, nobody's terribly excited about revenues or earnings for FY2014, which will likely be close to flat again. A hopeful reversal in currency misfortune, cost savings initiatives, and new initiatives in the home beverage and single-cup beverage market (notably, the company bought a 10 percent stake in single-cup licensor Green Mountain Coffee Roasters in late 2013) are expected to lift sales 4–5 percent in FY2015 and earnings a little over 5 percent. With steady 25–50 million-share buybacks yearly, earnings are projected in the $2.20–$2.30 range for FY2015, with 8–10 percent dividend increases annually.

Reasons to Buy

"I like to bet on sure things," Warren Buffett said, on why he'll never sell a single one of the 400 million shares of Coke stock he owns. That pretty much sums it up, and the reasons to buy Coke continue to be solid. The company has category leadership, especially globally, in soft drinks, juices and juice drinks, and ready-to-drink coffees and teas. They're number two globally in sports drinks, and number three in packaged water and energy drinks. In Coca-Cola, Diet Coke, Sprite, and Fanta, they own four of the top five brands of soft drink in the world.

The Coca-Cola name is probably the most recognized brand in the world and is almost beyond valuation. Indeed, Mr. Buffett once uttered the classic line about brand strength and intangibles in reference to Coke: "If you gave me $100 million and said take away the soft drink leadership in the world from Coke, I'd give it back to you and say it can't be done."

Coke has traditionally been a steady hedge stock and offers a solid dividend with a constant and recently accelerating track record of dividend growth. The company boasts—quite rightly—about having raised dividends in each of the past 52 years, and returned some $8.5 billion out of $10.5 billion in cash generated to shareholders in 2013. It is also as close to a pure play on international business as you'll find in a U.S. company. Finally, the low beta of 0.47 continues to confirm its low-volatility credentials.

Reasons for Caution

Sales in established markets—the U.S. and Europe, and now Latin America— are still flat or only slightly improving, probably caused in part by interest in health and reducing obesity. The company is largely past the bottling franchise acquisitions, but it is still a very complex business to manage. We're a bit concerned about the slowdown in Latin America, which was once the ace in the hole for growth. FY2013 unit volumes were up only 1 percent versus a 5 percent five-year compound annual growth rate. Could they be thinking "healthy" south of the border, too? Overall, this is a slow, steady growth story, which may be too slow for some, with new risks the company didn't face when Mr. Buffett bought in years ago.

As for the Coke-Pepsi debate (and Pepsi is a *100 Best* stock too) we think Coke's products and its marketing machine are better, as is its international brand strength, but Pepsi offers more diversity with its Frito-Lay snack food franchise and stronger non-carbonated products, particularly Gatorade. Take your pick—or just buy a couple of 12-packs of each.

SECTOR: **Consumer Staples**
BETA COEFFICIENT: **0.47**
10-YEAR COMPOUND EARNINGS PER-SHARE GROWTH: **8.5%**
10-YEAR COMPOUND DIVIDENDS PER-SHARE GROWTH: **10.0%**

	2006	2007	2008	2009	2010	2011	2012	2013
Revenues (mil)	24,088	28,857	31,944	30,990	35,123	46,554	48,017	46,854
Net income (mil)	5,568	5,981	7,050	6,824	8,144	8,932	9,019	9,374
Earnings per share	1.19	1.29	1.51	1.47	1.75	1.92	1.97	2.08
Dividends per share	0.62	0.68	0.76	0.82	0.88	0.94	1.02	1.12
Cash flow per share	1.40	1.54	1.79	1.75	2.09	2.41	2.46	2.58
Price:　　high	24.7	32.2	32.8	29.7	32.9	35.9	40.7	43.4
low	16.7	22.8	20.1	18.7	24.7	30.6	33.3	36.5

The Coca-Cola Company
One Coca-Cola Plaza
Atlanta, GA 30313
(404) 676-2121
Website: *www.coca-cola.com*

Colgate-Palmolive Company

Ticker symbol: CL (NYSE) □ S&P rating: AA- □ Value Line financial strength rating: A++
Current yield: 2.2% □ Dividend raises, past 10 years: 10

Company Profile

Colgate-Palmolive is the second-largest global producer of detergents, toiletries, and other household products. The company manages its business in two straightforward segments: Oral, Personal, and Home Care; and Pet Nutrition. The Oral, Personal, and Home Care division produces and markets a number of familiar brands and products: Ajax, Palmolive, Irish Spring, Softsoap, Mennen, and Speed Stick, as well as the familiar Colgate brand of oral care products. These brands are strong with substantial market share in most markets: Colgate owns 45 percent of the worldwide oral care market and 22 percent each of the personal care and home care markets. Colgate is also one of the leaders in the pet nutrition market; its Hill's pet food brand represents 13 percent of its total sales.

Colgate is also strong in the global consumer products market, with a presence in more than 200 countries and territories. About 80 percent of its business is international—down from 82 percent in FY2012—and about 50 percent of *that* business is in emerging markets (see our note on Venezuela below).

Financial Highlights, Fiscal Year 2013

After a strong FY2012, the company ran into some currency headwinds, headed by the drastic devaluation of Venezuela's currency. Venezuela? Yes, Colgate has a sizeable presence there, about 3 percent of revenues and 4 percent of total profits. Overall, currency headwinds took about 4 percent out of top-line and bottom-line results.

As a consequence, FY2013 revenues were up 2 percent even though volumes increased 5 percent and prices increased 1 percent. The math works out. At the same time, earnings softened due to increased advertising expenses and some one-time cost reduction initiatives to a dip of more than 9 percent to $2.2 billion. Per-share earnings didn't suffer much as about 16 million shares were bought back, or 1.7 percent of float; per share earnings dropped 7.8 percent. Continued geographic expansion and focus on higher-margined personal care lines, combined with some currency stabilization, should drive revenues 4 percent higher in FY2014 and FY2015. The "organic" business (without acquisitions and currency fluctuation) is thought capable of delivering 5–7 percent growth annually. Cost reduction programs will drive up to $300 million into the bottom line annually over FY2014 and FY2015, and combined with continued aggressive share buybacks, should bring per-share earnings forward 13 percent in FY2014 and perhaps more than 20 percent in FY2015. Decent dividend increases should accompany the ride.

Reasons to Buy

Colgate's brands are market leaders in most of the markets in which they operate. They have a 45 percent share of the global toothpaste market and 33 percent of the manual toothbrush market. They're number one or number two with many of their other brands, including Ajax and Softsoap, and have many other well-established brands. Strong brands lead to pricing power. The company's "first to market" global strategy has given them a formidable foothold in emerging markets such as China and India. Colgate is in a great position to benefit from the increased acceptance and use of dental care products and other toiletries in these markets.

Colgate is a conservatively run company that prefers slower organic growth over quick (but expensive) acquisitions. They rarely have a downside surprise—they tend to meet or beat their estimates. They plow money back into the company and achieve profitability through operational excellence, rather than paying for gross margins at any price. This is a solid defensive play with a good dividend, real earnings growth, and real earnings predictability. One of our recurring *100 Best* investment themes is to capture international exposure by buying firms that sell a lot overseas, rather than buying foreign firms, which are harder to understand and follow. With 80 percent of sales overseas and strength in emerging markets, Colgate-Palmolive could be a poster child for this strategy. That said, as we saw in FY2013, this strategy does bring some currency risk.

Looking at the bigger picture, Colgate is probably a safer, steadier alternative in the consumer staples marketplace than Procter & Gamble (another *100 Best Stock*), as it is less prone to reach for new, rapidly changing markets, such as cosmetics, and less apt to try to grow through acquisitions. This company is about slow, steady returns with little risk and little market volatility in bad times. The company touts not just ten but *50* consecutive years of dividend increases.

Reasons for Caution

Colgate participates in an increasingly competitive market, requiring more frequent new-product rollouts and related marketing expenses just to keep up. The Colgate business will not stimulate aggressive investors, and it could be that much of the forward good news is already priced into the stock—shop carefully.

SECTOR: **Consumer Staples**
BETA COEFFICIENT: **0.45**
10-YEAR COMPOUND EARNINGS PER-SHARE GROWTH: **8.5%**
10-YEAR COMPOUND DIVIDENDS PER-SHARE GROWTH: **12.5%**

	2006	2007	2008	2009	2010	2011	2012	2013
Revenues (mil)	12,238	13,790	15,330	15,327	15,564	16,734	17,085	17,420
Net income (mil)	1,353	1,737	1,957	2,291	2,203	2,431	2,472	2,241
Earnings per share	1.46	1.69	1.83	2.19	2.16	2.47	2.58	2.38
Dividends per share	0.63	0.70	0.78	0.86	1.02	1.14	1.22	1.33
Cash flow per share	1.85	2.10	2.27	2.64	2.57	2.97	3.10	2.91
Price: high	33.5	40.6	41.0	43.7	43.1	47.4	55.5	66.5
low	26.7	31.9	27.2	27.3	36.6	37.4	43.6	52.6

Colgate-Palmolive Company
300 Park Avenue
New York, NY 10022–7499
(212) 310-2000
Website: *www.colgate.com*

AGGRESSIVE GROWTH

Comcast Corporation

Ticker symbol: CMCSA (NASDAQ) ❑ S&P rating: BBB+ ❑ Value Line financial strength rating: A
Current yield: 1.8% ❑ Dividend raises, past 10 years: 4

Company Profile

Comcast is one of the nation's leading providers of communications services. The core business is Comcast Cable, the familiar cable TV network that has evolved into a conduit for delivering bundled high-speed Internet services, phone services, and on-demand content. This business has served some 23 million subscribers in 39 states.

In early 2014, the company announced a blockbuster acquisition of Time Warner Cable for some $35 billion, which would substantially increase the company's leadership in those markets. At the time of this analysis, this acquisition was far from complete and its effect far from known. The acquisition would expand U.S. pay-TV market share to about 30 percent and give a stronger presence across the country. It would also, of course, give the company not only scale but more negotiating power with content providers, but it is unclear whether the FCC would require the company to divest some subscribers to complete the acquisition.

Prior to early 2014, the company had been evolving its information and entertainment business gradually through its ownership of regional sports networks and national channels such as the Golf Channel, E! (an entertainment channel), Fandango (a moviegoer's website), and others. The company took a major leap forward as a content provider with the 2011 acquisition of 51 percent of NBCUniversal, almost instantly turning the company into a media powerhouse as well through its ownership of Universal Pictures. In March 2013, Comcast completed the purchase by acquiring the remaining 49 percent of NBCUniversal from General Electric. With that acquisition, Comcast became the largest integrated content development and distribution business in the United States.

The company has been building its Xfinity Internet portal brand to compete with satellite operators and such offerings as AT&T U-verse and Verizon FiOS. Customers can buy bundles of services including TV, on-demand video, and, on-demand TV through the Hulu application. With Xfinity, customers can also get up to 105 mbps Internet service, probably the best service for downloading large chunks of video content. In short, Comcast has evolved from being a lackluster cable TV service to a full-scale communications utility with some of the highest-performance products on the market. The company now has nearly as many Internet service customers (22 million) as it does cable subscribers (23 million), and more than 10 million phone service connections on top of that.

The vast majority of Comcast customers are residential, though the company offers a business class service, including fiber end-user connections and cloud storage, for small and mid-sized organizations. The company also owns the Philadelphia 76ers and Flyers and a series of Universal theme parks.

Financial Highlights, Fiscal Year 2013

The Time Warner Cable acquisition will obviously shake up the financials a bit, starting with some $1.5 billion in projected operating efficiencies. It's too early to project revenues and profits going forward, so we'll stick with what we know, which does not include the acquisition.

Continued strength from the NBCUniversal acquisition, healthy consumer subscriber gains (including 3 million new Xfinity customers), and continued strength in the Business Services segment made for a solid picture in FY2013. Revenues increased 5.8 percent, while a modest increase in operating margin drove net profit some 7.2 percent higher; share buybacks drove per-share earnings up some 12 percent. The company bought back some $4 billion in stock.

FY2014 and FY2015 look to be equally strong, acquisition aside, with revenues up 5.6 percent and 4.5 percent respectively. These are big numbers, so moderate percentages still suggest $3 billion plus in new revenue annually. Per-share earnings could change considerably with the acquisition but are now projected to grow 10 percent in FY2014 and close to 20 percent in FY2015.

In the wake of the Time Warner Cable acquisition, the company added $2.5 billion to its existing $3 billion share buyback, in part to deal with some 1 billion shares that could be issued to complete the acquisition. Possible cash infusions from required divestitures would support these buybacks and other returns to investors.

Reasons to Buy

The addition of Comcast to the 2013 *100 Best* list was one we debated out of concern about cable companies in general. However, it has paid off handsomely; the shares have more than doubled since our decision. The company continues to make intriguing moves to grow and increase its footprint well beyond traditional cable TV in key content delivery markets.

Recent decisions have challenged "net neutrality"—where every content provider and customer gets about the same terms for delivery regardless of the bandwidth required. We think Comcast would benefit substantially from a "less neutral" net; a recent deal with Netflix to pay an increased sum to use its broadband last-mile delivery highlights the point. Growth in market dominance, improved branding, and new revenues from deals like the Netflix deal from the increased adoption of Xfinity all bode well, as does what we think will become the eventual reality of on-demand content as a standard.

Reasons for Caution

The size and scale of the acquisition, regulatory scrutiny, mandated spinoffs, write-offs, etc., bring a large layer of uncertainty as the company attempts to solidify its number one position. While recent decisions on net neutrality now look to be a positive, they aren't a done deal, and we could be left with an Internet that can't charge any extra for handling heavy loads, which with the expected expansion of such loads, could become a problem. Too, if the company becomes too aggressive in the media content market, and particularly if it restricts others from using

its "last mile" of cable, that could bring some grief in the court of public opinion, not to mention regulation.

The company faces extreme competition in most of its markets, although it may have at least a bandwidth advantage at present. The Time Warner Cable acquisition could diminish this competition temporarily, but there will always be competing technologies and services. Speaking of technology, it could so evolve that companies serving portable devices like tablets and smartphones might get a share of the home market; on the other hand, we don't see Comcast serving mobile devices any time soon.

The high share count may go higher with the acquisition and will continue to be a drag, although the company is positioning well to do something about it.

SECTOR: **Telecommunications Services**
BETA COEFFICIENT: **1.14**
10-YEAR COMPOUND EARNINGS PER-SHARE GROWTH: **28.3%**
5-YEAR COMPOUND DIVIDENDS PER-SHARE GROWTH: **18.2%**

	2006	2007	2008	2009	2010	2011	2012	2013
Revenues (mil)	24,966	30,895	34,256	35,756	37,937	55,842	62,570	64,657
Net income (mil)	2,235	2,287	2,701	3,638	3,535	4,377	6,023	6,649
Earnings per share	0.47	0.74	0.91	1.26	1.29	1.58	2.29	2.56
Dividends per share	—	—	0.25	0.27	0.38	0.45	0.60	0.78
Cash flow per share	1.48	2.82	3.10	3.57	3.89	4.44	5.26	5.59
Price: high	28.7	29.6	22.5	17.3	21.2	27.2	38.2	52.1
low	16.2	17.3	12.1	10.3	14.3	19.2	24.3	37.2

Comcast Corporation
One Comcast Center
Philadelphia, PA 19103
(215) 286-1700
Website: *www.comcast.com*

GROWTH AND INCOME

ConocoPhillips

Ticker symbol: COP (NYSE) ❑ S&P rating: A ❑ Value Line financial strength rating: A++
Current yield: 3.6% ❑ Dividend raises, past 10 years: 10

Company Profile

Back in 2012, ConocoPhillips investors got a chance to make a choice. The options were to own a global energy production business, a global refining and marketing business, or shares of both. The "old" ConocoPhillips, like Marathon and a few others in the industry, split itself into an exploration and production unit that maintained the name, and a distribution and refining unit going by the name of Phillips 66, the name on its largest line of gas stations. This review covers the original ConocoPhillips, now a $54 billion multinational "E&P" company. The remaining "COP" is still headquartered in Houston, TX, and operates in 27 countries with about 18,400 employees and $54 billion in annual revenues (the "old" COP had about $240 billion in revenues), accounting for the shift in the numbers at the bottom of this review. The portion now represented by the "new COP" generated about half to three-quarters of the profit on one-quarter of the revenue, with different capital budgeting and working capital needs, management expertise, and other requirements.

"Set for Growth" and "Exclusively E&P" are the mottos of the new COP. The company's E&P operations are geographically diverse, producing in the United States, including a large presence in Alaska's Prudhoe Bay. The company also has a large presence in U.S shale "fracking" regions, including Eagle Ford and Permian regions in Texas and the Bakken region in North Dakota. The company also produces in Norway, the United Kingdom, western Canada, Australia, offshore Timor-Leste in the Timor Sea, Indonesia, Malaysia, China, Vietnam, Libya, Senegal, Nigeria, Algeria, and Russia.

ConocoPhillips has become a strong natural gas play, with approximately 54 percent of production equivalent in natural gas or natural gas liquids, 39 percent crude oil, and 7 percent bitumen. Production has an unusually high domestic concentration: 25 percent of crude oil production and about 37 percent of natural gas production occur in the Lower 48, with another 29 percent of crude oil production and 1 percent of natural gas coming from Alaska. About 44 percent of total proved reserves are in the Lower 48 or Alaska, with another 27 percent in Canada.

Like many other "big oil" concerns, ConocoPhillips completed the disposition of some "non-core" assets in non-concentrated regions like Trinidad and Tobago to raise cash and reduce costs. The company generated some $10.2 billion in asset sales in FY2013, which goes a long way toward explaining the revenue drop described shortly. On the other side, the company grew production in the Bakken and Eagle Ford regions some 60 percent during the year.

Financial Highlights, Fiscal Year 2013

It's tough to make a useful comparison between COP's FY2013 performance and that of earlier years. Divestitures and "right-sizing" brought revenues down to the $54.4 billion level; the company considers that a solid base for comparisons moving forward. Higher oil prices and realized efficiencies brought earnings forward about 7 percent despite the decline in revenues.

Going forward, new production and continued strength in energy prices give rise to a 13 percent projected revenue gain for FY2014 and another 5 percent in FY2015; per-share earnings should rise in the 8 percent range in FY2014 (slowed by higher development expenses) and a stronger 10–13 percent range in FY2015.

Reasons to Buy

There is a lot to like here. ConocoPhillips made a bold move to focus on what it does best, both operationally and geographically. The remaining business is less vulnerable to refining and pricing cycles. Beyond the split, the company has divested itself of about $12 billion in assets, moves that would on the surface cause some panic but in this case seem destined to improve focus, make a strong competitive run at the bigger integrated oil companies, and produce more profits. With a strong U.S. base, COP is less exposed to political risks, and it stands to benefit from any rise in oil and especially gas prices. Production is strong and effective; the company reports a 179 percent "organic reserve replacement ratio"—an excellent figure taken against declining reserves observed in other big oil players such as ExxonMobil and Royal Dutch Shell in recent years. Cash flow is strong, and the dividend is attractive and has grown persistently.

Reasons for Caution

It has taken more than a year for everything to settle down so that investors can really track and understand ongoing performance. As with most energy companies, the ambiguities of exploration and geopolitics add a bit more uncertainty to the risk profile. The company has not been a "buyback achiever" of late but could resume some share buybacks in the

near future as cash flows are strong.
The share price has risen considerably;
investors will have to seek good entry
points.

SECTOR: **Energy**
BETA COEFFICIENT: **1.23**
10-YEAR COMPOUND EARNINGS PER-SHARE GROWTH: **10.5%**
10-YEAR COMPOUND DIVIDENDS PER-SHARE GROWTH: **13.5%**

	2006	**2007**	**2008**	**2009**	**2010**	**2011**	**2012**	**2013**
Revenues (bil)	183.7	187.4	240.8	149.3	189.4	244.8	62.0	54.4
Net income (bil)	16.1	15.1	15.9	4.9	8.8	12.1	7.4	8.0
Earnings per share	9.99	9.14	10.68	3.24	5.92	8.76	5.91	6.43
Dividends per share	1.44	1.64	1.88	1.91	2.16	2.64	2.64	2.70
Cash flow per share	14.19	14.86	16.80	9.58	12.50	15.63	11.47	12.57
Price: high	74.9	90.8	96.0	57.4	68.6	77.4	78.3	74.6
low	54.9	61.6	41.3	34.1	48.5	68.0	50.6	56.4

ConocoPhillips
600 North Dairy Ashford Rd.
Houston, TX 77252
(281) 293-1000
Website: *www.conocophillips.com*

AGGRESSIVE GROWTH

Corning Incorporated

Ticker symbol: GLW (NYSE) ❑ S&P rating: NR ❑ Value Line financial strength rating: B++
Current yield: 1.9% ❑ Dividend raises, past 10 years: 4

Company Profile

When you think of Corning, you think of glass. All kinds of glass—drinking glasses, glass tableware, etc. If you were around in the 1960s, you may remember that well-known white cookware with the little blue flowers on the side.

Today's Corning is a premier technology materials company. If you use a smartphone, a tablet, a laptop PC, or a flat-panel television, chances are pretty good that the glass on the screen comes from Corning. A good amount of the data you see on that screen may have come through glass-based fiber-optic materials supplied by—guess who—Corning.

In fact, Corning operates in five segments, all centered on the glass business. Display Technologies (32 percent of FY2013 sales) makes a lot of those screens, actually referred to as "glass substrates for liquid crystal displays." Optical Communications (formerly Telecommunications) (30 percent) makes fiber-optic cable and an assortment of connectivity and other products related to fiber for telecommunications companies, LAN, and data center applications. Specialty Materials (15 percent) provides a wide assortment of high-tech, glass-based materials, including those specialty glass screens for smartphones, tablets, etc., which it has cleverly branded as Corning Gorilla Glass for its endurance characteristics. Also out of this division comes a new bendable display substrate known as Willow Glass and a host of glass and ceramic products and formulations used in the semiconductor industry, precision instruments, and even astronomy and ophthalmology. The Environmental Technologies segment (12 percent) makes ceramic substrates and filters for emission control systems, mostly for gasoline and diesel engines. The Life Sciences segment (11 percent) makes laboratory glass and plastic wares.

The company competes with a number of suppliers, mostly Japanese, but also has a 50–50 joint venture with Samsung in the display business (Samsung Corning). This venture will add $2 billion to the top line in FY2014, and offer significant cost savings particularly with a transfer of production to Korea, and form the base for other strategic joint ventures with that company. Corning also has had a joint venture with Dow Chemical for years, known as Dow Corning, a leader in silicon products and technologies producing high-quality sealants, lubricants, etc., from silicon materials. Recently the company announced a collaboration with

Atmel to develop ultrathin, ultrasensitive touchscreens to improve size and weight characteristics of mobile devices. Through this venture and others, we await the announcement of bendable, and curved glass displays into the market allowing us to literally wear our devices. Any day now—and Corning will likely lead this lucrative innovation.

Financial Highlights, Fiscal Year 2013

FY2013 was another strong year for Corning, with several crosscurrents affecting performance. Revenues actually declined slightly for the year due to a weaker product mix and price competition in key markets, especially glass displays. That price competition largely arose from the new "Abenomics" Japanese monetary policy, which significantly drove down the value of the yen, making Japanese suppliers more competitive. Corning will benefit some from that crosscurrent, particularly with the Samsung Corning joint venture. Despite the competitive crosscurrents, however, volumes and other manufacturing efficiencies led to a recovery in margins and 14 percent gain in net earnings, though still not to levels experienced earlier in the decade. A buyback of some 70 million shares—5 percent of float—led to a per-share earnings gain of 16.5 percent for FY2013.

The crosscurrents will continue in all operating segments into FY2014 and FY2015; however, in all, we expect the ship to sail through them just fine. Traditional display glass will continue to be competitive, and price decreases in that market appear to be accelerating, but cost savings and synergies are moving hand in hand, allowing this business to earn profits far greater, at 21.5 percent net margin, than the "commodity" business that such pricing dynamics would imply. The incorporation of Samsung Corning will bring revenues to the $10 billion mark in FY2014, not easily compared to FY2013, and with a 5 percent gain projected into FY2015. Per-share earnings are expected to rise 17 percent in FY2014 (again, with buybacks; the company just authorized another $1.25 billion) and another 6 percent in FY2015.

Reasons to Buy

We like companies that stand to benefit no matter how a market plays out. Our CarMax pick benefits whether Ford or Toyota or Hyundai wins; CarMax sells used cars no matter what. At least for glass displays, Corning is in the same position—whether Samsung or Apple comes out on top of the smartphone contest, Corning wins. Whether tablets or PCs lead the personal computing market, Corning wins. The explosion in smart devices and the new technologies Corning is likely to bring to that space create some excitement down the road. We think the eventual advent of wearable mobile computing devices will be a big spark for this company.

The core businesses aren't too shabby, either. The company endured a huge boom-bust cycle with the first buildout of the Internet during the dot-com bubble, and it suffered the consequences. But having a piece of the world's largest fiber-optic supplier and technology leader isn't such a bad thing, either. Across the board, Corning continues to invest a lot (in fact, 9.1 percent of revenues in R&D) to differentiate their products through innovation. The presence of competition, especially Japanese competition, reminds us from time to time that Corning doesn't own the "glass" niche outright, but it is close to owning the innovation in this area; for those who like pure plays in a strong and profitable technology segment, Corning is a good bet.

Finally, this company is profitable, with plenty of cash flow, and is returning plenty of cash to shareholders both in the form of dividends and in share buybacks; the dividend yield is quite decent for this type of company and is growing.

Reasons for Caution

While its product portfolio is broader than it was 15 years ago, the company is still subject to business and inventory cycles. Glass, without the right amount of innovation, is a commodity business, and the recent strengthening of Japanese competition through the lower yen continues to present a challenge. If you're concerned that price erosion through competition will outpace innovation and cost savings initiatives, Corning may not be the place to be.

SECTOR: **Information Technology**
BETA COEFFICIENT: **1.56**
10-YEAR COMPOUND EARNINGS PER-SHARE GROWTH: 11.5%
10-YEAR COMPOUND DIVIDENDS PER-SHARE GROWTH: NM

		2006	2007	2008	2009	2010	2011	2012	2013
Revenues (mil)		5,174	5,860	5,948	5,395	6,632	7,890	8,012	7,819
Net income (mil)		1,785	2,267	2,424	2,114	3,275	2,620	1,728	1,961
Earnings per share		1.12	1.41	1.53	1.35	2.07	1.76	1.15	1.34
Dividends per share		—	0.10	0.20	0.20	0.20	0.23	0.32	0.39
Cash flow per share		1.51	1.83	2.01	1.86	2.64	2.49	1.85	2.12
Price.	high	29.6	27.3	28.1	19.5	21.1	23.4	14.6	18.1
	low	17.5	18.1	7.4	9.0	15.5	11.5	10.6	11.6

Corning Incorporated
One Riverfront Plaza
Corning, NY 14831
(607) 974-9000
Website: *www.corning.com*

AGGRESSIVE GROWTH

Costco Wholesale Corporation

Ticker symbol: COST (NASDAQ) ❑ S&P rating: A+ ❑ Value Line financial strength rating: A+
Current yield: 1.2% ❑ Dividend raises, past 10 years: 10

Company Profile

Costco Wholesale Corporation operates a multinational chain of membership warehouses, mainly under the Costco Wholesale name, that carry brand-name merchandise at substantially lower prices than are typically found at conventional wholesale or retail sources. The warehouse sales model was designed to help small to medium-sized businesses reduce costs in purchasing for resale and for everyday business use, but as most know, the individual consumer has been their big growth driver. The company capitalizes on size and operational efficiencies, like "cross-docking" shipments directly from manufacturers to stores, to deliver attractive pricing to its customers. The company does not do delivery, nor does it run billing or accounts receivable for sales accounts—sales are "where is" for cash or cash equivalents. Costco is the largest membership warehouse club chain in the world based on sales volume, the fifth-largest general retailer in the United States, and the seventh-largest general retailer in the world.

Costco carries a broad line of product categories, including groceries, appliances, television and media, automotive supplies, toys, hardware, sporting goods, jewelry, cameras, books, housewares, apparel, health and beauty aids, tobacco, furniture, office supplies, and office equipment. The company also operates self-service gasoline stations at a number of its U.S. and Canadian locations. Approximately 56 percent of sales comes from food, beverages, alcohol, sundries, and snacks. Another 16 percent comes from hardlines—electronics, appliances, hardware, automotive, office supplies, and health and beauty aids—and 11 percent from softlines—primarily clothing, housewares, media, jewelry, and domestics. The rest, including gasoline, pharmacy, optical, and other services, form a catchall "other" category. The emergence of Costco as a grocer of choice cannot be missed.

Additionally, Costco Wholesale Industries, a division of the company, operates manufacturing businesses, including special food packaging, optical laboratories, meat processing, and jewelry distribution. A wide and growing variety of products are sold under its "Kirkland" private label.

Costco is open only to members of its tiered membership plan, the higher "Executive" tier gaining access to reward points on the accompanying American Express card. In all, there are 71 million members. As of early 2014 Costco has 648 locations: 461 in the United States and Puerto Rico (up from 449), 87 in Canada (versus 85), 33 in Mexico (unchanged), 25 in the U.K. (versus 24), 18 in Japan, 10 in Taiwan, and 9 in Korea (totaling 37, up from 33 reported for all of Asia), and 5 in Australia (versus 3). The company plans a bigger move into Europe with store openings in France and Spain in 2014; it also plans a big jump in stores in Japan through the next few years. All told, the company expects to open an additional 29 warehouse clubs through the end of FY2014 and 170 through the end of the decade, a 5 percent and 21 percent rise respectively.

The company also has a significant and growing e-commerce presence at *www.costco.com*, though it accounts for only 3 percent of revenues at this time.

Financial Highlights, Fiscal Year 2013

Total and same-store sales both increased about 6 percent in FY2013, comparable to the previous year's results. The "comp" would have been a bit better if there hadn't been an extra week in the FY2012 period. Gross margin ticked just slightly upward—7 basis points or 7 one-hundredths of a percentage point—but this is a big

deal in a $105 billion business, and total operating margin increased from 3.7 percent to 3.8 percent—again a big deal. As a consequence, net profit rose some 13.6 percent, with a comparable per-share earnings increase. For FY2014 and FY2015, the company expects top-line growth in the 10 percent range, with per-share earnings rising 4 percent in FY2014 and about 12 percent in FY2015.

Membership revenues increased 10 percent, and membership retention continued at 90 percent in North America and over 86 percent worldwide (if you're new to Costco, understand that membership fees account for more than half of the company's profit). This high retention comes despite a significant fee raise in late 2011.

Reasons to Buy

You have to admire a retailer that can get paid in cash and buy merchandise on credit. Costco claims that for a significant percentage of their inventory, the product is sold long before they have to pay for it.

Costco is in an attractive best-of-both-worlds niche: It is a price leader consistent with the attitudes of today's more frugal consumer, yet it enjoys a reputation for being more upscale than the competition. We've all heard the boast, "I got it at Costco," from even our most affluent and high-minded friends. And of course, there's everybody else.

We also continue to like the international expansion and think the formula will play well overseas. We expect international expansion will be one of the company's primary growth drivers over the next ten years. The company has a strong brand in a highly competitive sector, is gaining market share, and has a strong management track record. Although the 1.2 percent yield isn't that much of an attraction, the company has raised its dividend consistently since initiating it in 2004. Share repurchases are on the table, but may not happen until later in the decade.

Reasons for Caution

One concern is the dependence on low-margin food and sundry lines. With the ramp-up of Walmart and Target groceries and stiff competition elsewhere, Costco may not always be the food source of choice. That said, food does get customers into the store more often. Average sales per visit have been declining as a consequence, but overall the trend is probably favorable; more store traffic means more and more regular store sales overall.

Our biggest concern comes from the high share price, low margins, and dependence on membership fees for profitability. All three bring a measure of vulnerability to the stock and we seriously considered taking the company off our *100 Best* list. On the flip side, management has shown its ability to navigate through difficult periods, the brand is strong, and the prospects for a global footprint; all encouraging signs for the future. In light of those three items, we're keeping Costco.

SECTOR: Retail
BETA COEFFICIENT: 0.56
10-YEAR COMPOUND EARNINGS PER-SHARE GROWTH: 10.5%
10-YEAR COMPOUND DIVIDENDS PER-SHARE GROWTH: 22.7%

	2006	2007	2008	2009	2010	2011	2012	2013
Revenues (mil)	60,151	64,400	72,483	71,422	77,946	88,915	99,137	105,156
Net income (mil)	1,103	1,083	1,283	1,086	1,307	1,462	1,741	1,977
Earnings per share	2.30	2.37	2.89	2.57	2.93	3.30	3.97	4.49
Dividends per share	0.49	0.55	0.61	0.68	0.77	0.89	1.03	1.17
Cash flow per share	3.50	4.05	4.48	4.25	4.85	5.34	6.13	6.69
Price: high	57.9	72.7	75.2	61.3	73.2	88.7	106.0	126.1
low	46.0	51.5	43.9	38.2	53.4	69.5	78.8	98.6

Costco Wholesale Corporation
999 Lake Drive
Issaquah, WA 98027
(425) 313-8100
Website: *www.costco.com*

CONSERVATIVE GROWTH

CVS Caremark Corporation

Ticker symbol: CVS (NYSE) □ S&P rating: BBB+ □ Value Line financial strength rating: A
Current yield: 1.5% □ Dividend raises, past 10 years: 10

Company Profile

Stanley and Sid Goldstein were distributing health and beauty products in the early 1960s when they decided to branch out into retailing, opening their first Consumer Value Store in Lowell, MA, in 1963. The CVS chain had grown to 40 outlets by 1969, the year they sold the business to Melville Shoes. Melville underwent a restructuring in the mid-1990s, spinning off CVS and other retail units.

Stan and Sid should be proud. CVS is now the largest pharmacy health-care provider in the United States. Its flagship domestic drugstore chain operates 7,600 retail and specialty pharmacy stores in 42 states, Puerto Rico, and the District of Columbia. The company holds the leading market share in 32 of the 100 largest U.S. drugstore markets, more than any other retail drugstore chain. Over time, it has expanded through acquiring other players in the category—Osco, Sav-On, Eckerd, and Longs Drugs. CVS's purchase of Longs Drugs in 2008 vaulted the company into the lead position in the U.S. drug retail market, ahead of Walgreens.

Stores are situated primarily in strip shopping centers or free-standing locations, with a typical store ranging in size from 8,000 to 12,000 square feet. Most new units being built are based on either a 10,000-square-foot or 12,000-square-foot prototype building that typically includes a drive-thru pharmacy. The company says that about half of its stores were opened or remodeled over the past five years.

The Caremark acquisition in 2007 transformed CVS from strictly a retailer into the nation's leading manager of pharmacy benefits, the middleman between pharmaceutical companies and individuals with drug benefit coverage. The Caremark acquisition forms the core of the company's Pharmacy Benefits Management (PBM) operations, which have some 65,000 pharmacy outlets including hospitals and clinics as well as the previously mentioned retail stores. The company dispenses about a billion prescriptions a year to 63 million plan members, and the Pharmacy Services segment now makes up about 69 percent of sales.

The company's MinuteClinic concept is especially interesting in today's climate of managing health-care costs. CVS now has 800 clinics in 28 states offering basic health services like flu shots and such given by 2,200 nurse practitioners in a convenient retail environment. All but 12 of these clinics are located in CVS stores, naturally serving to drive traffic into the stores. Plans are to grow MinuteClinic into 1,500 locations in 35 states by 2017, and the service now has more than 30 major health affiliations; the concept gradually is gaining mainstream acceptance. The company also operates mail order and online pharmacies for regular and chronically ill patients and is working on a "Telehealth" service to accompany its platform of retail health services.

Perhaps as a gesture of thematic and ethical consistency, and clearly as a gesture of leadership in its market, the company announced the discontinuance of tobacco product sales effective October 2014. The change will adversely affect short-term revenues and profits but generated a considerable amount of positive PR, and several competitors have followed suit.

Financial Highlights, Fiscal Year 2013

CVS had a very good FY2013. Revenues rose a modest 2.6 percent but improved margins due to a slowdown in store expansion, increased private label sales, and general efficiency gains drove net profits some 11.6 percent higher; on top of that, a 50 million (4 percent) share buyback led to a 16.6 percent gain in per-share earnings.

For FY2014 and FY2015, the company faces some crosswinds as the stoppage of tobacco sales will shave some $2 billion (!) from the top line and 5–10 cents from per-share earnings; meanwhile, gains in health coverage through the Affordable Care Act, improved sales and margins from new initiatives like MinuteClinic, and continued aggressive share buybacks will usher in per-share earnings in the $4.30–$4.50 range in FY2014 (the midpoint is 10 percent higher) with similar gains in store for FY2015. The persistence of its market dominance and increased coverage of the ACA should produce similar gains for the next several years even without the tobacco products. In light of all of this, the company projects continued share buybacks in the 2–3 percent range annually, and just raised its dividend 40 percent (although with share price appreciation, the yield remained a modest 1.5 percent).

Reasons to Buy

This company is clearly a market leader and knows how to take advantage of that position without alienating customers or key health-care payers. What's more, its "retail" location in the health-care food chain positions it perfectly to capitalize on the initiatives of the Affordable Care Act: more patients getting more and lower-cost services. We think CVS and retail in general is less likely than other players in the health-food chain to be scrutinized in an effort to reduce costs. For example, efforts to reduce Medicare and Medicaid payments are more targeted to physicians and providers, not retailers or distributors of health-care products. This, of course, all comes on top of favorable demographics—an aging population; one also ever more willing to pay for convenience, and a growing acceptance of CVS as a local convenience store for needs beyond health- and personal-care products.

These moderate and steady gains have turned into plenty of return for shareholders both in the form of cash and as share price appreciation, and CVS is one of the surer bets on our list to continue this trend.

Reasons for Caution

The business model is intact and positioned for growth as the ACA becomes standard and as demographics shift in CVS's favor. That, of course, could change dramatically if political forces undermine ACA. To some degree, the company's potential has been built into the price of the stock already, and we haven't seen many short-term entry points in the past two years.

SECTOR: **Retail**
BETA COEFFICIENT: **0.95**
10-YEAR COMPOUND EARNINGS PER-SHARE GROWTH: **13.5%**
10-YEAR COMPOUND DIVIDENDS PER-SHARE GROWTH: **16.0%**

	2006	2007	2008	2009	2010	2011	2012	2013
Revenues (mil)	43,814	76,330	87,472	98,729	98,413	107,273	123,133	126,761
Net income (mil)	1,343	2,637	3,589	3,803	3,700	3,766	4,394	4,902
Earnings per share	1.60	1.92	2.44	2.63	2.67	2.80	3.43	4.00
Dividends per share	0.16	0.24	0.26	0.30	0.35	0.50	0.65	0.90
Cash flow per share	2.50	2.59	3.37	3.73	3.75	4.10	4.99	5.74
Price: high	36.1	42.6	44.3	38.3	37.8	39.5	49.8	72.0
low	26.1	30.5	23.2	23.7	26.8	31.3	41.0	49.9

CVS Caremark Corporation
One CVS Drive
Woonsocket, RI 02895
(401) 765-1500
Website: *www.cvs.com*

AGGRESSIVE GROWTH

Daktronics, Inc.

Ticker symbol: DAKT (NASDAQ) ❑ S&P rating: NR ❑ Value Line financial strength rating: B+
Current yield: 3.1% ❑ Dividend raises, past 10 years: 6

Company Profile

You're driving down the highway. You're thinking about getting rid of a month's worth of grime and dirt and crud from your car. Suddenly, in vivid Technicolor, you see a billboard ahead on your right. Not just any old indifferent and ignorable billboard displaying the same old thing months on end. It's brightly lit. It flashes an offer. Five Star Car Wash, at this exit, has a "Today Only—25 Percent Off" special. A few minutes ago you passed an electronic sign flashing "Road Work Ahead—Current Delay 30 Minutes." So, you tap the brakes, hit the right lane, and off the interstate you go. A win-win—you have a clean car, and the car wash, having a lighter day than usual, gets another unit through their system.

Hockey great Wayne Gretzky made famous the idea of "skating where the puck is going," and it's one of our favorite investing maxims. Like it or not, we think such real-time, highly visual signage is where the puck is going in marketing—real-time visual displays to complement your real-time mobile devices. Give it time, and it will come. Give it time, and there will be real-time visual graphic displays on park benches and subway entrances. Give it time, and there will be "digital street furniture" and such just about everywhere.

So how do you invest in this looming megatrend? We just happened to find a small company located literally in the middle of nowhere—Brookings, South Dakota—that makes this stuff. Chances are this company made both of the signs mentioned above. "Digital Street Furniture" is actually one of their product lines. Their core and founding business is really the large multimedia scoreboards in place in a growing number of sports arenas. Today, our new pick, Daktronics, has a hand in an assortment of places where digital display technology can make a difference in outdoor environments, from $40 million scoreboards to the variable dollars-and-cents-per-gallon digital displays outside your local gas station.

Daktronics is the world's leading supplier of electronic scoreboards, large electronic display systems, digital messaging solutions, and related software and support services for sporting, commercial, and transportation applications. The company offers everything from small signs and scoreboards costing under $1,000 to the large $40 million sports-complex scoreboards mentioned above.

Business segments include Commercial, Live Events, Schools and Theaters, Transportation, and International: These groups are organized around customer segments and are all set up to create and sell unique applications of the core product lines of the company, which include video display systems, scoring and timing systems, digital billboards, digital street furniture, and simpler message displays like price, time, and temperature displays. Most of the company's products are based on LED technology with low to high resolution and embedded digital controllers. Here is a bit more "color" on the five segments:

- Commercial (26 percent of 2013 revenue) sells a variety of digital signage to auto dealer, restaurant, gaming, retail petroleum (gas stations, mainly), and shopping center markets. Vivid video displays used for architectural or commercial purposes as part of the full building design is another emerging subsegment of this business.
- Live Events (31 percent) produces the traditional and some highly customized scoreboards, as well as signs for entertainment venues, including programmable displays, parking information

signs, and even specialized signs for places of worship.

- Schools and Theaters (13 percent). Included here are not only digital-age marquee signs for theaters and other venues but also for the box office, merchandise sales areas, and others. Continuously refreshed campus signs on high school and college campuses promote events and campus news and can show highlights from last Saturday's football game.
- Transportation (14 percent). You've seen the freeway signs; there is also plenty of digital signage in airports, train stations, and other mass transit facilities. Recent large installations were made at Los Angeles International Airport and for the New Jersey Turnpike Authority.
- International (14 percent) sells all applications into international markets.

The company has about 2,200 employees. Cofounder and chairman Aelred J. Kurtenbach, a PhD electrical engineer, owns 5.5 percent of the shares. The website, at *www.daktron ics.com*, is a fun and instructive ride.

Financial Highlights, Fiscal Year 2013

FY2013 started off with a relatively light backlog which picked up as prospects were converted to orders. At year's end, revenues increased about 7 percent, and more favorably, backlog increased about 29 percent to $170 million. Increased volume and operating efficiency led to a 10 percent increase in earnings. Forecasting such a small and variable business can be tricky, especially when sales of certain products like the large scoreboards can account for as much as 8 percent of annual revenue—but for now the company is forecasting top-line growth to continue in the 8–9 percent range, and per-share earnings, on the back of continued volume and operating leverage, to increase in the high teens. Annual dividend increases should roughly track the earnings trend.

Reasons to Buy

Since beaches and surf weren't part of the landscape, like any normal kids growing up in the Midwest we were fascinated with signs of all kinds. Daktronics takes signs to a new level. We feel such digital signage is a big part of the future of mass, real-time marketing communications—a "system" including your mobile device plus electronic signage—like it or not. We like situations where a core technology is applied successfully to an ever-larger number of end markets. Too, we think as such digital signage becomes more mainstream, the company will be able to produce in larger volumes, even mass-produce more of their applications, which should increase profitability.

Here, too, we have, more than anywhere else on our *100 Best* list, an opportunity to invest in what feels like your best friend's business next door. Founder Aelred Kurtenbach, PhD, is still very active in the company, owns a significant share of it, and seems not at all reluctant to share his success with shareholders. We see advantages in the location, too—a dedicated work force and low cost of doing business. Finally, the company has virtually no debt.

Reasons for Caution

We quote from the 2013 Annual Letter to Shareholders: "Our strategic focus is to be the industry leader in providing value to our customers through understanding their needs and expectations; we leverage our experience and technical knowledge through product innovation to create robust and configurable product platforms that meet or exceed customer expectations in performance, ease of use, quality, and reliability."

While we applaud the concepts, we found it surprisingly reflective of the drippy "say what they all say" business cliché stuff found in much larger, more bureaucratic organizations. We were surprised to find it at the close of management's letter and wonder whether the executives who signed the letter really wrote it—or think this way. We doubt both.

Setting this quip aside, we do see product and price competition in the form of major Japanese firms like Mitsubishi (and if you've been to Tokyo, you know how mainstream digital signage can be). We do also wonder if environmental movements will rise up to quell what could easily become overstimulating visual "pollution," but so far to our knowledge this hasn't happened on a large scale.

More conventionally, Daktronics clearly has a riskier profile than most of our picks. Order flow and timing can vary considerably, especially in the sports segment, but we think it will smooth out once electronic commercial signage becomes more mainstream.

SECTOR: Technology
BETA COEFFICIENT: 1.24
10-YEAR COMPOUND EARNINGS PER-SHARE GROWTH: 4.5%
10-YEAR COMPOUND DIVIDENDS PER-SHARE GROWTH: 23.0%

	2006	2007	2008	2009	2010	2011	2012	2013
Revenues (mil)	433	500	582	393	442	489	518	555
Net income (mil)	24.4	26.2	26.4	(7.0)	14.2	8.5	22.8	25.0
Earnings per share	0.59	0.63	0.64	(0.17)	0.34	0.20	0.53	0.60
Dividends per share	.06	.07	.09	.10	.10	.22	.23	.39
Cash flow per share	0.97	1.17	1.25	0.37	0.81	0.62	0.91	0.90
Price: high	40.1	39.5	23.1	10.5	17.3	16.7	11.9	16.1
low	13.9	19.8	5.7	5.9	7.1	8.0	6.3	9.4

Daktronics, Incorporated
201 Daktronics Drive
Brookings, SD 57006
(605) 692 0200
Website: *www.daktronics.com*

Deere & Company

Ticker symbol: DE (NYSE) ▫ S&P rating: A ▫ Value Line financial strength rating: A++
Current yield: 2.3% ▫ Dividend raises, past 10 years: 10

Company Profile

Founded in 1837, Deere & Company grew from a one-man blacksmith shop into a worldwide corporation that today does business in more than 160 countries and employs more than 66,000 people around the globe. Deere has a diverse base of operations reporting into three segments: Agriculture and Turf, Construction and Forestry, and Financial Services.

Deere has been the world's premier producer of agricultural equipment for nearly 50 years. The Agriculture and Turf segment produces and distributes tractors, loaders, combines, harvesters, seeding, mowers, hay baling, tilling, crop care and application, snow removal, and other equipment. If it's used on a farm and requires an engine, Deere likely offers it. With the Construction and Forestry segment, Deere is also the world's leading manufacturer of forestry equipment and a major manufacturer of heavy construction equipment (Caterpillar being the market leader in this segment). They're also the world leader in premium turf-care equipment and utility vehicles in both the commercial and consumer markets.

As the company reports it, revenue for the Agriculture and Turf segment is about 83 percent of the $35 billion in FY2013 revenue; the Construction and Forestry segment makes up the remainder. The Financial Services segment rolls its revenue into the other segments, and only segment profits are reported.

The Financial Services segment includes John Deere Credit, which is one of the largest equipment finance companies in the United States, with more than 1.8 million accounts, a managed asset portfolio of nearly $31 billion, and a contribution of $460 million in profits, or about 13 percent of the total. It provides retail, wholesale, and lease financing for agricultural, construction, and forestry equipment; commercial and consumer equipment, including lawn and ground care; and revolving credit for agricultural inputs and services. These services are available in all of Deere's largest markets, including Argentina, Australia, Brazil, Canada, France, and Germany. Overall, international sales continue to account for about 41 percent of the total.

Financial Highlights, Fiscal Year 2013

Despite the 2012 drought in the U.S., Deere's stellar international performance in that year made FY2013 a difficult comparison. Despite that, farm activity was very strong in 2013, and Deere brought home the bacon in record form in FY2013 as a consequence. Revenues rose 4.5 percent to $35 billion, and a full percentage point increase in operating margin to 10.1 percent drove net profits a full 15 percent higher than FY2012, itself a record year. The company clicked on all cylinders, and investors weren't left out with a 10 percent dividend increase and a 4 percent reduction in share count.

However, those gains have already been harvested, and FY2014 and beyond are projected to level off. Why? Because of lower crop prices. Prices of key agricultural commodities like corn have dropped as much as 40 percent. While it may be temporary, the company is projecting a modest decline in farm income and in farm balance sheets—two figures that it watches closely. As a consequence, the company forecasts a 6 percent drop in farm and turf equipment sales, mostly in North America and Europe. Offsetting that to a degree is a recovery in the construction industry, which will help its construction and forestry equipment segments, but as we've seen that is only 15 percent of the business. Current guidance calls for a 3–4 percent reduction in overall sales and a 6.5 percent drop in per-share earnings.

Reasons to Buy

"Nothing runs like a Deere" is the company's apt slogan, and as far as industrial companies go, Deere continues to be a poster child for U.S. industrial ingenuity and excellence. It has an outstanding brand (and one of the most popular logos for hats, jackets, and so on, worn by people who have barely seen a farm field!) and reputation in the agriculture industry, and we see the ag industry as strong and strategic far into the future as global living standards improve and emerging markets develop. Farm incomes continue to rise worldwide. The company is making good progress in developing markets, particularly in Brazil and India. Too, we think that innovation is a plus—Deere leads its competitors in R&D investment (more than 4 percent of sales), bringing the Internet and GPS to farming and farming machines; new engines also promise greater fuel economy and reduced emissions.

Beyond its products, Deere has established an almost unassailable brand leadership with its services and customer-centered innovations. Deere, more than others, puts its people in the field (literally) to figure out what agriculture professionals really need, and they work with their customers closely to sell their products through a solid dealer network.

Now the company appears to be navigating a flat period due to the aforementioned softness in crop prices, but are we really concerned? The past two years were exceptionally strong— a "reversion to the mean" in growth is hardly a reason to turn away from this company. Even with a slow FY2014, improving sales, profitability, and share buybacks have doubled per-share earnings from their 2007–2010 range; to underscore that point, the ten-year compound annual rate in earnings growth is 25 percent, one of the best on our list in that respect. We continue to believe that agriculture is a good place to be long term and that the current softness presents a solid buying opportunity.

Reasons for Caution

The company is, and always will be, vulnerable to cycles in the farm sector. The normal cycle, and in particular indelible memories of 1980s farm difficulties, can cause the farmers who buy this stuff to get cautious pretty quickly. The company's beta of 1.45 reflects this long-term volatility and cyclicality, although recently the stock has had little volatility. The U.S. government farm legislation, called the "farm bill" and typically passed every five years, has become more political of late because of its ties to food stamps and general welfare. As evidence of this trend it took two years longer to pass than usual, and future cutbacks could affect farmers although not immediately. All in all, farming will always be with us, and there will always be a demand for machines and especially smarter, more efficient ones—Deere has an enormous brand and long-term track record.

SECTOR: **Industrials**
BETA COEFFICIENT: **1.45**
10-YEAR COMPOUND EARNINGS PER-SHARE GROWTH: **25.0%**
10-YEAR COMPOUND DIVIDENDS PER-SHARE GROWTH: **13.0%**

	2006	2007	2008	2009	2010	2011	2012	2013
Revenues (mil)	19,884	21,489	25,804	20,756	23,573	29,466	33,501	34,998
Net income (mil)	1,453	1,822	2,053	1,198	1,865	2,799	3,065	3,533
Earnings per share	3.08	4.01	4.70	2.82	4.35	6.63	7.64	9.08
Dividends per share	0.78	0.91	1.06	1.12	1.16	1.52	1.79	1.99
Cash flow per share	4.09	5.12	6.01	4.05	5.72	8.34	9.56	11.45
Price: high	50.7	93.7	94.9	56.9	84.9	99.8	89.7	95.6
low	33.5	45.1	28.5	24.5	46.3	59.9	69.5	79.5

Deere & Company
One John Deere Place
Moline, IL 61265
(309) 765-8000
Website: *www.deere.com*

CONSERVATIVE GROWTH

NEW
FOR 2015

Devon Energy

Ticker symbol: DVN (NYSE) ❑ S&P rating: BBB+ ❑ Value Line financial strength rating: B++
Current yield: 1.3% ❑ Dividend raises, past 10 years: 7

Company Profile

Over the past two years, we pruned out Marathon Oil and ExxonMobil from our *100 Best Stocks* list; the former due to a company split we wanted to see bear fruit; the latter because of its sheer size and lack of success replacing reserves. That left us with Chevron, ConocoPhillips, and Total S.A.—good picks but they left us wondering whether we were underexposed to this key, cash-producing, strategic sector. So we went shopping in the oil patch for a new energy company for our list.

We had a few criteria in mind. First, we wanted a company well positioned to take advantage of the new "fracking" (hydraulic fracturing) boom producing a bounty of energy right here in North America. In line with that, we wanted a company with less international exposure, one comfortable with new technologies, one expanding its reserves faster than production, one qualifying as a good corporate citizen, and one with a sizeable presence in the natural gas business (which we think will recover from recent price softness).

If we hadn't found a company that qualified, we would probably have stuck with the three named

above. But indeed we did find one: Devon Energy.

Devon Energy drills almost exclusively in seven locations all within North America. Its biggest activities are in Texas in the Barnett Shale formations of east Texas and the Permian Basin farther west. Devon also has a sizeable presence in Oklahoma, Louisiana, Wyoming, and in Alberta, Canada—it is a pure play in North American energy production.

Devon is involved in "upstream" exploration and production and in "midstream" processing, mainly the separation of natural gas liquids (propane, butane, etc.) from the gaseous methane for sale and shipment. About 58 percent of proved reserves are natural gas. The company's strategies include investing in more profitable oil and natural gas liquids (NGL) production, and in keeping critical mass in relatively few areas to reduce operating costs and concentrate on knowledge of those areas. The company expects liquids and oil to make up 50 percent of the business in 2014, up from 34 percent in 2011. Adjacent to these strategies are an effort to sell off assets ("monetize non-core E&P properties") that don't fit this model, to partner with others in midstream operations (a new joint venture with midstream operator Crosstek), and to build more concentrated areas of exploration (through a $6 billion acquisition in the Eagle Ford shale area in south Texas).

Through creating these strategies and executing them well, the company has doubled its production since 2008, and in 2013 replaced about 180 percent of what it has produced with new reserves. Reserves are at a record level as the company exited that year. As a good corporate citizen, the company has been a supporter of transparency on the environmental front, especially in fracking activities, as one of the earliest supporters of fracking disclosure on the *fracfocus.org* website. For the eighth consecutive year Devon was named to *Fortune's* "100 Best Companies to Work For" award—rival Chesapeake Energy was the only other energy producer seen on this list.

Financial Highlights, Fiscal Year 2013

Reading much from the top and bottom line over the years has been a challenge, as the company has acquired and divested properties through the course of the past eight years; also the energy price spike in 2007–8, followed by the dip in the Great Recession, are more anomalous than predictive of future results. Better to focus on the near term and the future.

For FY2013, revenues advanced almost 10 percent, helped along by better-than-expected production— especially in the oil segment, which was 32 percent ahead of 2012 in volume—and firmer prices, especially in the natural gas segment. Top-line improvement, cost containment measures, and a favorable tax rate drove per-share earnings up almost 31 percent from FY2012.

For FY2014 the company expects continued exploration and production momentum, particularly in oil with Permian Basin developments and the new Eagle Ford property. Revenues are projected to rise 13 percent, with earnings advancing 25–30 percent. The incremental activity will slow to a more normal 3–5 percent top-line gain in FY2015 with a 10 percent gain in the bottom line.

Reasons to Buy

Devon gives us exposure to a highly efficient energy exploration and production machine right in our own back yard—translation: devoid of the international political risks that face most producers. They have made more of both "fracking" and conventional methods than most. While we like the expansion into NGLs and oil exploration, we also feel their stronghold in traditional natural gas will be a strength going forward, as prices inevitably rise as more and more major energy consumers, like power plants, step up gas usage.

Over the years we have not been terribly trusting of "big oil" and particularly the management of "big oil" companies. With that in mind, we found the company's 2013 Form 10-K annual report to be a notably informative read—more real facts and figures and less corporate BS than we're used to seeing. Kudos, management.

Reasons for Caution

Energy prices and the economy go hand in hand, and neither are a sure bet going forward—the company will always be exposed to economic and energy cycles. Gas prices could remain low for some time as new domestic energy reserves come on line, but we expect that new demand will meet if not exceed this new supply. While not facing international political issues, American energy companies are a favorite target of environmentalists and are prone to PR problems (and as BP showed us, some of these risks are real), but Devon not having its name on local gas stations, and not being known as a "big oil" giant, mitigates this.

Finally, while we see good returns on reinvested cash flows, we'd like to see a little more going to shareholders.

SECTOR: **Energy**
BETA COEFFICIENT: **1.39**
10-YEAR COMPOUND EARNINGS PER-SHARE GROWTH: **5.0%**
10-YEAR COMPOUND DIVIDENDS PER-SHARE GROWTH: **21.5%**

	2006	2007	2008	2009	2010	2011	2012	2013
Revenues (mil)	10,578	11,362	15,211	8,960	9,940	11,494	9,502	10,407
Net income (mil)	2,627	3,146	4,364	1,706	2,543	2,485	1,285	1,727
Earnings per share	0.85	1.12	1.41	1.53	1.35	2.07	1.76	1.15
Dividends per share	0.45	0.56	0.64	0.64	0.64	0.67	0.80	0.86
Cash flow per share	11.85	13.49	17.74	8.98	10.02	11.71	10.09	11.17
Price: high	74.8	94.8	127.4	75.1	78.9	93.6	76.3	66.9
low	48.9	62.8	54.4	38.6	58.6	50.7	50.9	50.8

Devon Energy
333 W. Sheridan Avenue
Oklahoma City, OK 73102-5015
(405) 235-3611
Website: *www.devonenergy.com*

GROWTH AND INCOME

E. I. du Pont de Nemours and Company (DuPont)

Ticker symbol: DD (NYSE) □ S&P rating: A □ Value Line financial strength rating: A++
Current yield: 2.7% □ Dividend raises, past 10 years: 6

Company Profile

"The miracles of science" is the slogan and rallying cry of this $36 billion-plus science and technology juggernaut originally founded in 1802 to make gunpowder. Although the company is known to many as a cyclical diversified chemical company making a host of lifeless chemical products and ingredients, many by the tank car–load, today's DuPont is reawakening as a world leader in science and technology with important end-product ingredients in a range of disciplines, including biotechnology, electronics materials and science, safety and security, and synthetic fibers. The company has always been a technology leader with such well-known inventions as Nylon and Rayon in earlier years, and Teflon and Kevlar more recently, but at least until lately has been taken in more as a commodity producer than an innovator. We see signs of change in that reputation, toward its own "market-driven science" business vision.

The company began a more deliberate evolution away from more commoditized chemicals and toward more higher-growth, less cyclical technology-based products with the 2012 divestiture of the Performance Coatings Division. In 2013, the company continued the trend by announcing the separation of the Performance Chemicals segment in a shareholder spinoff, a transaction that had yet to be completed as we prepared the 2015 list. We'll include the Performance Chemicals segment among the seven operating segments for now:

- The Agriculture (30 percent of FY2013 revenues) segment delivers a portfolio of products and services specifically targeted to achieve gains in crop yields and productivity, including Pioneer brand seed products and well-established brands of insecticides, fungicides, and herbicides. Pioneer develops, produces, and markets corn hybrid and soybean varieties and sells wheat, rice, sunflower, canola, and other seeds under the Pioneer and other brand names. DuPont also sells a line of crop protection products for field and orchard agriculture.

■ Electronics and Communications (7 percent) makes a line of high-tech materials for the semiconductor industry, including ceramic packages and LCD materials. E&C supplies differentiated materials and systems for photovoltaics (solar), consumer electronics, displays, and advanced printing.

■ Nutrition and Health (10 percent) consists of the recently acquired Danisco's specialty food ingredients business and Solae, a majority-owned venture with Bunge Limited, which is engaged in developing soy-based technologies. The segment is a provider of solutions for specialty food ingredients, health, and safety. Products include cultures, emulsifiers, gums, natural sweeteners, and soy-based food.

■ Industrial Biosciences (3 percent) is engaged in developing and manufacturing a wide range of enzymes, the biocatalysts that enable chemical reactions, on a large scale. The segment's enzymes add value and functionality to a broad range of products and processes, such as animal nutrition, detergents, food manufacturing, ethanol production, and industrial applications.

These first four businesses are relatively new and growing and add on to the traditional core businesses:

■ Performance Chemicals (21 percent) delivers a range of industrial and specialty chemical products such as fluorochemicals (refrigerants, Teflon), lubricants, solvents, propellants, fire suppression chemicals, and titanium-based pigments to a variety of industrial customers, including plastics and coatings, textiles, mining, pulp and paper, water treatment, and health-care manufacturers.

■ Performance Materials (19 percent) supplies high-performance polymers, films, plastics, and substrates to a variety of industries from automotive to aerospace and consumer durable goods manufacturers and many others.

■ Safety and Protection (11 percent) makes protective fibers and clothing, including bulletproof apparel; disinfectants; and protective building surfaces—Tyvek house wrap is one of the bigger brands here.

The sales breakdown is largely unchanged from FY2012, save for a 2 percent uptick in Agriculture and a balancing 2 percent downtick in Performance Chemicals, the division being spun off. The company has operations in 90 countries worldwide, and about 61 percent of consolidated net sales are made to customers outside the United States. Not surprisingly, innovation is an important theme at DuPont. The company has one of the largest R&D budgets of any company in the world and operates more than 150 R&D centers worldwide. DuPont's core research is concentrated at its Wilmington, Delaware, facilities. DuPont's modern research is focused on renewable bio-based materials, advanced biofuels, energy-efficient technologies, enhanced safety products, and alternative energy technologies. The company introduced some 1,800 new products in FY2013 and estimates $10 billion in revenues, a bit under a third of their total, from products introduced in the past four years.

Financial Highlights, Fiscal Year 2013

Including the divestiture of Performance Coatings, but not including the separation of Performance Chemicals, DuPont rang up a 3.2 percent top-line gain and a far stronger 15.8 percent gain in net earnings, brought forward by improvements in its higher-margin businesses pretty much across the board, in turn reflecting the evolution in its overall business strategy. The net profit margin gained a full 1.2 percent to 10.2 percent. Helped along by a moderate share buyback, per-share earnings

rose some 16.5 percent. For FY2014 and FY 2015, the company expects a strengthening top-line growth rate to about 5 percent, reflecting the continued business mix evolution and strength in emerging markets and in domestic manufacturing. Per-share earnings increases are projected in the 10–12 percent range, reflecting margin improvements and a recently sweetened $5 billion share buyback, which should gobble up 7–8 percent of its share count. Such figures make DuPont another member of our "5 and 10" club—steady 5 percent top-line and 10 percent bottom-line growth.

Reasons to Buy

DuPont continues to succeed in reinventing itself (and remarketing itself) as an innovation leader and to capitalize equally on innovation and product leadership in established categories. The product pipeline continues to be full, individual product margins remain strong, the product mix is improving, and the company's biggest moneymakers still dominate their markets. Slowly but surely, the company is exiting low-margin, cyclical commodity businesses.

The company continues to capitalize on "global megatrends"—population growth, alternative energy production, and so forth. The improvement of worldwide food production is at the center of its new growth initiatives. The company has brand leadership in many important categories, and is committed to total shareholder returns with a solid dividend track record and an aggressive share buyback program.

Reasons for Caution

The company still needs to overcome the stigma—and some of the behaviors—of a commodity producer. Too, some of the "new age" businesses like photovoltaic products haven't taken hold as expected, though that is starting to change. Finally, DuPont's fortunes are tied to hydrocarbon feedstocks and commodity prices in general; while the current picture is favorable, particularly with plentiful natural gas and soft prices, this scenario can change quickly.

SECTOR: Materials
BETA COEFFICIENT: 1.59
10-YEAR COMPOUND EARNINGS PER-SHARE GROWTH: 6.0%
10-YEAR COMPOUND DIVIDENDS PER-SHARE GROWTH: 2.0%

	2006	2007	2008	2009	2010	2011	2012	2013
Revenues (mil)	27,421	29,378	30,529	26,109	31,505	37,961	34,812	35,734
Net income (mil)	2,684	3,034	2,477	1,853	3,032	3,698	3,137	3,632
Earnings per share	2.88	3.28	2.73	2.04	3.28	3.93	3.33	3.68
Dividends per share	1.48	1.52	1.64	1.64	1.64	1.64	1.70	1.78
Cash flow per share	4.40	4.89	4.33	3.70	4.80	5.67	5.19	5.65
Price: high	49.7	53.9	52.5	35.6	50.2	57.0	57.5	65.0
low	37.6	42.3	21.3	16.0	31.9	37.1	4.7	45.1

E. I. du Pont de Nemours and Company
1007 North Market Street
Wilmington, DE 19898
(302) 774-1000
Website: www.dupont.com

CONSERVATIVE GROWTH

Eastman Chemical Company

Ticker symbol: EMN (NYSE) □ S&P rating: BBB □ Value Line financial strength rating: A
Current yield: 1.6% □ Dividend raises, past 10 years: 5

Company Profile

Spun off in 1993 from the recently bankrupted Eastman Kodak, Eastman Chemical is one of those "better living through chemistry" companies with a history of solving problems and providing standard, high-tech, and high-precision materials to industries ranging from food and beverage to toys to medical equipment to computers and electronics. The Eastman mission could be almost be refined into "better living through polymer chemistry"—the chemical building blocks, mostly sourced from petroleum and other feedstocks known as hydrocarbons that turn into all things useful such as plastics, paints, coatings, inks, and the like. Many of their products are "intermediaries," used to manufacture other chemicals and products. When speaking the language of the company you quickly pick up expressions like "olefin cycle" and "phthalate," among the more difficult concepts and spelling challenges, like "ophthalmology," we've encountered in the *100 Best Stocks* space.

The company is organized into five product segments, all of which have something more or less to do with petrochemicals:

- Advanced Materials (25 percent of 2013 sales) produces and markets specialty copolyesters, cellulose esters, and plastic and window film products into the automotive and transportation industries, building materials, LCD and display manufacturing, health and wellness, and durable goods industries.

- Additives & Functional Products (18 percent) produces chemical products for the coatings industry and for tires, paints, inks, building materials, durable goods, and consumables markets. Key technology platforms include rubber additives, cellulosic polymers, ketones, coalescents, polyester polymers olefins, and hydrocarbon resins.

- Fibers (16 percent) produces acetate tow, triacetin, and solution-dyed acetate yarns for the apparel, filtration, tobacco (filters), fabric, home furnishings, and other industries.

- Additives & Plasticizers (14 percent) produces intermediary products, mainly adhesive resins and plasticizers, sold into the consumables, building materials, health and wellness, industrial chemicals, and durable goods markets.

- Specialty Fluids and Intermediates (27 percent) is a catchall for other products that don't fall into the other segments, including new or custom-made polymer-based products for key customers.

Obviously there could be considerably more detail in these descriptions, but it would probably only be meaningful to those with a strong chemistry or materials background. The upshot: Eastman makes a lot of strategically important materials that support a lot of manufacturing processes for common and fairly high-volume items, such as beer bottles. Additionally, these materials are used in considerable amounts in overseas manufacturing. Eastman has adapted by setting up plants in 10 countries and driving foreign sales to 54 percent of the total. By region, sales are 46 percent from North America, 28 percent Asia-Pacific, 21 percent EMEA, and 5 percent Latin America.

Financial Highlights, Fiscal Year 2013

Increased global manufacturing activity, and particular strength in the automotive, construction, energy and energy efficiency, and emerging economies led to an excellent post-recession recovery year in FY2013. Helped along by these factors and the late 2012 acquisition of Solutia, a complementary maker of specialty chemicals, revenues advanced 15.4 percent to $9.35 billion, while improved operating leverage, cost synergies with the Solutia acquisition, and reduced input costs combined with slightly lower selling prices and unfavorable exchange rates, led to improved margins which in turn led to a full 25 percent gain in net earnings. For FY2014 and beyond, the company will finish the integration of Solutia and ride more operating efficiency and margin improvements, while making a few small acquisitions, all told generating sales gains in the 3–5 percent range and earnings gains in the 8–13 percent range. The company has stated a goal to grow per-share earnings to $8.00 in FY2015, which would be a 24 percent increase from FY2013's level.

Reasons to Buy

Although Eastman lies on the edge of the "buy businesses you understand" test, it's obvious from the numbers and especially the improving margins that the company really does produce things vitally important to manufacturing mainstream and advanced products. Successful product development has always been a key strength for Eastman, but the company has grown margins very steadily over the past few years through careful investments in business restructuring, cost-cutting measures, and additions to its output capacity. Eastman will benefit from the continued strength in domestic manufacturing, although its international operations, particularly in Asia, are also a source of strength. Eastman is well positioned for continued organic growth with excellent cash flow, solid projected earnings growth, and good liquidity.

Reasons for Caution

Eastman's fortunes will follow those of the larger manufacturing sector in general and, to a lesser extent, the feedstock (petroleum) market more specifically. Petro pricing is stable at the moment and is expected to remain so in the near term, but there is always risk of turmoil here, both political and speculative. The company is still carrying a heavy debt load and an increased share count from the Solutia acquisition, and continued prudence in paying that down and a focus on organic growth will be needed going forward. That will hamper share repurchases somewhat, but it's good to see them starting again with a recent $1 billion authorization alongside reasonably healthy dividend increases. That said, shareholder returns have a bit of catching up to do to match the rate of earnings increases, and share price increases, for that matter.

SECTOR: **Materials**
BETA COEFFICIENT: **1.84**
10-YEAR COMPOUND EARNINGS PER-SHARE GROWTH: **25.0%**
10-YEAR COMPOUND DIVIDENDS PER-SHARE GROWTH: **2.5%**

	2006	2007	2008	2009	2010	2011	2012	2013
Revenues (mil)	7,450	6,830	6,720	5,047	5,842	7,178	8,102	9,350
Net income (mil)	416	423	342	265	514	653	802	1,008
Earnings per share	2.50	2.53	2.25	1.82	3.48	4.56	5.38	6.45
Dividends per share	0.88	0.88	0.88	0.88	0.90	0.99	1.08	1.25
Cash flow per share	4.33	4.71	4.20	3.72	5.62	6.76	7.55	9.45
Price: high	30.6	39.2	39.1	31.0	42.3	55.4	68.2	83.0
low	23.7	28.8	12.9	8.9	25.9	32.4	39.2	63.5

Eastman Chemical Company
200 South Wilcox Drive
Kingsport, TN 37660
(423) 229-2000
Website: *www.eastman.com*

AGGRESSIVE GROWTH

Fair Isaac Corporation

Ticker symbol: FICO (NYSE) ❑ S&P rating: NR ❑ Value Line financial strength rating: B++
Current yield: 0.14% ❑ Dividend raises, past 10 years: 1

Company Profile

Fair Isaac Corporation provides decision support analytics, software, and solutions to help businesses improve and automate decision making and risk management. The most well-known and best example of these solutions is the FICO score—an analytic single-figure estimate of a consumer's creditworthiness used in the credit industry and for other purposes such as employment and insurance.

FICO provides its analytic solutions and services to a variety of financial and other service organizations, including banks, credit-reporting agencies, credit card–processing agencies, insurers, telecommunications providers, retailers, marketers, and health-care organizations. It operates in three segments: Applications, Scores, and Tools. The Applications segment provides decision and risk management tools, market targeting and customer analytics tools, and fraud detection tools and associated professional services. The Scores segment includes the business-to-business scoring solutions; myFICO solutions, delivering FICO scores for consumers; and associated professional services. The Tools segment provides software products and consulting services to help organizations build their own analytic tools.

The company actively works with customers in a variety of vertical markets to identify and apply their tools and applications; a recent application of the FICO Xpress Optimization Suite to a research arm of the Lawrence Livermore Laboratory to optimize power grids serves as a good example.

Financial Highlights, Fiscal Year 2013

FICO is well past the Great Recession crunch, which saw a sharp slackening of demand as financial services firms reduced spending and as credit and loan activity diminished altogether. The demand for traditional credit-scoring products has resumed, though not at previous levels, and revenues haven't reached the record $826.4 million achieved in 2006. But since then, the Applications unit, which represents about 61 percent of the business, has picked up some, but not all of the slack. The unit was a bit soft in FY2013 and early FY2014, but with fraud detection as 25 percent of this unit's business and the recent surge in credit card fraud at Target and other retailers, we have what could be aptly described as a mixed picture in the recent past and going forward.

FY2013 brought a decent 10 percent revenue gain but with a bit of margin softness, net profit and per-share earnings actually declined slightly. For FY2014 the company is guiding revenues 3–4 percent higher, reflecting some competitive pressure and continued softness in the Applications segment with a modest increase in reported earnings. The company will also accelerate share buybacks slightly. We expect FY2015 to be a stronger year as vertical market and "cloud" applications and fraud analytics provide tailwinds.

Reasons to Buy

"Big data" and related analytics are hot right now as more vertical industries (banking, retail, utilities, pharma, medical devices, health insurers, etc.) learn how to use them more efficiently and effectively to manage different parts of their business. There are a number of companies, large and small, in the analytics business, but few have the brand reputation, product packaging, and leadership enjoyed by FICO. The company is a pure play and is considered to be the gold standard for this type of product. It is more turnkey and easy for customers who don't have advanced mathematicians and software engineering staffs to buy. As a consequence, and with the brand recognition of the FICO score, the company has attained a pretty large moat on its brand and is a good example of how packaging and market definition can be as important as the product.

We also think a stabilizing financial industry with new rules, fewer workers, and a greater recognition for risk and risk management will bode well for the FICO product suite. Financial and other decision-making FICO products offer a good combination of streamlining and sophistication. Long term, we can easily see their modeling approaches being further extended to analyze customer behavior and provide decision support for insurability, employability, acceptance into schools, and even customer behaviors in stores or online, other areas well beyond a consumer's ability to repay extended credit. International demand for FICO's products continues to grow, too, notably in China, where fraud protection is a big business.

At less than $1 billion in revenues and with only 2,460 employees, this company has room to grow and offers a nice alternative to the much larger businesses on our *100 Best* list.

The dividend remains inconsequential, but it doesn't take a genius (or analytics) to figure out the company's policy of providing shareholder returns in the form of cash. Share counts have dropped from almost 70 million in 2004 to just under 34 million at present and are projected to drop into the 30 million range over the next few years.

Reasons for Caution

Most of the changes afoot in the credit card and financial services industry bode well for FICO, but we wonder if credit-scoring demand will ever be what it was in 2004–07. There is more competition in the scoring arena from the three major credit bureaus (who now act as both a channel and a competitor, always a delicate situation) and from a product called VantageScore being marketed by the bureaus, which looks a lot like a FICO score but isn't. That said, the company recently renewed its agreement with Equifax.

While FICO is a solid company with a solid product, there are other uncertainties. The company's business is still heavily tied to the financial industry and financial transaction volumes, although less so moving forward as analytics and big data take center stage—but the market for analytics is crowded and rapidly evolving. Software companies always run a certain amount of technology risk; this should also be considered. The ability to sell in a "cloud" environment and to maintain or increase margins by selling the right mix of products and channels will be key. There is some public concern that scoring models oversimplify lending and insurability decisions and should not be used or relied on so heavily. Finally, as we've seen, the company is vulnerable to economic downturns. In all, we feel the company will succeed on the basis of its brand, reputation, and market leadership.

SECTOR: **Business Services**
BETA COEFFICIENT: **1.32**
10-YEAR COMPOUND EARNINGS PER-SHARE GROWTH: **7.0%**
10-YEAR COMPOUND DIVIDENDS PER-SHARE GROWTH: **7.5%**

		2006	2007	2008	2009	2010	2011	2012	2013
Revenues (mil)		825.4	822.2	744.8	630.7	605.6	619.7	676.4	743.4
Net income (mil)		103.5	104.7	81.2	65.1	64.5	71.6	92.0	90.1
Earnings per share		1.50	1.82	1.64	1.34	1.42	1.79	2.55	2.48
Dividends per share		0.08	0.08	0.08	0.08	0.08	0.08	0.08	0.08
Cash flow per share		2.57	3.03	2.49	2.15	2.36	2.58	3.20	3.54
Price:	high	47.8	41.8	32.2	24.5	27.0	38.5	47.9	63.5
	low	32.5	32.1	10.4	9.8	19.5	20.0	34.6	41.3

Fair Isaac Corporation
181 Metro Drive
San Jose, CA 95110
Phone: (408) 535-1500
Website: *www.fairisaac.com*

FedEx Corporation

Ticker symbol: FDX (NYSE) □ S&P rating: BBB □ Value Line financial strength rating: A+
Current yield: 0.4% □ Dividend raises, past 10 years: 10

Company Profile

FedEx Corporation is the world's leading provider of guaranteed express delivery services and a major player in the overall small shipment and small package logistics market. The corporation is organized as a holding company, with four individual businesses that compete collectively and operate independently under the FedEx brand, offering a wide range of express delivery services for the time-definite transportation of documents, packages, and freight. The familiar FedEx Express operation offers overnight and deferred air service to 57,000 drop-off locations, operating 649 aircraft and approximately 50,000 ground vehicles to support this business. The company also offers freight services for less time-sensitive items and small or less-than-truckload (LTL) shipments under the FedEx Ground and FedEx Freight brands. FedEx Ground offers overnight service from 500 pickup/delivery terminals for up to 400 miles anywhere in the United States for packages weighing up to 150 pounds, while FedEx Freight offers standard and priority LTL service across North America mainly for business supply-chain operations. Finally, the company has

ventured into specialized logistics services with its comprehensive FedEx Services, which also includes the former Kinko's copy and office centers, now operating under the FedEx/Office brand.

In total, the company operates an enormous logistics network of 649 aircraft, 100,000 ground vehicles, over 690 World Service Centers, over 1,750 FedEx Office locations, nearly 6,300 authorized Ship Centers, and more than 37,000 Drop Boxes. The company has about 300,000 "team members"—employees and contractors. They serve over 375 airports in over 220 countries. Except for the number of countries served, all of these figures are slightly attenuated from previous years as the company weeds out unproductive and redundant locations in a drive for efficiency. In FY2013, the Express segment accounted for 61 percent of revenues, Ground 24 percent, Freight 12 percent, and Services 4 percent, representing a slight increase in the overall mix for the Ground service.

In 2013, *Fortune* magazine rated the company as number nine among "World's Most Admired Companies" and number one in the delivery industry segment.

Financial Highlights, Fiscal Year 2013

Following up on its strong rebound in FY2011 and FY2012, FY2013 revenue continued its steady climb of about 4 percent to just over $44 billion. However, soft international shipments and pricing, gradually rising fuel costs and other expenses, and a drop in fuel surcharges caused profits to dip their nose some 23 percent for the year. In the latter half of the year, the operating environment improved, and the company forecasts another 5 percent top-line growth in FY2013, with solid operating margin improvements delivered by pricing and operational adjustments and cost-cutting measures to the tune of a $6.80 per-share performance in FY2014 and $7.80 per share in FY2015. Such a recovery attests to good management and a healthy operating flexibility we like to see in a comprehensive business such as FedEx; it is also clear evidence of the growth in small single-shipment volume arising from e-commerce and time-sensitive delivery to support general U.S. and world commerce.

Reasons to Buy

After a fairly soft 2013, both for the company and its shareholders, the company's share fortunes and share price finally climbed through the clouds and reached cruising altitude by the end of the year. The integrated service offerings worked better together both for customers and the company, and we expect that trend to continue in the future. A strong tailwind of e-commerce business and greater need for a complete, economical, and partially time-sensitive logistics mix is the right place to be as American manufacturing activity and local sourcing increase—although this will dampen international shipments, a trend we've already seen. We like the company's partnerships with the U.S. Postal Service. The "SmartPost" service uses the USPS for economical final "last mile" delivery to residences, an attractive route for smaller e-commerce shipments. The company is also a key "wholesale" provider for the USPS express and overnight small package delivery services. Such alliances, or "co-opetition," between archrivals tend to be productive "win-win" arrangements for both carriers and customers as well.

With SmartPost and other business expansions, the Ground segment is approaching a 30 percent market share for such services, a position from which it can start to call the shots in the marketplace for lucrative e-commerce and time-sensitive ground business. Indeed, of late, the company has been able to raise prices while also gaining market share. FedEx has a strong brand and offers a diverse set of services, really a complete logistics solution, for a large group of customers. The continued resurgence in the economy and growth in online shopping and delivery will certainly help volumes and pricing, and the continuing shift to e-commerce gives a boost to this recovery. The resumption of strong U.S. exports not only helps volume but also helps fill up planes traveling from the United States. The logistics business is always ripe for innovation, and FedEx has long been an innovator in the transportation and small-package shipment business, not only with new transportation services, but also with new tools to help customers track shipments and manage their supply chains in real time; we expect this to continue.

Reasons for Caution

International volumes remain soft and will likely continue to do so in the near-term future, although the company is paring capacity in this segment.

Of course, any slowdown in business activity can and will hurt the company. The company is always vulnerable to fuel prices, particularly if cost increases come faster than they can be recovered in rates and fuel surcharges—as is often the case. While cash flows are strong, this company must occasionally purchase or lease aircraft, and this and other capital expenditures can put a big dent in cash flows.

To a degree, favorable trends have already been priced into the stock, so investors should be patient as they look for an entry point. We like the fact that the company has raised the dividend every year since starting to pay dividends in 2002, but we'd also like to see the company return more to shareholders, both in the form of dividends and share buybacks.

SECTOR: **Transportation**
BETA COEFFICIENT: **1.44**
10-YEAR COMPOUND EARNINGS PER-SHARE GROWTH: **8.0%**
10-YEAR COMPOUND DIVIDENDS PER-SHARE GROWTH: **20.0%**

	2006	2007	2008	2009	2010	2011	2012	2013
Revenues (mil)	32,294	35,214	37,953	35,497	34,734	39,204	42,680	44,287
Net income (mil)	1,885	2,073	1,821	1,173	1,184	1,452	2,032	1,561
Earnings per share	5.98	6.67	5.83	3.76	3.76	4.90	6.41	4.91
Dividends per share	0.33	0.37	0.40	0.44	0.44	0.48	0.52	0.56
Cash flow per share	11.13	12.39	12.13	10.09	10.01	11.13	13.08	12.41
Price: high	120.0	121.4	99.5	92.6	97.8	98.7	97.2	144.1
low	96.5	89.5	53.9	34.0	69.8	64.1	82.8	90.6

FedEx Corporation
942 South Shady Grove Road
Memphis, TN 38120
(901) 369-3600
Website: *www.fedex.com*

Fluor Corporation

Ticker symbol: FLR (NYSE) □ S&P rating: A- □ Value Line financial strength rating: A++
Current yield: 1.1% □ Dividend raises, past 10 years: 3

Company Profile

Want to build a big, expensive, technically complex plant to make, mine, or refine a lot of stuff? Like an oil refinery or liquefied natural gas (LNG) shipping terminal or a mine or a chemical or power plant? Or do you want to remodel or upgrade or expand one? Whom would you call? There aren't too many listings in the phone book for companies that do stuff like this. If you're into big, mostly private (but some public) infrastructure, you'll like Fluor.

Founded in 1912, Fluor is one of the world's largest publicly owned engineering, procurement, construction, maintenance, and project management companies. It provides a diverse portfolio of large-scale infrastructure development expertise and services, primarily for five industry segments:

■ Oil and Gas (41 percent of revenue, 37 percent of gross profit in 2013), where they serve all facets of the traditional energy industry, including upstream, downstream, and petrochemical markets, including oilfields, refineries, and pipelines.

■ Industrial and Infrastructure (40 percent of revenue, 39 percent of profits) is the most diverse organization, which includes transportation, mining, life sciences, telecom, manufacturing, and commercial and institutional projects. This segment also covers the emerging alternative energy projects, including major windmill farm developments and a new line of small nuclear reactors.

■ Government (10 percent of revenue, 13 percent of profits) addresses the U.S. Departments of Energy, Defense, and Homeland Security.

■ Global Services (5 percent of revenue, 10 percent of profits) provides operations and maintenance, supply chain, equipment services, and contract staffing.

■ Power (5 percent of revenue, 1 percent of profits) designs, builds, commissions, and retrofits electric generation facilities using coal, natural gas, and nuclear fuels.

About 64 percent of revenues come from outside the U.S., and

80 percent of contracts are "reimbursable" in contrast to fixed price, providing greater flexibility to avoid major losses on the projects.

Financial Highlights, Fiscal Year 2013

After a strong FY2012, business tailed off a bit in FY2013 due in large part to a slowdown in the mining industry and in particular, the cancellation of one large gold mine project. Revenues and earnings sagged slightly for the year in total, and backlogs were down just slightly from about $36.5 billion to about $35 billion. That said, business and backlogs shifted to the somewhat more profitable oil and gas and other segments (that segment's profits were up 32 percent during the year), and new bookings for large international projects including Canada's first LNG terminal bode well, as does an upcoming replacement of New York's Tappan Zee bridge.

The company projects FY2014 revenues to continue soft until the new oil and gas projects gain momentum, with another slight drop in the year but a healthy 5.6 percent gain in FY2015. Meanwhile a more profitable mix will drive projected FY2014 earnings about 5 percent higher and about 14 percent higher in FY2015—and moderate share buybacks will bring a faster acceleration in per-share earnings. FY2015 per-share earnings are expected to top $5.00/share. After a few flat spells

in dividend increases, the company expects to pick these up as well.

Reasons to Buy

Last year we touted Fluor's apparent recovery and strength on the basis that all five of its sectors were on positive ground; this year the softness in mining is dragging the Industrial and Infrastructure segment down. Backlogs in this segment were down $7 billion while overall backlog dropped just $1.9 billion—that tells us that other segments on the whole were pretty strong. So while strength across all parts of a diverse platform is a good thing, we like this company not only as a pure play in infrastructure (and one of the few players in the phone book) but also because of this diversity—when one business or sector is soft, the others can pick it up. It's like playing basketball with five players, rather than one or two.

We continue to feel that in total, infrastructure needs to be built and it needs to be replaced on an ever-increasing scale—and the increasing technical requirements and scale of these projects makes Fluor one of the few players that can do projects like this. We like the strong international footprint, too. Overall, Fluor has a strong market position and niche, and we like that.

Reasons for Caution

While Fluor is strong in its niche, it will always be vulnerable to economic cycles, and as we've seen, price soft-ness in key markets that consume its services. Right now, hard minerals have slumped, in part due to cooling China demand, which is attenuat-ing the mining business. Could oil and gas be next? Utility companies? Public sector budgets? It takes a lot of capital to fund Fluor-sized projects, and anything that contributes to a shortage of such capital, including a soft economy or interest rates, can have an effect. Too, while we like the slow, steady pace of share buybacks and moderate dividend increases, we would like to see a bit more of the strong cash flow returned to shareholders.

SECTOR: Heavy Construction
BETA COEFFICIENT: 1.55
10-YEAR COMPOUND EARNINGS PER-SHARE GROWTH: 15.0%
10-YEAR COMPOUND DIVIDENDS PER-SHARE GROWTH: 6.5%

		2006	2007	2008	2009	2010	2011	2012	2013
Revenues (mil)		14,079	16,691	22,326	21,990	20,849	23,381	27,577	27,352
Net income (mil)		264	410	673	685	358	594	722	679
Earnings per share		1.48	2.25	3.67	3.75	1.98	3.40	4.30	4.13
Dividends per share		0.32	0.40	0.50	0.50	0.50	0.50	0.64	0.64
Cash flow per share		2.21	3.14	4.61	4.85	3.11	4.71	5.76	5.49
Price:	high	51.9	86.1	101.4	50.5	67.3	75.8	64.7	80.4
	low	36.8	37.6	28.6	41.7	41.2	44.2	45.0	53.5

Fluor Corporation
6700 Las Colinas Blvd
Irving, TX 75039
Tel: (469) 398-7000
Website: *www.fluor.com*

FMC Corporation

Ticker symbol: FMC (NYSE) ❑ S&P rating: A- ❑ Value Line financial strength rating: A ❑ Current yield: 0.8% ❑ Dividend raises, past 10 years: 7

Company Profile

FMC Corporation is a diversified chemical company serving global agricultural, industrial, and consumer markets. Founded in 1883 as the Bean Spray Pump Company, FMC (it was also Farm Machinery Company at one point in its history) continues to serve the agricultural market in the largest of its three segments: Agricultural Solutions. At present, two other segments round out the picture: FMC Health and Nutrition, and FMC Minerals. That is about to change: Following the fashion of many companies in the chemical and pharmaceutical industries these days, FMC has announced the spinoff of the more commodity-oriented FMC Minerals business into a separate company by that name in 2015. While we normally shy away from such splits until the dust settles, we think it makes sense for FMC and will continue to carry the stock on our *100 Best* list; next year we'll evaluate whether both stocks will remain on the list. With that in mind, we'll describe the company in its current form:

FMC Agricultural Solutions (55 percent of FY2013 revenues) provides crop protection and pest-control products for worldwide markets. The business offers a solid portfolio of insecticides, herbicides, and seed protection products. Through two new acquisitions, the segment has entered the biological crop protection market to supplement its chemical protection solutions.

The FMC Health and Nutrition segment (20 percent of revenues) is the world's leading producer of alginate, carrageenan, and microcrystalline cellulose, which are key thickening, texturing, stabilizing, and fat substitute ingredients used in the food industry. The segment also produces active nutritional and pharmaceutical ingredients; a 2013 acquisition of Epac, a maker of premium omega-3 fish oil concentrates expanded—and exemplifies—this offering.

The FMC Minerals business, currently 25 percent and the part to be spun off in 2015, combines all of the company's lithium-based businesses and Alkali Chemicals business under one reporting segment. FMC Lithium is one of the world's leading producers of lithium-based products and recognized as the technology leader in specialty organolithium chemicals and related technologies. Among other things, the lithium compounds produced at FMC are key ingredients in many emerging battery technologies. FMC Alkali Chemicals is the world's largest producer of natural soda ash and is the market leader in North America. Downstream products include sodium bicarbonate, sodium cyanide, sodium sesquicarbonate, and caustic soda. You may not have heard of many of these products, which typically are used to manufacture things like glass, paper, detergents, tires, and electronic components, among other things—and shipped by the rail tank carload—but they are vital ingredients in a number of key industries worldwide.

Speaking of which, about 67 percent of the company's overall business comes from overseas; the sizeable international footprint includes a new Asia Innovation Center in China and a new microcrystalline cellulose plant in Thailand.

Financial Highlights, Fiscal Year 2013

With its Agricultural Solutions unit still in the lead, FMC had another good year in FY2013, although not at the same pace as FY2012. Revenues rose 3.4 percent, while net earnings rose at a healthier 9 percent, and helped along by a 5 million share (3.6 percent) buyback, per-share earnings rose a still-better 11.5 percent. Not all segments contributed equally— earnings in the "Ag" business rose

19 percent, while commodity price drops in key Minerals businesses led to a 26 percent decline in that segment. Health and Nutrition stands in the middle with a 6 percent earnings gain for the year.

Of course, the split will alter this, but the company is forecasting a more robust 13.5 percent revenue growth in FY2014, aided by acquisitions, and a further 11 percent rise in FY2015. Per-share earnings are expected to rise in the 15 percent range in both years, as agricultural demand continues to grow, commodity prices firm, and acquisitions bring more to the top and the bottom lines.

Reasons to Buy

Before and after the spinoff, FMC is well positioned in several areas of relative strategic importance in the chemical industry, in particular the agriculture, biopolymer, and lithium compounds businesses. The strength of the economic rebound, combined with these leadership positions in specialty markets, bodes well for the company. Pricing strength, improving margins, and strong international sales all add to a promising picture. The spinoff will allow each of the two new companies to focus more on their businesses and align their cost structures appropriately.

As an example of FMC's strategic portfolio, the company is the leading supplier of lithium-based compounds used in the lithium-ion battery industry. Lithium batteries are used extensively in technology products such as laptops, music players, tablets, and automobiles like the Tesla Model S, the Chevrolet Volt, and the Nissan Leaf. All of the early hybrid cars and many of those still in production use nickel metal hydride (NiMH) battery chemistry, but lithium batteries deliver higher power density at a much lower weight. They can also be recharged more quickly.

Up until now, the company has deployed its strong cash flow for acquisitions and to return to shareholders mostly through buybacks, but dividend increases have picked up recently. It remains to be seen how this will evolve with the split.

Reasons for Caution

Mergers and spinoffs both make us nervous. They cost money, and worse, gobble up management bandwidth and can confuse customers and key channel partners. Many companies merge to leverage their infrastructure and overhead, thus reducing costs—when you go the other way, you may have to duplicate some overhead. While we see these risks to a degree with this spinoff, we do think it makes sense and look forward to next year's evaluation of the split enterprises. Fortunately or unfortunately, the markets seem to agree that the split is a good idea and have sent the shares up handsomely since the announcement—new investors might wait for a pullback or to pick one of the two evolving businesses at a more opportune time.

SECTOR: **Materials**
BETA COEFFICIENT: **1.16**
10-YEAR COMPOUND EARNINGS PER-SHARE GROWTH: **16.5%**
10-YEAR COMPOUND DIVIDENDS PER-SHARE GROWTH: **17.0%**

	2006	2007	2008	2009	2010	2011	2012	2013
Revenues (mil)	2,347	2,633	3,115	2,826	3,116	3,378	3,748	3,875
Net income (mil)	216.4	132.4	351	305	353	429	483	528
Earnings per share	2.74	3.40	4.63	4.15	4.83	5.98	3.48	3.88
Dividends per share	0.18	0.21	0.24	0.25	0.25	0.30	0.35	0.54
Cash flow per share	2.27	2.62	3.27	2.97	3.41	3.98	4.51	4.93
Price: high	19.5	29.5	40.1	31.6	41.0	46.5	59.4	75.7
low	12.5	17.8	14.2	17.5	25.4	31.9	42.9	55.2

FMC Corporation
1735 Market Street
Philadelphia, PA 19103
(215) 299-6000
Website: *www.fmc.com*

NEW
FOR 2015

General Electric Company

Ticker symbol: GE (NYSE) ❑ S&P rating: AA+ ❑ Value Line financial strength rating: B++
Current yield: 3.3% ❑ Dividend raises, past 10 years: 8

Company Profile

Few companies in the history of the world have seen their strength—and their shareholders' fortunes—sapped so severely as GE's were during the Great Recession. The company made some serious strategic mistakes, pursuing growth in such non-core activities as financing and television; at one point, a colleague of ours referred to the company as a "hedge fund that happens to make jet engines." The vast financial empire soured in 2008 and almost brought the company down with it.

That was then (and we took the company off our *100 Best* list in 2010 as a consequence), and, we feel, this is now. The company is once again positioned to "bring good things to light"—and to bring good things to shareholders.

Formed in 1892 as a major producer of all things electric, GE evolved over the years into a massive conglomerate producing aircraft engines, power generation, railroad locomotives, household appliances, energy infrastructure, alternative energy equipment, medical imaging equipment, oilfield service equipment, and a vast array of other products—in addition to its General Electric Capital Services financial arm.

In total, the company has eight operating segments—seven industrial plus the GE Capital arm. By segment and percent of FY2013 revenues in the order GE presents them: Power & Water (17 percent), Oil & Gas (11.5 percent), Energy Management (5 percent), Aviation (15 percent), Healthcare (12 percent), Transportation (4 percent), and the still-gigantic GE Capital (30 percent—and down from 37 percent in FY2010). We should also note that GE Capital still produces about a third of total segment net profits. The goal is to continue a balance of 70 percent "premier infrastructure" and 30 percent "specialty finance."

International sales account for about 53 percent of revenues. Innovation is a big deal: The company spends about $4.8 billion annually on R&D and has spent $43 billion in the past decade on six global research centers. The company presents itself as a leader in helping customers realize efficiencies through its "Power of 1%" campaign—1 percent reduction in fuel consumption or other efficiencies saves the aviation industry $30 billion, the power industry $66 billion, the rail industry $27 billion, $63 billion for health care, and $90 billion for the oil and gas industries. The numbers aren't important, but the strategy and messages are compelling; recall this is the company that invented the "Six

Sigma" quality improvement philosophy as well.

The company has always been active in the acquisitions market, acquiring smaller businesses as well as larger ones such as Dresser Industries in the Oil & Gas production sector, and more recently, a move to acquire Alstom S.A., the large French energy equipment business. Recently, more activity has been on the divestiture side, with the significant announcement of selling the consumer credit card business recently and its NBC Universal business three years ago.

Financial Highlights, Fiscal Year 2013

Because of the shifting business mix, FY2013 is difficult to compare with previous years, and some of that difficulty will persist going forward. Crosswinds of acquisitions, divestitures, and currency effects left revenues essentially flat for the year, but a favorable tax rate on top of a less favorable business mix drove earnings up 6 percent, and per-share earnings, with the help of buybacks, up about 8 percent.

For FY2014, "industrial" earnings are expected to grow 10 percent on organic revenue growth in the 4–7 percent range—and that's a good thing, because the financial businesses that the company is downsizing *were* fairly profitable. All told, the company predicts revenue gains in the 1–3 percent range through FY2015, with slightly improving margins and per-share

earnings growth in the 6–8 percent range. We think the earnings growth figures could better these numbers if the company gets more aggressive with buybacks, which we think will happen in time as it de-emphasizes acquisitions. In FY2013 the company returned $18 billion to investors through cash dividends and repurchases, repurchasing some 61 million shares during the year—a large number but a small percentage of its 10 billion share base.

Reasons to Buy

The company is returning to its roots as a colossal infrastructure play. It is downsizing, rightsizing, and trimming businesses all over, specifically in its financial services arm. The company openly shares its "look of a simpler company" goals to downsize HQ operations by 45 percent, reduce the new product introduction cycle time by 30 percent, create 30 percent fewer internal P&Ls, and reduce the number of enterprise resource planning (ERP) systems by 80 percent.

The company is returning to, and strengthening, its industrial roots, and we believe the distractions of acquisition and divestiture, while always there, will decrease going forward. The new focus is centered on improvements in its industrial businesses. It is investing in new technologies such as intelligent machinery, which not only provide new efficiencies to customers but also help GE manage its sales cycle by providing sales leads for new and replacement equipment. The company is leveraging its already successful brand in key infrastructure markets such as jet engines and locomotives. With much of the financial sector distraction out of the way, it can focus on things such as improving efficiency and increasing margins. It predicts industrial margins will grow by 1.5 percent to 17 percent in the next three years—huge on such a large business base. Steady earnings and cash flow growth should turn into steady dividend growth on top of an already decent payout for a business with a growing top and bottom line.

Reasons for Caution

Reasons for caution are plenty, but we think they will gradually diminish over time. Most obvious is the continued exposure to the financial sector, but we think this business will continue to stabilize or generate more cash to repurchase shares if all or part is sold. The company is still active in the acquisitions market, and overall we wonder if it is even possible to manage a company this size for its best performance—management is taking the right steps but would we accept the job as CEO? Never, not in a million years. That said, we also like the continuity provided by the tenure of Jeffrey Immelt. Finally, one of our biggest concerns is the gigantic share count—10 billion—one of the biggest we're aware of. It's hard to generate meaningful per-share gains when new sales and profits are divided up into so many little slices. We would hope the company gets even more aggressive in this opportunity, as other share giants like Microsoft and Cisco already have.

SECTOR: **Industrials**

BETA COEFFICIENT: **1.51**

10-YEAR COMPOUND EARNINGS PER-SHARE GROWTH: **NM**

10-YEAR COMPOUND DIVIDENDS PER-SHARE GROWTH: **NM**

	2006	2007	2008	2009	2010	2011	2012	2013
Revenues (bil)	163.3	172.7	182.5	156.8	150.2	147.3	147.4	146.0
Net income (bil)	20.7	22.5	18.1	11.4	12.6	14.9	16.1	16.9
Earnings per share	1.99	2.20	1.78	1.03	1.15	1.31	1.52	1.64
Dividends per share	1.03	1.15	1.24	0.61	0.46	0.61	0.70	0.79
Cash flow per share	2.90	3.28	2.81	2.07	2.13	2.28	2.44	2.65
Price: high	38.5	42.2	38.5	17.5	19.7	21.7	23.2	28.1
low	32.1	33.9	12.6	5.7	13.8	14.0	18.0	20.7

General Electric

3135 Easton Turnpike

Fairfield, CT 06828

(203) 373-2211

Website: *www.ge.com*

GROWTH AND INCOME

General Mills, Inc.

Ticker symbol: GIS (NYSE) ❑ S&P rating: BBB+ ❑ Value Line financial strength rating: A+
Current yield: 3.1% ❑ Dividend raises, past 10 years: 9

Company Profile

General Mills is the second-largest domestic producer of ready-to-eat breakfast cereals and the sixth-largest food company in the world. Sales are broken out into three major segments, organized by channel: U.S. Retail (60 percent of revenues), International (29 percent), and Convenience Stores and Foodservice (11 percent).

Major cereal brands, most of which bear the Big G label, include Cheerios, Wheaties, Lucky Charms, Total, and Chex. The company owns Pillsbury, which it acquired in 2001. Other consumer packaged food products include baking mixes (Betty Crocker and Bisquick); meals (Betty Crocker dry packaged dinner mixes); Progresso soups; Green Giant canned and frozen vegetables; Hamburger Helper; snacks (Pop Secret microwave popcorn, Bugles snacks, and grain and fruit snack products); Pillsbury refrigerated and frozen dough products, including frozen breakfast products, and frozen pizza and snack products; organic foods; and other products, including Nature Valley, Yoplait (which was acquired in 2011 along with Go-Gurt), and Colombo yogurt. The company's holdings include many other brand names, such as Häagen-Dazs ice cream and a host of joint ventures.

In the International sector, General Foods sells numerous local brands, in addition to internationally recognized brands such as Häagen-Dazs ice cream, Old El Paso Mexican foods, and Green Giant vegetables. The company is in a 50–50 joint venture with Nestlé known as Cereal Partners Worldwide. International accounts for about $5.2 billion in sales, or 29 percent of the total, with Europe holding the largest share (43 percent) followed by Canada (23 percent), and Asia Pacific and Latin America, both with 17 percent of the International total.

The Convenience Store and Foodservice sector is mainly a distribution channel targeting convenience stores, hotels and restaurants, and wholesale and grocery store bakeries.

The company offers a breakdown of its business by type of product to better understand this relatively diverse food business:

- 21 percent ready-to-eat cereal
- 15 percent yogurt
- 15 percent "Convenient Meals"
- 10 percent snacks

- 10 percent dough
- 10 percent baking aisle products
- 8 percent super-premium ice cream
- 6 percent vegetables
- 5 percent other

It's not hard to see that General Mills is a solid part of any well-stocked pantry.

Financial Highlights, Fiscal Year 2013

Historically General Mills has been a slow, steady climber producing single-digit business gains with double-digit dividend increases and decent share buybacks—we've liked the combination. FY2013 was a little bit of a break-out year, with revenues up almost 7 percent and earnings up a more moderate 4.7 percent, hurt a bit by high commodity prices experienced in 2012 and much of 2013. FY2014 and beyond look to be even more promising, although there's some softness in the highly competitive and price-sensitive cereal market, and the rapid-growth days of the yogurt market might be over. That said, commodity prices have come down, operational improvements have taken effect, and emerging market sales have some promise, all shifting the growth emphasis a bit more toward profits. Revenues are projected to grow in the 2.5–3.5 percent range, with earnings growing in the 5–6 percent range and per-share earnings, helped along by buybacks, growing in the 7–9 percent range.

Reasons to Buy

General Mills continues to enjoy solid brand strength and a strong position in a very competitive cereal and packaged food market. Recent trends have pointed to brand leveraging (e.g., Chocolate Cheerios, Wheaties Fuel), and the results have been encouraging. While the company has already grown its international business effectively in recent years, at 29 percent of the business we feel there is still some opportunity.

Earnings, operating margins, and cash flows have all followed a slow but steady and cash-rich track upward and in tune with management guidance. The long-term policy aimed at share repurchases has brought the share count down from 758 million in 2004 to 640 million recently; after a pause related to the Yoplait acquisition, sizeable repurchase looks to continue with decent dividend increases adding some icing to the cake. Finally, General Mills continues to be a notably safe and stable "sleep at night" stock with a beta of 0.15—the lowest on our *100 Best Stocks* list.

Reasons for Caution

While commodity prices have moderated, the company is strongly affected by commodity prices and cycles. Recent profit projections, a solid yield and—possibly—some takeover interest more clearly rumored with store shelf neighbor Kellogg (another *100 Best* stock) have brought the shares up to a new trading range; they aren't the bargain they were a year ago. Shop carefully.

SECTOR: **Consumer Staples**
BETA COEFFICIENT: **0.15**
10-YEAR COMPOUND EARNINGS PER-SHARE GROWTH: **9.0%**
10-YEAR COMPOUND DIVIDENDS PER-SHARE GROWTH: **8.5%**

	2006	2007	2008	2009	2010	2011	2012	2013
Revenues (mil)	11,640	12,442	13,652	14,691	14,796	14,880	16,658	17,754
Net income (mil)	1,090	1,144	1,288	1,367	1,571	1,652	1,707	1,789
Earnings per share	1.45	1.59	1.78	1.99	2.30	2.48	2.56	2.69
Dividends per share	0.67	0.72	0.79	0.86	0.96	1.12	1.22	1.32
Cash flow per share	2.13	2.30	2.50	2.78	3.09	3.29	3.47	3.71
Price: high	29.6	30.8	36.0	36.0	39.0	40.8	41.9	53.1
low	23.5	27.1	25.5	23.2	33.1	34.5	36.6	40.4

General Mills, Inc.
One General Mills Blvd.
Minneapolis, MN 55426
(763) 764-7600
Website: *www.generalmills.com*

AGGRESSIVE GROWTH

Harman International Industries

Ticker symbol: HAR (NYSE) ❑ S&P rating: BBB- ❑ Value Line financial strength rating: B++
Current yield: 1.1% ❑ Dividend raises, past 10 years: 2

Company Profile

When we pick a company for our *100 Best* list, we're usually quite content with a steady incremental gain of, say 10 or 20 percent in the price of its shares, along with the usual signs of shareholder recognition in the form of cash returns and steadily improving business performance to support both. This is our core model for success, and the best we can expect is that most of our "good ideas" deliver this way. But sometimes we find a real gem among our "good ideas," and the results can be exhilarating. It turns out that Harman International was just such a find. It was our number-one pick for 2014, rising some 137 percent from $44 to $104 in our one-year measurement period. So the question is, do we take our money and put it elsewhere? Sell when there's something better to buy? We pondered this hard in Harman's case . . . and decided that the same story that got us here in 2014 would keep on going through 2015 and beyond. "When you find a good horse, keep riding it" is the operative phrase.

Harman International is one of the world's leading producers of audio and infotainment solutions for an increasingly mobile society. That sounds like marketing copy, but it's a true depiction of this company. Harman, probably more than any other supplier in the world, has made a partner out of its former customer, the automobile manufacturer. How? By selling a branded product in the car. Where there used to be only one logo, one brand, in the interior of an automobile, now there are two the manufacturer's and brands offered by Harman. It's not unusual to find Infinity, JBL, Mark Levinson, and several other Harman brands front and center on the dashboard of over half of the popular car lines today.

The company divides its business into three overlapping segments. The Infotainment business (51 percent of FY2013 revenues) sells built-in, digital, and integrated information and entertainment systems for automobiles, allowing drivers to listen, talk, navigate, and connect to the outside world. Lifestyle (31 percent), more what Harman is known for, manufactures and markets audio components traditionally for home environments, but now automotive and other "mobile" apps have become a big share of that business, too. Brands range from the high-middle-end JBL, Harman/Kardon, and Infinity to the high-end Mark Levinson, Lexicon, and recently, through license, Bowers

& Wilkins. The Professional segment (16 percent) builds loudspeakers and amplifications systems for professional musicians.

Indeed, Harman is really an automotive company, with about 75 percent of sales altogether coming from this business. Key customers include most of the major brands: Audi/Volkswagen, BMW, Chrysler, Toyota, Lexus, Porsche, Daimler, GM, Hyundai, Kia, and Honda to name a few—and even Harley Davidson. Not only is Harman expanding its presence across most brands, it is also penetrating into more mid-market offerings; its infotainment systems are no longer exclusively a "premium" offering suited only for luxury cars. Too, success in the automotive sector has breathed some life into its home entertainment (Lifestyle) brands, with sales in home and multimedia businesses up 23 percent in a year. Design wins have driven current backlog to over $19 billion heading into 2014 from $16 billion last year. The company continues to move ahead in integrated digital technologies for automotive applications with a new software engineering center and the acquisition of Interchain Solution, a producer of Android-based infotainment systems, and other small acquisitions to boost the technology portfolio.

Financial Highlights, Fiscal Year 2013

After a strong FY2012, we would like to turn down the volume a bit on FY2013—a relatively slow year due to weakness in European and Asian markets, notably China, and currency effects. Although the company gained market share, revenues were down about 2 percent, with earnings off about 8 percent, clearly not something to write home about after a 40 percent earnings increase in FY2012. However, the company expects to convert the market share gains, strong market, modest cost reductions, margin improvement, and share buybacks into a gain north of 20 percent in revenues for FY2014, continuing with another 7 percent in FY2015, with per-share earnings north of 40 percent in FY2014 and another 20–25 percent in FY2015.

Reasons to Buy

Harman has virtually created a new market for high-end, integrated automotive systems and has stepped into the automotive market with some of the most respected brands in traditional home electronics, creating a nice win-win for themselves and the automakers. More recently, Harman has added a lot of innovation to this thrust. Automotive infotainment and connectivity design is highly specific in its application and is "designed in" from the beginning, and Harman owns a substantial piece of this market. They partner with the auto companies at the design stage to provide infotainment systems—those integrated systems that all work together to provide sound, video, wireless communications, navigation, Internet access, and climate control on demand and in all parts of the vehicle. As Harman evolves, the integration of digital automotive electronics with personal digital devices (e.g., the iPod), and now with the "cloud," offers a huge opportunity. The company is also leveraging this idea to "smart" hotel room adaptations, where you can plug in your device to get your music and tap into your chosen personal information, and we expect the company to bring more innovative integrated designs to the home as well. Automobile purchases appear to be on the rebound worldwide, not just in the U.S. but now in Europe and China too, making the scenario one of increasing share in an increasing market with an increasing "value add" brought through innovation and technology—a marketplace triple play that is hard to resist. Financials and cash returns, in the form of a doubling of the dividend plus a $200 million share buyback, are showing strength in lockstep with the marketplace gains.

Reasons for Caution

We can't deny it: There is some risk here. Harman is vulnerable to economic cycles and particularly those in the auto industry, and downturns in discretionary consumer audio purchases will amplify auto industry woes. Audio and infotainment tastes can be fickle, so the company will have to quickly embrace the latest trends. Recent successes have been built into the stock price, but we feel that Harman is more than just a one-trick pony.

SECTOR: **Consumer Discretionary**
BETA COEFFICIENT: **1.81**
10-YEAR COMPOUND EARNINGS PER-SHARE GROWTH: **9.0%**
10-YEAR COMPOUND DIVIDENDS PER-SHARE GROWTH: **20.5%**

	2006	2007	2008	2009	2010	2011	2012	2013
Revenues (mil)	3,248	3,551	4,112	2,891	3,364	3,772	4,364	4,298
Net income (mil)	268	25	146	(56)	60	149	211	194
Earnings per share	3.94	4.14	2.35	(1.01)	0.85	2.08	2.83	2.78
Dividends per share	0.05	0.05	0.05	0.05	0.05	0.05	0.30	0.60
Cash flow per share	6.02	6.17	5.10	1.32	2.70	3.89	4.96	4.74
Price: high	115.9	125.1	73.8	40.3	53.4	52.5	52.8	85.8
low	74.6	69.5	9.9	9.2	28.1	25.5	34.1	40.5

Harman International Industries
400 Atlantic St.
Stamford, CT 06901
(203) 328-3500
Website: *www.harman.com*

GROWTH AND INCOME

Health Care REIT, Inc.

Ticker symbol: HCN (NYSE) □ S&P rating: BBB □ Value Line financial strength rating: B+
Current yield: 5.4% □ Dividend raises, past 10 years: 10

Company Profile

Health Care REIT, as the name clearly conveys, is a real estate investment trust investing primarily in senior living and medical care properties primarily in the U.S. For 2014, it was our first venture into the REIT space and is still intended as a steady growth plus income investment and to provide some exposure to real estate in our *100 Best Stocks* portfolio. We feel that it not only offers good exposure to a secure and growing segment of the real estate market but that it also exhibits qualities of a good business in addition to its core real estate asset holdings.

The trust operates in three primary business segments. The first and largest is referred to as the Seniors Housing "triple net" segment and is involved primarily in owning senior housing properties, including independent, continuing care, and assisted living facilities, and leasing them to qualified operators in return for a steady income stream. This segment currently owns 620 properties, almost all in the U.S., concentrated in high-cost urban areas mostly on the coasts, and contributes about 27 percent of net operating income. There are also 19 facilities in the U.K.

The second and fastest-growing segment is the Seniors Housing Operating segment, which operates some of the facilities owned by the REIT and others owned by third parties. It operates 127 properties in 35 states, Canada, and the U.K. and contributes about 33 percent to net operating income. The third major segment is Medical Facilities, which operates office space set in 213 facilities for medical purposes, inpatient and outpatient medical centers, and life science laboratories in 36 states, contributing about 15 percent to NOI. Skilled nursing and post-acute facilities contribute another 18 percent.

The REIT owns and/or operates some 1,199 properties in all in three countries, and operates assisted living, skilled nursing, independent living, and the medical centers just mentioned.

Health Care REIT employs a conscious and stated strategy of being in markets with high barriers to entry and with a more upscale, affluent retiree base—this is part of why we feel it is a good business, not just a real estate play. Markets such as Boston, New Jersey, Seattle, and major coastal California cities are territories for Health Care REIT. The average revenue per occupied room for this REIT is $6,228 per month, some 43 percent higher than the national senior housing industry average. In the markets in which HCN operates, the cost of the average single-family home runs 60 percent higher than the national average, and household incomes are 40 percent higher. Eighty percent of facilities are in the 31 most affluent U.S. metropolitan areas. The facilities are newer, more attractive, and desirable, as a trip through the company's website at *www.hcreit.com* will show.

REITs, obviously, play on the real estate market, and in this case, in the high-value-add segment of health care. So by investing in such a REIT, you are investing in real estate and in the health-care industry, and with the property mix owned by Health Care REIT, you're investing in the aging population. In this case in particular, you're investing in the willingness of the more affluent segments of the elderly population to spend for a pleasant retirement. REITs are typically good income producers, as they are required by law to pay a substantial portion of their cash flow to investors. The accounting rules are different, and REIT investors should focus on Funds From Operations (FFO), which is analogous to operating income; net income figures have depreciation expenses deducted, which can vary in timing and not always be realistic. Funds From Operations (FFO) support the dividends paid to investors.

Financial Highlights, Fiscal Year 2013

The 2012 acquisition of Sunrise Senior Living added to an already healthy portfolio. Net operating income (NOI)—another pure measure of REIT activity—rose 3.5 percent on a same-store basis. Per-share Funds From Operations (FFO) rose about 8 percent over FY2012, while the dividend was raised 3.4 percent. Guidance for FY2014 calls for an FFO of $4.00 per share and $4.30 per share in FY2015 as recent acquisitions continue to take root. As the REIT structure implies, those FFO increases should readily turn into similar increases. The company added a modest number of shares to achieve a goal of 60 percent equity as noted below.

Reasons to Buy

"At the intersection of Resiliency and Growth" is their stated theme, and we agree. Health Care REIT is a solid way to play the steady growth of the health-care industry and the aging demographic. REITs are a relatively risk-free, income-oriented way to play the steady growth of this intersection of trends. Rents—and rent growth—are better than average, and its income payout is stable and growing. The company estimates that senior housing rent growth will exceed inflation by 1.7 percent, and that the U.S. population over 75 years of age will grow some 88 percent over the next

20 years—both factors supporting a healthy growth story.

Some 83 percent of revenues are derived from private pay sources; with the concentration on private-pay services, Health Care REIT will avoid some of the exposure to Medicare utilization management initiatives and related cutbacks that many others in the sector are exposed to. The company also avoids exposure to debt and interest costs better than most REITs, with a target debt of 40 percent of total capital.

Reasons for Caution

Because of their differences from ordinary corporations, it may be difficult to understand this investment, particularly the financial performance of REITs, especially a complex REIT such as this one, which has both traditional property investments and operating company investments. Okay, we'll be more to the point—this company is complex and hard to understand.

One could also question, going forward, whether retirees will be as well-heeled as they are today, with deterioration in retirement savings and increased costs. Finally, while real estate prices have rebounded well since the Great Recession, any hiccup in any sector of real estate is likely to affect this issue.

SECTOR: **Health Care**
BETA COEFFICIENT: **0.60**
10-YEAR COMPOUND FFO PER-SHARE GROWTH: **2.5%**
10-YEAR COMPOUND DIVIDENDS PER-SHARE GROWTH: **2.5%**

	2006	2007	2008	2009	2010	2011	2012	2013
Revenues (mil)	322.8	486.0	551.2	569.0	680.5	1,421	1,822	2,880
Net income (mil)	103.5	125.2	150.3	161.6	84.4	155.9	294.8	93.3
Funds from operations per share	2.97	3.12	3.38	3.13	3.08	3.41	3.52	3.80
Real estate owned per share	56.3	58.6	55.9	49.3	58.4	72.5	66.9	74.9
Dividends per share	2.54	2.62	2.70	2.72	2.74	2.84	2.96	3.06
Price: high	43.0	48.6	54.0	46.7	52.1	55.2	62.8	80.1
low	32.8	35.1	30.1	25.9	38.4	41.0	52.4	52.4

Health Care REIT, Inc.
4500 Dorr Street
Toledo, OH 43615
(419) 247-2800
Website: *www.hcreit.com*

AGGRESSIVE GROWTH

Honeywell International

Ticker symbol: HON (NYSE) ❑ S&P rating: A ❑ Value Line financial strength rating: A++
Current yield: 1.9% ❑ Dividend raises, past 10 years: 8

Company Profile

Honeywell is a diversified international technology and manufacturing company operating in four business segments, engaged in the development, manufacturing, and marketing of aerospace products and services (32 percent of FY2013 sales); control technologies for buildings, homes, and industry (42 percent); automotive products (10 percent); and specialty materials (17 percent).

The Aerospace segment primarily makes cockpit controls, power generation equipment, and wheels and brakes for commercial and military aircraft and for airports and ground operations. It also makes jet engines for regional and business jet manufacturers. Products include avionics, auxiliary power units (APUs), aircraft lighting, and landing systems.

Honeywell's Automation and Control Solutions segment is best known as a maker of home and office climate-control equipment. It also makes home automation systems; thermostats; sensing and combustion controls for heating, A/C, and other environmental controls; lighting controls; security systems and sensing products; and fire alarms. This segment produces most of the components of what is known in the trade and advertising lingo as a "smart building." The company estimates that its products are at work in some 150 million homes and 10 million commercial buildings worldwide. This part of the business also produces a number of factory automation products.

The Performance Materials and Technologies operation makes a wide assortment of specialty chemicals and fibers, plastics, coatings, and semiconductor and electronics materials, which are sold primarily to the food, pharmaceutical, petroleum refining, and electronic packaging industries. Petroleum refining catalysts and carbon fiber materials are among the more important and fastest-growing products in this segment.

The Transportation System segment consists of a portfolio of parts and supplies for the automotive, railroad, and other industries. Products include brake system and cooling system components, turbochargers, and an assortment of other products. With the sale of its retail consumer automotive brands, this group is now focused on OEM components such as sensors and braking systems.

The company has a considerable international footprint, with technology and manufacturing centers located outside the U.S.; five such centers are located in China along with a similar number in India. The company estimates some 55 percent of its business to be done outside the U.S, with 14 of that 55 percent made up of U.S. exports and the rest by foreign manufactured products.

Financial Highlights, Fiscal Year 2013

While sales grew a moderate 4 percent in FY2013, the company still calls it a "weakish" year. Per-share earnings, on the back of moderately increased profit margins, increased about 11 percent over FY2012. Management identifies the year as another "… opportunity to continue our seed planting … products, technologies, restructuring, geographies, services, processes, new capacity … to ensure that growth continues far into the future."

For 2014, those seeds are expected to germinate into another 4 percent sales increase, followed closely by a 5 percent gain in FY2015. Per-share earnings are expected to advance 11 percent in both years, more or less qualifying the company for our "5 and 10" list: steady 5 percent revenue gains, 10 percent earnings growth.

Reasons to Buy

Honeywell is a "best in class" producer of a wide variety of business and consumer products with an underlying technology theme—not really "high tech" but using advanced technologies, or, in some cases, supporting them. The company shows many of the traditional signs of being well managed, with a strong focus on cash flow and operational efficiency and a healthy respect for transparency, as evidenced by its informative annual reports and other corporate materials.

Honeywell has outlined its key growth vectors as international ("globalization"), safety and security, energy efficiency, and energy generation. We like this diverse but timely set of focal points. In particular, Honeywell is positioned well with regard to the growing awareness of the value of energy efficiency. The company also has a valuable distribution network and existing customer base in all of its businesses. The company has a solid balance sheet and participates almost exclusively in high-margin businesses, particularly with the divestiture of the consumer auto business.

Reasons for Caution

Many of the industries Honeywell sells to—in particular, the aerospace industry—will probably always be low-growth businesses. However, as we've seen, the focus on profitability will make the most of these businesses. That said, the inherent low growth makes the company a bit hungry for acquisitions, although to date it has made none of great size or risk to the company as a whole—we would hope for that to continue. The stock has been on a long run, more than doubling since 2011; investors looking for a big share price gain from here might have to be patient.

SECTOR: **Industrials**
BETA COEFFICIENT: **1.31**
10-YEAR COMPOUND EARNINGS PER-SHARE GROWTH: **5.0%**
10-YEAR COMPOUND DIVIDENDS PER-SHARE GROWTH: **6.0%**

	2006	2007	2008	2009	2010	2011	2012	2013
Revenues (mil)	31,367	34,589	36,556	30,908	33,370	36,500	37,665	39,055
Net income (mil)	2,078	2,444	2,792	2,153	2,342	2,998	3,552	3,965
Earnings per share	2.52	3.16	3.75	2.85	3.00	3.79	4.48	4.97
Dividends per share	0.91	1.00	1.10	1.21	1.21	1.37	1.53	1.68
Cash flow per share	3.59	4.39	5.03	4.07	4.27	5.11	5.72	6.32
Price: high	45.8	62.3	63.0	41.6	53.7	62.3	64.5	91.6
low	35.2	43.1	23.2	23.1	36.7	41.2	52.2	64.2

Honeywell International
101 Columbia Road
P.O. Box 2245
Morristown, NJ 07962–2245
(973) 455-2000
Website: *www.honeywell.com*

CONSERVATIVE GROWTH

Illinois Tool Works Inc.

Ticker symbol: ITW (NYSE) ❑ S&P rating: A+ ❑ Value Line financial strength rating: A++
Current yield: 2.1% ❑ Dividend raises, past 10 years: 10

Company Profile

Illinois Tool Works is a longstanding multinational conglomerate involved in the manufacture of a diversified range of industrial products, mainly components, fasteners, and other "ingredients" for manufacturers. Customers include the automotive, machinery, construction, food and beverage, and general industrial markets. The company currently operates some 800 decentralized and modestly sized business units in 58 countries, employing approximately 60,000. Some of the products are branded and familiar, like Wolf and Hobart kitchen equipment and Paslode air power tools; most are obscure and only known to others in their industries. Overseas sales account for about 57 percent of the total.

In early 2014 the company announced the spinoff of the Industrial Packaging segment to the private equity firm Carlyle Group for $3.2 billion, subject to regulatory approval. That operation accounted for some 14 percent of revenues in FY2012 and has been removed from the FY2013 results numbers presented below, hence the apparent downdraft in sales, profits, and especially per-share earnings. The company has declared its intention to buy back some 35 million shares (10 percent of float) with the proceeds to help mitigate long-term impact on per-share results.

The remaining segments are presented below with approximate figures for percentages of total ITW revenues—the company had not posted its own post-divestiture estimates at the time of this writing:

- Specialty Products (16 percent)— is a hodgepodge of brands and businesses that includes Diagraph (industrial marking and coding systems), Fastex (engineered components for the appliance industry), and Zip-Pak reclosable plastic packaging.

- Test & Measurement and Electronics (15 percent) supplies equipment and software for testing and measuring of materials and structures, solder, and other materials for PC board manufacturing and microelectronics assembly. Brands include Brooks Instrument, Buehler, Chemtronics, Instron, Magnaflux, and Speedline Technologies.

- Automotive OEM (15 percent) includes transportation-related components, fasteners, and polymers, as well as truck remanufacturing and related parts and service for the automotive manufacturer market. Important brands include Drawform ("high volume, highly toleranced deep drawn metal stampings"), and Deltar Interior Components, which makes things like interior door handles.

- Polymers and Fluids (15 percent) businesses produce adhesives, sealants, lubrication and cutting fluids, and hygiene products for an assortment of markets. Their primary brands include Futura, Krafft, Devcon, Rocol, and Permatex and such brands as Rain-X and Wynn's for the automotive aftermarket.
- Food Equipment (12 percent) produces commercial food equipment and related services, including professional kitchen ovens, refrigeration, mixers, and exhaust and ventilation systems. Major brands include Hobart, Traulsen, Vulcan, and Wolf.
- Construction Products (12 percent) concentrates on tools, fasteners, and other products for construction applications. Their major end markets are residential, commercial, and renovation construction. Brands include Ramset, Paslode, Buildex, Proline, and others.
- The Welding segment (12 percent of revenues) produces

equipment and consumables associated with specialty power conversion, metallurgy, and electronics. Their primary products include arc-welding equipment and consumables, solder materials, equipment and services for electronics assembly, and airport ground support equipment. Primary brands include AXA Power, Hobart, and Weldcraft.

Financial Highlights, Fiscal Year 2013

The Industrial Packaging divestiture makes the FY2013 picture a bit cloudy, but in every way ITW continues to enjoy both a recovery in the economy and in U.S. manufacturing activity. Although adjusted revenues dipped to $14.13 billion, "organic" growth remained in the 3 percent range. Business is healthy in the remaining segments, particularly the Automotive OEM segment where segment revenues are up an estimated 11 percent driven by the automotive rebound in the U.S. and Europe and some market share gains. Construction products and food equipment also benefitted from current economic trends.

For FY2014, the company projects a total revenue growth in the 2–4 percent range with per-share earnings (after the aforementioned share repurchase) between $4.20–$4.50. The company has embarked on an efficiency campaign projected to increase operating and net profit margins in the 1–2 percent range, an action that bodes well for future profitability and cash returns for investors.

Reasons to Buy

The company is well diversified and serves many markets, some with end products, some with components, some in cyclical industries such as automotive and construction, some in steady-state industries like food processing. The company has solid models for making acquisitions and seems to do better than most conglomerates historically in choosing candidates and then managing them. The company seems to do an equally good job of turning opportunity into cash flow and using that cash flow to enhance shareholder returns, as exemplified by

the steady record of dividend increases each year since 1994. The balance sheet is strong and net profit margins are projected to rise a healthy figure. Finally, the company appears to be slowing down its acquisitions, which should reduce distractions and costs in absorbing new businesses.

Reasons for Caution

ITW is by nature tied to some of the more volatile elements of the business cycle, so it may not be the best pick for investors living in fear of the next downturn. Conglomerates are notoriously difficult to manage (it's hard enough to manage one business, let alone 800 of them); that said, the company is working to streamline management structure and is also putting fewer new acquisitions on its plate.

SECTOR: **Industrials**
BETA COEFFICIENT: **1.12**
10-YEAR COMPOUND EARNINGS PER-SHARE GROWTH: **9.5%**
10-YEAR COMPOUND DIVIDENDS PER-SHARE GROWTH: **13.0%**

	2006	2007	2008	2009	2010	2011	2012	2013
Revenues (mil)	14,055	16,169	15,869	13,876	15,870	17,787	17,924	14,135
Net income (mil)	1,717	1,826	1,583	969	1,527	1,852	1,921	1,629
Earnings per share	3.01	3.36	3.05	1.93	3.03	3.74	4.06	3.63
Dividends per share	0.71	0.91	1.15	1.24	1.27	1.38	1.46	1.60
Cash flow per share	3.87	4.44	4.56	3.27	4.17	5.06	5.55	5.20
Price: high	53.5	60.0	55.6	51.2	52.7	59.3	63.3	84.3
low	41.5	45.6	28.5	25.6	40.3	39.1	47.4	59.7

Illinois Tool Works Inc.
3600 West Lake Avenue
Glenview, IL 60026
(847) 724-7500
Website: *www.itwinc.com*

CONSERVATIVE GROWTH

International Business Machines

Ticker symbol: IBM (NYSE) ❑ S&P rating: AA ❑ Value Line financial strength rating: A++
Current yield: 2.0% ❑ Dividend raises, past 10 years: 10

Company Profile

Big Blue is the world's leading provider of computer hardware, software, and services. Really—we should say services, software, and hardware. Get the drift? IBM makes a broad range of computers, mainframes, and network servers. But the company has morphed over the years into a software and services company. Nobody talks about an "IBM computer" anymore; as we'll see, they talk about an "IBM business solution" or some such.

IBM is divided into four principal business units and a financing unit. The largest, at 37 percent of revenues, the Global Technology Services unit, is really an IT service, offering cloud computing, analytics, and other applications outsourcing. The Global Business Services unit (18 percent) is also a service unit but now provides its service on customer sites through consulting, application design, systems integration, and similar services. The Software unit (27 percent) supplies rather unexciting "middleware" products that make everything in an IT environment work together, and the more interesting "big data" and business analytics that is starting to emerge as a leading new offering for the company. The Systems and Technology group, which is the unit that most closely harkens back to the "Big Iron" days, is now just 14 percent of the business (was 17 percent in FY2012 and poised to drop further—note what follows about the Lenovo sale). Finally, the Financing unit (4 percent) helps the company market it all. Overseas sales make up about 65 percent of revenues. It's not hard to see how the company has evolved from the old "Big Blue" maker of mainframes. It still produces high-margin commercial servers and enterprise-level installations, but in recent years, it has "reinvented" itself away from lower-margin, commodity computing hardware businesses, exiting the PC, laptop, and hard drive businesses entirely during the past 15 years, and recently announcing plans to exit the midrange server business through a $2 billion sale to China's Lenovo. The company has kept "strategic" (as opposed to commoditized) large systems and is now starting to offer integrated hardware/software/service solutions for diverse needs such as business analytics cloud service providers. The company, more than most in the industry, lives up to a common industry promise to provide "solutions," not just products.

Financial Highlights, Fiscal Year 2013

Big Blue continues down a predictable results path as it has for the past several years. Revenues stay mostly flat, going up a little, down a little; FY2013 was one of those slight "down" years. But not to worry: The business mix continues to shift to more profitable software services, and with this shift net profit margins have grown from the high single digits to the high teens over the course of ten years. A 10 percent growth in net margins on a revenue base the size of IBM's—you start not to care that the revenue isn't growing so much. Indeed, net profit, while hitting a pothole in FY2013 due to weak China demand and a soft hardware market, has doubled from the $8 billion a year range in 2005 to $16.5 billion now. Not too surprisingly, the accompanying cash flows have been used to take a 40 percent whack out of share count over this same two-year period. So, again, who cares about revenues when per-share earnings triple over a ten year period, the dividend grows some five-fold—well, you get the idea.

For FY2014 and into FY2015, revenues will likely continue in the doldrums, aside from the effects of the Lenovo sale. Net profit and per-share earnings will be the story and should grow steadily in the 6–10 percent range over this time. Again, such a percentage means a lot on a business base of this size and as share counts continue to fall.

Reasons to Buy

Once viewed as a teetering giant of the computer industry with a massive intellectual property portfolio but an uncertain product strategy, IBM has, over the past decade, successfully reinvented itself as a go-to solutions powerhouse. Not long ago, many companies felt they had to have in-house information technology departments to service their IT needs. Now, most have found that it's far more efficient to contract those services out to someone who can provide data warehousing, website development and maintenance, regional/national/global IT infrastructure, etc., without requiring a commitment in fixed assets—not just "cloud" services but fully integrated IT solutions. This is where IBM has leveraged its expertise, and as this trend continues and as businesses increase their reliance on these services, IBM benefits. We also feel that as the common architecture becomes more cloudlike, IBM will benefit as an integrated solution provider. IBM offers an excellent way to play the growth in world economies through a U.S.-based business.

Despite the revenue softness, the company is very tenacious about its goals and strategies, as we've observed in the exit of its mainstay hardware businesses. Not too long ago they promised $20 per share in earnings for FY2015; this goal now looks in jeopardy but we wouldn't be surprised to see them pull it off. The company returned about $15 billion in 2013 to investors in the form of dividends and buybacks, and looks to continue along this track.

Reasons for Caution

Innovation in the IT business can be rapid and disruptive, and margins can shrink precipitously as a result. IBM will have to stay ahead of the curve with innovative and compelling products and defensive product strategies in order to maintain revenue and grow profitability. To do that, in part, the company tends to acquire or partner with numerous small companies to fill in holes in its product offering. We're glad it has avoided large-scale acquisitions thus far, but we do get concerned about too much growth through acquisition and the rather unwieldy task of managing it all.

IBM does have a larger exposure to governments and government contracts than many of its competitors. While this can be stabilizing in hard times, this time we feel that a massive and widespread public sector belt tightening could hurt the company. Finally, IBM has a reputation, somewhat deserved, of being big, bureaucratic, laden with headcount, and not very nimble, which can be a serious negative in the tech world—but unlike many big, unwieldy tech companies, IBM has demonstrated a clear go-forward strategy and the ability to execute on it.

SECTOR: **Information Technology**
BETA COEFFICIENT: **0.72**
10-YEAR COMPOUND EARNINGS PER-SHARE GROWTH: **13.0%**
10-YEAR COMPOUND DIVIDENDS PER-SHARE GROWTH: **19.0%**

	2006	2007	2008	2009	2010	2011	2012	2013
Revenues (bil)	91.4	98.8	103.6	95.8	99.9	106.9	104.5	99.8
Net income (bil)	9.4	10.4	12.3	13.4	14.8	15.9	16.6	16.5
Earnings per share	6.01	7.18	8.93	10.01	11.52	13.06	14.37	14.94
Dividends per share	1.10	1.50	1.90	2.15	2.50	2.90	3.30	3.70
Cash flow per share	9.56	11.28	13.28	14.11	16.01	17.77	19.04	20.07
Price: high	97.4	121.5	130.9	132.3	147.5	194.9	211.8	215.9
low	72.7	88.8	69.5	81.8	116.0	146.6	177.3	172.2

International Business Machines Corporation
New Orchard Road
Armonk, NY 10504
(914) 499-1900
Website: *www.ibm.com*

Itron, Inc.

Ticker symbol: ITRI (NASDAQ) □ S&P rating: BB □ Value Line financial strength rating: B+
Current yield: Nil □ Dividend raises, past 10 years: NA

Company Profile

From worst to first? We're hoping so. We must admit, this stock was the worst performer on our 2014 *100 Best Stocks* list, losing some 25 percent of its value without even a compensating dividend. This, and the reasons supporting such a performance, would typically indicate a quick dismissal. But, as with a difficult teenager you expect to grow up into an outstanding adult, sometimes you stick with something that may turn out well in the long term. For us, and for now at least, Itron is just such a story. Stay tuned.

Itron is the world's largest provider of standard and intelligent metering systems for residential and commercial gas, electric, and water usage, primarily to the utility industry. Intelligent meters, in addition to tracking raw usage over a period of time, can also measure at the point of use operating parameters such as pressure, temperature, voltage, phase, etc. This information can be extremely valuable to the supplying utility but has in the past been difficult and expensive to obtain.

Itron supplies a range of products from basic meters that are read manually to meters that act as network devices and transmit their data in real time to the managing utility and/or to the consuming customer. Products and systems are produced and sold in three groupings:

- Standard metering—basic meters that measure electricity, gas, or water flow by electrical or mechanical means, with displays but no built-in remote reading or transmission capability.

- Advanced metering—these units, depending on the country and the communications technologies available— transmit usage data remotely through telephone, cellular, radio frequency (RF), Ethernet, or power line carrier paths. Among other value-adds, these meters transmit usage data for billing, thereby eliminating the need for onsite meter reading—a big savings for utility companies.

- Smart metering—smart meters collect and store interval data and other detailed info, receive commands, and interface with other devices through assorted communication paths to thermostats, smart appliances, and home network and other advanced control systems.

Itron also sells a range of software platforms for utilities and building managers for the management of the installed base and the analysis and optimization of usage, and it is active in developing so-called "smart grid" solutions for utilities and utility networks. The company also markets advanced metering initiative (AMI) contracts to utilities, where it installs devices and monitors and optimizes power usage for a utility.

The company was founded in 1977 and in 2004 acquired the electric meter operations of Schlumberger, which at the time was the largest global supplier of this equipment. At present, electric meters represent about 43 percent of the business, gas meters about 29 percent, and water meters the remaining 28 percent. The company has about 8,000 customers in 130 countries, and about 52 percent of the business comes from overseas. In 2012 the company acquired SmartSynch, a provider of metering and communications systems using cellular technology—an indicator of the kinds of innovative technologies to come.

Financial Highlights, Fiscal Year 2013

We anticipated a slump in Itron's fortunes when we first added the stock to our *100 Best* list in 2013, due to the completion of five "advanced metering initiative" contracts in 2012. That slump happened, but we didn't anticipate continued weakness in 2013 as some contracts were postponed and public sector and utility infrastructure investments were attenuated due to budget constraints. Also not helping were new supplies of "cheap" energy, which both dampened demand for energy-saving product concepts and soaked up utility budgets for gas power plant conversions. If these weren't enough, the company faced currency headwinds in its growing international business. All in all, not a good mix—FY2013 revenues dropped a bit more than 10 percent, and earnings, hit by the loss of volume and operating leverage, skidded some 65 percent.

Normally the story would end right there, and frankly, projections do not appear to bring a full recovery even out through FY2015. The departure of the CFO didn't help, either.

However, we see some help coming from the international sector, and in the first quarter of FY2014, the company reported a 30 percent increase in net backlog and a rise in its "book to bill" ratio—orders to shipments—to 1.6. Forecasts call for earnings in a wide range: $1.30–$1.80 per share, not great but a step in the right direction, with far stronger cash flows. We expect the trend to improve—possibly faster than the company does—into FY2015 based on new products, cost reductions, and strength in emerging markets. We hope our value picking "meter" is calibrated correctly.

Reasons to Buy

Can you picture a day when you might manage your energy consumption, device by device, in your home using your smartphone? Even if you're away from the home? And the day when utilities can monitor usage in real time to shift supply of a resource such as electricity that virtually cannot be stored? When solar energy generated from one locale on a sunny day is moved to another with clouds and rain?

If you believe that the need for managed energy efficiency will only grow in the future, Itron is a good place to be. As utilities modernize, reduce costs, and replace infrastructure, Itron products and networks will be in the sweet spot. Internationally, utilities are adding infrastructure, as well as replacing it, and Itron is positioned well for that, too. Public policy will provide some tailwinds too, as the European Union is committed to reduce energy use by 2020. Recent droughts will probably bode well for water conservation and smart metering, too. Worldwide, only about 12 percent of 2.5 billion meters are "smart" or "advanced."

Conceptually, these ideas make for a fine story, but as with so many similar companies they retain the question, "Yeah, but does this company make money?" In Itron's case, even though it is in a flat spot currently, the answer in general is yes, with decent earnings and especially cash flows even now, and we think this company will do better as time goes on and more utility infrastructure is replaced. This technology, and its cost savings, is proven. Over time, this company, like the utility industry it supports, has been relatively stable for a technology stock, and at recent prices, the stock continues to look like a good growth holding to sock away for the future. At the same time, while there is no dividend for the moment, the company continues to repurchase shares at a moderate rate—$50 million authorized in 2014 would retire more than 3 percent of the modest 39 million share float.

Reasons for Caution

Needless to say, Itron is one of our more risky picks—but in today's markets, we feel there's more risk than usual in a lot of stocks; might as well pick one that has already suffered the bad news and can be had at a relatively low price, right? For sure, companies that sell good ideas don't always grow, particularly if the size of their markets is limited or they are particularly conservative about spending money; that might describe the utility industry, which has been spending money on a lot of other things lately, including new gas-fired plants. Energy credits and subsidies are always subject to change. The next few years will be a test of whether the company can size its business properly to the conditions, and bring more good ideas to more markets successfully.

SECTOR: **Information Technology**
BETA COEFFICIENT: **1.64**
10-YEAR COMPOUND EARNINGS PER-SHARE GROWTH: **17.0%**
10-YEAR COMPOUND DIVIDENDS PER-SHARE GROWTH: **NA**

	2006	2007	2008	2009	2010	2011	2012	2013
Revenues (mil)	644	1,464	1,909	1,687	2,259	2,434	2,178	1,949
Net income (mil)	56.4	87.3	117.6	44.3	133.9	156.3	128.5	45.0
Earnings per share	2.16	2.78	3.36	1.15	3.27	3.85	3.22	1.14
Dividends per share	—	—	—	—	—	—	—	—
Cash flow per share	2.79	4.24	4.96	2.53	4.85	5.56	4.84	2.60
Price: high	73.7	112.9	109.3	69.5	81.9	64.4	50.3	48.4
low	39.4	51.2	34.3	40.1	52.0	26.9	33.3	37.0

Itron, Inc.
2111 North Moller Rd.
Liberty Lake, WA 99019
(509) 924-9900
Website: *www.itron.com*

GROWTH AND INCOME

The J.M. Smucker Company

Ticker symbol: SJM (NYSE) ❑ S&P rating: NR ❑ Value Line financial strength rating: A++
Current yield: 2.4% ❑ Dividend raises, past 10 years: 10

Company Profile

"With a name like Smucker's, it has to be good!" This ad jingle says it all about this eastern Ohio–based firm, a leading manufacturer of jams, jellies, and other processed foods for years. Thanks in large part to divestitures from the Procter & Gamble food division and other companies, it has grown itself into a premier player in the packaged food industry.

Smucker manufactures and markets products under its own name, as well as under a number of other household names such as Crisco, Folgers, Millstone, Laura Scudder's, Hungry Jack, Eagle, Pillsbury, Jif (why not sell the peanut butter if they sell the jelly?), and naturally, Goober (a combination of peanut butter and jelly in a single jar), and Uncrustables (why not just sell the whole sandwich?). The company also produces and distributes Dunkin' Donuts coffee and produces an assortment of cooking oils, toppings, juices, and baking ingredients. The company has revitalized such brands as Folgers and Jif through improved marketing, channel relationships, and better focus on the packaging and delivery of these brands to the customer. In the coffee business, for example, for custom blends, K-cup offerings, etc., "Coffee Served Your Way" is their motto, and there are new convenience packages for peanut butter, jelly, and other spreads as well. Overall, the company aims to sell the number one brand in the various markets it serves.

The company is organized into three reporting segments: Retail Coffee (41 percent of revenues, 50 percent of profits), Retail Consumer Foods (38 percent revenues, 34 percent profits), and International, Foodservice, and Natural Foods (which contributes the remaining 21 percent of revenues and 16 percent of profits). Operations are centered in the United States, Canada, and Europe, with about 10 percent of sales coming from overseas.

Even as a nearly $6 billion a year enterprise, the company still retains the feel of a family business, with brothers Tim and Richard Smucker sharing the CEO responsibilities as chairman and president respectively.

Financial Highlights, Fiscal Year 2013

The jelly was spread a little bit thinner than we expected in FY2013, with significant competition in all markets and lingering effects of high commodity prices. FY2013 was a bit of a down year, with revenues dipping a bit over 3 percent, while earnings remained essentially flat. FY2013 was a year of fine-tuning product lines, operations, and marketing strategies, which should bear fruit in FY2014 and beyond, although higher coffee prices in early 2014 are a concern. The company is guiding revenues of $5.82 billion in FY2014, which would just a little more than recapture the setback in FY2013, with a similar 3.7 percent rise forecast for FY2015. Per-share earnings, helped along with a regular 2–3 percent buyback, are forecast ahead about 6 percent in FY2014 and a stronger 9 percent in FY2015.

After several years of moderate acquisitions, mostly from the food businesses of Procter & Gamble and Pillsbury, all was quiet on the acquisition front in 2013, but there were a few small divestitures. The company has stated an overall goal to grow net sales by 6 percent and per-share earnings by 8 percent long term, with "organic" growth from current products or products invented from within to be in the 3–4 percent range, so modest acquisitions are likely part of the long-term picture.

Reasons to Buy

This is a very well-managed company with an excellent and lasting reputation in its markets. In recent years, it has a proven track record in buying and revitalizing key brands, the most prominent being former Procter & Gamble food brands, Sara Lee food-service coffee and beverage brands, and a few International Multifoods brands. We expect this trend to continue. The company's aggressive moves into coffee and other beverages were well timed and have provided a boost to the bottom line.

The base for steady growth in cash flows and investor returns is well established over the long term. Steady and safe: Smucker is the peanut butter and jelly sandwich of the investing landscape.

Reasons for Caution

The prepared-food business is very sensitive in the short term to commodity and energy costs. As the company relies more and more on coffee products for earnings growth, it will find itself exposed to instability in the cost of raw materials and transportation and to changes in consumer tastes. Yes, these are costs that also affect all of their competitors, but Smucker is in competition with a number of low-margin brands and has customers (such as Walmart) that have enormous buying power. Smucker will need to rely on brand strength and breadth should the economy slow again.

SECTOR: Consumer Staples
BETA COEFFICIENT: 0.70
10-YEAR COMPOUND EARNINGS PER-SHARE GROWTH: 12.0%
10-YEAR COMPOUND DIVIDENDS PER-SHARE GROWTH: 10.5%

	2006	2007	2008	2009	2010	2011	2012	2013
Revenues (mil)	2,148	2,525	3,758	4,605	4,826	5,526	5,897	5,615E
Net income (mil)	164.6	178.9	321.4	520.3	566.5	535.6	584	610E
Earnings per share	2.89	3.15	3.77	4.15	4.79	4.73	5.37	5.55
Dividends per share	1.14	1.22	1.31	1.40	1.68	1.88	2.06	2.26
Cash flow per share	3.94	4.42	3.73	5.60	7.06	6.75	7.85	8.10E
Price: high	50.0	64.3	56.7	62.7	66.3	80.3	89.4	114.7
low	37.2	46.6	37.2	34.1	53.3	61.2	70.5	86.5

The J.M. Smucker Company
One Strawberry Lane
Orrville, OH, 44667
(330) 682-3000
Website: *www.smuckers.com*

GROWTH AND INCOME

Johnson & Johnson

Ticker symbol: JNJ (NYSE) ❑ S&P rating: AAA ❑ Value Line financial strength rating: A++
Current yield: 2.8 percent ❑ Dividend raises, past 10 years: 10

Company Profile

With FY2013 sales of $71 billion, Johnson & Johnson remains the largest and most comprehensive health-care company in the world. JNJ offers a broad line of consumer products, over-the-counter drugs, and various other medical devices and diagnostic equipment.

The company has three reporting segments: Consumer Health Care ($14.7 billion in FY2013 sales), Medical Devices and Diagnostics ($28.5 billion), and Pharmaceuticals ($28.2 billion). In those segments, Johnson & Johnson has more than 275 operating companies in 60 countries, selling some 50,000 products in more than 175 countries. Among Johnson & Johnson's premier assets are its well-entrenched brand names, which are widely known in the United States as well as abroad. And as a marketer, JNJ's reputation for quality has enabled it to build strong ties to commercial health-care providers.

In the Consumer segment, the company's vast portfolio of well-known trade names includes Band-Aid adhesive bandages; Tylenol; Stayfree, Carefree, and Sure & Natural feminine hygiene products; Mylanta;

Pepcid AC; Motrin; Sudafed; Zyrtec; Neosporin; Neutrogena; Johnson's baby powder, shampoo, and oil; Listerine; and Reach toothbrushes. Names in the Pharmaceutical segment are less well-known but include major entries in the areas of antiseptics, antipsychotics, gastroenterology, immunology, neurology, hematology, contraceptives, oncology, pain management, and many others distributed both through consumer and health-care professional channels. Medical Devices and Diagnostics products include professionally used cardiovascular, orthopedic, diabetic, neurologic, and surgical products among others.

The company is typically fairly active with acquisitions, acquiring small niche players to strengthen its overall product offering. In early FY2014, however, the company announced a fairly large divestiture in the form of a spinoff of the Ortho-Clinical Diagnostics business to private equity firm Carlyle Group for $4.2 billion, subject to regulatory approval which should come well in advance of the FY2015 fiscal year. The company is already actively retiring shares, and this divestiture may accelerate that trend.

Financial Highlights, Fiscal Year 2013

Johnson & Johnson continues to own a dominant and stable franchise in a secure and lucrative industry. We like the model of steady, recurring income from solid consumer brands such as Tylenol combined with more aggressive and lucrative ventures into pharmaceuticals and surgical products. In 2012 the company generated 25 percent of sales from products introduced in the past five years, and new offerings and growth particularly in the Pharmaceutical and MD&D segments continue to lead the way.

FY2013 saw a slight strengthening in the top line to a 6 percent growth rate and a stronger per-share earnings growth rate of 8.2 percent. This performance, and a recognition that things would have been still better without currency headwinds, brought the stock out of a three-year flat spot on the chart, as the FY2013 share price high was some 30 percent ahead of that for any of the past three years. The price factors in a promise for future steady growth and relief from the currency headwinds, and the recently announced FY2014 guidance, always conservative from this company, calls for a 6 percent EPS growth for the year and a stronger 7.7 percent growth into FY2015.

Reasons to Buy

A term we don't hear much anymore in the investment arena is "blue chip." A name taken from the highest-value poker chip on the table, it was used to describe a stock into which you could put your money without fear. A blue-chip stock was where you put money that you would normally put in a bank, if banks would only pay dividends and occasionally offer you more than a toaster as an incentive to stick around. Johnson & Johnson has been a blue chip for as long as there have been blue chips.

JNJ is fundamentally a conservatively run company whose growth prospects are on the lower end of this book's scale, but clearly the company has great appeal in the investment community. Even if it's more often unexciting for the growth and momentum investor, JNJ's business model reminds us of the blue chips—steady earnings and cash flow combined with a healthy dividend and share repurchases, leading to very gratifying total shareholder returns. Dividends, by the way, have not only been raised ten consecutive years, but the increases continue to be substantial, 5–10 percent or more each year with another 17 percent expected over the next two years (are your wage increases this large?). Even with the recent price runup, we feel this is a strong and well-managed company with less chance for a downside surprise than most.

Reasons for Caution

While we still think JNJ is a good, steady horse for a relatively long race, it has picked up some speed of late, enhancing the chance of getting winded somewhere along the way. The P/E, a figure we don't rely on heavily but do look at, has expanded from 14–15 to the 16–17 range, adding a bit of downside risk to the mix. It's still a good horse, but investors might wait for it to settle back into the pack a bit and gather steam for another pull toward finishing in the money.

SECTOR: **Health Care**
BETA COEFFICIENT: **0.53**
10-YEAR COMPOUND EARNINGS PER-SHARE GROWTH: **13.0%**
10-YEAR COMPOUND DIVIDENDS PER-SHARE GROWTH: **12.5%**

	2006	**2007**	**2008**	**2009**	**2010**	**2011**	**2012**	**2013**
Revenues (mil)	53,324	61,095	63,747	61,897	61,587	65,030	67,224	71,312
Net income (mil)	11,053	10,576	12,949	12,906	13,279	13,867	14,345	15,576
Earnings per share	3.73	4.15	4.57	4.63	4.76	5.00	5.10	5.52
Dividends per share	1.46	1.62	1.80	1.93	2.11	2.25	2.40	2.56
Cash flow per share	4.60	5.23	5.70	5.69	5.90	6.25	6.45	7.10
Price: high	69.4	68.8	72.8	65.9	66.2	66.3	72.7	96.0
low	56.6	59.7	52.1	61.9	56.9	64.3	61.7	70.3

Johnson & Johnson
One Johnson & Johnson Plaza
New Brunswick, NJ 08933
(732) 524-0400
Website: *www.jnj.com*

Johnson Controls Inc.

Ticker symbol: JCI (NYSE) □ S&P rating: BBB+ □ Value Line financial strength rating: A
Current yield: 1.9% □ Dividend raises, past 10 years: 9

Company Profile

The name may only describe a portion of the business, but Johnson Controls is a large manufacturer of automotive parts and subassemblies, heating, ventilation, and air conditioning (HVAC) and other energy controls, and an assortment of battery technologies. Its products are found in more than 12 million homes, 1 million commercial buildings, and are installed in more than 30 million new vehicles every year. The company operates in three segments: Automotive Experience, Building Efficiency, and Power Solutions.

Automotive Experience (51 percent of FY2013 revenues, 39 percent of profits) is one of the world's largest automotive suppliers, providing seating and overhead systems, door systems, and floor consoles. The business, including affiliates, has 240 plants and produces automotive interior systems for original equipment manufacturers (OEMs) and operates in 33 countries worldwide. Additionally, the business has partially owned affiliates in Asia, Europe, North America, and South America. An automotive interior electronics business, primarily responsible for displays and phone link products, was sold in early FY2014.

Building Efficiency (34 percent of revenues, 30 percent of profits) is the original business at its founding in 1900 and the source of the company's name. The unit is a global leader in delivering integrated control systems, mechanical equipment, services, and solutions designed to improve the comfort, safety, and energy efficiency of buildings with operations in more than 125 countries.

The Power Solutions business (15 percent of revenues, 31 percent of profits) produces lead-acid automotive batteries, serving both automotive equipment manufacturers and the vehicle battery aftermarket. They also offer absorbent glass mat, nickel metal hydride, and lithium-ion battery technologies to power hybrid vehicles.

Financial Highlights, Fiscal Year 2013

In the past few years, all three of JCI's businesses have come into favor. The automotive industry has recovered, even in Europe, the last weak link in the chain. Construction is better than it was during the Great Recession; however, it has softened a bit just recently (cheaper energy?) and a mix of divestitures and acquisitions has also affected the numbers. All that considered, FY2013 was a decent year, with revenues up 1.8 percent and, with the effects of a better product mix and some efficiency measures, earnings were up 4.8 percent. Going forward, JCI projects steadily increasing revenues in the 2–3.5 percent range through FY2015; efficiency and fine-tuning measures will grow net profit margins into the 5–6 percent range from FY2013's 4.3 percent; that in turn will bring earnings increases in the 15–20 percent range. A recently approved $3 billion increase in share repurchases could retire as much as 10 percent of the stock.

Reasons to Buy

JCI was one of the great recovery stories coming out of the Great Recession and continues to be well positioned for the auto and building industry recoveries worldwide. While cyclical, their place in the auto industry supply chain is secure, and we like the worldwide footprint. We also think JCI is a strong long-term play in energy efficiency, with leadership both in building energy controls and in batteries and battery technologies—these should do well in the long term. The company is well managed, with an ever-greater portion of its success dropping to the bottom line.

Reasons for Caution

A significant portion of JCI's success is tied to the automotive industry. Currently the domestic auto industry is selling 17 million cars a year, but if this drops back to the 12 million pace experienced during the Great Recession or anything close, this company will suffer. JCI's business has a strong cyclical component, both in domestic and foreign markets.

SECTOR: Industrials
BETA COEFFICIENT: 1.98
10-YEAR COMPOUND EARNINGS PER-SHARE GROWTH: 9.5%
10-YEAR COMPOUND DIVIDENDS PER-SHARE GROWTH: 12.0%

	2006	2007	2008	2009	2010	2011	2012	2013
Revenues (mil)	32,235	34,624	38,062	28,497	34,305	40,833	41,995	42,730
Net income (mil)	1,028	1,252	1,400	281	1,365	1,665	1,749	1,833
Earnings per share	1.75	2.09	2.33	0.47	2.00	2.42	2.54	2.66
Dividends per share	0.37	0.44	0.52	0.52	0.52	0.72	0.74	0.76
Cash flow per share	2.95	3.34	3.63	1.48	3.00	3.45	3.68	4.07
Price: high	30.0	44.5	36.5	28.3	40.2	42.9	35.9	51.9
low	22.1	28.1	13.6	8.4	25.6	24.3	23.4	30.3

Johnson Controls Inc.
5757 North Green Bay Ave.
Milwaukee, WI 53201
(414) 524-1200
Website: www.johnsoncontrols.com

GROWTH AND INCOME

Kellogg Company

Ticker symbol: K (NYSE) ❑ S&P rating: BBB+ ❑ Value Line financial strength rating: A
Current yield: 2.7% ❑ Dividend raises, past 10 years: 10

Company Profile

Founded in 1906, Kellogg is the world's leading producer of breakfast cereal, the second-largest producer of cookies and crackers, and a leading producer of convenience foods, including toaster pastries, cereal bars, frozen waffles, meat alternatives, pie crusts, and cones. The company's brands include Kellogg's, Keebler, Pop-Tarts, Eggo, Cheez-It, Nutri-Grain, Rice Krispies, Special K, Murray, Austin, Morningstar Farms, Famous Amos, Mother's, Carr's, Plantation, Kashi, and, as of June 2012, Pringles. Kellogg's cereal brands include a long list of familiar names: Corn Flakes, All-Bran, Cocoa Krispies, Corn Pops, Froot Loops, Rice Krispies, Raisin Bran, Smart Start, Special K, Mueslix, Low Fat Granola—just to name a few. The company sells most of these brands and variations thereof in overseas markets.

The company operates in two segments: Kellogg North America (NA) and Kellogg International, with International generating about 44 percent of revenue. NA operations are further divided into Morning Foods (about 23 percent of FY2013 revenues), Snacks (also 23 percent), and Specialty (8 percent) categories. The company produces more than 1,500 different products, manufactured in 19 countries and marketed in more than 180 countries around the world. The company operates manufacturing facilities in 16 countries in addition to the United States.

Financial Highlights, Fiscal Year 2013

Reported results for FY2013 were mixed; on the surface, revenues rose about 4.3 percent, but 4 of that 4.3 percent was due to the Pringles acquisition; "organic" growth was basically flat. International sales and sales in the Specialty operations were strong but offset by softness in U.S. Morning Foods (mainly packaged cereal) and Snacks. Reported net income increased 6 percent, but again three-quarters of this increase was due to the addition of Pringles. So . . . pretty much a flat year.

Going forward the company expects stabilizing commodity costs, international expansion, and a cost reduction program called "Project K," which will bring a series of internal process improvements: facility and supply-chain fine-tuning with annual savings in the $400–500 million range a few years out, two-thirds of which will improve cost of goods sold, and thus operating margins. For FY2014 and FY2015 the company expects moderate 4–6 percent per-share earnings gains on revenue gains of 2–3 percent—all "organic" this time.

Cash flow and cash returns to shareholders are the real highlights: In early 2014 the company hiked its quarterly dividend 7 percent, a larger raise than most were expecting. The company also authorized a $1.5 billion share repurchase, enough to retire about 6 percent of its float—again more than expected.

Reasons to Buy

Kellogg owns just over a third of the U.S. market for ready-to-eat cereals, which makes it the most recognized brand and market leader in probably the most mature food category in the world. However, having invented it more than 100 years ago, the company continues to respond to customer demand for new and interesting products, many with a health bent, with various new versions of Mueslix, Granola, Special K, and other brands. Brand and market leadership, and at the other end of the value chain, strong cash flows, are the company's real strengths; operational and some marketing fine-tuning are set to start improving margins and profitability with gradually increasing effect going forward—we like the

shift from market share wars to product and process innovation and profitability. The company is particularly focused on supply-chain efficiency, and vows to "build the global supply chain of the future." The company was rumored as an acquisition target in early FY2014; we can see why.

We like Kellogg's growth in international markets. As discretionary income rises, so does consumption of prepared foods, and the international markets will reward companies that have the right products. Special K, for example, is growing at double-digit rates internationally and at triple-digit rates in India. Finally, management seems to take seriously its commitment to return cash to shareholders.

Reasons for Caution

Slowing growth in the all-important packaged cereals segment, and to a lesser extent, the snacks segment, are a cause for concern, particularly as people continue the trend toward healthier foods and less expensive store-brand alternatives. The company will have to fight this trend by lowering costs (and maybe prices a little) and by keeping the innovation machine running with new, appealing, healthy morning foods and snacks. We think it can be successful, but there are some risks. Project K also brings some distraction, disruption, up-front cost, and risks, but it seems to be well thought out and on track.

SECTOR: **Consumer Staples**
BETA COEFFICIENT: **0.48**
10-YEAR COMPOUND EARNINGS PER-SHARE GROWTH: **8.0%**
10-YEAR COMPOUND DIVIDENDS PER-SHARE GROWTH: **5.5%**

	2006	2007	2008	2009	2010	2011	2012	2013
Revenues (mil)	10,907	11,776	12,822	12,575	12,397	13,175	14,197	14,792
Net income (mil)	1,004	1,103	1,148	1,212	1,247	1,225	1,297	1,380
Earnings per share	2.51	2.76	2.99	3.17	3.30	3.35	3.37	3.77
Dividends per share	1.14	1.24	1.30	1.43	1.56	1.67	1.74	1.80
Cash flow per share	3.41	3.78	3.99	4.35	4.48	4.55	4.83	5.27
Price: high	51.0	56.9	58.5	54.1	56.0	57.7	57.2	68.0
low	42.4	48.7	35.6	35.6	47.3	48.1	46.3	56.0

Kellogg Company
One Kellogg Square
P. O. Box 3599
Battle Creek, MI 49016–3599
(269) 961-2000
Website: *www.kelloggcompany.com*

GROWTH AND INCOME

Kimberly-Clark

Ticker symbol: KMB (NYSE) □ S&P rating: A □ Value Line financial strength rating: A++
Current yield: 3.0% □ Dividend raises, past 10 years: 10

Company Profile

Kimberly-Clark develops, manufactures, and markets a full line of personal care products, mostly based on paper and paper technologies. Well-known for its ubiquitous Kleenex brand tissues, KMB also is a strong player in bath tissue, diapers, feminine products, incontinence products, industrial and, for now, health care–related paper products. The company was founded in 1872 and is headquartered today in Dallas, TX, with a historical, technology, and manufacturing base in the Fox River Valley in Wisconsin. About 51 percent of the company's sales originate outside North America.

For the moment, the company operates in four segments: Personal Care, Consumer Tissue, K-C Professional & Other, and Health Care. The Personal Care segment (45 percent of FY2013 revenues) provides disposable diapers, training and youth pants, and swim pants; baby wipes; and feminine and incontinence care products, and related products. Brand names include Huggies, Pull-Ups, Little Swimmers, GoodNites, Kotex, Lightdays, Depend, and Poise. Baby care is the single largest business category with $6 billion in revenues—about 28 percent of the business—mostly sold under the Huggies brand.

The Consumer Tissue segment (31 percent) offers facial and bathroom tissue, paper towels, napkins, and related products for household use under the Kleenex, Scott, Cottonelle, Viva, Andrex, Scottex, Hakle, and Page brands. Ah (choo), there's Kleenex, a $2 billion business in itself, almost 10 percent of the total. But Scott is no softie either, accounting for another 10 percent.

The K-C Professional & Other segment (16 percent) provides paper products for the away-from-home, that is, commercial/institutional marketplace under Kimberly-Clark, Kleenex, Scott, WypAll, Kimtech, KleenGuard, Kimcare, and Jackson brand names.

The fourth segment is the Health Care segment, which offers disposable health-care products, such as surgical drapes and gowns, infection control products, face masks, exam gloves, respiratory products, pain management products, and other disposable medical products. The company is in the final stages of a formal separation of this business into a new company called Halyard Health, a tax-free distribution of shares to current KMB shareholders.

This segment accounts for about 8 percent of Kimberly-Clark's current business and some 16,500 of 57,000 employees (28 percent—is this what inspired the move?). The spinoff will allow KMB to focus on more core and more manufacturing-oriented businesses, and if approvals go as planned, should happen at the end of FY2014. We see it as a neutral for the KMB business and its shareholders as a whole.

Financial Highlights, Fiscal Year 2013

We see it all the time, companies talking about increasing operating efficiencies. But very few realize the benefits that Kimberly-Clark has with its ongoing Focus on Reducing Costs Everywhere (FORCE) program. The company cut some $250 million from FY2012 operating costs, and rang in with another $300 million in FY2013. As a result, with the help of some moderating commodity costs, Kimberly-Clark delivered a 22 percent increase in net profit on a most lackluster, currency-hampered half a percent growth in sales. This is on top of a strong FY2012.

Going forward, the company is shifting its emphasis back to growing the top line through new product development and increased marketing spend; the FORCE will stay with us but probably not deliver much in the way of incremental performance. FY2014 and FY2015 revenues are projected 2.5–3 percent ahead, still not quite up to the company's stated 4 percent long-term objective. Earnings growth will flatten out in the 1–2 percent growth range, but the company hopes for better with its marketing initiatives, and none of this includes the effects of the healthcare business separation.

The company has budgeted another $1.2 billion for share buybacks and increased the dividend three times in the last year to a level 13.5 percent ahead of a year ago. KMB has reduced its share count from 501 million in 2003 to about 380 million at the end of 2013.

Reasons to Buy

Kimberly-Clark has shown itself to be a steady and solid business in all kinds of economic climates. The company has focused on profits of late, with great success; if you think business is about generating profits and passing them back to shareholders, then KMB ought to look attractive.

The relatively high yield and strong track record of raising dividends and buying back shares is a definite plus. Strong cash flow has financed strategic business investments, including international expansion in emerging markets, product innovations, and strategic marketing. If the Halyard Health separation pans out, that should help with focus and perhaps with cost structure, given the number of employees involved. The company continues to be rock solid, with a microscopic beta of 0.25 and with shareholder interests a consistent priority.

The company has stellar brands and should do well expanding into overseas markets. Also, compared to some peers, especially Procter & Gamble, the company is less inclined to go for "glamour" markets, choosing instead to add to margins through operating efficiencies and scale. Safety-oriented investors may find this approach preferable. In addition, Value Line gives the company an A++ for financial strength and a top rating for safety, the latter of which it has maintained since 1990.

Reasons for Caution

So many companies are splitting or spinning off businesses lately; while there are typically gains from greater focus, these events can be distracting and can also disrupt cost structures. After all, many companies merge or acquire other companies just to improve fixed cost leverage and to consolidate operations, so when it goes the other way, the net effect can go the other way too—higher costs.

While the paper products business is steady, it isn't easy to see where substantial additional growth would come from. The company, rightly so, is targeting international expansion, but competition and currency fluctuation make the results far from certain. The cost of pulp and paper raw materials will always be volatile. Companies like KMB have sometimes come to rely on acquisitions for growth; KMB has, so far, largely resisted this temptation but that could change. Finally, investors and the markets have recognized KMB's consistent excellence and continue to bid up the share price in response to all the good earnings news.

SECTOR: Consumer Staples
BETA COEFFICIENT: 0.25
10-YEAR COMPOUND EARNINGS PER-SHARE GROWTH: 3.5%
10-YEAR COMPOUND DIVIDENDS PER-SHARE GROWTH: 9.5%

	2006	2007	2008	2009	2010	2011	2012	2013
Revenues (mil)	16,747	18,266	19,415	19,115	19,746	20,846	21,063	21,182
Net income (mil)	1,844	1,862	1,698	1,884	1,843	1,591	1,750	2,142
Earnings per share	3.90	4.25	4.14	4.52	4.45	3.99	4.42	5.53
Dividends per share	1.96	2.08	2.27	2.38	2.58	2.76	2.92	3.24
Cash flow per share	6.10	6.34	5.98	6.40	6.53	6.78	6.70	7.89
Price: high	68.6	72.8	69.7	67.0	67.2	74.1	88.3	111.7
low	56.6	63.8	50.3	43.1	58.3	61.0	70.5	83.9

Kimberly-Clark Corporation
351 Phelps Drive
Irving, TX 75038
(972) 281-1200
Website: www.kimberly-clark.com

The Kroger Company

Ticker symbol: KR (NYSE) □ S&P rating: BBB □ Value Line financial strength rating: B++
Current yield: 1.5% □ Dividend raises, past 10 years: 7

Company Profile

Kroger is the nation's largest retail grocery store operator, with about 2,640 supermarkets, 768 convenience stores, and 320 specialty jewelry stores operated around the country. Supermarket operations account for about 94 percent of total revenue and are located in 34 states with a concentration in the Midwest (where it was founded) and in the South and West, where it grew mostly by acquisition. The company is dominant in the markets it serves, with a number one or two market share position in 36 of its 44 major markets.

Kroger operates through a series of store brands many of you will be familiar with but probably did not associate with the Kroger name, including King Soopers, City Market, Fred Meyer, Smiths, Fry's, Ralph's, Dillons, Smith's, Baker's, Food 4 Less, and an assortment of others totaling about two dozen business names. The company recently completed a merger with Harris Teeter, a large supermarket chain mainly in the mid-Atlantic and Southeast regions; this acquisition is not yet reflected in the store counts we present.

The typical Kroger supermarket is full service and well appointed with higher-margin specialty departments such as health foods, seafood, floral, and other perishables. The Fred Meyer stores carry a large assortment of general merchandise in addition to groceries, turning them into modern-era big-box department stores; the company has 128 stores in all that meet this format, mostly in the West. There are also 146 "warehouse" stores under the Food 4 Less brand and 78 "marketplace" stores with expanded offerings similar to Fred Meyer to complement the supermarkets. About 1,240 "supermarket fuel centers" and 1,949 pharmacies round out the supermarket picture. Finally, the company has a considerable presence in manufacturing its own store-branded food items, with 38 such plants located around the country.

Financial Highlights, Fiscal Year 2013

Kroger boasts that same-store supermarket sales have grown for 41 consecutive quarters, and this is a good track record particularly in light of the Great Recession and more recently, heightened competition from the likes of Wal-Mart, Target, and others. Same-store sales grew about 3 percent in FY2013, and in all, FY2013 revenues grew 1.8 percent—not bad for this type and size of business. Net earnings increased less than 1 percent, but this was due to a tough compare in FY2012, which had an extra week in the period and some beneficial accounting changes. More important are projections going forward, which now call for a 4.3 percent gain in FY2014 revenues and a 14 percent gain in per-share earnings. All of this has been helped along by substantial share buybacks, which have dropped share counts some 20 percent, or 130 million shares just since 2009. The buyback program will stop temporarily due to the Harris Teeter acquisition, but should resume once that's completed. The dividend, which commenced in 2006, should also continue to rise.

Reasons to Buy

Kroger has done a good job in a tough market. Major discount retailers like Wal-Mart and Target have stepped into the grocery business with a fairly significant price advantage, yet so far Kroger has been able to fend them off by focusing on product breadth, the shopping experience, and strategic price reductions. We also like the Fred Meyer quality grocery-plus-department-store format, a more pleasant and balanced shopping experience than either Walmart or Target and a format that Kroger would do well to roll out nationwide. The company also has a good toehold in the low-price warehouse food business with Food 4 Less.

This success has finally been recognized in the share price, which too has been helped along by the dramatic share buybacks. All told, this is a well-managed company that continues to dominate its niches.

Reasons for Caution

You can't think "full-service grocer" without raising the fear of competition from discounters, and the recent recession trained a lot of shoppers to look for the lowest possible prices, even if they had to go to two or three stores to complete a week's shopping. If the conventional grocery store format is condemned to the dustbin of retail history, Kroger could be vulnerable, but we feel it has enough clout and experience in new formats to adapt. The razor-thin 1.5 percent profit margins characteristic of this industry leave little room for error. The fact that the stock market has finally recognized Kroger's success makes the shares more volatile and less of a bargain—shop carefully.

SECTOR: **Retail**
BETA COEFFICIENT: **0.59**
10-YEAR COMPOUND EARNINGS PER-SHARE GROWTH: **3.5%**
10-YEAR COMPOUND DIVIDENDS PER-SHARE GROWTH: **NM**

	2006	2007	2008	2009	2010	2011	2012	2013
Revenues (bil)	66.1	70.2	76.0	76.7	82.1	90.4	96.7	98.5
Net income (mil)	1,115	1,181	1,249	1,122	1,118	1,192	1,423	1,445
Earnings per share	1.54	1.69	1.90	1.73	1.74	2.00	2.63	2.80
Dividends per share	0.26	0.30	0.36	0.37	0.40	0.44	0.53	0.63
Cash flow per share	3.39	3.83	4.15	4.12	4.38	5.05	5.98	6.10
Price: high	24.5	31.9	31.0	26.9	24.1	25.8	27.1	43.8
low	18.0	22.9	22.3	19.4	19.1	21.1	21.0	25.2

The Kroger Company
1014 Vine Street
Cincinnati, OH 45202
(513) 762-4000
Website: *www.kroger.com*

AGGRESSIVE GROWTH

Macy's, Inc.

Ticker symbol: M (NYSE) ❑ S&P rating: BBB- ❑ Value Line financial strength rating: B+ ❑ Current yield: 1.8% ❑ Dividend raises, past 10 years: 6

Company Profile

Macy's is now by far the largest operator of department stores in the U.S. The company operates under two brand names, Macy's and Bloomingdale's, and operates about 850 stores in 45 states, Puerto Rico, and Guam. Macy's has been assembled over the years from a large assortment of famed department store predecessors including Marshall Field, May, and a portfolio of names once under ownership of Federated Department Stores, including Lazarus, Weinstocks, Dillard, Abraham & Straus, I. Magnin, and others. The company, in current form, was assembled after Federated emerged from bankruptcy in 1992.

In addition to department stores, Macy's operates its own credit card operations and an internal merchandising group that, among other things, develops or licenses and markets a number of familiar proprietary brands such as Charter Club, Club Room, Hotel Collection, Tommy Hilfiger, Ellen Tracy, the Martha Stewart Collection, and more recently, Finish Line activewear. Private label brands now account for 20 percent of sales. The company has also embarked on a deliberate strategy to target the "millennial" age group (born between 1982 and 2001) with selected styles and brands—an important growth strategy as the department store demographic typically leaves this group out.

The company also operates 90 specialty stores including outlets and furniture stores. The sales mix is approximately 61 percent women's clothing, shoes, and accessories; 23 percent men's and children's; and 16 percent home and miscellaneous.

The online presence, macys.com, continues to grow and is strategically more integrated with the sales process, what it calls "omnichannel" shopping. It's easy to shop online, then see the product, pick it up, and importantly, pay the online price at the store. Such store pickups are thought to lead to more sales when at the store picking up merchandise. Also, omnichannel shopping, when done correctly, expands available stock, colors, and sizes, and produces logistical and supply-chain efficiencies, as orders can be flexibly filled from nearby stores if that makes sense.

Financial Highlights, Fiscal Year 2013

Macy's continues to ride a combination of economic recovery and a series of internal operational improvements to find a successful new growth trajectory in a business that many had given up on. That said, FY2013 top-line growth slowed a bit. The company reports comparable store sales gains of 2.8 percent, in line with expectations; the numbers below don't reflect that because of calendar adjustments. Net earnings, however, charged ahead 9 percent, and a substantial 5 percent share repurchase led to a 16 percent increase in per-share earnings. Gross margin ticked downward slightly; most earnings gains have come from operating costs, not gross margin improvements, suggesting that retail price competition (and discounting) are still substantial. The company is guiding for earnings per share in the $4.40–$4.50 range in FY2014 on 2.5–3 percent sales growth, and per-share earnings 12 percent ahead of that figure on similar sales gains through FY2015. Share buybacks continue to be a big part of the story, projected to continue at a 2–3 percent pace per year.

Reasons to Buy

Justifiably perhaps, most investors would perceive Macy's and the department store business to be yesterday's news, as big-box retailers and the Internet have taken over. True, those players have snatched important parts of the retail business, but the department store idea has made a comeback with more affluent, brand-conscious, and experience-conscious shoppers. The stores have been upgraded, merchandise assortments made more exciting and targeted to younger buyers, and service has improved. Merchandise assortments have been localized and are now more exciting and edgier and more aimed at the younger set. Department stores aren't just for grandma any longer. The company has managed its image and product well and has turned the new interest and a more scientific approach to management and execution into solid bottom-line results.

The integration of online and physical stores into a unified experience is one of the best such efforts we've seen. New technologies, such as large-screen digital displays and tablets in the hands of store personnel, are expanding the sales experience. We think the merchandise localization efforts (referred to by the company as "My Macy's") are working well. Additionally, the company has achieved savings by merging back-end inventories between stores and online channels—online orders can be filled with excess merchandise from stores, for example. Recent stumbles and lackluster market performance by competitors, notably J.C. Penney, have also helped.

In sum, we find a lot to like about the company's strategy, particularly in an industry where that word doesn't seem to be used as much as it could be. Cash flow continues to almost double reported per-share earnings and, through dividend increases and share buybacks, Macy's continues to lure investors through its front doors.

Reasons for Caution

The economy, of course, is always a risk, and any return to higher levels of unemployment, foreclosures, taxes, or any other factors that would make customers feel less flush will hurt. Macy's still relies heavily on promotional discounts and special sale events, which probably have become habitual shopping practice among many customers; we suspect that relatively few customers actually pay full price for most of what they buy. While Macy's is increasing its appeal to the younger set, the Internet is still a big contender here, although the growth in macys.com is encouraging.

SECTOR: **Retail**
BETA COEFFICIENT: **0.94**
10-YEAR COMPOUND EARNINGS PER-SHARE GROWTH: **6.0%**
10-YEAR COMPOUND DIVIDENDS PER-SHARE GROWTH: **13.0%**

	2006	2007	2008	2009	2010	2011	2012	2013
Revenues (mil)	26,970	26,313	24,892	23,489	25,003	26,405	27,686	27,931
Net income (mil)	1,147	970	543	595	867	1,238	1,410	1,539
Earnings per share	2.16	2.18	1.29	1.41	2.03	2.88	3.45	4.00
Dividends per share	0.52	0.53	0.20	0.20	0.20	0.35	0.80	0.90
Cash flow per share	4.85	5.42	4.33	4.29	4.77	5.61	6.34	7.01
Price: high	45.0	46.7	28.5	20.6	26.3	33.3	42.2	54.1
low	32.4	24.7	5.1	6.3	15.3	21.7	32.3	36.3

Macy's, Inc.
7 West Seventh St.
Cincinnati, OH 45202
(513) 579-7000
Website: *www.macys.com*

McCormick & Company, Inc.

Ticker symbol: MKC (NYSE) □ S&P rating: A- □ Value Line financial strength rating: A □ Current yield: 2.1% □ Dividend raises, past 10 years: 10

Company Profile

McCormick manufactures, markets, and distributes spices, herbs, seasonings, flavors, and flavor enhancers to consumers and to the global food industry. It is the largest such supplier in the world. Customers range from retail outlets and food manufacturers to foodservice businesses.

McCormick's U.S. Consumer business (about 62 percent of sales), its oldest and largest, manufactures consumer spices, herbs, extracts, proprietary seasoning blends, sauces, and marinades. Spices are sold under an assortment of recognizable brand names: McCormick, Lawry's, Zatarain's, Thai Kitchen, Simply Asia, Clubhouse, Billy Bee, Produce Partners, Golden Dipt, Old Bay, and Mojave. The company estimates its retail market share to be four times the nearest competitor.

Industrial customers include foodservice, food-processing businesses, and retail outlets. The Industrial segment was responsible for 81 percent of sales.

Many of the spices and herbs purchased by the company, such as black pepper, vanilla beans, cinnamon, and herbs and seeds, must be imported from countries such as India, Indonesia, Malaysia, Brazil, and the Malagasy Republic. Other ingredients such as paprika, dehydrated vegetables, onion, garlic, and food ingredients other than spices and herbs originate in the United States.

The company was founded in 1889 and has approximately 10,000 full-time employees in facilities located around the world. Major sales, distribution, and production facilities are located in North America and Europe. Additional facilities are based in Mexico, Central America, Australia, China, Singapore, Thailand, and South Africa. International sales account for about 43 percent of the total, and the company's products reach consumers in 125 countries. Emerging markets accounted for 15 percent of sales, up from 10 percent two years ago.

McCormick has been investing in more informative print and web content with recipes and other information to spur cooking with spices. The company recently sponsored a contest to mark their one hundred and twenty-fifth anniversary to collect 1.25 million stories about flavor. The company reports a 94 percent increase in recipe views on its U.S. website and a 24 percent increase in Europe. There is a lot of innovation in the area of flavors and flavor trends, and we also like a new packaging initiative—called Recipe Inspirations—to sell prepackaged spices set to cook a particular meal; this launch has been successful. All of these initiatives broaden the market to reach the millions of plain folks like us who weren't born with a wooden spoon.

Financial Highlights, Fiscal Year 2013

A 5 percent increase in Consumer sales, led by a China acquisition that increased sales more than 60 percent in that country, as well as some price adjustments and new products, in turn led the way to a 3 percent overall sales increase in FY2013. That was on top of a much larger 10 percent increase in FY2012 as people began eating at home more in response to the global recession; it seems like at least some of this shift has stuck. Industrial and foodservice revenues dropped 1 percent, however—due in part to the same shift, as sales particularly in the fast food segment softened.

Led by a modest buyback, per-share earnings increased about 3 percent after a similarly strong year in FY2012. For FY2014 and FY2015, the company expects marketing investments, product introductions, and international strength to spice up revenues and earnings, with revenues growing in the 4–6 percent range and earnings, while still a bit soft in FY2014 at 3 percent, up a stronger 9–10 percent in FY2015. This company looks like another of our "5 and 10" entries—10 percent earnings growth on 5 percent steady sales growth—and nothing appears to us more steady than the spice business.

Reasons to Buy

As a strong pure play in the seasonings business, McCormick is the largest branded producer of seasonings in North America, and the largest private-label producer of seasonings as well, giving the company a substantial level of price protection. McCormick is not just a producer, however—it also creates new seasoning products. In fact, every year since 2005, 13–18 percent of its industrial business sales have come from new products launched in the preceding three years. Keeping up with changing tastes requires McCormick to produce that new, hot flavor and to come up with new and interesting flavors and blends of existing seasonings. The company has also tapped existing niches, for example, reporting a 40 percent increase in flavorings sold into the Hispanic market since 2006. The company continues to acquire in the Asian market, this year with the agreement to acquire WAPC, more than doubling its reach in China.

On the consumer side, as amateur cooks ourselves we continue to feel that people would use more spices if they only knew how to use them. The website and its recipe offerings and the prepackaged Recipe Inspirations meal kits will get the less-experienced cooks using spices more effectively in their own cooking. Doesn't that prepackaged Country Herb Chicken & Dumplings, which deploys six prepackaged McCormick spices, sound good? In our view, these initiatives, combined with continuing growth in the health-conscious segment by learning to replace fat flavoring with spice flavoring, will add to a solid business base for the company.

McCormick's sales have increased every year for the past 50 years, and the company has paid a dividend every year since 1925. In 2013, it raised the dividend for the twenty-eighth consecutive year, and the size of the hikes is increasing. The profitability, stability, and defensive nature of the company and its business continue to present an attractive combination for investors.

Reasons for Caution

Downsides include the rising cost of ingredients and the sourcing of many of these ingredients in geopolitically unstable regions. Top-line growth is likely to remain moderate except by acquisition. While earnings and share-price growth have been steady, they don't add a lot of "spice" to an aggressive portfolio; too, in the past three years the price of the stock has been spiced up a bit by its success and the strength of the stock market. All that said, we don't see people's tastes in taste diminishing anytime soon.

SECTOR: **Consumer Staples**
BETA COEFFICIENT: **0.39**
10-YEAR COMPOUND EARNINGS PER-SHARE GROWTH: **9.0%**
10-YEAR COMPOUND DIVIDENDS PER-SHARE GROWTH: **11.5%**

	2006	2007	2008	2009	2010	2011	2012	2013
Revenues (mil)	2,716	2,916	3,177	3,192	3,339	3,650	4,014	4,123
Net income (mil)	202	230	282	311	356.3	380	408	418
Earnings per share	1.72	1.92	2.14	2.35	2.65	2.80	3.04	3.13
Dividends per share	0.72	0.80	0.88	0.96	1.04	1.12	1.24	1.36
Cash flow per share	2.45	2.64	2.83	3.08	3.39	3.55	3.85	4.00
Price: high	39.8	39.7	42.1	36.8	47.8	51.3	66.4	75.3
low	30.1	33.9	28.2	28.1	35.4	43.4	49.9	60.8

McCormick & Company, Inc.
18 Loveton Circle
P. O. Box 6000
Sparks, MD 21152–6000
(410) 771-7301
Website: *www.mccormick.com*

McDonald's Corporation

Ticker symbol: MCD (NYSE) ❑ S&P rating: A ❑ Value Line financial strength rating: A++ ❑ Current yield: 3.4% ❑ Dividend raises, past 10 years: 10

Company Profile

McDonald's Corporation operates and franchises the ubiquitous golden arches McDonald's restaurants. At 2013 year-end, there were approximately 35,429 restaurants in 118 countries, a 4 percent rise from 34,010 at the end of 2012. Some 81 percent of these restaurants are operated by franchisees; the remainder by the company. Franchisees pay for and own the equipment, signs, and interior of the businesses and are required to reinvest in them from time to time. The company owns the land and building or secures leases for both company-operated and franchised restaurant sites.

Revenues to the company come in the form of sales from company-owned stores and rents, fees, royalties, and other revenue streams from the franchisees. The company continues to sell off company stores to increase the dominance of the franchising business, which benefits cash flow and reduces operational costs and exposure to commodities prices.

The company continues to dominate the fast food segment overall, with market share approaching 50 percent in the hamburger subsegment. That said, as is obvious for anyone living almost anywhere near a McDonald's restaurant, competition is fierce, and new ideas like Chipotle (a McDonald's spinoff in 2006) are giving the company a run for its money. "Healthy eating" trends have also led the company to tinker with its menu, and the relatively modest employment and income advances in its principal clientele have provided some headwinds of late.

McDonald's, however, is one of the strongest brands in the business and continues to benefit from a strong international presence. An iconic brand worldwide, the company generates about 69 percent of its revenue and 57 percent of profits outside the United States.

Financial Highlights, Fiscal Year 2013

FY2013 was another mixed deal for McDonald's. Sales eked out another paltry 2 percent gain to $28.1 billion, and per-share earnings, helped along by a 2.5 percent share buyback, resumed a rise of about 3.5 percent. Increased food costs and operating expenses related to store remodels and modest expansion also reduced operating and net margins slightly. For FY2014 the company will continue to expand the franchise model, experiment with new menu innovations, remodel restaurants, and reduce share counts, but it will still encounter the headwinds of competition and relatively paltry income gains among its primary consumer base. On the positive side, economic recovery in Europe should reverse a trend of modest declines in that geography. The company will continue its international expansion with its first opening in Vietnam. These many moving parts are expected to lead to a slightly more healthy revenue gain approaching 4 percent, with per-share earnings advancing about 5.5 percent to $5.85, including the effects of another 1.5 percent share repurchase.

Reasons to Buy

McDonald's continues to be a slow but steady market leader in this business, albeit with some growth headwinds tied to popularity of its menus with younger, more affluent, and more health-conscious constituents. We've been through this cycle before, where the company hits a flat spot both in the marketplace and in the financial markets, only to break forward with a stronger cycle. In 2003, the company ran into an unprecedented low of $12 (recently, $95) in one of these troughs, and while the vultures circled, McDonald's responded with menu changes,

store format improvements, and a new strategy aimed at strengthening its franchisee base. In addition, the company has always led in innovative operational models, including food preparation technology, staffing and sourcing models, and promotional campaigns—we expect this to continue. We don't think they'll succeed in becoming the next Starbucks (as they once tried to) but will be the best at what they do do as time goes on, in our opinion.

Meanwhile, the company continues to dish up strong cash returns to shareholders, retiring almost a quarter of its share count since 2003 and increasing its dividend some eight-fold during this time. McDonald's continues to be an iconic name in overseas markets and continues to offer "quality, service, convenience, and value" to restaurant-goers worldwide—and good value to shareholders in the process.

Reasons for Caution

If the reasons behind the current flat spot turn out to be permanent, that is, if people permanently abandon the standard fast-hamburger-served-up-in-plastic-environs format regardless of menu additions, the slowdown may become chronic. Too, restaurant remodels are expensive, and high food ingredient prices and expanding menu complexity may affect margins, though in total margins are projected to be stable for the near future. There are far more exciting plays in the restaurant sector, but we also feel that most of them go stale in rather short order; McDonald's is a strong cash return play for the longer term with a historically decent growth pattern and ability to bounce back from periods of malaise.

SECTOR: **Restaurants**
BETA COEFFICIENT: **0.28**
10-YEAR COMPOUND EARNINGS PER-SHARE GROWTH: **14.0%**
10-YEAR COMPOUND DIVIDENDS PER-SHARE GROWTH: **27.0%**

	2006	**2007**	**2008**	**2009**	**2010**	**2011**	**2012**	**2013**
Revenues (mil)	21,586	22,787	23,522	22,745	24,075	27,008	27,567	28,106
Net income (mil)	2,873	3,522	4,201	4,451	4,970	5,503	5,465	5,586
Earnings per share	2.30	2.91	3.67	4.11	4.60	5.27	5.36	5.55
Dividends per share	1.00	1.50	1.63	2.05	2.26	2.53	2.87	3.12
Cash flow per share	3.43	4.06	4.85	5.20	5.95	6.75	6.95	7.30
Price: high	44.7	63.7	67.0	64.8	80.9	101.0	102.2	103.7
low	31.7	42.3	45.8	50.4	61.1	72.1	83.3	89.3

McDonald's Corporation
One McDonald's Plaza
Oak Brook, IL 60523
(630) 623-3000
Website: *www.mcdonalds.com*

McKesson Corporation

Ticker symbol: MCK (NYSE) ❑ S&P rating: A– ❑ Value Line financial strength rating: A++
Current yield: 0.5% ❑ Dividend raises, past 10 years: 5

Company Profile

McKesson Corporation is America's oldest and largest health-care services company and engages in two distinct businesses to support the health-care industry. Pharmaceutical and medical-surgical supply distribution is the first and by far the largest business: The company is the largest such distributor in North America. The company delivers to approximately 40,000 pharmaceutical outlets as well as hospitals and clinics throughout North America from 28 domestic and 17 Canadian distribution facilities.

Second, and not to be ignored, is a technology solutions business that provides clinical systems, analytics, clinical decision support, medical necessity and utilization management tools, electronic medical records, physical and financial supply-chain management, and connectivity solutions to hospitals, pharmacies, and an assortment of health-care providers. While the distribution business continues to provide 97 percent of the company's revenue, the information technology business is no less important and is a $3.4 billion business all by itself. McKesson's software and hardware IT solutions are installed in some 76 percent of the nation's

hospitals with more than 200 beds and 52 percent of hospitals overall.

The company offers products and services covering most aspects of pharmacy and drug distribution, including not only physical distribution and supply-chain services but also a line of proprietary generics and automated dispensing systems, record-keeping systems, and outsourcing services used in retail and hospital pharmacy operations.

McKesson has been busy acquiring other related businesses, large and small—and all good fits in our opinion. In late 2010, the company completed a $2.16 billion acquisition of U.S. Oncology, a distributor of products targeted at the cancer-care industry. With that acquisition, McKesson became the leading supplier of materials, technology, and operational platforms to the oncological community, and that acquisition has performed well. In early 2012, the company acquired the Katz Group Canada, a major distributor supplying more than 1,000 Canadian pharmacies. The company finalized the acquisition of medical supplies distributor PSS World Medical during FY2013. Finally, in early 2014, the company completed the acquisition of German pharmaceutical distributor Celesio, gaining a strong entry into the international wholesale, retail, and generic distribution markets, particularly in Europe.

Financial Highlights, Fiscal Year 2013

The McKesson business is a pure play in health care and about as close to recession-proof as one can become, and on top of that, exhibited its healthy growth and growth potential in 2013. Revenues were up a bit over 8 percent, although some of this is due to acquisitions. As a high-volume, low-margin business, a very slight improvement in net profit margins from 1.2 percent to 1.4 percent delivered a hefty 12.7 percent increase in net profit. Similar gains in margins are projected over the next few years, along with projected share buybacks, which in ten years' time will lower share counts by approximately a third. That said, per-share earnings guidance for FY2014, which had previously been given at $8.40–$8.70, was lowered to $8.05–$8.20 primarily due to a Canadian tax issue and a charge in the Technology Solutions segment due to some regulatory delays on a new software platform. Neither of these reasons for lowering guidance indicates declining operational performance.

Reasons to Buy

The distribution business has proven to be rock solid and will likely continue that way. Demographics and the addition of millions to the insured health-care rolls will keep demand moving in the right direction, and acquisitions have strengthened that position in domestic and especially international markets. McKesson dominates its niches and is a go-to provider of much of what hospitals and clinics need to operate. It holds market leader position in several important market categories, including number one in pharmaceutical distribution in U.S. and Canada, number one in generic pharmaceutical distribution, number one in hospital automation, number one in medical management software and services to payers—you get the idea.

Additionally, hospitals and other health-care providers are starting to get the memo that it is time to improve utilization and operational efficiency, and McKesson's technology solutions are hard to ignore, although many might do so at first glance, as they are only 3 percent of the business. As most distributors do, McKesson operates on very thin margins; the expansion of technology services and generic equivalent drugs should eventually become a growth driver as efficiency measures continue to catch on. The company has a strong track record of stability and operational excellence and is well managed; the stock has many of the characteristics of a true long-term equity holding.

Reasons for Caution

Some, and perhaps much, of the optimism previously mentioned has already been priced into the stock, and truly it's been one of our best performers in the three-year residence on our *100 Best Stocks* list, almost tripling in value over that time frame. As for many of the stocks on our list, this indicates one should be patient to find a good entry point. The relatively deliberate growth pace in its two primary businesses suggests the temptation of acquisitions; the company has done okay here thus far but there is always some danger. Additionally, and as mentioned, the company does operate on thin margins and as such has a low tolerance for mistakes or major changes in the health-care space that could be brought on by legislation or regulation. While we applaud the aggressive buyback strategy, we'd like to see a bit more return to shareholders in the form of cash dividends; that said, the company has quadrupled the indicated dividend since 2007.

SECTOR: **Health Care**
BETA COEFFICIENT: **0.63**
10-YEAR COMPOUND EARNINGS PER-SHARE GROWTH: **14.5%**
10-YEAR COMPOUND DIVIDENDS PER-SHARE GROWTH: **12.0%**

	2006	2007	2008	2009	2010	2011	2012	2013
Revenues (mil)	92,977	101,703	106,632	108,702	112,084	121,010	122,455	132,650
Net income (mil)	881	1,021	1,194	1,251	1,316	1,463	1,516	1,920
Earnings per share	2.89	3.43	4.28	4.58	5.00	6.05	6.33	8.50
Dividends per share	0.24	0.24	0.48	0.48	0.72	0.76	0.80	0.96
Cash flow per share	3.99	5.03	6.03	6.37	7.18	8.40	9.30	11.15
Price: high	55.1	68.4	68.4	65.0	71.5	87.3	100.0	166.6
low	44.5	50.5	28.3	33.1	57.2	66.6	74.9	96.7

McKesson Corporation
One Post Street
San Francisco, CA 94104
(415) 983-8300
Website: *www.mckesson.com*

AGGRESSIVE GROWTH

Medtronic, Inc.

Ticker symbol: MDT (NYSE) □ S&P rating: A+ □ Value Line financial strength rating: A++
Current yield: 1.9% □ Dividend raises, past 10 years: 10

Company Profile

Medtronic is the world's largest manufacturer of implantable medical devices and is a leading medical technology company, providing lifelong solutions to "alleviate pain, restore health, and extend life," primarily for people with chronic diseases.

The company is organized into two product groups: the Cardiovascular Group (which accounts for 52 percent of revenues) and the Restorative Therapies Group (48 percent). There are four segments within each group. First, the Cardiovascular Group:

■ Cardiac Rhythm Disease Management (30 percent of FY2013 sales) develops products that restore and regulate a patient's heart rhythm as well as improve the heart's pumping function, such as implantable pacemakers, defibrillators, Internet and non-Internet–based monitoring and diagnostic devices. A new implantable cardiac monitor 80 percent smaller than competing products was recently approved by the FDA, exemplifying the company's R&D leadership in this industry.

■ The Coronary segment (11 percent) includes therapies to treat coronary artery disease and hypertension, including balloon angioplasty catheters, guide catheters, diagnostic catheters, and guidewires.

■ The Structural Heart segment (7 percent) produces products and therapies to treat heart valve disorders and to repair and replace heart valves, some through catheters without chest incisions. The unit also markets tools to assist heart surgeons during surgery, including circulatory support systems, heart positioners and tissue stabilizers, and ablation tools.

■ The Endovascular segment (5 percent) produces stent graft and angioplasty systems to treat various heart and arterial conditions.

The Restorative Therapies Group includes:

■ Spine (19 percent) develops and manufactures products that treat a variety of disorders of the cranium and spine, including traumatically induced conditions, deformities, herniated discs and other disc diseases, osteoporosis, and tumors. The Biologics business is the global leader in biologics regeneration and pain therapies across a variety of musculoskeletal applications including spine, orthopedic trauma, and dental.

- Neuromodulation (11 percent) employs technologies used in heart electrical stimulation to treat diseases of the central nervous system. It offers therapies for movement disorders; chronic pain; urological and gastroenterological disorders, including incontinence, enlarged prostate, and gastroesophageal reflux disease (GERD); and psychological diseases.
- Diabetes (9 percent) offers advanced diabetes management solutions, including insulin pump therapy, glucose monitoring systems, and treatment management software.
- Surgical Technologies (9 percent) develops therapies for ear, nose, and throat–related diseases and certain neurological disorders; among them are precision image-guided surgical systems.

The company operates in 140 countries, with about 45 percent of revenues coming from outside the U.S. and 11 percent from emerging markets. Research and Development expenses are about 10 percent of sales,

and 38 percent of revenues on average come from products introduced in the past three years.

Financial Highlights, Fiscal Year 2013

Cost containment measures, currency effects, and some increased competition continued to hold the top line to low- to mid-single-digit increases; FY2013 was no exception with a 2.5 percent revenue increase realized for the year, and increases projected in the 3.5–4 percent range going into FY2015. Hurt as much as anything by the new 2.3 percent Affordable Care Act medical device tax but helped along a bit by share repurchases, per-share earnings logged a historically modest 2.7 percent increase. The company continued its regular 7–8 percent dividend increases. Helped along by efficiency measures and stronger operating margins, increased demand due to the ACA, and continued share repurchases in the 1.5 percent per year range, per-share earnings look to be on track to grow in the 6–8 percent range through FY2015.

Reasons to Buy

The name Medtronic continues to be synonymous with medical technology; the company remains one of the pure plays in the health-care technology space. That said, its solid financials and steady growth make it far different from a typical tech stock. The company gets 45 percent of its sales overseas, and international expansion continues to be part of the story, especially in emerging markets, as MDT-supported medical procedures become mainstream. The R&D footprint, with 9,000 employed scientists and 9.4 percent of revenues spent on R&D, also bode well for the future, and there are a number of important new products in the pipeline.

The company is a pioneer technology leader and a successful innovator in many surgical and implant technologies. The company's DBS (Deep Brain Stimulation) systems treat disorders by modulating the nervous system with electrical stimulation, chemicals, and biological agents delivered in precise amounts to specific sites in the brain and spinal cord. This system has been used successfully to treat the most severe symptoms of conditions such as Parkinson's disease, and this and other new products, especially in the neuromodulation segment, should enhance prospects.

Reasons for Caution

Medtronic may be entering the mature life-cycle phase of many of its product lines, meaning future growth opportunities may be harder to come by. The trend toward improved utilization (translation: medical cost abatement) in the United States is probably here to stay, but deferred procedures will be made up at some point. Sales and earnings growth are steady but both lackluster. This is a slow, steady performer, and we continue to hope that the company doesn't get too aggressive with acquisitions and instead focuses on making the most of its internally generated new products and international growth opportunities.

SECTOR: **Health Care**
BETA COEFFICIENT: **1.07**
10-YEAR COMPOUND EARNINGS PER-SHARE GROWTH: **11.0%**
10-YEAR COMPOUND DIVIDENDS PER-SHARE GROWTH: **16.0%**

	2006	2007	2008	2009	2010	2011	2012	2013
Revenues (mil)	12,299	13,515	14,599	15,817	15,933	16,184	16,590	17,000
Net income (mil)	2,798	2,984	3,282	3,576	3,647	3,447	3,857	3,890
Earnings per share	2.21	2.41	2.61	2.92	3.22	3.46	3.75	3.85
Dividends per share	0.41	0.47	0.63	0.82	0.90	0.97	1.04	1.12
Cash flow per share	2.96	3.22	3.45	3.96	4.16	4.13	4.60	4.70
Price: high	59.9	58.0	57.0	44.9	46.7	43.3	44.6	58.8
low	42.4	44.9	28.3	24.1	30.8	30.2	35.7	41.2

Medtronic, Inc.
710 Medtronic Parkway
Minneapolis, MN 55432–5604
(763) 514-4000
Website: *www.medtronic.com*

AGGRESSIVE GROWTH

Microchip Technology, Inc.

Ticker symbol: MCHP (NASDAQ) ❑ S&P rating: NR ❑ Value Line financial strength rating: B++
Current yield: 3.0% ❑ Dividend raises, past 10 years: 10

Company Profile

Your washing machine senses the load, adjusts the wash time and temperature accordingly, and tells you when it's done. Your refrigerator expands or contracts its power cycle according to outside temperature and the time of day to save on peak power costs. Your car shows you what it's about to back up into and may even prevent such a collision in the first place. Lighting comes on automatically as you walk by the freezer case in the grocery. And why not, someday, in every room of your house?

This "Internet of things," this Star Wars world of all of our stuff connected to all our other stuff and doing our thinking for us is really coming. Wave your hands the right way and the force will be with you, or perhaps a Microchip Technology–powered sensor will turn the lights on for you. We don't know for sure if your washing machine will ever talk directly to your refrigerator, but that aside, the application possibilities are almost endless.

Microchip Technology is a leading manufacturer and supplier of specialized semiconductor products primarily embedded as controllers, processors, or memory into products, mostly products other than computers. The company's devices, many of which are customizable, custom-made, or programmable, sense motion, temperature, touch, proximity, and other environmental conditions, process the information and control the device accordingly. Applications number literally in the thousands but are concentrated in automotive, communications, consumer product, appliance, lighting, medical, safety and security, and power and energy management products. Microchip products are typically small in size (the smallest is 1.5–2.5 millimeters), low power, low cost, and capable of operating reliably in extreme conditions. The company offers a full suite of design assistance, tools, and consulting services to help customers, usually OEM manufacturers, develop the best applications. They position these services as "low-risk product development" resources for their customers. Microchip owns most of its manufacturing capability in four plants, two in Arizona, one in Oregon, and one in Thailand, as part of a deliberate strategy to increase process yields and shorten cycle times.

Most but not all products are shipped "off the shelf" with short cycle times or as a scheduled production. R&D accounts for about 16 percent of revenues. As the company sells primarily to other OEM electronic product manufacturers, about 83 percent of sales are to international customers; about 27 percent are to China. Technology licensing accounts for about 5 percent of revenues.

Financial Highlights, Fiscal Year 2013

Design wins, market share gains, a general uptick in the manufacturing economy, and a 5 percent rise in average selling prices led to a 15.8 percent sales gain in FY2013. However, it should be noted that acquisitions accounted for about two-thirds of that gain. Net income, again helped by acquisitions, rose about 30 percent, while a slight increase in share count held the per-share earnings increase to 27 percent. Going forward into 2015, the company projects about a 7 percent top-line growth rate with earnings ahead in the 7–10 percent range each year. Microchip has made three moderate-sized acquisitions in the past two years to fill out its product offerings.

Reasons to Buy

The Internet of things is upon us, or at least, just around the corner. One doesn't have to look hard to find "smart" products. They're almost everywhere. Not just your smartphone, but your appliances, car, climate control system, alarm system, and in elevators, airplanes, airports, hospitals—you name it. We like companies that make the things that make things work, and Microchip seems well positioned as a leading supplier of all this intelligence as "smart" moves far beyond the "smartphone."

We were hesitant to include a semiconductor company on our list. Development and manufacturing costs are high, especially if a company owns its own "fabs"—manufacturing facilities—and product cycles are short. There is plenty of competition everywhere for most products, much of it from lower-cost producers in Asia. Inventory cycles can also play havoc with semiconductor producers, who do best by producing in large quantities. Microchip, in our view, has overcome a lot of that by choosing high value-add niches and by offering plenty of design and technical support to go along with the product.

All that said—and for many of these reasons—it has also become a tradition for capital-intensive semiconductor companies to not pay dividends or much else in the way of cash returns to shareholders. Capital is gobbled up internally for what seems to be endless new investments in fab capacity, design tools, and ever more expensive materials and supplies. Microchip has bucked that trend—how many semiconductor firms have paid a dividend, let alone raised it, for ten consecutive years?

Reasons for Caution

Despite what we said above, semiconductor makers will always endure the burdens of high capital requirements, short product cycles, inventory cycles of OEMs and distributors, and to no small degree the economy as a whole. Competition, especially from low-cost foreign suppliers, is keen in all semiconductor markets, although again Microchip has worked hard to make its offering more "whole" with design assistance and short lead times, both of which have pleased its customers. Intellectual property is also a risk, as the company has already encountered overseas reverse-engineered copies of its products.

SECTOR: **Technology**
BETA COEFFICIENT: **1.10**
10-YEAR COMPOUND EARNINGS PER-SHARE GROWTH: **12.5%**
10-YEAR COMPOUND DIVIDENDS PER-SHARE GROWTH: **21.0%**

	2006	2007	2008	2009	2010	2011	2012	2013
Revenues (mil)	1,040	1,036	903	948	1,487	1,383	1,606	1,920
Net income (mil)	305	304	206	213	430	337	389	505
Earnings per share	1.36	1.43	1.11	1.14	2.21	1.65	1.89	2.40
Dividends per share	0.97	1.21	1.35	1.36	1.37	1.39	1.41	1.42
Cash flow per share	1.94	2.19	1.66	1.63	2.83	2.26	3.02	3.50
Price: high	36.6	42.5	38.4	29.6	36.4	41.5	38.9	44.9
low	30.6	27.5	16.3	16.2	25.5	29.3	28.9	32.4

Microchip Technology, Inc.
2355 West Chandler Blvd.
Chandler, AZ 85224
(480) 792-7200
Website: *www.microchip.com*

Monsanto Company

Ticker symbol: MON (NYSE) ❑ S&P Rating: A+ ❑ Value Line financial strength rating: A+
Current yield: 1.5% ❑ Dividend raises, past 10 years: 9

Company Profile

Monsanto was once a major chemical company with a broad pedigree ranging from saccharine to sulfuric acid to Agent Orange and DDT. Monsanto was absorbed into Pharmacia & Upjohn in 2000, which kept its pharmaceutical products and spun off the agricultural products business into a "new" Monsanto in 2002. Today's Monsanto provides a set of leading-edge, technology-based agricultural products for use in farming in the United States and overseas. The company broadly views its business as providing a system of seeds, biotechnology trait products, and herbicides mainly to farmers to produce better-quality and healthier foods and animal feedstocks while expanding yields and reducing the costs of farming.

The company has two primary business segments: Seeds and Genomics, and Agricultural Productivity. The Seeds and Genomics segment (70 percent of FY2013 revenues) produces seeds for a host of crops, most importantly corn and soybeans, but also canola, cotton, and a variety of vegetable and fruit seeds. Most of the seed products are bioengineered to provide greater yields and to be more resistant to insects and weeds. Familiar to many consumers, especially those who travel in the Midwest, is the DeKalb seed brand, but there are many others.

The Agricultural Productivity segment (30 percent) offers glyphosate-based herbicides, known as Roundup to most of us, for agricultural, industrial, and residential lawn and garden applications. Beyond this market-leading product, the division also offers other selective herbicides for control of pre-emergent annual grass and small seeded broadleaf weeds in corn and other crops. Monsanto owns many of the major brands in both seed and herbicide markets. The company also partners with other agricultural and chemical companies such as Cargill, BASF, and Biotechnology, Inc. to develop other high-tech agricultural and food-processing solutions.

In recent years, the company underwent some upheaval as patents on its flagship Roundup herbicide system expired, almost immediately followed by reports that certain weeds were developing immunity to it anyhow, and cheaper foreign competitors were starting to invade its garden. Beyond that, Monsanto alienated some of its farmer base with pricing and marketing practices for its seed and herbicide systems. These reports and a sag in earnings brought the stock price from the 70s to the mid-40s in mid-2010. Since then, the company has taken steps to modernize its herbicide offerings and become less dependent on them, to develop the core seed businesses further, and to focus on developing markets like Latin America and China, making it less dependent on the "one-trick" Roundup pony. The company also diversified into the agricultural consulting, analytics, and decision support business by acquiring the Climate Corporation.

Financial Highlights, Fiscal Year 2013

After a weak and somewhat unsettling year in FY2010, Monsanto started its comeback to previous levels in FY2011 but the comeback started first on the top line, while profits lagged as the Roundup franchise lost some of its luster. In FY2012, the comeback really started to grow and bear fruit, led by the Seeds and Genomics segment and international expansion, particularly in Latin America. The drought, which increased demand for genetically modified seed stocks, created a strong "macro" environment for Monsanto products. Interestingly, the post-drought glut in farm production and the resulting decline of crop price through 2013 and into 2014 have led to more of the same—farmers seek Monsanto solutions to reduce costs and produce efficiently and more

farmers in more regions of the world are adopting Monsanto solutions as demand for farm products increases.

All of that led to a strong FY2013, really a strong three-year stretch after the 2010 doldrums, with earnings ahead more than 20 percent three years in a row. Sales climbed 10 percent in FY2013, while per-share earnings, helped by a modest buyback, rose 22.7 percent. The company generated some $2 billion in free cash flow, a sizeable figure on $15 billion in sales.

For FY2014 the company sees revenue growth in the 7–8 percent range, slowing a bit in FY2015; per-share earnings, helped along by moderate share buybacks and operational efficiencies, up in the 14–16 percent range annually.

Reasons to Buy

Monsanto will provide business schools with an excellent case study in becoming too dependent on one product and watching that product decline—and responding by retrenching back to its core strengths for a resurgence. The company continues to lead in innovation and technology applied to agricultural use and continues to advance in biotech applications in its Seeds and Genomics segment while advancing its products in the Agricultural Productivity segment with glyphosate-related products as well. All of this is working in the backdrop of growing food demand from growing middle classes on a growing global scale. Monsanto doesn't own the "agriculture tech" space outright but clearly plays a leadership role; the company has stated a goal to grow corn, soybean, cotton, and canola yields by 2030, thus becoming a leading agent of efficiency and change. When that formula is also profitable, great things can happen, and they have up to now—revenues, margins earnings, cash flow, and dividends are all moving in the right direction at an accelerating pace. The company surprised many by coming out ahead financially even with the U.S. drought, and then as crop prices fell in the wake of the drought.

Reasons for Caution

Not everyone—including its customer base of farmers—is happy with Monsanto. Many have been outspoken for years about the power and practices of the company, and some of that angst has turned into possible legal headwinds. More recently—and a bit more concerning—is the global movement against "GMO" foods, that is, genetically modified food products. The movement has strengthened markets for organically grown products and created an upswell of negative perceptions about the Monsanto system (and those of competitors as well). To date, these issues are presenting little more than a PR challenge for the company, which has started to incorporate "health" into its research and marketing messages, but it all bears watching. We'd also like to see a little more cash returned to investors as dividends or share buybacks, but we can also see that the company is investing its profits in its own business successfully.

SECTOR: Industrials
BETA COEFFICIENT: 1.40
10-YEAR COMPOUND EARNINGS PER-SHARE GROWTH: 20.0%
10-YEAR COMPOUND DIVIDENDS PER-SHARE GROWTH: 18.5%

	2006	2007	2008	2009	2010	2011	2012	2013
Revenues (mil)	7,344	8,563	11,365	11,724	10,502	11,822	13,516	14,861
Net income (mil)	722.1	1,027	1,895	2,448	1,327	1,615	1,997	2,450
Earnings per share	1.31	1.98	3.39	4.41	2.41	2.93	3.70	4.54
Dividends per share	0.34	0.55	0.83	1.01	1.08	1.14	1.28	1.56
Cash flow per share	2.28	2.85	4.50	5.49	3.57	4.07	4.90	5.79
Price: high	53.5	116.3	145.8	93.4	87.1	78.7	94.8	116.8
low	37.9	49.1	63.5	66.6	44.6	58.9	69.7	94.0

Monsanto Company
800 North Lindbergh Boulevard
St Louis, MO 63167
(314) 694-1000
Website: www.monsanto.com

Mosaic Company

Ticker symbol: MOS (NYSE) ❑ S&P rating: BBB ❑ Value Line financial strength rating: A ❑ Current yield: 2.1% ❑ Dividend raises, past 10 years: 3

Company Profile

We generally shy away from commodities producers. Why? Because it's hard to establish a brand or a competitive advantage. Typically the business becomes a race to the bottom, where the low-cost producer wins. But if you're the low-cost producer, you probably aren't making much money—and you probably won't stay the low-cost producer for long.

We prefer companies that have other routes to establishing—and maintaining—a competitive advantage. But there are commodities, and then there are *strategic* commodities. What do we mean by that? Well, some commodities are more important—and in more constrained supply—than others. If a company can invest itself wholly in these commodities, can own the largest and most efficient mines and establish a dominant market share and position, it will establish a competitive advantage. It can further that advantage by drip-irrigating a little innovation into the mix, as Mosaic has done by introducing a hybridized multi-ingredient fertilizer, nutrient, and pH control tablet known as "Microsessentials."

Although these strategies suffered something of a setback late in FY2013 (and we'll get to that), that's where the Mosaic Company comes in. Mosaic, formed in 2004 through a merger of Cargill's fertilizer operations with IMC Global, is the dominant world producer in the so-called "P+K" market—that's phosphorus and potassium, for those of you who shied away from high school chemistry. And in case you're not clear on why P and K are important, they are vital fertilizer ingredients and hence essential to most of the world's agriculture production. Plants require more potassium than any other nutrient besides nitrogen, and it is important to root-system development and many processes that form plant starch and proteins. Potassium is mined and sold in its oxide form known more popularly as potash. Phosphorus is a vital component of photosynthesis for plant metabolism and growth.

Mosaic is the largest combined P+K producer in the world. About two-thirds of the business is phosphorus and a third potash. Both minerals are produced commercially in a limited number of places in the world. Mosaic has interests in the important locations in North and South America, notably Florida phosphorus mines and potash mines in Saskatchewan, Michigan, New Mexico, and Peru. Through a network of processing and packaging plants in several countries, the company sells its product in approximately 40 countries. As a percentage of FY2013 sales, North America accounted for 51 percent, Asia 31 percent, Latin America 15 percent, and the rest 3 percent. The company is particularly enthused about growth in Brazil, and recently acquired a fertilizer distribution business there from Archer Daniels Midland (another *100 Best* stock).

Although the company suffered a bit with the 2012 drought in the U.S., the waters were calm and the sailing was smooth in the potash markets until Russia's Uralkali, a major producer, apparently got into a tiff with Belarus's Belaruskali, another major producer, and broke their cartel agreement. Uralkali announced a new business strategy emphasizing volume over price, leading to stiff 25–40 percent declines in world potash prices, undercutting Mosaic. (Actually Mosaic's own potash cartel formed with Potash Corp of Saskatchewan and Agrium known as "Canpotex.") Anyway, the new strategy disrupted world potash prices and lured away lucrative long-term contracts particularly in Asia, causing a 20 percent dent in Mosaic's stock price, putting it near the bottom of our performance

list, and casting some doubt about the future. We think global potash markets will eventually recover, particularly as higher-cost producers take product off the market and as Uralkali reevaluates its strategy. Until then, we'll continue to nourish this pick on our *100 Best Stocks* list.

As if this wasn't enough news, the company acquired the phosphate business of CF Industries for $1.2 billion, adding almost 20 percent to its phosphate mining capacity, a foresighted move to increase operating efficiency and reduce future capital expenditures as phosphate prices eventually recover.

Financial Highlights, Fiscal Year 2013

Not surprisingly, Mosaic's fortunes are driven by what is happening in the agriculture world and the news from down on the farm. It was bad in 2012, then especially good as the 2013 planting season unfolded, a welcome recovery from 2012. Only problem is that so much was planted that crop prices faltered, some 40 percent for corn alone. Farmers who get less for their crops spend less on fertilizer; that with the Uralkali strategy left FY2013 pretty much a year to plow under, as it were.

As such, FY2013 revenues shriveled up some 10 percent, and earnings wilted a similar amount—not a year to write home about. Although world prices for potash and phosphate materials stayed soft all year, volumes started to improve late in the year, as did prices, as did production efficiencies, as did a working off of old distributor inventories left over from 2012, particularly in China and India. Revenues will likely be flat to slightly up for FY2014, and recovering most of the 10 percent lost in FY2013 out in FY2015. While margins will remain somewhat diminished by historical standards, production efficiencies and firming prices are likely to return the company to well past the current level of sales and earnings a few years from now.

The company, which bought back 5 percent of its shares in FY2011, switched shareholder return "horses," doubling its dividend twice during FY2012 to an indicated $1.00 per share per year. That dividend is expected to increase in the 15 percent range annually, and the company also announced a resumption of its share repurchase program with a $1 billion commitment and a projected reduction of 10–15 percent of its shares over the next few years.

Reasons to Buy

Particularly for those interested in investing in commodities, we think this is some of the most fertile ground on which to stand. Demand for food will only increase over time, and Mosaic is the largest of ten world producers of P+K. The combination of prime mining sites, size, and operational efficiency in its processing and distribution operations should lead to at least maintaining, if not expanding, market share. We enthusiastically applaud the dividend hikes and the dedication to returning cash to shareholders in general, whatever form that may take.

Reasons for Caution

Commodity markets and commodity producers are inherently volatile, and any reduction in planting or backup in inventory, not to mention overall global economic weakness or short-term droughts as experienced in the U.S., can drive prices down in a heartbeat. Worse, a commodity volume and price war such as the one that erupted during FY2013 can be particularly damaging if it blows the assumptions of the most carefully laid business plans and strategies. We think the Uralkali disruption will go away sooner than many expect, particularly if crop prices firm again; the natural economics of world food demand and supply will take over.

SECTOR: **Materials**
BETA COEFFICIENT: **1.52**
10-YEAR COMPOUND EARNINGS PER-SHARE GROWTH: **19.5%**
10-YEAR COMPOUND DIVIDENDS PER-SHARE GROWTH: **NM**

	2006	**2007**	**2008**	**2009**	**2010**	**2011**	**2012**	**2013**
Revenues (mil)	5,304	5,774	9,812	10,298	6,759	9,937	11,108	9,974
Net income (mil)	82.6	342.5	1,962.2	1,909.7	862.8	1,942.2	1,930	1,744
Earnings per share	0.18	0.80	4.38	4.28	1.93	4.34	4.42	4.09
Dividends per share	—	—	—	0.20	0.20	0.20	0.28	1.00
Cash flow per share	1.15	1.67	5.20	5.11	2.94	5.35	5.73	5.51
Price: high	23.5	97.6	103.3	62.5	76.9	59.5	62.0	64.6
low	13.3	19.5	21.9	31.2	37.7	44.9	44.4	39.8

The Mosaic Company
Atria Corporate Center
Suite E490
3033 Campus Drive
Plymouth, MN 55441
(763) 577-2700
Website: *www.mosaicco.com*

NextEra Energy, Inc.

Ticker symbol: NEE (NYSE) □ S&P rating: A- □ Value Line financial strength rating: A □ Current yield: 3.1% □ Dividend raises, past 10 years: 10

Company Profile

NextEra is a full-service utility, power-generating unit, and utility services provider built around the utility stalwart Florida Power & Light, which formally changed its name to NextEra in 2010. NextEra not only represents an evolution in name but also a hint about how the company does business and expects to do business in the future as a leader in clean and large-scale alternative energy sourcing for the power market.

Headquartered in Juno Beach, FL, NextEra's principal operating subsidiaries are NextEra Energy Resources, LLC, and the original Florida Power & Light Company, one of the largest rate-regulated electric utilities in the country. FP&L serves 8.9 million people and 4.6 million customer accounts in eastern and southern Florida. Through its subsidiaries, NextEra collectively operates the third-largest U.S. nuclear power generation fleet and has a significant presence in solar and wind generation markets.

As a nonregulated subsidiary, NextEra Energy Resources, LLC (or "NEER"), is a wholesale energy provider and a leader in producing electricity from clean and renewable fuels and, unlike many other alternative-energy-driven businesses, is a viable standalone business entity. It has 4,700 employees at 115 facilities in 26 states and has solar and wind farms, nuclear energy facilities, and gas infrastructure operations not just in Florida but in 22 states and Canada. NEER's energy-producing portfolio includes 8,569 megawatts of wind-generation facilities in 17 states and Canada, which is estimated to comprise 17 percent of the entire wind power–generating capacity in the U.S., 14 percent of utility-scale solar power production, and 6 percent of total U.S. nuclear power production. All told, the combined fuel mix of alternative energy and natural gas not only reduces fuel costs (36 percent of revenues, compared to 40s and 50s in much of the industry), but it also produces levels of sulfur dioxide (the cause of acid rain) some 90 percent below the average for the U.S. electric industry, a nitrous oxide emission rate 80 percent below the industry, and a carbon dioxide (CO_2) emission rate 51 percent below industry averages. NEER subsidiary accounts for nearly a third of NextEra's total revenue—and nearly half of its profits—a healthy return for an alternative energy–based operation. Recently the NEER subsidiary has redirected its business toward longer-term contracts, which can hurt short-term profitability but help stabilize future revenues and earnings.

The company has a few small but promising nonregulated subsidiaries, offering design and consulting services for other alternative and conventional utility providers. Its FPL FiberNet subsidiary specializes in high-bandwidth data transmission from telecommunications locations to cell phone towers, mainly in Florida, Texas, and other areas in the South. Finally, the company is a regular winner of awards for most green, most ethical, and most admired companies.

Financial Highlights, Fiscal Year 2013

Revenues in FY2013 charged ahead to $15.13 billion, some 6.2 percent ahead of FY2012, while per-share earnings advanced a similar amount. The company expects decent growth in FY2014 with earnings in the $5.05–5.45 range and has also projected a 5–7 percent annual earnings growth through FY2015, as energy use and demographic patterns improve and as the regulatory environment continues to be generally favorable for rates.

Reasons to Buy

For those who believe that alternative energy is the future for large-scale power generation, NextEra continues to be the best play available. The Recovery Act of 2009 contains a number of tax incentives for the deployment and use of renewable and nuclear sources, and NextEra is well positioned to take advantage. The company continues to grow alternative energy capacity on all fronts, particularly wind and solar, and continues to make money on these efforts. All of this adds to the solid and traditional FP&L regulated utility base; this company has the steady feel of a traditional utility with a bit more interest in the form of alternative energy plays and leading-edge power utility technology. There is also a chance that the company may spin off certain operations to separate regulated and nonregulated segments (yield focused and growth focused) as others in the industry have done or have considered—this could unlock some shareholder value. Cash flow is very strong and supports both hearty dividend increases and continued investments in alternative energy production but hasn't, as noted below, been used to reduce share counts.

Reasons for Caution

The company's FPL subsidiary is still a regulated utility and may not always receive the most accommodating treatment. Additionally, alternative energy tax credits may not be around forever. The dividend yield, while still healthy for a company with future growth prospects in an up-and-coming industry, is still a little low by current utility standards—reflecting in part the fact that investors have already put a lot of energy into this stock, and the price accounts for its prospects. Unlike many companies on the list, NEE has not only not been retiring shares but has been adding shares in an effort to deleverage (reduce debt) slightly, recently selling 11 million shares in the open market. This is a dynamic, growth-oriented utility company, but buyers should continue to look for good entry points—a $100 utility stock is unusual to say the least.

SECTOR: **Utilities**
BETA COEFFICIENT: **0.44**
10-YEAR COMPOUND EARNINGS PER-SHARE GROWTH: **8.5%**
10-YEAR COMPOUND DIVIDENDS PER-SHARE GROWTH: **7.0%**

	2006	2007	2008	2009	2010	2011	2012	2013
Revenues (mil)	15,710	15,263	16,410	15,646	15,317	15,341	14,256	15,136
Net income (mil)	1,261	1,312	1,639	1,615	1,957	2,021	1,911	2,062
Earnings per share	3.23	3.27	4.07	3.97	4.74	4.82	4.56	4.83
Dividends per share	1.50	1.64	1.78	1.89	2.00	2.20	2.40	2.64
Cash flow per share	6.77	6.85	8.03	8.75	9.60	9.29	8.70	10.65
Price: high	55.6	72.8	73.8	60.6	56.3	61.2	72.2	89.8
low	37.8	53.7	33.8	41.5	45.3	49.0	58.6	69.8

NextEra Energy, Inc.
700 Universe Boulevard
Juno Beach, FL 33408
(561) 691-7171
Website: *www.nexteraenergy.com*

AGGRESSIVE GROWTH

Nike, Inc.

Ticker symbol: NKE (NYSE) □ S&P rating: A+ □ Value Line financial strength rating: A++
Current yield: 1.3% □ Dividend raises, past 10 years: 10

Company Profile

Nike's principal business activity is the design, development, and worldwide marketing of footwear, apparel, equipment, and accessory products. Nike is the largest seller of athletic footwear and athletic apparel in the world, but a big part of the story is how it is extending beyond traditional footwear and apparel. Its products are sold through retail accounts, Nike-owned retail outlets, its website, and a mix of independent distributors and licensees in more than 190 countries around the world. Recently, the company has experimented with specialized destination "Running Stores" and has expanded reach with more "Direct-to-Consumer," or DTC outlets, carrying its traditionally strong product innovation to the channel and retail marketplace.

Nike does no manufacturing—virtually all of its footwear and apparel items are manufactured by independent contractors outside the United States, while equipment products are produced both in the United States and abroad.

Nike's shoes are designed primarily for athletic use, although a large percentage of these products are worn for casual or leisure purposes. The shoes are designed for men, women, and children for running, training, basketball, and soccer use, although the company also carries brands for casual wear.

Nike sells apparel and accessories for most of the sports addressed by its shoe lines, as well as athletic bags and accessory items. Nike apparel and accessories are designed to complement its athletic footwear products, feature the same trademarks, and are sold through the same marketing and distribution channels. All Nike-branded products are marketed with the familiar "swoosh" logo, one of the most recognized and successful branding images in history.

Nike has a number of wholly owned subsidiaries, or "affiliate brands," including Converse, Hurley, Jordan Brand, and Nike Golf, which variously design, distribute, and license dress, athletic, and casual footwear, sports apparel, and accessories. In FY2013, these subsidiary brands accounted for just under 10 percent of total revenues, down from 15 percent, after a sale of the Umbra and Cole Haan subsidiaries in FY2012.

Of the total $23 billion in 2013 Nike brand revenues (excluding subsidiaries), approximately 45 percent comes from North America, 16 percent from Western Europe, 11 percent from China, 6 percent from central and eastern Europe, 3.5 percent from Japan, and 16 percent from other emerging markets. Growth was strongest in North America, central and eastern Europe, and emerging markets.

Financial Highlights, Fiscal Year 2013

FY2013 revenues jogged ahead 8 percent to just over $25 billion. While labor and material costs have risen, the company also leveraged newer, higher-margined products and operating efficiencies into a slight improvement in operating margins to bring a 10.8 percent gain in net income. That and a 2.4 percent share buyback combined as a point guard and a power forward would to deliver a per-share earnings growth of 13.5 percent. The company reports that demand for its products continues to be strong in all regions, but it was particularly pleased with business in the U.S., which many had given up on as a growth vector. Brand strength and expanded channels, notably direct-to-consumer and factory stores, grew the U.S. business some $1.5 billion over FY2012— about 60 percent of the company's total FY2013 growth. That's a good thing, because international markets, especially China, were unusually soft for the year, in part due to currency. Including currency effects, China was effectively flat for the year.

On a constant currency basis, the company expects FY2014 top-line growth somewhere around 10 percent, with earnings per share expected to grow in the low to mid-teens, with similar growth rates projected into FY2015.

Reasons to Buy

Why buy Nike? In a word, brand. The Nike brand and its corresponding swoosh continue to be one of the most recognized—and sought after—brands in the world. It is a lesson in simplicity and image congruence with the product behind it. Nike doesn't sit still with it; rather, the company is learning to leverage it into more products outside the traditional athletic wear circuit—golf clubs, golf balls, even a new line of GPS watches and apps to find, say, a new route for your run and to track your performance right on your phone. The company continues to invest in innovation in all of its segments, including new fabrics, colors, uniform materials, and digital linkages to make active lifestyles more productive and fun—and it is now extending this innovation further into marketing and retail. As well, Nike doesn't just limit the brand appeal to athletes: Slogans like "Just Do It" and "If you have a body, you're an athlete" emphasize the appeal and lifestyle across all segments of the population. We think this is drop-dead smart.

Of course, solid brand and brand reputation lead to category leadership and, hence, higher profitability, and Nike has finished far ahead of the pack in this area, too. The brand and the moat created by the brand seem to have nowhere to go but forward, and improved manufacturing efficiencies, strong channel relationships, and international exposure all keep the company moving faster in the right direction. Despite its size, the company continues to deliver double-digit earnings, cash flow, and dividend growth. We continue to like the combination of protected profitability through brand excellence with a clean conservative balance sheet, providing a good combination of safety and growth potential—and we like the fact that the company is returning more of the proceeds to shareholders.

Reasons for Caution

Two things could put hurdles in Nike's path. The first is higher labor and commodity input prices. Second, the company is continually in the news—and the rumor mill—for unfair labor practices and child labor violations in some of its foreign manufacturing plants. The company doesn't actually own or operate these plants, but the rumors can stick nonetheless. Finally, while we think its image and marketing extend well into a direct-to-consumer selling strategy, the potential for conflict with existing channels is always a cause for concern.

SECTOR: **Consumer Discretionary**
BETA COEFFICIENT: **0.90**
10-YEAR COMPOUND EARNINGS PER-SHARE GROWTH: **14.5%**
10-YEAR COMPOUND DIVIDENDS PER-SHARE GROWTH: **19.0%**

		2006	2007	2008	2009	2010	2011	2012	2013
Revenues (mil)		14,955	16,326	18,627	19,176	19,014	20,862	24,128	25,313
Net income (mil)		1,392	1,458	1,734	1,727	1,907	2,133	2,223	2,464
Earnings per share		1.32	1.43	1.72	1.76	1.93	2.20	2.37	2.69
Dividends per share		0.30	0.36	0.44	0.49	0.53	0.60	0.70	0.81
Cash flow per share		1.60	1.72	2.07	2.12	2.23	2.60	2.83	3.25
Price:	high	25.3	34.0	35.3	33.3	46.2	49.1	57.4	80.3
	low	18.9	23.7	21.3	16.1	30.4	54.7	42.6	51.4

Nike, Inc.
One Bowerman Drive
Beaverton, OR 97005
(503) 671-6453
Website: *www.nikeinc.com*

CONSERVATIVE GROWTH

Norfolk Southern Corporation

Ticker symbol: NSC (NYSE) ❑ S&P rating: BBB+ ❑ Value Line financial strength rating: A
Current yield: 2.3 ❑ Dividend raises, past 10 years: 10

Company Profile

Norfolk Southern Corp. was formed in 1982 as a holding company when the Norfolk & Western Railway merged with the Southern Railway. Including lines received in the split takeover (with CSX) of Conrail, the current railroad operates 20,000 route-miles of track in 22 eastern and southern states. It serves every major port on the East Coast of the United States and has the most extensive intermodal network in the east.

Company business in FY2012 was about 23 percent coal, coke, and iron ore (down from 26 percent, more on that in a minute); 21 percent intermodal; 13 percent agricultural and consumer products; 12 percent metals and construction; and 29 percent other. Within those categories, the railroad transports the usual mix of raw materials, intermediate products such as parts, and manufactured goods.

In the late 1990s, the company split the acquisition of northeastern rail heavyweight Conrail with rival CSX corporation, so it has considerable operations in the Northeast and Midwest in addition to its traditional southern base. The heaviest traffic corridors are New York–Chicago;

Chicago–Atlanta; Appalachian coalfields to the port of Norfolk, VA, and Sandusky, OH; and Cleveland–Kansas City. The company has a diverse base of large Midwestern factories and large and smaller southern factories and basic materials producers in the coal and lumber industry, giving a well-diversified traffic base.

The company has been an innovator in the intermodal business, that is, combining trucking and rail services—with its Triple Crown services, centered on the Roadrailer, a train of coupled-together highway vans on special wheelsets. At the terminal, a cab simply backs up to the van and drives it off.

The company provides a number of logistics services and has substantial traffic to and from ports and overseas destinations. The company has an active program to attract lineside customers to build freight volumes.

Financial Highlights, Fiscal Year 2013

It's common knowledge that the recent oil and gas boom has caused a major shift in energy markets. In particular, cheaper and more plentiful natural gas and a continued shift in basic metals manufacturing have to a degree derailed the lucrative coal traffic enjoyed by the railroads; Norfolk Southern with its geography has been front and center in this shift. As a portion of the company's revenues, coal dropped from 31 percent in FY2011 to 26 percent in FY2012 and 23 percent in FY2013. Although this loss has been partially offset by the oil boom and tank-train shipments to East Coast and southern refineries, the real story is the broadening of the traffic mix especially into intermodal—and a continued benefit from a forward-looking series of improvements in infrastructure all begun years ago. As a consequence of all of this, revenues have flattened somewhat, but the all-important cost structure has more than kept up. In fact, the company's operating ratio—variable costs to total costs—declined to 71.0 percent, down from 71.7 percent last year and 75.4 percent in 2009. So, in total, revenues are up less than 1 percent in two years, but per-share earnings, also helped along by buybacks, have risen a steady 5–6 percent. Improved oil, automotive, and chemical shipments will begin to more than offset the decline in coal, bringing a 4–5 percent annual revenue increase and a more substantial 10–12 percent rise in per-share earnings. Too, the dividend has more than tripled since 2006.

Reasons to Buy

NSC and its competitors have all been hurt by the coal slowdown, but there are some silver linings, both short and long term. For the short term, increased exploration and production of crude oil in places like North Dakota have changed around oil supply chains in the U.S., and since there are no pipelines to serve the need, trainloads of oil are moving from this and a few other booming regions to eastern refineries. The boom has also brought new business moving other commodities used in the new fracking extraction process. Longer term, a widening of the Panama Canal will expand Asian trade into southern and eastern ports (a lot of which now comes into the West Coast). Norfolk Southern continues to do an excellent job sizing its physical plant and managing costs, as evidenced by the operating ratio mentioned earlier. NSC has proven over the past 30 years that it can compete effectively for long-haul truck business with its intermodal offerings and has some of the most competitive service and terminal structures in the business. It has gained market share from trucks, and general merchandise volume increased some 4 percent during 2013 with over 62 percent of merchandise traffic originating on its own lines.

Additionally, NSC serves some of the more dynamic and up-and-coming manufacturing markets in the United States, namely, Asian and other foreign-owned manufacturing facilities found particularly in the Southeast. The company has created a Heartland Corridor time freight and double-stack container routing between Chicago and the East Coast, reducing distance by 250 miles and, more importantly, transit times from four to three days. Similar improvements have occurred on its Crescent Corridor between Louisiana and New Jersey. Such innovations will further assert the company's leadership. Additionally, we like the strength and diversity coming from serving the domestic and especially the foreign-owned auto industry—the company serves plants for (in alphabetical order) BMW, Chrysler, Ford, General Motors, Honda, Isuzu, Mazda, Mercedes-Benz, Mitsubishi, Nissan, Subaru, Suzuki, and Toyota.

Finally, cash flow continues to be strong, dividend raises are consistent, and the company continues down the share repurchase track.

Reasons for Caution

While the coal slowdown seems to be under control, it is still a very important commodity; a further major decline would hurt the business. The decline in coal traffic, which mostly supports electric utilities, also exposes the company more to general economic downturns as the remaining mix is more economically sensitive. Too, increased oil shipments expose the company to headline risk and accidents.

SECTOR: **Transportation**
BETA COEFFICIENT: **1.10**
10-YEAR COMPOUND EARNINGS PER-SHARE GROWTH: **17.0%**
10-YEAR COMPOUND DIVIDENDS PER-SHARE GROWTH: **21.5%**

	2006	2007	2008	2009	2010	2011	2012	2013
Revenues (mil)	9,407	9,432	10,661	7,969	9,516	11,172	11,040	11,245
Net income (mil)	1,481	1,464	1,716	1,034	1,498	1,853	1,749	1,850
Earnings per share	3.58	3.68	4.52	2.76	4.00	5.27	5.37	5.85
Dividends per share	0.68	0.96	1.22	1.36	1.40	1.68	1.94	2.04
Cash flow per share	5.58	5.90	6.88	5.07	6.48	8.22	8.49	8.96
Price: high	57.7	59.6	75.5	54.8	63.7	78.4	78.5	93.2
low	39.1	45.4	41.4	26.7	46.2	57.6	56.1	62.7

Norfolk Southern Corporation
Three Commercial Place
Norfolk, VA 23510–2191
(757) 629-2600
Website: *www.nscorp.com*

AGGRESSIVE GROWTH

NEW FOR 2015

Oracle Corporation

Ticker symbol: ORCL (NYSE) □ S&P rating: A □ Value Line financial strength rating: A++
Current yield: 1.4% □ Dividend raises, past 10 years: 3

Company Profile

Oracle Corporation is best known as the producer and marketer of . . . the Oracle database. Why rename your company after your mainline product? Well, with the possible exception of Coca-Cola, maybe no single product has meant as much to one company as this database has meant to Oracle. It put the company on the map and fueled all of its growth for the first three decades of its existence. Licenses and support revenue for this product continue to be the most profitable segment of the company's business, which, as these things tend to do, has become both a blessing and a curse. More on that later.

Led by tech pioneer Larry Ellison, who still owns 25 percent of the company, Oracle is a global provider of database and applications software, "engineered systems" (Oracle hardware pre-configured with Oracle software), and services. Software licenses, renewals, and support constitute roughly 75 percent of revenue, with nearly 60 percent of revenue coming from outside the United States.

The acquisition of Sun Microsystems in 2010 brought with it what was to become Oracle's first hardware products. These were basically little more than standard Sun servers with Oracle software installed. These product lines have now been pared down and customized into Oracle's "Exadata" machines, which are very large standalone installations with enormous storage capacity.

If you think of corporate data as a restaurant, the Oracle database is sort of the line cook—it prepares the basics of the order by cooking the food and letting the waiter know it's ready. The waiter is the customer interface in this model, and he represents the application layer. His job is to make the meal more attractive and user-friendly. He adds the serving plate, drops in the parsley and the pie chart, makes sure the food matches the order, and then delivers the data with a friendly face. For decades Oracle's business model was to sweat over a hot stove, preparing and plating data and letting its tens of thousands of partner companies deliver the meal—that is, the application.

Things have definitely changed over the past ten years, however. Oracle, through internal development and acquisition (over 100 companies in the past decade) has grown its in-house applications and middleware to where they now account for a significant percentage of revenue.

As well, Oracle is ubiquitous. Its database, middleware, and applications, which include everything from sales to accounting to supply chain to human resources management products, hold the top spots in retail, banking, manufacturing, financial services, the public sector, and several other industry segments. Increasingly, these products and services are being delivered through the "cloud" as SaaS (Software as a Service) and PaaS (Platform as a Service) offerings.

Financial Highlights, Fiscal Year 2013

For FY2013 total revenues were up just 3 percent to $38.3 billion. Software and cloud revenues were up 5 percent, with cloud SaaS and PaaS revenues up a healthy 23 percent to $1.1 billion. New software licenses revenues and hardware system revenues were flat at $9.4 billion and $5.4 billion respectively, while software license updates and product support revenues were up 6 percent to $18.2 billion. Earnings per share was $2.38, up 5 percent compared to last year. In all, not a stellar year, but then again no troubling signs, either. The strong growth in SaaS and PaaS revenues is encouraging.

Reasons to Buy

For several years now, people have viewed Oracle as a company that just doesn't get it. Why design and market an Exadata machine for a data center when no one builds their own datacenter anymore? Why not just use Amazon Web Services? Why continue to market a giant database which requires a large staff of expensive professionals to configure? Everybody knows the sexy part of the market is in small, targeted application software.

These are valid questions and would be reasons for concern if Oracle were just now getting into the business, but the simple truth is there are over 300,000 Oracle database customers, including nearly all of the *Fortune* 100. Oracle database support and licensing revenues are a massive cash cow. This large installed base brings with it a large population of very skilled practitioners, people who have made their entire careers out of installing, configuring, and supporting this software. Understanding that, the company continues to update its namesake product with new capabilities.

However, Oracle also recognizes the trend among small and mid-sized companies toward lower capital investment in data services. Many startups and even mature companies are moving to cloud service schemes such as SaaS and PaaS. Oracle has responded with a dual approach of internal development programs and targeted acquisitions. As a result, Oracle is now the second-largest (by revenue) SaaS vendor in the world.

Oracle continues to be aggressive in acquisitions and, as we go to press, they've announced another rather large ($4.6 billion, net of cash) purchase: Micros Systems. Micros is a large vertical player in the point-of-sale business with over 100,000 customers in retail, restaurants, and hotels. The company has a very attractive niche, with a customer base that should be a good fit for Oracle's existing products.

We like Oracle's financials, its steady share price growth, and its wallet—if you plan to grow by acquisition, it's good to have $35 billion in cash. Share price increases have not been stellar over the years, but through share buybacks the company expects to have reduced share counts by a billion shares—about 20 percent—in a ten-year period ending in 2015. The company also instituted a dividend in 2009, which has grown steadily since.

Reasons for Caution

In spite of Oracle's history of steady, if not spectacular, share price increases, questions about its future profitability remain: Can Oracle compete effectively in an increasingly mobile and cloud-based computing environment? Is it too dependent on its cash-cow database products? Are the company's acquisitions hitting the right segments, and is it buying at the right price? We also have some concerns about Oracle's ability to quickly and effectively integrate the larger acquisitions; it took more than a year for operating margins to recover from the Sun purchase in 2010. Oracle's strategy with Micros will bear watching.

SECTOR: **Information Technology**
BETA COEFFICIENT: **1.0**
10-YEAR COMPOUND EARNINGS PER-SHARE GROWTH: **19.0%**
10-YEAR COMPOUND DIVIDENDS PER-SHARE GROWTH: **NA**

	2006	2007	2008	2009	2010	2011	2012	2013
Revenues (mil)	14,771	18,208	22,609	23,495	27,034	35,850	37,221	37,253
Net income (mil)	4,246	5,295	6,799	7,393	6,494	11,385	12,520	12,958
Earnings per share	0.80	1.01	1.30	1.44	1.67	2.22	2.46	2.68
Dividends per share	—	—	—	0.05	0.20	0.20	0.24	0.30
Cash flow per share	0.85	1.09	1.37	1.53	1.75	2.32	2.65	2.91
Price: high	19.8	23.3	23.6	25.1	32.3	36.5	34.3	38.3
low	12.1	16.0	15.0	13.8	21.2	24.7	25.3	29.9

Oracle Corporation
500 Oracle Parkway
Redwood Shores, CA 94065
(650) 506-7000
Website: *www.oracle.com*

GROWTH AND INCOME

Otter Tail Corporation

Ticker symbol: OTTR (NASDAQ) ❑ S&P rating: BBB- ❑ Value Line financial strength rating: B+
Current yield: 4.1% ❑ Dividend raises, past 10 years: 5

Company Profile

Otter Tail Corporation is a holding company and a mini-conglomerate operating primarily in the upper Midwest. The conglomerate is centered on and stabilized by the Otter Tail Power Company, a regulated utility serving about 130,000 customers in rural western Minnesota, the eastern half of North Dakota, and the eastern quarter of South Dakota. (In case you're wondering, these areas just miss the vast energy exploration territories of western North Dakota.) About 46 percent of electric revenues come from Minnesota, 43 percent from North Dakota, and 9 percent from South Dakota. The utility accounted for about 42 percent of the total business in FY2013.

Extensive use of wind generation and hydro power, and lower grades of coal available in the region, have driven fuel costs down to 13.8 percent of revenues, a very low figure for the industry. (By comparison, Xcel Energy, which supplies electricity to surrounding areas in North Dakota and Minnesota as well as other Great Plains locations, Colorado, and Texas, spends 50 percent of revenues on fuel.) Approximately 19 percent of power generation is from wind power

sources; another 1 percent comes from hydro.

Beyond the utility, the company, which has sold six fairly good-sized businesses in the past two years, now continues to operate six non-utility companies in three other business segments, accounting for the other 58 percent of the business. The company now refers to these assets by the name of "Varistar"; they play largely but not wholly in the area of infrastructure construction and replacement:

- The Manufacturing segment (23 percent of revenues) houses two smaller businesses. BTD Manufacturing is a metal stamping, fabricating, and laser-cutting shop supplying custom parts for agriculture, lawn care, health and fitness, and the RV industry. T.O. Plastics supplies packaging and handling products for the horticultural industry.
- The Plastics segment (19 percent) has two operations supplying commercial and utility-grade PVC and other plastic pipe and accessories. The two operating companies are Northern Pipe Products, which

produces PVC water and sewer pipes up to 24 inches in diameter, and VinylTech, a producer of a similar line of utility-grade PVC products.

■ The Construction segment (about 17 percent) also has two companies primarily aligned to infrastructure construction and management. Aevenia offers energy and electrical construction, installation, and maintenance services, including transmission and distribution, substations, fiber optics and urban telecom. The Foley Company is a specialty contractor involved in industrial power, water and wastewater, and other complex construction projects.

Overall, the company has 2,336 employees, and most operations are centered in the upper Midwest.

Financial Highlights, Fiscal Year 2013

FY2012 was a difficult compare to FY2011 because of the divestitures: FY2013 was more straightforward and came with decent gains in revenues and earnings. Strength in all businesses led to a 4 percent gain in the top line to $893 million, while earnings increased a healthy 29 percent despite a one-time loss on an early debt retirement. Through FY2015, revenues are projected to rise in the 4–5 percent range, with earnings increases in the 10 percent range—another "5 and 10" stock for our *100 Best* list. Cash flows are notably strong and have supported the dividend for some time even though reported per-share earnings didn't; continued strong cash flows and earnings that also cover dividends well should lead to a resumption of regular dividend increases.

Reasons to Buy

When we first added Otter Tail to the 2012 *100 Best Stocks* list, admittedly we were taken by its Berkshire Hathaway–like construct of a basic business around a steady core, the electric utility. We also liked its commitment to the wind energy business. However, aside from reducing energy input costs to the utility, the wind business wasn't working well, and the other businesses may have been a bit too far-flung to manage effectively so the company retrenched, trimmed the branches, so to speak, and continued on with a company still more or less constructed around this model. The resulting non-utility core is centered on infrastructure construction and materials, and we like that.

Otter Tail still appears to be a good way to participate in several well-managed businesses while getting a decent current return with solid cash flows and dividends. It is indeed like a "small town" company in contrast to "big city" corporate America.

Reasons for Caution

The utility is stable but not likely to be helped along by population growth, and the Varistar businesses are cyclical. The company is on a much more solid footing than it was a few years ago, but it still doesn't have the reserve strength of larger companies. We compared Otter Tail to Berkshire Hathaway but should note that Berkshire is more diversified and has much larger anchor businesses.

SECTOR: **Utilities/Industrial**
BETA COEFFICIENT: **0.81**
10-YEAR COMPOUND EARNINGS PER-SHARE GROWTH: **-9.5%**
10-YEAR COMPOUND DIVIDENDS PER-SHARE GROWTH: **1.5%**

	2006	2007	2008	2009	2010	2011	2012	2013
Revenues (mil)	1,105	1,239	1,311	1,040	1,118	1,078	859.2	893.3
Net income (mil)	50.8	54.0	35.1	26.0	13.6	16.4	39.0	50.2
Earnings per share	1.88	1.78	1.09	0.71	0.38	0.45	1.05	1.37
Dividends per share	1.15	1.17	1.19	1.19	1.19	1.19	1.19	1.19
Cash flow per share	3.39	3.55	2.81	2.76	2.82	2.39	2.71	3.03
Price: high	31.9	39.4	46.2	25.4	25.4	23.5	25.3	31.9
low	25.8	29.0	15.0	18.5	18.2	17.5	20.7	25.2

Otter Tail Corporation
P.O. Box 496
215 S Cascade Street
Fergus Falls, MN 56538
(866) 410-8780
Website: *www.ottertail.com*

AGGRESSIVE GROWTH

Pall Corporation

Ticker symbol: PLL (NYSE) ❑ S&P rating: BBB ❑ Value Line financial strength rating: A+ ❑ Current yield: 1.3% ❑ Dividend raises, past 10 years: 9

Company Profile

Pall Corporation supplies filtration, separation, and purification technologies for the removal of solid, liquid, and gaseous contaminants from a variety of liquids and gases. Its products are used in thousands of industrial and clinical settings: removal of contaminants from gas reagents in every semiconductor production facility in the world, removal of bacteria and virus spores from water in hospitals and other clinical settings, and detection of bacteria in blood samples. Its products range in scale from simple in-line filters, sold 100 to the carton, to entire graywater treatment systems with capacities up to 150,000 gallons/day. The company holds a market leading position in most of its filtration, separation, and purification markets.

Pall's product and customers fall into two broad categories that each make up about half of the business: Life Sciences and Industrial. The Life Sciences category breaks down further into Biopharma (33 percent of FY2013 revenues), Medical (8 percent), and Food & Beverage (9 percent). The company's Life Sciences technologies are used in the research

laboratory, pharmaceutical and biotechnology industries, in blood centers, and in hospitals at the point of patient care. Certain medical products improve the safety of the use of blood products in patient care and help control the spread of infections in hospitals. Pall's separation systems and disposable filtration and purification technologies are critical to the development and commercialization of chemically synthesized and biologically derived drugs and vaccines.

The Industrial segment includes Process Technologies (31 percent of FY2013 sales), Aerospace and Transportation (9 percent), and Microelectronics (10 percent). Industrial markets include, but aren't limited to, consumer electronics, municipal and industrial water, fuels, chemicals, energy, pulp and paper, automotive, and food and beverage markets. Using food and beverage as an example, Pall sells filtration solutions to wine, beer, soft drink, bottled water, and food ingredient producers. Additionally, the company sells filtration and fluid monitoring equipment to the aerospace industry for use on commercial and military aircraft, ships, and land-based military vehicles to help protect critical systems and components. Pall also sells filtration and purification technologies for the semiconductor, data storage, fiber optic, advanced display, and materials markets, and a line of contamination-control products for an assortment of industries.

Pall is the leader in almost all of these markets. International sales account for 68 percent of the total. The company is fairly active in acquiring smaller complementary fish in the filtration business every year; it has acquired broadline filtration supplier Filter Specialists and medical and pharmaceutical filtration suppliers Medistad, Solohill Engineering, and the life sciences business of ATMI, Inc. The company continues to invest in new research centers, applications, engineering capability, and distribution channels in emerging markets.

Financial Highlights, Fiscal Year 2013

After a mixed FY2012, slowed up a bit by the absorption of distributor inventories, FY2013 was another mixed bag, as a slowdown in emerging market growth and ongoing currency effects dampened an otherwise stronger market performance in places such as Europe that had been in decline. Revenues fell a bit less than 1 percent to $2.65 billion. Operating efficiencies delivered by an ongoing minor restructure delivered much stronger operating margins: over 20 percent versus 18.6 percent in FY2012. That,

combined with a 3 percent share buyback, produced a 6.6 percent increase in per-share earnings.

The *real* good news appears to be going forward, as the new acquisitions and operational improvements shift into higher gear. Revenues are forecasted to gain in the mid to high single digits, while the net profit margin is projected to increase by a full percentage point to 13.5 percent—producing a per-share earnings increase to $3.40, 17.6 percent ahead of FY2012, and a 15 percent increase into FY2015. The dividend was increased 17 percent in FY2013, and similar future increases look likely. The company also authorized another $250 million (3 percent) share repurchase in 2014.

Reasons to Buy

As the company puts it, "sophisticated filters are rarely discretionary." We like companies with a dominant position in their marketplaces or market niches, particularly when there is little to "cloud" the demand for their product. We also like industrials with a diversified customer base, and we like companies that have a strong and ongoing base of repeat business. Pall delivers on all three principles. The company sells into the medical, biopharma, energy, and water-process technologies; aerospace; and microelectronics spaces, among others. These sectors will continue to show consistency and strength over time. Further, Pall's products are consumables used consistently within the lab and manufacturing processes they sell into; they do not depend greatly on capital spending decisions and are relatively less sensitive to economic cycles, although they can be affected by inventory cycles as mentioned. Some 90 percent of Pall's sales are repeat-purchased consumables; this makes the company a little more recession proof, and with a dominant market position.

All that can be seen in the strong net profit margin performance cited above; the net profit margin has roughly doubled to 14 percent over the past seven years. In fact, the forward projections reflect a company that seems to be doing an excellent job of patiently turning a strong market position into profits—which

arc being returned to shareholders at an accelerating rate. We also like the company's strong international footprint.

Reasons for Caution

While its presence in the consumables side of the business attenuates the effects of economic cycles somewhat, the company is still sensitive to economic downturns. The recent strength in the business and business model has been noticed by others, too. This may attract more competition (or who knows, a takeover bid?) from the likes of 3M or a similar company. The strength continues to be reflected in the share price; new investors should look to buy on dips.

SECTOR: **Industrials**
BETA COEFFICIENT: **1.35**
10-YEAR COMPOUND EARNINGS PER-SHARE GROWTH: **12.0%**
10-YEAR COMPOUND DIVIDENDS PER-SHARE GROWTH: **5.5%**

	2006	2007	2008	2009	2010	2011	2012	2013
Revenues (mil)	2,017	2,250	2,572	2,392	2,402	2,741	2,672	2,658
Net income (mil)	146	128	217	196	241	315	319	330
Earnings per share	1.16	1.02	1.76	1.64	2.03	2.67	2.71	2.89
Dividends per share	0.44	0.48	0.51	0.58	0.64	0.70	0.88	1.03
Cash flow per share	1.97	1.81	2.60	2.44	2.90	3.60	3.77	3.90
Price: high	35.6	49.0	43.2	37.3	44.7	59.5	65.8	85.6
low	25.3	33.2	21.6	18.2	31.8	39.8	50.0	61.3

Pall Corporation
25 Harbor Park Drive
Port Washington, NY 11548
(516) 484-5400
Website: *www.pall.com*

AGGRESSIVE GROWTH

Patterson Companies, Inc.

Ticker symbol: PDCO (NASDAQ) □ S&P rating: NR □ Value Line financial strength rating: A
Current yield: 2.0% □ Dividend raises, past 10 years: 4

Company Profile

Patterson Companies is a value-added distributor operating in three segments—Dental Supply, Veterinary Supply, and Medical Supply. Dental Supply (about 65 percent of sales) provides a range of consumable dental products, equipment, and software; turnkey digital solutions; office design and setup; and value-added services to dentists and dental laboratories primarily for the North American market. Veterinary Supply (21 percent) is the nation's second-largest distributor of consumable veterinary supplies, equipment, diagnostic products, vaccines, and pharmaceuticals to companion-pet veterinary clinics. Medical Supply (14 percent) distributes medical supplies and assistive products, primarily for rehabilitation and sports medicine, globally to hospitals, long-term-care facilities, clinics, and dealers.

Patterson has one-third of the dental supply market. Their main competitors are HSIC (Henry Schein), which also has about a one-third share, and Dentsply (a former *100 Best* stock). The remaining share is fragmented among a number of smaller players. As one of the lead dogs, Patterson has the clout to negotiate a number of exclusive distribution deals. It is sole distributor for the industry's most popular line of dental chairs and also has an exclusive on the CEREC 3D dental restorative system, an increasingly popular alternative to traditional dental crowns. Patterson is also the leading provider of digital radiography systems, which create instant images of dental work, superior to the images generated by traditional x-ray equipment. The company also supplies and supports dental practice financial and supply-chain management software, and offers physical and system design and consulting services to dentists.

Patterson's veterinary business, Webster Veterinary, is the second-largest distributor of consumable veterinary supplies to companion-pet veterinary clinics. Its line also includes equipment and software, diagnostic products, and vaccines and pharmaceuticals.

In FY2013 the company made a couple of small acquisitions to grow practice management software and its international business.

Financial Highlights, Fiscal Year 2013

It's human nature to delay trips to the dentist as long as possible regardless of economic times, and the "dental lag" gets even longer in a recession. The soft economy gave patients plenty of reasons (and excuses) to defer elective and even not-so-elective procedures, and dentists, as a result, drew down their inventories and delayed capital purchases for things like dental chairs and digital imaging systems.

Despite the economic recovery, the dental industry continues to be one of the most lagging of many lagging industries after a recession, and the scenario continued through early 2014. Patterson and others in the business have had to be quite patient with modest 4–5 percent sales gains, partially driven by acquisitions, and almost flat net profit figures. The company hopes (and expects) the decay to stop, while in the meantime it has been practicing good hygiene in the form of steady share buybacks. Since 2006, Patterson has bought back almost 30 percent of its shares and surprised investors with a 25 percent dividend increase for 2014—all in anticipation of the day when dentists—and their patients—finally resume a normal level of activity. We expect, if not this year, in the very near term per-share earnings could almost double. All that said, the company projects a modest per-share earnings increase to the $2.30–$2.40 net of acquisition costs.

Reasons to Buy

We think that dental lag will subside sooner rather than later, and dental procedures, capital investment, and inventory replenishment will all return to more normal levels. When this happens, it may not be too much to expect a "hockey stick"-shaped trajectory for sales, earnings, cash flow, and, yes, the stock price—although some would probably prefer to avoid using the hockey stick analogy to describe a dental supply stock!

While there have been some improvements in the art of long-term dental care, such as more widespread fluoride use, we see the need for replacement crowns as well as more expensive and material-intensive implant restorations continuing, if not growing, as the population ages and as dental care becomes a bigger industry overseas.

The aforementioned CEREC 3D is an imaging and milling system that allows the dentist to take an image of the area to be restored and in less than 30 minutes produce a crown, inlay, or other device that is then fitted to the patient's existing dental structure. It's a compelling proposition for high-volume offices where patient throughput is at a premium and the equipment can be fully utilized. Sales of this high-ticket item have been very good and generate ongoing supplies revenue. Patterson's exclusive license for this product is a powerful foot in the door for new accounts.

We like the company's moves into the companion-pet veterinary and rehabilitation markets, both of which are driven by a growing and profitable demographic. Today the company is primarily focused on the North American market, with promised 24- to 48-hour delivery for most items. It has established an international beachhead with the Patterson Medical group in the U.K. and France and intends to leverage this presence to expand the dental and veterinary businesses; last year's acquisition of Dechra Pharmaceuticals expands this beachhead.

The company continues to aggressively return cash to its investors, making significant share repurchases and now, better than expected dividend increases. Share repurchases may approach 5 percent again this year. Patterson is one of a small handful of mid-cap companies on our *100 Best Stocks* list, so it may be of interest to investors looking for something in that size range to complement our mostly large-cap-dominated list.

Reasons for Caution

Competition in this arena is strong, and the company will have to stay sharp to take advantage once dental lag subsides; otherwise, it could lose share to competitors. We believe that the number of companies offering good dental insurance is declining, and any factor that makes dental procedures more "elective" will likely work against Patterson. Some of the expected recovery from dental lag may already be priced into the stock; rosier times may require some patience and entry points should be chosen carefully. While the wait may be long, we also believe this stock to have little real downside.

SECTOR: **Health Care**
BETA COEFFICIENT: **0.82**
10-YEAR COMPOUND EARNINGS PER-SHARE GROWTH: **10.5%**
10-YEAR COMPOUND DIVIDENDS PER-SHARE GROWTH: **NM**

	2006	2007	2008	2009	2010	2011	2012	2013
Revenues (mil)	2,798	2,998	3,094	3,237	3,415	3,536	3,637	3,800
Net income (mil)	208	225	200	212	225	213	210	220
Earnings per share	1.51	1.69	1.70	1.78	1.91	1.92	2.03	2.15
Dividends per share	—	—	—	0.10	0.42	0.50	0.58	0.66
Cash flow per share	2.05	1.88	2.00	2.04	2.20	2.31	2.43	2.70
Price: high	38.3	40.1	37.8	28.3	32.8	39.9	37.6	44.4
low	29.6	28.3	15.8	16.1	24.1	26.2	29.0	34.3

Patterson Companies, Inc.
1031 Mendota Heights Road
St. Paul, MN 55120–1419
(651) 686-1660
Website: *www.pattersoncompanies.com*

AGGRESSIVE GROWTH

Paychex, Inc.

Ticker symbol: PAYX (NASDAQ) ❑ S&P rating: NR ❑ Value Line financial strength rating: A
Current yield: 3.3% ❑ Dividend raises, past 10 years: 8

Company Profile

Paychex, Inc. provides payroll, human resource, and benefits outsourcing solutions for small- to medium-sized businesses with 10–200 employees. Founded in 1971, the company has more than 100 offices and serves over 570,000 clients in the United States, and an additional 2,000 clients in Germany. Some 85 percent of its customers are the small- to medium-sized businesses mentioned above. The company has two sources of revenue: service revenue, paid by clients for services, and interest income on the funds held by Paychex for clients.

Paychex offers a portfolio of services and products, including:

■ Payroll processing
■ Payroll tax administration
■ Employee payment services, including expense reporting, reimbursements, etc.
■ Regulatory compliance services (new-hire reporting and garnishment processing)
■ Comprehensive human resource outsourcing services
■ Retirement services administration
■ Workers' comp insurance
■ Health and benefits services

■ Time and attendance solutions
■ Medical deduction, state unemployment, and other HR services and products

The company's products are marketed primarily through its direct sales force, the bulk of which is focused on payroll products. In addition to the direct sales force, the company uses its relationships with existing clients, CPAs, and banks for new client referrals. Approximately two-thirds of its new clients come via referrals.

Larger clients can choose to outsource their payroll and HR functions or to run them in-house using a Paychex platform.

In addition to traditional payroll services, Paychex offers full-service HR outsourcing solutions; custom-built solutions including payroll, compliance, HR, and employee benefits sourcing and administration; outsourcing management; and even professionally trained onsite HR representatives. The company also manages retirement plans and other benefits, including pretax "cafeteria" plans, and has a subsidiary insurance agency. About 21,000 of the 570,000 clients use the full Human Resource Services offering. The company has recently made a push to implement web-based and mobile versions of its key products, adding to convenience and reducing paperwork for its clients.

The company has three primary growth strategies: First, offer a more complete service, such as HR; second, acquire smaller companies offering similar local services; and third, create more cloudlike services to enable clients to switch from homegrown to Paychex solutions. The company again made a few small acquisitions during the year and will probably continue to do so.

Financial Highlights, Fiscal Year 2013

As the global economy continues to strengthen after the Great Recession, employment expansion helps Paychex's business. That said, the prospects of a "jobless recovery" loom large, and with that too, what employee growth there is tends to lag the economy, at least in so far as adding them to payroll systems. That has moderated revenue gains over the past few years, but the company has started to emerge from the doldrums with a 4.2 percent revenue gain in FY2013 and is on track for a 6.2 revenue gain in FY2014, reflecting increases in hiring and some pricing increases. The company's customers, in a nutshell, are in better shape, and that helps the company both in volume and in pricing. Extremely low short-term interest rates on cash deposits continue to attenuate what might otherwise be stronger profit numbers. That too is

showing some signs of turning around with Fed tapering putting some mild upward pressure on short-term rates.

The company now projects a 9–10 percent increase in net income, 1 percent ahead of previous guidance, and has resumed buying back about 1 percent of its shares annually.

Reasons to Buy

A bet on Paychex is a bet on two things: continued improvement in the economy and an eventual increase in interest rates (so they can make money on the float). In the meantime, you get a decent yield and little downside risk if you own the stock.

Paychex's primary market is companies with fewer than 100 employees. This is one of the primary reasons that Paychex lost clients during the recession. That trend has turned around with the economy; in fact, small business is leading the way while larger businesses are focused on reducing cost, which also helps Paychex as a provider of outsourced services. Beyond that, the cost of switching and a generally good client relationship has made for a loyal client base. We continue to think the trend to outsource payroll and HR activities will not only continue but accelerate as easier Internet-based solutions come more into favor.

The company is conservatively run, well managed, and well financed. Margins are significantly higher than its closest competitor, Automated

Data Processing (ADP). It carries no long-term debt and should have little difficulty funding the generous dividend, even at its current payout level of 80–90 percent of earnings. Fragmentation in the market and Paychex's strong financial position will allow the company to continue to grow market share through acquisition. The company is also expanding in Europe and in South America, a move that could blossom into more business down the road. Finally, sooner or later short-term interest rates must tick upward; when that happens the company will once again be able to profit from the float. Such an increase in interest income would likely fund greater dividend increases and share repurchases; this is one of the few stocks on our list that can tangibly benefit from *moderate* interest rate increases.

Reasons for Caution

This company will always be vulnerable to economic swings, and did hit the slow-growth wall in 2009 with only a slow recovery. The company's acquisition strategy makes sense, as those acquisitions will increase market share, but they do come with costs and risks. Finally, while most analysts consider the dividend payout secure, it does account for a substantial fraction of the company's cash flow, and increases may be hard to come by for the immediate future, particularly if short-term interest rates remain low. Also, the high yield and moderate growth prospects, always tied to employment levels, will moderate near-term share appreciation.

SECTOR: **Information Technology**
BETA COEFFICIENT: **1.00**
10-YEAR COMPOUND EARNINGS PER-SHARE GROWTH: **7.5%**
10-YEAR COMPOUND DIVIDENDS PER-SHARE GROWTH: **12.5%**

		2006	2007	2008	2009	2010	2011	2012	2013
Revenues (mil)		1,675	1,887	2,066	2,083	2,001	2,084	2,230	2,326
Net income (mil)		465	515	576	534	477	516	548	569
Earnings per share		1.22	1.35	1.56	1.48	1.32	1.42	1.51	1.56
Dividends per share		0.61	0.79	1.20	1.24	1.24	1.24	1.27	1.31
Cash flow per share		1.40	1.54	1.82	1.72	1.56	1.67	1.78	1.83
Price:	high	42.4	47.1	37.5	32.9	32.8	33.9	34.7	45.9
	low	33.0	36.1	23.2	20.3	24.7	25.1	29.1	31.5

Paychex, Inc.
911 Panorama Trail South
Rochester, NY 14625–0397
(585) 385-6666
Website: *www.paychex.com*

CONSERVATIVE GROWTH

PepsiCo, Inc.

Ticker symbol: PEP (NYSE) ❏ S&P rating: A ❏ Value Line financial strength rating: A++
Current yield: 2.6% ❏ Dividend raises, past 10 years: 10

Company Profile

PepsiCo is a global beverage, snack, and food company. It manufactures, markets, and sells a variety of salty, convenient, sweet, and grain-based snacks; carbonated and noncarbonated beverages; and foods in approximately 200 countries, with its largest operations in North America (United States, Canada, and Mexico); the United Kingdom; and now Russia. Most of the major PepsiCo brands, such as the familiar Pepsi Cola, are likely to show up in abundance in your refrigerator and kitchen cupboard at any time. About 49 percent of current sales come from outside the U.S.

PepsiCo is organized into four business units, as follows:

- PepsiCo Americas Foods (37 percent revenue, 52 percent profit) which includes two major foods groups, formerly reported as separate operating segments. The first is the familiar Frito-Lay, which makes and distributes the too-familiar snack brands—Fritos, Doritos, Lay's, Cheetos, Tostitos, Ruffles, SunChips, and various dips and spreads to go with these products—and popular local brands like Sabritas in Mexico. The second is Quaker Foods which came to Pepsi in 2001 and sells Quaker Oats, Aunt Jemima, Cap'n Crunch, Life cereal, Rice-A-Roni, Mother's Cookies, and Near East, to name a few.

- PepsiCo Americas Beverages (32 percent revenue, 26 percent profit), the flagship business, includes PepsiCo Beverages North America and all of the Latin American beverage businesses, and brings to market Tropicana and Gatorade products, Lipton teas, Aquafina bottled water, SoBe, and Naked juices, in addition to several familiar soft drink brands like Pepsi, Mountain Dew, Sierra Mist, and 7-UP outside the United States. There are 14 billion-dollar brands in all. The Beverages unit also distributes Dr Pepper, Crush, and Rockstar energy drinks, and handles all beverage distribution in the Latin American market, including specialized local brands like Sabritas and Gamesa in the Mexican market.

- PepsiCo Europe (21 percent revenue, 12 percent profit) which includes all PepsiCo businesses in the United Kingdom and the rest of Europe. The Europe and "AMEA" segments, (Asia, Middle East, and Africa) explained next, distribute not only U.S.-branded products but also many that are formulated and branded for local markets, similar to the Sabritas and Gamesa examples cited above.
- AMEA—Asia, Middle East, and Africa (10 percent revenue, 10 percent profit) handles distribution of PepsiCo products in these regions as just described.

Many of PepsiCo's brand names are more than 100 years old, but the corporation is relatively young. PepsiCo was founded in 1965 through the merger of Pepsi-Cola and Frito-Lay. PepsiCo now has 18 brands in total that generate over $1 billion in retail sales. The top two brands are Pepsi-Cola and Mountain Dew, but beverages constitute less than half of Pepsi's sales. It is primarily a snack company. Frito-Lay brands alone account for more than half of the U.S. snack chip industry. Note also that the snack businesses are relatively more profitable and contribute a larger share of the company's total profits.

PepsiCo began its international snack food operations in 1966. Today, with operations in more than 40 countries, it's the leading multinational snack chip company, with more than a 25 percent market share of international retail snack chip sales. Brand Pepsi and other Pepsi-Cola products—including Diet Pepsi, Pepsi One, Mountain Dew, Slice, Sierra Mist, and Mug brands—account for nearly one-third of total soft drink sales in the United States. Pepsi-Cola also offers a variety of noncarbonated beverages, including Aquafina bottled water, Lipton ready-to-drink tea, and Frappuccino ready-to-drink coffee through a partnership with Starbucks.

PepsiCo acquired Tropicana, including the Dole juice business, in August 1998 and now markets these products in 63 countries. Tropicana Pure Premium is the third-largest brand of all food products sold in grocery stores in the United States. Gatorade, acquired as part of the Quaker Oats Company merger in 2001, is the world's leading sports drink.

Financial Highlights, Fiscal Year 2013

Strategic shifts, new investments, and rising commodity costs kept the fizz out of Pepsi's earnings in FY2012. The company implemented a series of price increases to recover increasing commodity costs, and those may not have gone over well with customers—a bag of Doritos can now set you back over 4 dollars. The company put into place major initiatives to improve organizational and operational efficiency in 2012, which have borne fruit to the tune of $3 billion in cost savings through 2014, and has a target to save another $1 billion annually through productivity improvements by 2019.

As such, the fizz started to come back in FY2013. "Organic" revenues grew 4 percent and per-share earnings for FY2013 rose 9 percent on a constant currency basis suggesting some results from the operational improvements. Operating margins rose more than a full percentage point to 19.3 percent. To offset the higher costs of those Doritos, the company did hand out a 5 percent dividend increase and has committed to continue strong cash returns to shareholders, announcing plans for a 35 percent increase in cash returns to shareholders in 2014 as a mixed bag of dividend increases and accelerated share buybacks. Although currency translation is still a headwind, and the restructuring plan is still on, the company is guiding both revenue and earnings growth in the mid-single digits, which it considers its long-term target through FY2015 and beyond.

Reasons to Buy

PepsiCo continues to offer a compelling combination of steady and predictable earnings, dividend, and cash flow growth with a strong measure of safety, as the low beta of 0.32 suggests. If you want to compare Pepsi with archrival Coke, Pepsi's food business adds some diversification, channel strength, and profitability that rival Coke does not have, and its noncarbonated drink segments, led by Gatorade, Tropicana, and Lipton, are probably stronger, while Coke has stronger international brand recognition and a stronger brand equity overall, in our opinion.

That said, the company is taking an aggressive approach to geographical expansion, localization, and brand recognition, and it expects continued solid growth in international markets especially as middle classes expand in emerging regions. Recently, for example, the company opened a food and beverage R&D center in Shanghai to address the Asian market. International growth combined with new operational efficiencies should bode well for the long term. Mainly through efficiencies, the company has resumed earnings growth from a pretty flat few years 2010 through 2012, and has increased its dividend for 41 straight years.

Reasons for Caution

The puck is still moving to more innovative and health-conscious drinks and food products, and while the company recognizes the need to "improve the nutritional profile," PepsiCo will need to invest aggressively in this area. They have many new and reformulated products in the works that use healthier ingredients and reduced levels of sodium and trans fats, but the competition for this segment is intense.

The newly formed Global Nutrition Group is addressing this challenge, as a recent release of Tropicana Farmstand 100 percent fruit and vegetable drinks exemplifies. While Pepsi is investing heavily in international markets, there is no guarantee that they will displace Coke, although the food offering will help get attention and valuable shelf space. Finally, the food business may be a drag depending on which way commodity prices run; for instance, most snack products are heavily influenced by corn prices.

SECTOR: **Consumer Staples**
BETA COEFFICIENT: **0.32**
10-YEAR COMPOUND EARNINGS PER-SHARE GROWTH: **9.0%**
10-YEAR COMPOUND DIVIDENDS PER-SHARE GROWTH: **13.5%**

	2006	2007	2008	2009	2010	2011	2012	2013
Revenues (mil)	35,137	39,474	43,251	43,232	57,938	66,504	65,492	66,415
Net Income (mil)	5,065	5,543	5,142	5,946	6,320	6,379	6,178	6,823
Earnings per share	3.00	3.34	3.21	3.77	3.91	3.98	3.92	4.37
Dividends per share	1.16	1.43	1.60	1.75	1.89	2.03	2.13	2.24
Cash flow per share	3.95	4.38	4.30	4.84	5.47	5.83	5.74	6.20
Price: high	66.0	79.0	79.8	64.5	68.1	71.9	73.7	87.1
low	56.0	61.9	49.7	43.8	58.8	58.5	62.2	68.6

PepsiCo, Inc.
700 Anderson Hill Road
Purchase, NY 10577–1444
(914) 253-2000
Website: *www.pepsico.com*

Perrigo Company

Ticker symbol: PRGO (NASDAQ) ❑ S&P rating: NR ❑ Value Line financial strength rating: A
Current yield: 0.3% ❑ Dividend raises, past 10 years: 10

Company Profile

Perrigo is the world's largest manufacturer of over-the-counter pharmaceutical products for the store-brand market. They also manufacture generic prescription pharmaceuticals, nutritional products, and active pharmaceutical ingredients (APIs). As we'll describe below, the company entered into an $8.6 billion merger agreement with Irish pharmaceutical maker Elan to be consummated in 2014; so what follows describes the pre-merger Perrigo.

The company operates in four segments: Consumer Healthcare, Nutritionals, Rx Pharmaceuticals, and API. Consumer Healthcare is by far the largest segment, generating about 59 percent of Perrigo's revenue in 2013, while Nutritionals brings in 14 percent, Rx Pharma 20 percent, and APIs 5 percent.

The company's success depends on its ability to manufacture and quickly market generic equivalents to branded products. It employs internal R&D resources to develop product formulations and manufacture in quantity for its customers. It also develops retail packaging specific to the customer's needs.

If you have bought a store-branded over-the-counter medication such as ibuprofen, acetaminophen, skin remedies, or cough medicine at a store like Target or Walmart in the past year, there's a good chance (a 75 percent chance, in fact) that it was made by Perrigo. The company's Consumer Healthcare business produces and markets over 1,800 store-brand products in 8,300 individual SKUs to approximately 1,000 customers, including Wal-Mart, CVS, Walgreens, Kroger, Target, Safeway, Dollar General, Costco, and other national and regional drugstores, supermarkets, and mass merchandisers. Wal-Mart is its single largest customer and accounts for 19 percent of Perrigo's net sales.

The Nutritionals segment is relatively new as a standalone segment and includes store-brand infant formula, vitamins, and minerals. The segment distributes 400 store-brand products in 2,500 SKUs to more than 150 customers.

The Rx Pharma operations produce generic prescription drugs (in contrast to the over-the-counter drugs produced in the Consumer Healthcare segment), obviously benefiting when key patented drugs run past their patent protection. Rx Pharma markets approximately 300 generic prescription products, many of them topicals and creams, with over 760 SKUs, to approximately 120 customers, while the API division markets an assortment of active ingredients to other drug manufacturers as well as for the company's own products, including a number of active ingredients that we'd have trouble spelling correctly, so we won't even try. The company's products are manufactured in nine facilities around the world. Its major markets are in North America, Mexico, the U.K., and China. About 33 percent of sales are overseas.

In mid-2013 the company announced the acquisition of Elan Corporation, a high-profile pharmaceutical manufacturer based in Ireland, and formed a new holding company located in that country. Elan is mainly a developer and marketer of prescription pharmaceuticals with strong products in multiple sclerosis, neuropsychiatrics, and other specialty drugs. The acquisition will give Perrigo a stronger foothold in the prescription segment and in international markets.

Financial Highlights, Fiscal Year 2013

Again, these results do not include Elan. For FY2013, the company posted another good year with a healthy 11.5 percent growth in revenues and a 7 percent growth in per-share earnings. Going forward, the picture is murky due to the merger and differences in accounting standards. Currently the company is giving guidance for "adjusted" earnings in the $6.45–$6.70 range. The company financed most of the Elan purchase by issuing shares, which will certainly not put it on this year's "buyback achievers" list. There will be some adjustments and divestitures, including an $80 million stake in a company that Elan owned before the merger; we'll see if the proceeds are used to retire some of the issued shares or for other purposes. The Elan merger was probably intended to improve overall gross margins, which were already on the upswing, and reduce operating expenses. If the projections are right there could be a sizeable improvement in earnings and cash flow—and dividends and buybacks.

Reasons to Buy

Perrigo is a real success story of solid niche dominance (store-branded medications) with a couple of high-growth, high-margin businesses mixed in. Steady growth in sales combined with a steady growth in margins have a multiplicative effect, and the company has enjoyed well-above-average profit growth in this industry. Frankly, we had some doubts about the Elan merger and whether it would dilute Perrigo's focus on its core niche businesses, but we've been fans of this company and its management team for a while and have more trust than usual that things will come out right.

Not only does Perrigo currently dominate a niche, it is a growing niche. The company calls it "Quality Affordable Healthcare Products." People are becoming more sensitive to their own health-care costs and spending in general and are opting more often for the store brand; after all, 200 mg of ibuprofen is 200 mg of ibuprofen. This all sits on top of the demographic tailwind of the aging population.

Reasons for Caution

Perrigo broke most of our rules in making a major acquisition of a complex business, then moving to another country where accounting standards make business evaluation more difficult. Normally we would have dropped the company right then and there, but again, we like its track record and niche dominance. If anything, the confusion around the merger provided a buying opportunity in FY2014. We hope—and expect—to be able to write a clearer story next year; we admit there is more risk to this stock now than there was in the past.

SECTOR: **Health Care**
BETA COEFFICIENT: **0.80**
10-YEAR COMPOUND EARNINGS PER-SHARE GROWTH: **21.0%**
10-YEAR COMPOUND DIVIDENDS PER-SHARE GROWTH: **10.5%**

	2006	2007	2008	2009	2010	2011	2012	2013
Revenues (mil)	1,366	1,447	1,822	2,007	2,269	2,765	3,173	3,540
Net income (mil)	74.1	78.6	150	176	263	341	411	442
Earnings per share	0.79	0.84	1.58	1.87	2.83	3.64	4.37	4.68
Dividends per share	0.17	0.18	0.21	0.22	0.25	0.27	0.32	0.35
Cash flow per share	1.41	1.46	2.35	2.67	3.69	4.78	5.84	6.41
Price: high	18.7	36.9	43.1	61.4	67.5	104.7	120.8	157.5
low	14.4	16.1	27.7	18.5	37.5	62.3	90.2	98.6

Perrigo Company
Treasury Building
Lower Grand Canal St.
Dublin 2, Ireland
+353 (1) 6040031
Website: *www.perrigo.com*

Philips Electronics, N.V.

Ticker symbol: PHG (NYSE) □ S&P rating: NR □ Value Line financial strength rating: B+ □ Current yield: 3.5% □ Dividend raises, past 10 years: 6

Company Profile

Philips is a global electronics-based conglomerate serving consumer and professional markets in three primary and adjacent segments: health care, consumer lifestyle, and lighting.

The company's markets are worldwide but centered outside the U.S., which accounts for only 28 percent of its sales, and the company is considered an innovation leader in most of its key markets.

The Healthcare business (41 percent of FY2013 revenues) supplies a variety of imaging systems, home health care and clinical patient care, and informatics systems. Products deploy high degrees of technology and range from health monitors to radiation oncology and CT scanner and MRI systems to fluoroscopy systems, ventilators, ultrasound, interventional x-ray and surgery systems—you get the idea. The company also supplies analytical services, telehealth and other workflow systems, and "health-care transformation services" to modernize health-care delivery.

The Consumer Lifestyle business (20 percent) provides an assortment of mostly small home appliances, personal care, and convenience products, like razors, coffeemakers, etc.

The Lighting segment (36 percent) supplies stock and custom lighting products, including fixtures, lighting systems, bulbs, and LED components to all markets.

A smaller Group & Services segment (3 percent) provides innovation and lab services for internal and external customers.

Philips is one of the few companies on our list not domiciled in the U.S. As such, it represents an effort to diversify our base a little and to choose a company with strong non-U.S.-based brands in key and growing overseas markets, as well as the more traditional ones like Western Europe that are showing signs of being in investment and spending mode once again.

Financial Highlights, Fiscal Year 2013

The economic environment remained a challenge in many global markets, particularly Europe, through FY2013. Nominal sales declined 1 percent but increased by 3 percent on a comparable basis (comparable business base and currency). Comparable-based Healthcare sales were flat, hurt by a modest decline in imaging systems, while Lighting rose 3.2 percent and Consumer Lifestyle was up about

10 percent. The bright spot within Lighting was LED products, which rose about 36 percent over FY2012. Increased productivity and margin gains brought pre-tax earnings (EBITDA) forward by 10.5 percent.

Going forward the company has identified numerous productivity improvements, new products, and partnerships as part of a self-declared "Path to Value." Revenues are projected ahead 4–6 percent on a comparable basis, while earnings should grow in the 7–12 percent range (currency among other things makes these forecasts difficult) and we think we could see more if share buybacks accelerate a little with cash flow gains on top of an already healthy per-share cash flow base. Overall, we think Philips qualifies for our "5 in 10" list—10 percent earnings growth on 5 percent revenue growth long term.

The company bought back about $2.7 billion in shares and has authorized another $2 billion over the next three years, which would represent a 7 percent reduction in capitalization. Long-term debt levels run a safe and frugal 14.3 percent of total capital, a favorable figure for this type of company.

Reasons to Buy

Philips is emerging from several years of mixed operating performance culminating with the Great Recession and continued European malaise after the recession. Like its competitor General Electric (another new *100 Best* entry for 2015), it has embarked on a multiyear program to restructure and fine-tune its business mix, operational and channel efficiency with a major internal initiative called "Accelerate!" Unlike GE, Philips didn't have to deal with an oversized financial arm. The global brand is strong. Our bet on this company is mainly based on technology and innovation, improved global markets, and above all else, gaining its feet and keeping them with significant and persistent operational improvements over the near term. It's a play on creating value and delivering strong and persistent gross margins, profits, and ultimately cash to shareholders as it completes its transformation.

Reasons for Caution

Health-care technology markets are competitive and constrained in many areas like the U.S. that are trying to rein in health-care costs; taxes on medical technology players don't help, either. The decline in FY2013 imaging systems revenue probably reflects this. Going forward, this is still a complex company to manage in a complex set of markets and geographies. We hope it doesn't get too acquisition-happy to meet growth targets. If our bets on getting the ducks to fly in formation don't work out, we may lose a few feathers on this flight and become the "quacks" of the investment idea space. This one may take a little more patience than others, but we think it's worth taking a flyer.

SECTOR: **Industrials**
BETA COEFFICIENT: **1.50**
10-YEAR COMPOUND EARNINGS PER-SHARE GROWTH: **28.5%**
10-YEAR COMPOUND DIVIDENDS PER-SHARE GROWTH: **11.5%**

	2006	2007	2008	2009	2010	2011	2012	2013
Revenues (bil)	35.6	39.1	36.7	31.3	34.0	29.2	32.8	32.1
Net income (mil)	1,442	2,381	545	572	1,943	211	346	1,611
Earnings per share	1.22	2.17	0.54	0.61	2.05	0.19	0.37	1.75
Dividends per share	0.54	0.81	0.97	0.94	0.93	1.11	0.94	0.98
Cash flow per share	2.30	3.40	2.38	2.76	4.06	2.26	2.45	3.80
Price: high	38.0	45.9	42.9	30.5	36.1	34.1	26.8	37.0
low	27.4	35.3	14.7	13.9	26.5	16.3	17.2	26.3

Philips Electronics N.V.
Amstelplein 2
Breitner Center
1070 MX Amsterdam, The Netherlands
+3120 59 77777
Website: *www.philips.com*

Praxair, Inc.

Ticker symbol: PX (NYSE ❑ S&P rating: A ❑ Value Line financial strength rating: A ❑ Current yield: 2.0% ❑ Dividend raises, past 10 years: 10

Company Profile

Praxair, Inc. is the second-largest supplier of industrial gases in the world. The company, which was spun off to Union Carbide shareholders in June 1992, supplies a broad range of atmospheric, process, and specialty gases; high-performance coatings; and related services and technologies.

Praxair's primary products are atmospheric gases—oxygen, nitrogen, argon, and rare gases (produced when atmospheric air is purified, compressed, cooled, distilled, and condensed) and process and specialty gases—carbon dioxide, helium, hydrogen, and acetylene (produced as by-products of chemical production or recovered from natural gas). Customers include makers of primary metals, metal fabricators, petroleum refiners, and producers of chemicals, health-care products, electronics, glass, pulp and paper, and environmental products.

The gas products are sold into the packaged-gas market and the merchant market. In the packaged-gas market, bulk gases are packaged into high-pressure cylinders and either delivered to the customer or to distributors. In the merchant market, bulk gases are liquefied and transported by truck to the customer's facility.

The company also designs, engineers, and constructs cryogenic and noncryogenic gas supply systems for customers who choose to produce their own atmospheric gases onsite. This is obviously a capital-intensive delivery solution for Praxair but results in lower delivered cost to the customer and higher returns for Praxair, as all operational costs are paid by the customer. Contracts for these installations can run to 20 years.

Praxair Surface Technologies is a subsidiary that applies wear-, corrosion-, and thermal-resistant metallic and ceramic coatings and powders to metal surfaces in order to resist wear, high temperatures, and corrosion. Aircraft engines are a primary market, but it serves others, including the printing, textile, chemical, and primary metals markets, and provides aircraft engine and airframe component overhaul services. About 62 percent of Praxair's sales come from outside the U.S.

Financial Highlights, Fiscal Year 2013

FY2013 results saw a recovery from a flat FY2012 as demand related to a resurgence of U.S. manufacturing and strength in the energy and chemical sectors worldwide took hold. Meanwhile, Europe, another important market, also started to recover. Sales resumed their upward path, rising 6.2 percent over FY2012. Per-share earnings did not quite hold that line due to acquisition costs and some exchange-rate fluctuations, but improved pricing and some cost reductions will likely carry the day to a more impressive figure in FY2014. Sales are anticipated to rise another 7.3 percent with per-share earnings in the $6.25–$6.55 range, the midpoint of which would represent a 9 percent increase. At the same time cash flow has been rising almost 10 percent a year. As a consequence, the company is planning to resume its more aggressive share repurchase tack to around 2 percent annually. It has steadily raised its dividend 20 cents a year and may increase the rate of increase to something closer to 30 cents or even more.

Reasons to Buy

It's nice to own a few "golf-clap" stocks in companies that show high margins, steady growth, and no surprises. Par, par, birdie, par—not a bad round, and Praxair continues to be the sort of company that can deliver that.

Praxair is the largest gas provider in the emerging markets of China, India, Brazil, Mexico, and Korea and continues to invest heavily in plants in these regions. In general, the international presence is more balanced and diversified than most of its competitors, and it is not as dependent upon growth in China. The company is a big player in the petroleum industry and especially the heavy crude segment; equally if not more importantly, the company is a strong and pure play in the re-emergence of U.S. manufacturing.

We especially like the company's high margins (31 percent and growing) and cash flow generation—and the willingness to share it with shareholders, with steady 10 percent dividend increases over the past five years and likely to increase in years to come, with decent share repurchases thrown in for good measure.

Reasons for Caution

Competitors are strong, and getting stronger with the recent Air Products–Airgas merger and a consolidation of smaller players in the industry. As hydrocarbon energy products are feedstock for many of Praxair's products, the company is sensitive to increases in energy prices, and the price of natural gas in particular, an important feedstock, has fluctuated considerably while being historically low. The strong international presence means that results are sensitive to currency headwinds, but those headwinds may subside or even turn into tailwinds. Finally, the markets have recognized Praxair's recent score card and are still giving a low handicap in the form of a high share price continuing at 20 times earnings, difficult to sustain for a high single-digit growth rate—new investors should thus look for favorable entry points. That said, this company continues to regularly make its putts and has been one of the more dependable performers on our list.

SECTOR: **Materials**

BETA COEFFICIENT: **0.91**

10-YEAR COMPOUND EARNINGS PER-SHARE GROWTH: **12.5%**

10-YEAR COMPOUND DIVIDENDS PER-SHARE GROWTH: **19.5%**

	2006	2007	2008	2009	2010	2011	2012	2013
Revenues (mil)	8,324	9,402	10,796	8,956	10,118	11,252	11,224	11,925
Net income (mil)	988	1,177	1,335	1,254	1,195	1,672	1,692	1,755
Earnings per share	3.00	3.62	4.19	4.01	3.84	5.45	5.61	5.87
Dividends per share	1.00	1.20	1.50	1.60	1.80	2.00	2.20	2.40
Cash flow per share	5.25	6.18	8.63	6.85	6.95	8.95	9.10	9.70
Price: high	63.7	92.1	77.6	86.1	96.3	111.7	116.9	130.5
low	50.4	58.0	53.3	53.3	72.7	88.6	100.0	107.7

Praxair, Inc.

39 Old Ridgebury Road

Danbury, CT 06810–5113

(203) 837-2000

Website: *www.praxair.com*

CONSERVATIVE GROWTH

The Procter & Gamble Company

Ticker symbol: PG (NYSE) ❑ S&P rating: AA- ❑ Value Line financial strength rating: A++ ❑ Current yield: 3.2% ❑ Dividend raises, past 10 years: 10

Company Profile

Procter & Gamble dates back to 1837, when William Procter and James Gamble began making soap and candles in Cincinnati, OH. The company's first major product introduction took place in 1879 when it launched Ivory soap. Since then, P&G has continually created a host of blockbuster products, added some key acquisitions, exited the food business and a few others, and, in total, has some of the strongest, most recognizable consumer brands in the world.

P&G is a uniquely diversified consumer products company with a strong global presence. P&G markets its broad line of products to nearly 5 billion consumers in more than 180 countries.

The company is a recognized leader in the development, manufacturing, and marketing of quality laundry, cleaning, paper, personal care, and health-care products, including prescription pharmaceuticals.

To understand Procter, it's worth a look at how the company is organized. That organization has evolved as the company reexamines its business mix and realigned its sectors accordingly. The company is now organized into four more or less equally sized "industry-based" sectors: Global Beauty, Global Fabric and Home Care, Global Health and Grooming, and Global Baby, Feminine, and Family Care. This sector split may not rattle right off your tongue but will become clearer as we examine the business mix:

- Global Beauty (24 percent of FY2013 sales, 21 percent of profits) includes shampoo, skin care, and bar soap products, including such traditional brands as Head & Shoulders, Ivory soap, Safeguard, Secret, Pantene, Vidal Sassoon, Cover Girl, and Old Spice, and some newer and edgier brands like Olay, HUGO BOSS, 007 Men's Fragrances, Gucci, and Dolce & Gabbana. There are 36 brands in all.
- Global Fabric and Home Care (32 percent, 27 percent) covers many of the familiar laundry and cleaning brands—Tide, Cheer, Dawn, Febreze, Downy, Bounce, Era, Mr. Clean, and a handful created for international markets—34 brands in all.

- Global Health and Grooming (24 percent, 33 percent) includes oral care products like Crest and Scope, shaving products like Gillette and Braun, and an assortment of other over-the-counter personal care products like Metamucil, Prilosec, Vicks, and Pepto-Bismol—18 brands in all.
- Global Baby, Feminine, and Family Care (20 percent, 19 percent) markets mostly paper products like Puffs, Charmin, Pampers, Bounty, Always, and Tampax—11 brands in all.

The company recently announced the sale of its global pet food business (the "IAMS" brand) for $2.9 billion to privately held Mars; it's not hard to see that this operation did not fit the mix, particularly as much of this product sells through pet food specialty stores, not the traditional grocery or discount channels. It's a logical continuation of a long series of food divestitures—for example, solid brands like Folgers and Jif—many to friendly rival J.M. Smucker, another *100 Best* stock.

Procter has always been a hallmark example of brand management and building intrinsic brand strength—that is, strength not from the company name but through the brand's own name and reputation. It is described as a "house of brands," not a "branded house," although we're starting to see the "P&G" name more prominently in its marketing and advertising. The company tells us that its 50 "Leadership Brands" are some of the world's most well-known household names, that 90 percent of its business comes from these 50 brands, and that 25 of them are billion-dollar businesses.

The company has a strong international presence, with 61 percent of sales originating outside the U.S. The company also manufactures locally in its largest international markets.

Financial Highlights, Fiscal Year 2013

Despite a fairly strong currency headwind, P&G cleaned up fairly well in FY2013. Revenues were up just shy of 1 percent, although the company reported "organic" sales up 3 percent—you get the idea about currency. The company also reported crosscurrents including stronger volumes and pricing, manufacturing cost savings and other efficiencies (they've been outsourcing major manufacturing operations for years, even bringing outside operators onto their own factory sites), and higher commodity costs. The crosscurrents led to a modest decline in operating margins to 22.3 percent (from 22.6 percent) but improved volumes resulted in a 4.6 percent gain in net earnings anyway. A modest share buyback brought a 5.2 percent rise in per-share earnings.

For FY2014 and FY2015, the company expects commodity prices

to moderate, pricing to continue to strengthen as the economy picks up and people return to traditional brands, to realize stronger emerging market growth, and to buy back $6 billion in shares—all told, bringing revenue growth back to a reported 2–3 percent range and per-share earnings growth into the high single digits.

Reasons to Buy

Regardless of developments in the world economy, people will continue to shave, bathe, do laundry, and care for their babies, and P&G is the global leader in baby care, feminine care, fabric care, and shaving products. Everyone should consider at least one defensive play in their portfolio, and P&G continues to deserve a spot at the top of the list.

P&G is extending its reach to capture share in channels and markets that are currently underserved. Developing markets are a huge opportunity, representing 86 percent of the world's population, and P&G feels it can be a leader in many product categories. Emerging markets now represent 39 percent of their revenue, up from 32 percent in 2011 and 20 percent in 2002. P&G is also broadening its distribution channels to pursue opportunities in drug and pharmacy outlets, convenience stores, export operations, and even e-commerce.

As the company continues to evolve its organizational structure (and we think they're about done),

it has departed from its traditional model of managing brands as wholly separate businesses with brand-specific advertising budgets, product research labs, and so forth. Synergies from combining ads and ad strategies alone should reduce total costs across the company's many portfolios. Recent cost-cutting moves (which are expected to save $10 billion annually by 2016) will grow the profit base faster than the moderately strong growth in the sales base—all a good combination. The move to bring back former CEO A.G. Lafley for what appears to be a short-term assignment to finalize the organization structure, groom his successor, and tune up the innovation machine appears to be working. In short, we continue to like the brand, marketplace, and financial strength; sure and steady dividend growth (the company has raised its dividend 58 straight years); and short- and long-term prospects.

Reasons for Caution

The recent recession made consumers much more price conscious, and many switched to generics. That switch has reversed to a degree, but not everyone will come back on board, and the company has added some lower-priced subbrands as a result. Rising commodity costs can affect P&G, and the expansion into the health and beauty business brings more exposure to often-fickle consumer tastes and shorter brand life than the company may be used to. Finally, we think the steady stream of reorganizations has been a distraction (it's been distracting to us) but it appears that such activity may be coming to an end now.

SECTOR: **Consumer Staples**
BETA COEFFICIENT: **0.46**
10-YEAR COMPOUND EARNINGS PER-SHARE GROWTH: **8.0%**
10-YEAR COMPOUND DIVIDENDS PER-SHARE GROWTH: **11.0%**

	2006	2007	2008	2009	2010	2011	2012	2013
Revenues (mil)	68,222	76,476	83,503	79,029	78,938	82,559	83,680	85,500
Net income (mil)	8,684	10,340	12,075	11,293	10,946	11,797	11,344	11,869
Earnings per share	2.64	3.04	3.64	3.58	3.53	3.93	3.85	4.05
Dividends per share	1.15	1.28	1.45	1.64	1.80	1.97	2.14	2.29
Cash flow per share	3.51	4.25	4.97	4.65	4.87	5.21	5.20	5.33
Price: high	64.2	75.2	73.8	63.5	65.3	67.7	71.0	85.8
low	52.8	60.4	54.9	43.9	39.4	57.6	59.1	68.4

The Procter & Gamble Company
1 Procter & Gamble Plaza
Cincinnati, OH 45201
(513) 983-1100
Website: *www.pg.com*

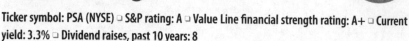

Public Storage

Ticker symbol: PSA (NYSE) ❑ S&P rating: A ❑ Value Line financial strength rating: A+ ❑ Current yield: 3.3% ❑ Dividend raises, past 10 years: 8

Company Profile

You have stuff. We have stuff. We all have stuff. Stuff to store somewhere. Stuff from our families, stuff from our kids, stuff from our past. Boats, RVs, and extra vehicles. And we all need to store that stuff somewhere. But where? As more of us live in houses with smaller yards and devoid of basements, where? As more of us choose to rent rather than buy, where? As more of us, especially the younger Millennials among us, choose to live closer to the centers of larger cities, where? As the retirees among us downsize, where? As the elderly give up their primary residences, where?

You get the idea. There is more personal stuff for most of us to store, and less space to do it. That's where Public Storage comes in.

Public Storage is a real estate investment trust owning and operating 2,200 self-storage properties in 38 states and another 188 facilities in seven countries in Europe. The company also owns a 42 percent interest in another trust called PS Business Parks, which owns 108 rentable properties in eight states.

Most are probably familiar with the format—small unfinished, generally not-climate-controlled lockers rentable on a month-to-month basis for personal and business use. They range in size from 25 to 400 square feet, and there are typically 350 to 750 storage spaces in each facility. Some include covered parking for vehicle, boat, and RV storage. On average the company nets about $1 per square foot per month—a rather handsome sum considering these units do not come with any of the finish or comfort of an apartment which may rent for something similar depending on the market.

Not surprisingly, the largest concentrations are in California, Texas, and Florida (since these are centers of retirees), and most are near a major U.S. or European city. The three largest markets are New York, San Francisco, and Los Angeles. Branding in the U.S. is "Public Storage"; in Europe it is "Shurgard."

The key strategies are revenue and cost optimization, market share growth in major markets, and building brand recognition. The company has a centralized call center and a website to help market its product and facilitate transactions. Acquisitions are also an important part of the strategy; the current market is fragmented with PSA only owning 10–20 percent of the market at most, and good properties come up regularly. The company acquired 121 such properties in 2013 and expects to grow its property base a steady 1–2 percent annually.

Public Storage represents our second *100 Best* venture into the REIT market; the first was Health Care REIT last year. Our principle here remains the same; we're not looking for just real estate, we want to own a good business that *just happens* to own a lot of real estate. REITs are typically good income producers, as they are required by law to pay a substantial portion of their cash flow to investors. The accounting rules are different, and REIT investors should focus on Funds From Operations (FFO), which is analogous to operating income; net income figures have depreciation expenses deducted, which can vary in timing and not always be realistic. FFO supports the dividends paid to investors.

Financial Highlights, Fiscal Year 2013

FY2013 was a strong and steady year. Revenues grew about 8 percent in all, while the core self-storage business grew 5.3 percent on a same-store basis. Net income grew about 26 percent; about 19 of that 26 percent came from increased profits in the self-storage business, with non-recurring items making up most of the rest of it. Total funds from operations increased just over 19 percent.

For FY2014 and FY2015, the company projects revenue growth, aided by acquisitions, in the 10 percent and 7 percent ranges respectively, with per-share FFO growth in the 6–8 percent range.

Reasons to Buy

As stated above: we aren't just looking for a real estate play, we're looking for a good business. With Public Storage, we're pretty sure we've found one. PSA has the best brand and highest operating efficiency in the business, and the core business model and need for its product is sustained and growing. No matter how easy it is to sell stuff on craigslist, it's also too easy to acquire stuff, and we don't see people getting out of that habit anytime soon. At the same time, real estate is trending away from large suburban McMansions with extra space and more toward city digs, patio homes, cluster homes, and the like. All point to strong, steady business prospects for providers of flexible storage solutions, and as PSA strengthens its brand and market-share foothold, more of that business will go its way. The dividend has risen substantially in recent years and is well funded; too, there is less debt than usually found in a real estate investment business.

Reasons for Caution

Real estate is real estate, and is more subject to ups and downs than was once thought. Increased dividends and general strength of this business have stored away some pretty healthy gains for the stock—unlock the door and enter carefully.

SECTOR: **Real Estate**
BETA COEFFICIENT: **0.77**
10-YEAR COMPOUND FFO PER-SHARE GROWTH: **18.5%**
10-YEAR COMPOUND DIVIDENDS PER-SHARE GROWTH: **11.0%**

	2006	2007	2008	2009	2010	2011	2012	2013
Revenues (mil)	1,381	1,616	1,746	1,628	1,647	1,752	1,826	1,982
Net income (mil)	314	457	636	835	672	824	670	845
Funds from operations								
per share	4.16	4.74	5.17	5.03	5.22	5.93	6.31	7.53
Real estate owned								
per share	56.74	56.61	46.48	46.48	44.51	43.35	42.71	47.97
Dividends per share	2.00	2.00	2.20	2.20	3.05	3.656	4.40	5.15
Price: high	98.1	117.2	102.5	85.1	106.1	136.7	152.7	176.7
low	67.7	68.1	52.5	45.3	74.7	100.0	129.0	144.4

Public Storage
701 Western Ave.
Glendale, CA 91201
(818) 244-8080
Website: *www.publicstorage.com*

AGGRESSIVE GROWTH

Quest Diagnostics Inc.

Ticker symbol: DGX (NYSE) ❑ S&P rating: BBB+ ❑ Value Line financial strength rating: B++
Current yield: 2.2% ❑ Dividend raises, past 10 years: 5

Company Profile

If you have gone for any kind of medical test, either at the recommendation of a doctor or as required by an employer or insurance company, chances are you got that test in a lab operated by Quest Diagnostics. Quest is the world's leading provider of diagnostic testing, information, and services to support doctors, hospitals, and the care-giving process.

The company operates more than 2,200 labs and patient service centers including about 150 smaller "rapid-response" labs in the U.S., and has facilities in India, Mexico, the U.K., Ireland, and Sweden. It provides about 150 million lab test results a year and serves physicians, hospitals, employers, life and health-care insurers, and other health facilities. The company estimates that it serves more than half the hospitals and physicians in the United States.

The company offers diagnostic testing services covering pretty much the gamut of medical necessity in its testing facilities. It also offers a line of diagnostic kits, reagents, and devices to support its own labs, home and remote testing, and other labs. The company offers a series of "wellness and risk management services,"

including tests, exams, and record services for the insurance industry. The company also does tests and provides other support for clinical research and trials, and finally, through its information technology segment, offers a Care360 platform to help physicians maintain charts and access data through its network, which has about 200,000 physicians enrolled.

The company has begun to provide "insourced" solutions to hospitals that formerly ran their own labs. More progressive hospitals and hospital systems have been trying to cut costs and are starting to look at independent labs to run some of their in-house functions. The company recently acquired parts of the UMass Memorial Medical Center and California's Dignity Health's (formerly Catholic Healthcare West) "outreach" lab business, that is, labs located off hospital premises.

The company has also been a leader in developing so-called "moderate complexity" direct molecular testing procedures, where more complex diagnostic tests can be performed in "moderate complexity" environments—i.e., a "retail" lab format such as Quest operates. Such a new test for encephalitis was cleared by the FDA in March 2014—a first, and a strong endorsement of this type of procedure delivery. The company is also a leader in "gene based" and "esoteric" testing and has launched an assortment of molecular genetics tests supporting new trends in the health industry toward individualized medicine—medicine based on a patient's own unique gene makeup and characteristics.

Financial Highlights, Fiscal Year 2013

Medicare cutbacks and competition in the lab diagnostic business have softened results through FY2012 and 2013: Current financials are far short of a highlight for this company. For FY2013, total revenues dropped some 3.2 percent to $7.1 billion, while margins also stalled out and sent earnings down some 12.6 percent. A 14 million share buyback, about 1 percent of float, moderated per-share earnings declines to just over 8 percent.

The current business is expected to turn around slowly, and management has been very conservative about adding any benefits in from the Affordable Care Act. Revenues and profits are forecast generally flat through FY2014 with a gradual return of margins through operating efficiency and leverage to a 5 percent per-share earnings gain in FY2015. We think this is too conservative—ACA changes and an increased emphasis on complex tests done in

independent labs like Quest will bring stronger than forecast results in our opinion. We'll see.

Reasons to Buy

Granted, increased utilization initiatives, particularly on the Medicare front, have softened results. But going forward and especially into FY2015, we think the company stands to benefit from the Affordable Care Act as 30 million more patients get access to "free" or subsidized health care. Additionally, an ever greater emphasis on wellness and preventative care is likely to send more people for routine checkups, particularly if insurance carriers offer benefits (like free tests or lower coinsurance) to motivate such preventative care.

But even more, we're excited about the innovative new tests performed at the retail lab level for molecular level and gene-based diagnostics, which bode well for the future—the company is advancing to higher, more profitable levels of the diagnostic food chain. When the company announced FDA approval of the encephalitis test, it woke the stock up to a 12 percent gain that day and garnered a considerable amount of positive attention in the markets and marketplace.

We're also fans of the ancillary businesses—clinical trials, insurance qualifications, employer testing, and IT services—which all should do well in an environment favoring greater cost control and outsourcing of distinct services as Quest provides. The company is a leader in its industry and has a beta of 0.66 indicating relative safety. Finally, shareholder returns have become considerably more attractive in the past few years. The dividend was raised almost 50 percent in 2013 and the company has bought back a third of its float in the past ten years. We see continued improvement going forward.

We admit that we're taking a rare stance of betting on a business to do better than its own management predicts, but here we see an opportunity, as several factors in the ongoing evolution of health care and health-care cost management seem to line up right for this company, and the cash returns give us a cushion if we turn out to be wrong.

Reasons for Caution

Of course, we could be wrong about the ACA and the improving value-add in the health-care food chain. Without these levers, the business is pretty unexciting; the company has been forced to reach for growth through acquisitions, which don't always work out, and through hospital partnerships, which can lead to some revenue sharing and thus pressure on margins. Medicare cuts are likely to continue, although we see that trend stabilizing and perhaps reversing in favor of wellness and preventative care. The company may also face more competition as large group physician practices get larger and bring some of their lab operations in-house—although that trend may be countered by hospitals and other large organizations getting out of this relatively easily outsourced business.

SECTOR: **Health Care**
BETA COEFFICIENT: **0.66**
10-YEAR COMPOUND EARNINGS PER-SHARE GROWTH: **11.0%**
10-YEAR COMPOUND DIVIDENDS PER-SHARE GROWTH: **8.5%**

		2006	2007	2008	2009	2010	2011	2012	2013
Revenues (mil)		6,269	6,705	7,249	7,455	7,400	7,511	7,468	7,146
Net income (mil)		641.4	553.8	640.0	730.3	720.9	728.7	700.0	612.0
Earnings per share		3.22	2.84	3.27	3.88	4.05	4.53	4.43	4.00
Dividends per share		0.40	0.40	0.40	0.40	0.40	0.47	0.81	1.20
Cash flow per share		4.32	4.08	4.75	5.52	5.00	6.42	6.23	6.22
Price:	high	64.7	58.6	59.9	62.8	61.7	61.2	64.9	64.1
	low	48.6	48.0	38.7	42.4	40.8	45.1	53.3	52.5

Quest Diagnostics Inc.
3 Giralda Farms
Madison, NJ 07940
(973) 520-2700
Website: www.*questdiagnostics.com*

AGGRESSIVE GROWTH

NEW FOR 2015

Ralph Lauren Corporation

Ticker symbol: RL (NYSE) □ S&P rating: A □ Value Line financial strength rating: A+ □ Current yield: 1.2% □ Dividend raises, past 10 years: 5

Company Profile

Follow the pony. The Polo pony. And this isn't a one-trick pony, either, it's been a tradition for (believe it or not, in the fashion industry) almost 50 years. Ralph Lauren Corporation is a leader in the design, marketing, and distribution of premium lifestyle products in four categories: apparel, home, accessories, and fragrances. Since 1967, the year it was founded by Ralph Lauren himself (who is still the President, Chairman, and CEO of the company), Ralph Lauren's reputation and distinctive image have been consistently developed across an expanding number of products, brands, and international markets. The company's brand names, which include Polo by Ralph Lauren, Ralph Lauren Collection, Ralph Lauren Purple Label, Black Label, Blue Label, Lauren by Ralph Lauren, RRL, RLX, Ralph Lauren Childrenswear, Denim & Supply Ralph Lauren, Chaps, and Club Monaco, constitute one of the world's most widely recognized families of consumer brands.

The brands reflect a lifestyle of luxury, understated elegance, distinct design, and quality, widely available to but aspirational for most consumer segments. Typical designs are understated but colorful, traditional but somewhat attention getting, well made, and well fit. When you see someone wearing a Polo or other Ralph Lauren product, you recognize it right away. It's the sort of fashion you can wear days in a row almost anywhere.

The company is divided up into three segments: Wholesale, Retail, and Licensing. The Wholesale segment is the "traditional" sales channel, selling primarily to more than 10,000 department stores and other retail shops worldwide, representing 45 percent of FY2013 revenues. The Retail segment (52 percent) operates approximately 388 standalone stores and 494 concession-based "shop-within-shop" outlets primarily in North America, Europe, and Asia, some through licensed partners. The Licensing unit allows third parties, such as makers of sunglasses and fragrances, the right to RL trademarks, and accounts for 3 percent of revenues. The company also sells directly through ralphlauren.com.

About 37 percent of the business originates outside the U.S., and the Lauren family owns some 83 percent of voting power through ownership of a Class B stock. Ralph Lauren himself is still involved in product design along with an internal design staff; much of the marketing and advertising material is also generated internally.

Financial Highlights, Fiscal Year 2013

Total net revenues for the year 2013 (which the company calls FY2014 as it ends in February 2014) were some 7 percent higher than 2012 and 9 percent higher absent the effects of currency and some discontinued operations. Wholesale growth was strongest, reflecting overall economic progress, strength with some key channel partners like Macy's (another *100 Best* stock), and a recovery in Europe. Sales in the retail segment were relatively flat on a same-store basis. Licensing revenues declined mainly due to the transfer of some Chaps products and Australia/New Zealand from a license to a direct model. Profit margins were hampered some by currency effects and a small mix effect from integrating Chaps, and helped some by operating leverage (higher volume) and the absence of some restructuring costs; all told net income increased about 1.8 percent to $776 million.

Although the company forecast a healthy top-line growth for FY2014 in the 8 percent range, it backed off on its earnings projections in an early 2014 earnings announcement, mostly due to some increased restructuring expenses and marketing and advertising. However, it still projects something in the 8–10 percent range. The company recently announced a $500 million share repurchase and has dropped share counts steadily, totaling about 15 percent since 2005. The dividend has advanced handsomely from 20 cents in 2009 to $1.80 for 2014, signaling a higher priority placed on shareholder returns.

Reasons to Buy

The Ralph Lauren story is all about brand and all about the enduring taste and quality that support that brand. As it's supposed to, the brand makes a promise of tradition and quality, and it delivers. Over and over. People of almost all walks of life, around the world, covet the brand; the only question is whether they want to pay for it and whether they want to substitute something more trendy. Ralph Lauren is our first, and admittedly rather conservative, venture into the often-fickle fashion industry—which we'll admit we don't on the whole really understand—but we do understand this brand and the products and images that go with it. And we like the rapidly growing shareholder returns.

Reasons for Caution

Fashion is fashion, and tastes do change. On a personal level, we see products that might be a little too bright and colorful at least for our doughty tastes—if they work in today's markets, fine, but we don't want to see too many leftover RL products in our Ross Stores (another *100 Best* pick). We're putting some faith and trust in fashion, something we don't have much faith and trust in, but RL has developed one of the steadiest and most enduring approaches to running any business—fashion or otherwise.

Fierce competition in the fashion industry could ultimately knock RL off its "full price" horse into discounting mode; once that starts it's hard to stop. The shares have been marked down a bit recently due to slowing profit growth projections, probably presenting a buying opportunity. Without this opportunity the shares might be, like their products, a bit out of reach for daily consumption.

SECTOR: **Consumer Discretionary**
BETA COEFFICIENT: **1.31**
10-YEAR COMPOUND EARNINGS PER-SHARE GROWTH: **15.0%**
10-YEAR COMPOUND DIVIDENDS PER-SHARE GROWTH: **NM**

	2005	2006	2007	2008	2009	2010	2011	2012
Revenues (mil)	4,295	4,880	5,018	4,980	5,660	6,859	6,944	7,415
Net income (mil)	401	420	406	479	568	681	762	776
Earnings per share	3.74	3.99	4.01	4.73	5.75	7.13	8.13	8.40
Dividends per share	0.20	0.20	.020	0.30	0.60	0.80	1.60	1.70
Cash flow per share	5.25	6.24	5.95	6.73	8.06	9.78	10.94	11.35
Price: high	83.1	102.6	82.0	83.5	115.3	164.5	182.5	192.0
low	45.7	60.4	31.2	31.6	71.1	102.3	134.3	149.3

Ralph Lauren Corporation
650 Madison Avenue
New York, NY 10022
(212) 318-7000
Website: *www.ralphlauren.com*

AGGRESSIVE GROWTH

NEW FOR 2015

ResMed, Inc.

Ticker symbol: RMD (NYSE) □ S&P rating: NR □ Value Line financial strength rating: A □ Current yield: 2.0% □ Dividend raises, past 10 years: 1

Company Profile

By this point, some of you may consider *The 100 Best Stocks to Buy in 2015* to be an excellent cure for sleep disorders. But for the tens of millions who don't own our book, there is another solution, a solution growing fast in application and ease of use. Perhaps you know someone using a CPAP (continuous positive airway pressure) machine to alleviate SDB (sleep-disordered breathing) or OSA (obstructive sleep apnea). As we age and tend to gain weight, the devices above are becoming a much more mainstream way for folks (and their partners) to get some much- needed sleep. If we still have your attention, read on . . .

Formed in 1989, ResMed develops, manufactures, and distributes medical equipment for treating, diagnosing, and managing sleep-disordered breathing and other respiratory disorders. Products include diagnostic products, airflow generators, headgear, and other accessories. The original and still largest product line of CPAP machines delivers pressurized air through a mask during sleep, to prevent collapse of tissue in the upper airway, a condition

common in people with narrow upper airways and poor muscle tone—in many cases, people who are older and overweight. Estimates are that 46 million adults age 30–70 (that's 26 percent) have some form of sleep apnea. A great many, who exhibit the typical symptoms of daytime sleepiness, snoring, hypertension, and irritability, have yet to be diagnosed.

CPAP machines and their cousins VPAP (Variable Positive Airway Pressure) and others were at one time massive, clunky machines restricting movement and very difficult to travel with. No more: The new machines are smaller, lighter, cheaper, and easier to use. We don't like solutions that are worse than the problem, and CPAP has turned the corner on that with the new machines, becoming more acceptable, less expensive, and more mainstream. We think the company's four-pronged strategy is a good one— make the machines easier to deal with (and afford), increase clinical awareness and the rate of diagnosis, expand into new applications including stroke and congestive heart failure treatment, and expand internationally. The company has executed effectively on all fronts.

The company markets its products in 100 countries and makes them in five countries outside the U.S., and invests 8 percent of revenues in R&D.

Financial Highlights, Fiscal Year 2013

For FY2013, net revenues increased 11 percent to $1.51 billion, a figure that would have been 15 million, or 1 percent higher, without currency effects. Unit volumes were higher across the board, and growth in the U.S. outpaced international growth, probably indicating initial diagnosis and acceptance of the company's newer, more compact product lines. A more favorable product mix led earnings some 20 percent higher, and the company initiated a new 68 cent per share dividend, which was raised rather quickly to $1.00 annually.

Through FY2015, the company projects top-line growth in the 6–9 percent range, and per-share earnings, aided by operating margin improvements and a new 20 million share buyback authorization, to rise in the upper teens to the 20 percent range annually.

Reasons to Buy

We believe that the company's four-pronged strategy, outlined above, is right on. As these machines, and the diagnosis of the condition they're designed for, become more mainstream, we expect more people in the market, and the lower prices and reduced inconvenience should open up larger and larger slices of the market for the company. Demographics are a plus, too—as people get older and heavier, these machines will find more potential users. It's a niche business, and ResMed dominates the niche and is the only company solely focused on this market (Philips N.V., another new *100 Best* pick, is also a player). While we tend not to look for this out of the gate, we feel the company is a good acquisition candidate for a larger provider of health-care technology products. The new dividend is substantial and share buybacks have already been a healthy source of shareholder return, with outstanding shares projected to drop to 132 million in FY2014 from 152 million in 2011, and an authorization to repurchase another 10 million.

Reasons for Caution

One of the bigger issues facing CPAP and related technologies is the eligibility for reimbursement or coverage through Medicare/Medicaid and through private insurers. The current landscape is a mixed bag: Many non-Medicare health insurance plans do not cover the machines (which range from about $600 to $1,900 in price), and Medicare has driven payment rates down through competitive bidding and across-the-board cuts. Too, ResMed has been hit by the 2.3 percent medical equipment maker excise tax that is part of the Affordable Care Act, but on the positive side the company also sees more business driven their way by universal coverage. Health-care reform continues to be a wild card, which may benefit or hurt the company; probably it will be a mix of the two.

SECTOR: **Health Care**
BETA COEFFICIENT: **0.72**
10-YEAR COMPOUND EARNINGS PER-SHARE GROWTH: **20.5%**
10-YEAR COMPOUND DIVIDENDS PER-SHARE GROWTH: **NM**

	2006	2007	2008	2009	2010	2011	2012	2013
Revenues (mil)	607	716	835	921	1,092	1,243	1,368	1,514
Net income (mil)	92.5	108.1	114.1	146.4	190.1	227.0	254.9	307.1
Earnings per share	0.61	0.69	0.73	0.95	1.23	1.44	1.71	2.10
Dividends per share	—	—	—	—	—	—	—	0.68
Cash flow per share	0.88	1.01	1.14	1.33	1.66	1.96	2.40	2.71
Price: high	25.6	28.1	26.2	26.7	35.9	35.4	42.9	57.3
low	18.4	19.2	14.5	15.7	25.0	23.4	24.4	42.0

ResMed, Inc.
9001 Spectrum Center Blvd.
San Diego, CA 92123
(858) 836-5000
Website: *www.resmed.com*

AGGRESSIVE GROWTH

Ross Stores, Inc.

Ticker symbol: ROST (NASDAQ) □ S&P rating: BBB+ □ Value Line financial strength rating: A
Current yield: 1.2% □ Dividend raises, past 10 years: 10

Company Profile

"Always a Great Bargain" is the motto of Ross Stores, the second-largest off-price retailer in the United States. Ross and its subsidiaries operate two chains of apparel and home accessories stores. As of 2013 the company operated a total of 1,276 stores, up from 1,125 in 2011, of which 1,168 were Ross Dress for Less locations in 33 states, D.C., and Guam and 108 were dd's DISCOUNTS stores in four states. Just under half the company's stores are located in three states—California, Florida, and Texas.

Both chains target value-conscious women and men between the ages of 18 and 54. Ross's target customers are primarily from middle-income households, while the dd's DISCOUNTS target customers are typically from lower- to middle-income households. Merchandising, purchasing, pricing, and the locations of the stores are all aimed at these customer bases. Ross and dd's DISCOUNTS both offer first-quality, in-season, name-brand and designer apparel, accessories, and footwear for the family at savings typically in the 20–60 percent range off department store prices (at Ross) or 20–70 percent off (at dd's DISCOUNTS). The stores also offer discounted home fashions and housewares, educational toys and games, furniture and furniture accents, luggage, cookware, and at some stores jewelry.

Ross's strategy is to offer competitive values to target customers by offering a well-managed mix of inventory with a strong percentage of name brands and items of local and seasonal interest at attractive prices.

Financial Highlights, Fiscal Year 2013

The Great Recession was nothing but good news for this company, bringing in newly cost-conscious customers by the busload. The question was—what would happen after that? Would people feel they were on more solid footing and abandon Ross in droves for more fully priced favorites? The answer, so far, appears to be "no."

Helped along by an expanding store presence, FY2013 sales grew 5.2 percent, and about 3 percent on a same-store basis. While this was down from figures experienced in the wake of the downturn, it's still pretty healthy by retail standards. A slight uptick in gross and operating margins led to a 6.5 percent increase in net earnings; a 3.2 percent "markdown" in the number of shares due to buybacks propelled per-share earnings forward to a fairly handsome 10 percent increase.

FY2014 looks to be pretty much more of the same. The company continues to expand its footprint, both in existing and new geographies. Plans call for opening 95 new stores in all: 75 Dress for Less and 20 of the dd's DISCOUNTS in 2014. This new infrastructure, plus two new distribution centers and the expiration of state hiring tax credits will attenuate earnings growth modestly to about 8 percent higher on a per-share basis, on revenues continuing about 6 percent higher. We expect more of the same in FY2015 and beyond—steady mid-to-high single-digit growth in revenues, steady high single digits to near 10 percent growth in earnings, qualifying Ross for our "5 and 10" club: 10 percent earnings growth on 5 percent sales growth. We should also note that from 2003 forward, the company has consistently reduced share counts some 30 percent from 302 million to 213 million, and has raised its dividend by a factor of 10 over the same period.

Reasons to Buy

The recession apparently helped Ross gain mainstream appeal across a wider set of customers. While some of those customers defected back to full-price retail stores as things improved, a greater number have shown that they will continue to shop at the stores. At the same time, the company was successful with operational changes begun in 2009 to improve merchandising and inventory management, which led to better stocking of a more favorable mix of goods and better inventory turnover. The higher store count has increased operating leverage as well—more volume through the same infrastructure and cost base. These marketplace and operational changes have led to the financial success one would expect and then some, and the company continues to improve its inventory management and should see greater profitability almost regardless of the economic environment.

The company plans to expand the formula into the Midwest and other regions, which should be a good match for the offering. There are still no stores in the upper Midwest, Ohio, Michigan, or most of the Northeast; the company sees enough geography and enough market to grow to 2,500 stores long term, about twice the current footprint. Nothing is mentioned about international expansion, but we wonder if there too lies an opportunity.

As mentioned, the company has done plenty for its shareholders. There is lots of room in the cash flow to increase the payout, and the company has almost no long-term debt. The company boasts that it has repurchased stock as planned (which doesn't always happen for many companies) every year since 1993—it's a strong commitment. Moderate expansion, operational excellence, sustained shareholder returns; it's an attractive formula.

Reasons for Caution

One concern is that the company is dependent on the actions of others—mainly first-line apparel retailers—for its success. There are still questions about Ross's ability to acquire the same quantity and quality of merchandise as the economy picks up and full-price retailers begin to see higher levels of foot traffic. Such inventory follows a cycle, and if full-price retailers cut back on orders, there is less for everyone—and if the economy picks up, they will sell more, so less for Ross. Upshot: Inventory management improvements at full-price retailers could make things tougher for the company. On top of that, the company still depends to a degree on store expansion, which carries its own risks, and could make supply constraints hurt even more.

SECTOR: **Retail**
BETA COEFFICIENT: **0.65**
10-YEAR COMPOUND EARNINGS PER-SHARE GROWTH: **16.5%**
10-YEAR COMPOUND DIVIDENDS PER-SHARE GROWTH: **26.0%**

		2006	**2007**	**2008**	**2009**	**2010**	**2011**	**2012**	**2013**
Revenues (mil)		5,570	5,975	6,486	7,184	7,866	8,608	9,721	10,230
Net income (mil)		241	261	305	443	555	657	787	837
Earnings per share		0.85	0.95	1.77	1.77	2.32	2.84	3.53	3.88
Dividends per share		0.13	0.16	0.20	0.25	0.35	0.47	0.59	0.71
Cash flow per share		1.26	1.42	1.76	2.45	3.03	3.65	4.42	4.89
Price:	high	15.9	17.6	20.8	25.3	33.3	49.2	70.8	82.0
	low	11.1	12.2	10.6	14.0	21.2	30.1	47.1	53.0

Ross Stores, Inc.
5130 Hacienda Drive
Dublin, CA 94568
(925) 965-4400
Website: *www.rossstores.com*

Schlumberger Limited

Ticker symbol: SLB (NYSE) □ S&P rating: A+ □ Value Line financial strength rating: A++
Current yield: 1.6% □ Dividend raises, past 10 years: 8

Company Profile

Schlumberger Limited is the world's leading oilfield services company. It provides technology, information solutions, and integrated project management services with the goal of optimizing reservoir performance for its customers in the oil and gas industry. Founded in 1926, today the company has a large international footprint, employing more than 123,000 people in 85 countries, with 69 percent of revenue generated outside of North America. The company operates in three primary business segments:

- The Reservoir Characterization Group (27 percent of FY2013 revenues, 38 percent of pretax income) is mostly a consulting service, applying many digital and other technologies toward finding, defining, and characterizing hydrocarbon deposits. Interestingly, the company compares the electronic characterization of a hydrocarbon-producing zone to the imaging of a human body, using an assortment of technologies (for example, a technology referred to as a "Saturn 3D radial fluid sampling probe") to identify what you can't see directly.

- Not surprisingly, the Drilling Group (38 percent of revenues, 35 percent of pretax income) does the actual drilling and creation of wells for production, both in onshore and offshore environments. Again, a number of new drilling, drillbit, and drilling fluid technologies are in play, and naturally, so-called "fracking" is an important new part of the product offering.

- The Reservoir Production Group (37 percent of revenues, 27 percent of pretax income) completes and services the well for production, maintaining and enhancing productivity through its life.

Throughout the petroleum production process, the company not only provides physical onsite services but also substantial consulting, modeling, information management, total cost, yield, and general project management around these activities. In short, SLB offers a full outsourced supply chain for oil and gas field development and production.

Schlumberger manages its business through 28 GeoMarket regions, which are grouped into four geographic areas, fairly evenly split according to the pretax profits delivered: North America (20 percent); Latin America (21 percent); Europe, Commonwealth of Independent States, and Africa (21 percent); and Middle East and Asia (25 percent). The GeoMarket structure provides a single point of contact at the local level for field operations and brings together geographically focused teams to meet local needs and deliver customized solutions.

The company made the big-ticket acquisition of oil services giant Smith International, which was integrated into the operations and financials during FY2011.

Financial Highlights, Fiscal Year 2013

Beyond the Smith acquisition, which added about $12 billion to a $27 billion revenue base in FY2011, Schlumberger continues to ring up decent growth numbers, with FY2013 revenues some 8 percent ahead of FY2012, earnings ahead 14 percent, and per-share earnings ahead almost 16 percent of FY2012 levels. The company bought back some 21 million shares and appears to be trying to reduce share counts to something close to pre-Smith acquisition levels sometime in the next few years—175 million shares were issued in that 2011 acquisition; 54 million have retired so far, if you're keeping score.

Global oil exploration and production spend rates continue to move ahead nicely as big oil attempts to replenish reserves, as new "fracking" production is developed, and as global consumption levels slowly rise. Revenues are projected to rise in the 8–10 percent range annually through FY2015, while per-share earnings are projected in the high teens to 20 percent higher.

The company announced a 28 percent dividend increase to $1.60 annually in early 2014, following a 16 percent increase in 2013.

Reasons to Buy

The first page of Schlumberger's 2009 annual report began with: "The age of easy oil is over." The sentence seems prescient and, along with its size and complete offering to the exploration and production industry, it is perhaps the most succinct statement of Schlumberger's advantages in the E&P business. Its expertise is most valuable in the most technically challenging projects, such as the several recent sub-salt offshore finds in Brazil, West Africa, and the Gulf of Mexico.

We were concerned about the many crosscurrents in the petroleum industry: softer prices, hazardous (but profitable) offshore exploration and new regulations thereon, and the possible boom-bust cycle of fracking. But the uncertainties of all three have moderated, and when you look at the results, it's clear that the company manages such crosscurrents well and performs strongly even during down cycles. That, combined with the strong and likely growing imperative for big oil companies to replace reserves, should benefit the company over the long haul. We continue to admire the way SLB develops and deploys new technologies in the E&P business, which are all, taken together, a competitive advantage and "moat" protecting the franchise. In all, we continue to like SLB for the long term.

Reasons for Caution

The shifts and uncertainties just mentioned could get larger, and that plus competition could put a bigger dent in the oil service industry. The current dip in natural gas prices—if it starts to really eat into production—could become a firm "down" story, although that's been moderating of late. The company continues to face the traditional risks of oil drilling—particularly offshore drilling—that culminated in the BP disaster of 2010.

SECTOR: **Energy**
BETA COEFFICIENT: **1.55**
10-YEAR COMPOUND EARNINGS PER-SHARE GROWTH: **19.5%**
10-YEAR COMPOUND DIVIDENDS PER-SHARE GROWTH: **11.5%**

	2006	2007	2008	2009	2010	2011	2012	2013
Revenues (mil)	19,230	23,277	27,163	22,702	27,447	39,540	42,149	45,266
Net income (mil)	3,747	5,177	5,397	3,142	3,408	3,954	5,439	6,210
Earnings per share	3.04	4.18	4.42	2.61	2.70	3.51	4.06	4.70
Dividends per share	0.48	0.70	0.81	0.84	0.84	0.96	1.06	1.25
Cash flow per share	4.51	5.94	6.42	4.70	4.55	6.05	6.73	7.55
Price: high	74.8	114.8	112.0	71.1	84.1	95.6	80.8	94.9
low	47.9	56.3	37.1	35.1	54.7	54.8	59.1	69.1

Schlumberger Limited
5599 San Felipe, 17th Floor
Houston, TX 77056
(713) 513-2000
Website: *www.slb.com*

NEW FOR 2015

Schnitzer Steel Industries, Inc.

Ticker symbol: SCHN (NASDAQ) ❑ S&P rating: NR ❑ Value Line financial strength rating: B
Current yield: 2.8% ❑ Dividend raises, past 10 years: 3

Company Profile

Welcome to the only stock on our *100 Best* list to post a loss. In the last year, no less. And it's a new stock for the 2015 list. What were we thinking? What were we drinking?

Truth of the matter is, while we don't like companies that are too vulnerable to economic cycles, we do like companies that know how to make the best of them. And we like companies in commodity industries that occupy niches in their industries and add relatively more value than their larger competitors. We like companies that think shareholders are important and who return lots of cash to them. Finally, we wanted to offer another "small cap" stock for those who might like to feel as if they own a bigger part of a smaller but successful and dynamic business.

Founded in 1946, Schnitzer Steel is mainly a collector and recycler of ferrous and non-ferrous scrap, with smaller operations that collect, dismantle, and market auto and truck parts and a steel mill "mini-mill" finished steel product business. The Metals Recycling business (about 77 percent of FY2013 revenues) collects, recycles, processes, and brokers scrap steel and non-ferrous metals to domestic and foreign markets. Larger scrap mills are located in Oregon; Washington; Oakland, CA; and Massachusetts, with smaller mills in Rhode Island, Puerto Rico, Hawaii, and Alaska, all with adjacent deep-water ports, correctly suggesting an orientation toward international export of scrap metal for foreign mills. Indeed, that is true—some 50 percent of ferrous shipments go to Asia, 25 percent to Europe/Africa/Middle East, and 25 percent to U.S. steel mills. The company operates 60 metals recycling facilities ("scrapyards," in popular vernacular) in 15 states, mostly on the coasts and in the south, seven in Canada and five in Puerto Rico. The operation adds value in part by sorting and shredding input scrap into homogenous materials well suited to the needs of downstream customers.

The Auto Parts business (11 percent of revenues) operates 61 self-serve locations and remarketing centers, some co-located with Metals Recycling facilities, in 16 states with a concentration in California. Some of these centers operate under the "Pick-n-Pull" franchise. This operation processes about 350,000 cars per year. Inventories of scrapped autos and common parts from those autos are posted online and updated as new inventory is received.

The Steel Manufacturing business (12 percent of revenues) operates an electric arc furnace mini-mill in McMinnville, Oregon, producing rebar, wire rod, merchant bar, and other specialty products, of course from scrap steel available from the company's own Metals Recycling facilities.

The numbers for the whole operation are fascinating—here is a quick snapshot for 2013:

4.3 million tons of ferrous metal and 520 million pounds of non-ferrous metal shipped; 900 million pounds of metal from crushed auto bodies; 9.6 million pounds of catalytic converters, 1.2 million gallons of fuel, 800,000 gallons of motor oil, 7.5 million pounds of batteries, and 838,000 tires and wheels from all those cars.

The synergies between the three businesses are obvious; the company is also thought to have some of the better locations and especially port facilities in the industry.

Financial Highlights, Fiscal Year 2013

FY2013 was not a particularly good year for the company, and the reason was fairly obvious—low steel prices in turn caused by a slowdown in Pacific Rim growth and a global supply glut. Recycled steel prices averaged $359 per ton after averaging $417 per ton in FY2012, while finished steel went for $680 per ton, down from $715. Volumes exported to the major importing countries—China, South Korea, and Turkey—declined some 20 percent for the year. The company was able to offset this somewhat with greater domestic sales for the year. The fourth quarter of FY2013 was weakest but finished strong into FY2014; we think global steel inventories and demand will stabilize into FY2014 and especially FY2015 as auto, appliance, and nonresidential construction activity increases both in the U.S. and abroad. Non-ferrous metals prices have remained fairly stable at just under $1.00 per pound through both years, but saw a similar volume decrease driven primarily by export demand weakness.

All taken together, revenues declined about 22 percent from FY2012, and earnings dipped just barely into the red. However, the company maintained cash flow above $3.00 per share and actually raised its dividend 82 percent to 75 cents per share.

Going forward, the company expects somewhat firmer prices and new operational efficiencies to expand both the top line and margins somewhat, with a 4 percent increase in revenues in FY2014 widening out a bit to 15 percent in FY2015—almost a full recovery to FY2012 levels. Per-share earnings are expected in the $1.50 range in FY2015, with continued dividend increases and moderate buybacks. The company has retired 15 percent of its shares since 2006 and has only 26 million shares outstanding today.

Reasons to Buy

There are a lot of mom-and-pop scrap dealers around the world, but few have the size, operating leverage, and remarketing abilities of Schnitzer. The company is a strong and recognized brand in a fragmented and unbranded industry, offering advantages both on the sales and operational side. When prices and markets are soft, the company loses a little, but as we saw particularly in 2008, when markets are strong, the company does really, really well. Schnitzer is well managed, adds a lot of value in a relatively non-value-add industry, and knows how to preserve its success to get through tough times—and is also learning how to reward shareholders. There have been only three dividend increases in the past ten years, but they've been recent and large.

Reasons for Caution

Schnitzer is very sensitive to global steel and non-ferrous metals markets and the ups and downs of pricing. While its size and marketing advantages serve it well in tough times, inventory is inventory, and the company can get caught with a lot of it purchased at higher prices if the markets don't move to its advantage. It does okay in bad economic climates, but the company is really a bet on recycling value-add and on good times in global manufacturing. If you buy in, you'll want to watch global steel and other metals prices. Too, while the company has a good track record, there are always some environmental risks and costs in this sort of business. The high beta of 1.94 reflects some of this risk and the volatility inherent in the relatively low share count.

SECTOR: **Industrials**
BETA COEFFICIENT: **1.94**
10-YEAR COMPOUND EARNINGS PER-SHARE GROWTH: **9.0%**
10-YEAR COMPOUND DIVIDENDS PER-SHARE GROWTH: **20.0%**

	2006	2007	2008	2009	2010	2011	2012	2013
Revenues (mil)	1,855	2,572	3,641	1,900	2,301	3,459	3,341	2,621
Net income (mil)	105	131	249	(32.2)	67	119	30	(2.0)
Earnings per share	3.42	4.32	8.61	(1.14)	2.86	4.24	1.10	(0.07)
Dividends per share	—	—	0.10	0.20	0.20	0.20	0.23	0.32
Cash flow per share	1.17	1.51	1.83	2.01	1.86	2.64	2.49	1.85
Price: high	22.0	29.6	27.3	28.1	19.5	21.1	23.4	14.6
low	10.6	17.5	18.1	7.4	9.0	15.5	11.5	10.6

Schnitzer Steel Industries, Inc.
3200 N.W. Yeon Avenue
Portland, OR 97210
(503) 224-9900
Website: *www.schnitzersteel.com*

NEW FOR 2015

The Scotts Miracle-Gro Company

Ticker symbol: SMG (NYSE) ❑ S&P rating: BB+ ❑ Value Line financial strength rating: B+
Current yield: 3.0% ❑ Dividend raises, past 10 years: 5

Company Profile

Scotts Miracle-Gro, formerly Scotts Co., formerly O.M. Scott & Sons, is a 146-year-old provider of mostly packaged lawn- and garden-care products for consumer markets. Originally it was a seed company; today lawn-care products include packaged, pre-mixed fertilizers and combination fertilizer, weed-, and pest-control products marketed mainly under the Scotts and Turf Builder brand names. The company also markets packaged grass seed and a line of individually packaged pest- and disease-control products mainly under the Ortho brand, acquired in 1997, and a line of specialty garden fertilizers and pest-control products under the Miracle-Gro name, acquired in 1995. The company also markets a line of home protection pest-control products. Through a series of small acquisitions, the company has entered the Lawn Service business, which now operates out of 26 company-operated and 93 franchised locations. Consumer businesses account for about 90 percent of revenues, Lawn Service another 9 percent.

Scotts is a study in branding in an otherwise highly fragmented market. The attractive core brands of Scotts, Turf Builder, and Ortho are being leveraged into other businesses, such as lawn service under the Scotts LawnService brand and home pest control under the Ortho brand. The vision is interesting: "To help people of all ages express themselves on their own piece of the earth." While this sounds pretty groovy, it also connotes the possibilities to expand markets. Further trendy elements in this business include an ongoing demographic shift—more returning to cities—different styles of gardening, more specialty products—a shift that may prove positive but will take some work. The company has created a dedicated team to address this segment. People are also seeking organic gardening products in consumer packages; Scotts is testing a new line of organic Miracle-Gro products to address this need.

Financial Highlights, Fiscal Year 2013

Revenues didn't quite "green up" as the company expected in FY2013 and remained flat for the year with a small downtick in volume offset by a slight uptick in price. The company cited a variety of factors, including political gridlock, that kept consumers from opening their wallets, and the sort of discretionary expense that many Scotts products represent are probably not at the top of the list when times get better and people finally have more disposable income. As such, the company turned its focus to profitability with such mundane initiatives as better inventory management and with price decreases in key potash and phosphate fertilizer components (to the chagrin of Mosaic, another *100 Best* pick). All told, Scotts managed to nourish some pretty good gains; net earnings were up some 43 percent from FY2012 (admittedly, an easy compare) and per-share earnings were up a similar amount. The company raised its dividend 15 percent and started off FY2014 with a 21 percent raise; clearly there is more "green" in shareholder returns these days.

The company expects to get a little closer to the top of consumer wish lists in FY2014 and beyond, with sales gains projected in the 3–5 percent range through FY2015. Profitability continues to be a big focus, and soft-input commodity prices should continue to help. Scotts recently reaffirmed guidance of $3.00–$3.20 per-share earnings, which would be some 23 percent ahead of FY2013; projections call for another 11 percent gain in FY2015.

Reasons to Buy

There are a lot of tailwinds that should help this well-established consumer brand. First on the list is the economy and resurgence in housing: Evidence

that people are spending more on their homes is sprouting up everywhere. We see more emphasis on quality landscapes over quantity and size of lawn, which should help Scotts. Too, we see help coming from changing demographics and aging clientele with disposable income and physical limitations who want easier, more complete solutions like Scotts Lawn Service and similar services we think will take root. The company has seen some recent market share gains in its core products and is a mainstay at key channel partners like Home Depot, Lowe's, and Wal-Mart. The brand remains strong and trusted, and we expect to see it in more places and connected to higher-margined services; Ortho pest-control services is but one example. It wouldn't surprise us to see a branded Scotts "store within a store" like Apple's stores in consumer electronics retailers or Ralph Lauren's Polo shops within major department stores. Fresh marketing and advertising are also a plus; we like the new Scotsman "Feed Your Lawn Now—Feed It!" campaigns.

We also think there will be some opportunity in the international sector for these same reasons and with the growing middle classes and urban gardening formats that could become mainstream in emerging market regions. Finally, cash returns for investors have provided a pretty good nutrient base for investors awaiting future extension of the brand and expansion of profitability.

Reasons for Caution

Scotts isn't the only brand in town, and the company does face some competition from less expensive house brands such as those sold at Ace Hardware and elsewhere. Lawn and garden spend is naturally sensitive to sluggish economies, but we do think that there is a baseline level people will drop to and remain at; they want to maintain their lawns and provide pleasant stay-at-home environments if they can't do much else. Finally, the demographic shifts away from the suburbs noted above, including downsizing and increases in renting versus owning could hurt the traditional bagged fertilizer and lawn goods business; that's where the new products and services in new niches will come into play.

SECTOR: **Materials**
BETA COEFFICIENT: **0.92**
10-YEAR COMPOUND EARNINGS PER-SHARE GROWTH: **6.0%**
10-YEAR COMPOUND DIVIDENDS PER-SHARE GROWTH: **27.0%**

	2006	2007	2008	2009	2010	2011	2012	2013
Revenues (mil)	2,697	2,672	2,983	3,141	3,139	2,835	2,826	2,819
Net income (mil)	132.7	113.4	(10.9)	153.3	212.4	121.9	113.2	161.2
Earnings per share	1.91	1.69	(0.17)	2.32	3.14	1.84	1.62	2.58
Dividends per share	0.50	0.50	0.50	0.50	0.63	1.05	1.23	1.41
Cash flow per share	3.00	2.82	0.91	3.23	4.07	3.00	2.86	3.87
Price: high	54.7	57.4	40.7	44.3	55.0	60.8	55.9	62.6
low	37.2	33.5	16.1	24.9	37.5	40.0	35.5	42.0

The Scotts Miracle-Gro Company
14111 Scottslawn Rd.
Marysville, OH 43041
(937) 644-0011
Website: *www.scotts.com*

Seagate Technology

Ticker symbol: STX (NASDAQ) □ S&P rating: BB+ □ Value Line financial strength rating: B+
Current yield: 3.3% □ Dividend raises, past 10 years: 8

Company Profile

About 30 years ago, you could buy a 5-megabyte hard disk drive from a major computer manufacturer like IBM or HP. It was about the size of a washing machine, cost several thousand dollars, and made little grunting noises that would have driven R2D2 into a frenzy.

Today, you can store about 200,000 times the information—1 terabyte—on an inexpensive hard drive measuring about 2.5" × 3", about 7mm thick, that makes no noise whatsoever, retrieves information almost instantly, and never breaks. These hard drives fit into laptops, netbooks, or even smaller devices, and you scarcely know they're even there. Or they can be assembled into racks and arrays to provide huge storage capability for enterprise servers and data centers—and most importantly, major and minor hubs in the cloud.

At the heart of the evolution, as well as a dominant force in producing these devices today, is Seagate Technology—the world's largest producer of computer hard disk drives and related storage media. Seagate offers a range of internal (that is, built-in) and external (packaged standalone) drive devices for enterprise, cloud, client, and noncomputer environments, such as DVRs, video game consoles, and the like.

Computer hard disk drives have become a high-volume commodity. Seagate shipped around 226 million drives in FY2013. Roughly two-thirds are for client applications—PCs, notebooks, external storage for PCs, workstations, and similar. About 20 percent are for the noncomputer market—DVRs, video game consoles, and so forth—and 13 percent currently are for enterprise storage applications.

So why would we be interested in a commodity business, one in which the majority of its volume has traditionally supported a mature, if not declining, PC industry? In an industry known for intense price competition and one where brand has meant less and less as time goes on?

The reasons are fairly simple. First—as has happened with other commodity industries in the past like oil refining, agricultural processing, and others—the industry eventually consolidates from many smaller players into a few larger, more powerful ones. During the PC boom, numerous small, nameless, mostly Asian manufacturers got on the bandwagon, creating oversupply and driving prices down. As prices dropped and profits disappeared, and as OEMs like HP and Dell wanted more reliable sourcing, the weak hands left the market. Now—particularly after Seagate's 2011 purchase of Samsung's hard drive business—two companies pretty much control the market: Seagate and Western Digital.

The second and perhaps the bigger factor driving long-term profitability is the in-progress change in the computing landscape toward cloud computing. While the cloud may temper client demand somewhat, those cloud server centers will need huge amounts of larger, more efficient, cooler running—and more profitable storage devices. Consumers and businesses, large and small, are adopting the cloud as their storage solution, and this extends storage makers' reach far beyond the PC ecosystem, as tablet devices, smartphones, etc., will produce and consume images, video, music, etc., all stored somewhere in the cloud. According to estimates, data creation rises some 35 percent per year, and storage capacity will rise in the 20–25 percent range yearly to accommodate (obviously, this assumes that some data is deleted). Amazon, Google, and Microsoft alone are apparently prepared to spend $18 billion on their data centers in 2015, double last year's total. Seagate estimates that by 2020, some 60 percent of storage will be delivered to the cloud compared to 25 percent recently.

Innovation will once again drive this business, and Seagate is in a good position to lead this innovation. Seagate is also leading the way in hybrid drive (a hard disk plus a solid-state memory array) and solid-state hard drive (SSHD) technology, which will replace mechanical drives in many applications with simpler, more energy-efficient units. The company, in all, sells ten lines of disk drives, ranging from larger-capacity high-performance 3.5" Cheetah drives for high-performance data warehousing environments down to its 2.5" Pipeline Mini drives used in gaming consoles and home entertainment devices—with the gamut of data center, PC, notebook, tablet, gaming, DVR, and other devices covered in between. The technology continues to improve, with the attainment of 1 terabyte (1 trillion bits or 1,000 gigabytes) per inch storage capacity through new recording technology announced during FY2012. The company projects 3.5", 60-terabyte drives to be available within ten years.

Innovation also means finding new vertical markets and channels for its products. The company recently introduced something called a "Surveillance HDD," targeted specifically to video surveillance and analytics applications with 4 terabytes of storage.

While the cloud continues to be the growth driver, traditional PC demand is still significant and accounts for two-thirds of the revenue, although this is down from 72 percent last year. As one of two major players in its market, the company has more pricing power than was inherent in the industry just a few years ago. The largest concentrations of manufacturing capacity are in Thailand, Singapore, and China, respectively, and not surprisingly, as it is the locus of PC manufacturing, about 58 percent of sales are to Asian customers.

Financial Highlights, Fiscal Year 2013

FY2013 revenues and earnings were expected to dip as an industry price bulge related to Thailand flooding subsided. Gross margins declined—as expected, as average selling prices declined—from 31 percent to 27 percent. The ASP drop hit the top line almost 4 percent, but it is still some 31 percent ahead of FY2011. Likewise, net earnings dipped some 32 percent, but are still well ahead of any year except FY2012. So . . . let's delete FY2012 as a comparison. FY2014 and FY2015 continue mostly on a flat line for revenues, margins, and net earnings, although substantial share buybacks will help earnings per share. Flat may be good as the company transitions into a cloud storage company; revenues and earnings from the PC-dominant days tended to vary a lot with commodity supply conditions. We think it could happen more quickly than the company projects.

Reasons to Buy

Seagate is one of the more volatile and aggressive stocks on our *100 Best* list, but we think the future is bright and probably more stable. We've already shared most of the "buy side" story—a shift to a suppliers market with Seagate and Western Digital in charge, larger long-term contracts, higher-value-add technology, and an evolving computing and network architecture that should drive more high-value demand. The company seems to be capitalizing on these trends well, is improving its technology, and over time will achieve a healthy and profitable steady state. In the meantime, it continues to return substantial cash to shareholders both through dividends and buybacks.

Reasons for Caution

The biggest concern—and it's clearly reflected in the numbers—is whether the cloud and enterprise storage markets will grow fast enough to compensate for the inevitable decline of the PC business. We think it will, but wish the cloud ramp-up would come a little sooner. The largest customers continue to be PC makers but also see that no matter what the device, data will have to be stored in ever-increasing volumes with greater miniaturization—Seagate will play well no matter where this puck goes.

This industry is noted for its "dreaded diamonds"— where scant supply triggers over-ordering, which eventually triggers overproduction into a softening market; on top of that, the excess orders get cancelled, supply balloons, and prices drop. With only two suppliers and a healthy and broadening technology demand, most don't see this happening in the near future as the company becomes less tied to the fortunes of the PC business. But one must always question the "it's different this time" viewpoint. This will, by nature, be a more volatile play than most on the *100 Best Stocks* list (the beta of 2.51 serves as evidence), but we do think that volatility will decline from years past and is compensated for by the strong cash flows paid to investors.

SECTOR: **Information Technology**
BETA COEFFICIENT: **2.51**
10-YEAR COMPOUND EARNINGS PER-SHARE GROWTH: **16.0%**
10-YEAR COMPOUND DIVIDENDS PER-SHARE GROWTH: **39.5%**

	2006	2007	2008	2009	2010	2011	2012	2013
Revenues (mil)	9,208	11,380	12,708	9,805	11,395	10,971	14,939	14,351
Net income (mil)	840	822	1,415	(231)	1,609	578	2,977	2,028
Earnings per share	1.60	1.40	2.63	(0.47)	3.14	1.09	6.75	5.31
Dividends per share	0.32	0.40	0.42	0.27	—	0.18	0.86	1.40
Cash flow per share	2.52	3.13	4.63	1.42	5.08	3.14	9.57	8.01
Price: high	28.1	28.9	25.8	18.5	21.6	18.5	35.7	57.1
low	19.2	20.1	3.7	3.0	9.8	9.0	16.2	30.3

Seagate Technology
39 Fitzwilliam Square W
Dublin 2, Ireland
+353 (1) 234-3136
Website: *www.seagate.com*

AGGRESSIVE GROWTH

Sigma-Aldrich Corporation

Ticker symbol: SIAL (NASDAQ) ❑ **S&P rating: A+** ❑ **Value Line financial strength rating: A+**
Current yield: 1.0% ❑ **Dividend raises, past 10 years: 10**

Company Profile

If you've been reading through our *100 Best* stock selections in the chemical industry, you may have just finished reading about Praxair, which we described as a "golf-clap" stock—steady gains, most greens in regulation, all putts made, steady, predictable achievement, steady and predictable performance. Now we move to the next hole to review Sigma-Aldrich—which fits that definition to a tee (sorry)—perhaps even more so.

Sigma-Aldrich is a manufacturer and reseller of the world's broadest range of high-value-add chemicals, biochemicals, laboratory equipment, and consumables used in research and large-scale manufacturing activities. The company sells more than 230,000 reagents and chemicals and manufactures about a third of the items itself, comprising about 60 percent of sales. It also stocks more than 45,000 laboratory equipment items. Most of the company's 97,000 customer accounts are research institutions that use basic laboratory essentials such as solvents, reagents, and other supplies, mostly in small but repeated quantities. Sigma-Aldrich products support a range of activities, including

R&D, diagnostics, pilot plant, and small-scale high-tech manufacturing. The company also sells chemicals in large quantities to pharmaceutical companies, but no single account provided more than 2 percent of Sigma-Aldrich's total sales. Sigma-Aldrich's business model is to provide its generic and specialized products with expedited (in most cases, next day) delivery. The company sells in 166 countries and obtains about 67 percent of its sales internationally.

Sigma-Aldrich recently redefined its business into three business units more aligned to its customers than its products: Research, Applied, and SAFC Commercial. Research (52 percent of revenues) targets pharmaceutical, biotech, academic, government, and hospital lab research activities mainly with a full line of organic chemicals, biochemicals, analytical reagents, chromatography consumables, reference materials, high-purity products, and various biotech and molecular biology materials. Applied (22 percent of revenues) supplies diagnostic labs and others delivering a service (as opposed to research) with chemicals, supplies, and lab equipment. The SAFC

(Sigma-Aldrich Fine Chemicals) Commercial segment (26 percent) supplies industrial and manufacturing markets with larger quantities of high-quality, high-purity materials and active ingredients for pharmaceutical manufacturers and similar businesses. At the end of FY2012, the company entered the biochemical analytic service business through the acquisition of BioReliance—such assay services being an important new offering for the company.

In early 2014, the company was named for the first time to the "Global 100 Most Sustainable Corporations in the World" list and ranked twentieth by the World Economic Forum.

Financial Highlights, Fiscal Year 2013

We continue to like Sigma-Aldrich's scorecard, which rang up a "4–7–19" performance—a 4 percent revenue gain which exceeded both peers and estimates, a 7 percent gain in profits, and a 19 percent gain in free cash flow—a good round overall. With 38 percent of its sales going to Europe, and 67 percent overall international, one would have expected softer results, especially with currency translation. FY2014 projections currently call for another 4.7 percent revenue growth with an 8 percent gain in per-share earnings—really, a similar, steady performance like the year just past.

Reasons to Buy

Sigma has been a very steady performer in several high-value-add segments of the chemical and health-care business, including pharmaceuticals and bio-tech. The company is big enough and broad enough to dominate this lucrative niche and has a good brand and sterling reputation both in domestic and international markets. For investors, it is a safe, steady grower in a solid business in a solid industry, and the stock price trajectory is about as even-up-and-to-the-right as any we've researched.

Reasons for Caution

The company's growth is tied to the state of research in the chemical and bio/pharmaceutical industries, and while this has been steady, economic and political factors can create doubts from time to time. Rapid growth in existing businesses isn't likely; when a company depends on acquisitions to grow, that brings some risks with it. While Sigma gets high marks for regular dividend raises, we still feel that a company in this industry with such a steady business and cash flow could pay out a little more to share-holders. Share buybacks have stalled at near zero over the past five years after steady activity up until 2008, but with improving margins and cash flows, that could change.

SECTOR: **Industrials**
BETA COEFFICIENT: **1.01**
10-YEAR COMPOUND EARNINGS PER-SHARE GROWTH: **15.0%**
10-YEAR COMPOUND DIVIDENDS PER-SHARE GROWTH: **16.0%**

	2006	2007	2008	2009	2010	2011	2012	2013
Revenues (mil)	1,798	2,039	2,201	2,148	2,271	2,505	2,623	2,704
Net income (mil)	276	311	342	347	384	457	460	491
Earnings per share	2.05	2.34	2.65	2.80	3.12	3.72	3.77	4.06
Dividends per share	0.42	0.46	0.52	0.58	0.64	0.72	0.80	0.86
Cash flow per share	2.74	3.09	3.60	3.61	3.95	4.59	4.89	5.24
Price: high	39.7	56.6	63.0	56.3	67.8	76.2	78.3	94.8
low	31.3	37.4	34.3	31.5	46.5	58.2	61.7	73.2

Sigma-Aldrich Corporation
3050 Spruce Street
St. Louis, MO 63103
(314) 771-5765
Website: *www.sigma-aldrich.com*

The Southern Company

Ticker symbol: SO (NYSE) □ S&P rating: A □ Value Line financial strength rating: A □ Current yield: 4.65% □ Dividend raises, past 10 years: 10

Company Profile

This year, we "cleaned house" on utility stocks just a bit, taking our list down from five to three with the departure of Dominion Resources and Duke Power. We felt that five was too many. With NextEra and Otter Tail, we get exposure to some of the more dynamic and innovative players in the industry; alongside the two we wanted to keep at least one more traditional, "sure bet" utility that made money the old-fashioned way and continued to pay a bit more every year to shareholders without fail, without regulatory resistance, and without complex business acquisitions, spinoffs, and separations looming in the air, like at Dominion and Duke. We also like innovation. So we decided to let Southern Company anchor our utility selections for another year, at least.

Through its four primary operating subsidiaries—Georgia Power, Alabama Power, Mississippi Power, and Gulf Power—Southern Company serves some 4.4 million customers in a large area of Georgia, Alabama, Mississippi, northern Florida, and parts of the Carolinas. The company also wholesales power to other utilities in a wider area.

The service area includes the Atlanta metropolitan area and a large base of modern manufacturing facilities in the region such as the many Asian-owned manufacturing facilities, including large auto plants. The fuel mix is increasingly diverse and less vulnerable to price fluctuations than some, and the company followed the industry trend of converting some coal plants to natural gas. Fuel costs total 38 percent of revenues, less than many traditional competitors, with 35 percent coal (was 49 percent), 38 percent oil and gas (was 28 percent), 16 percent nuclear, 2 percent hydroelectric, and 6 percent purchased.

Additionally, the company plans to deploy two of 40 worldwide copies of the new and more efficient Westinghouse AP1000 nuclear reactors for its massive Vogtle power stations in Georgia, purchased with an $8.3 billion loan guarantee from the U.S. Department of Energy. These plants, which serve as a showcase for the industry, are under construction and on track and received their operating license from the Nuclear Regulatory Commission in February 2012. They will add 1,000 megawatts of capacity to a 43,555mW-generating base and are expected to come on line in 2017. The company is also investing in alternative energy, along with partner Ted Turner's Turner Renewable Energy, most recently in an already-built 20mW photovoltaic grid project in Nevada purchased during 2012.

SO is also building a leading-edge technology "integrated gasification combined-style (IGCC)" coal plant, one of only three in the country, which creates synthetic gas from coal, removes impurities before combustion, and captures the resulting carbon dioxide, all dramatically reducing emissions and lowering total cost, including emissions mitigation, of typical coal plant operation. The technology is complex and eligible for Department of Energy and other tax subsidies. SO has had construction problems and cost overruns with its version in Mississippi, which have had a material effect on results. Still, this pursuit of new technology (and new nuclear technology) is pretty typical for Southern.

The company also has engaged in telecommunications services, operating as a regional wireless carrier in Alabama, Georgia, southeastern Mississippi, and northwest Florida and operating some fiber-optic networks co-located on company rights of way. The company also provides consulting services to other utilities.

Financial Highlights, Fiscal Year 2013

Southern ran into some speed bumps with its construction projects in FY2013, both with the Mississippi IGCC plant and with the new Georgia Power Vogtle nuclear units. Revenues powered ahead some 3.3 percent—not bad in this industry, but profits were dampened by the write-offs and were largely flat. The company raised the dividend seven cents as it had been doing for the past five years and looks to continue doing into the future. FY2014 and FY2015 should be better as construction costs (and variability) recede; the company is predicting earnings growth in the 5 percent range and per-share earnings growth slightly less as a few shares are tacked onto the float to pay for some of these projects.

Reasons to Buy

Southern serves a growing, diverse, and economically stable customer base and operates in a cooperative regulatory environment. The dividend, which has been raised about as steadily and dependably as kudzu on a Georgia power pole, remains a major attraction. The return won't put you into a yacht, but if you've already got one, it will certainly help you keep it. The solid history and relationship with local regulatory bodies makes the dividend and its annual raises look secure for the future. The stock price, too, has been very stable over time with one of our lowest beta coefficients on our list, recently at a microscopic 0.07.

We like the balanced production, enhanced by a few innovative efforts to complement a more traditional power base. In today's environment the IGCC plant and new nuclear facilities do add some risk, but we feel this is a good economic move for the future. So the risk is there, but shareholders get rewarded with higher-than-average yield while still retaining the defensive stability and steady income growth most of its investors seek.

Reasons for Caution

Electric utilities are always subject to rate and other forms of regulation, and one never knows what will happen in that arena. As noted, there is some construction risk present today and into 2015, and regulators may not always let the company pass these on; in fact a $700 million uncovered write-down has already been taken. Additionally, utilities are always vulnerable to capital costs and the attractiveness of alternative fixed-income investments and are sensitive to rising interest rates, especially if they rise quickly.

SECTOR: Utilities
BETA COEFFICIENT: 0.07
10-YEAR COMPOUND EARNINGS PER-SHARE GROWTH: 3.5%
10-YEAR COMPOUND DIVIDENDS PER-SHARE GROWTH: 3.5%

	2006	2007	2008	2009	2010	2011	2012	2013
Revenues (mil)	14,356	15,353	17,127	15,743	17,456	17,657	16,537	17,087
Net income (mil)	1,608	1,782	1,807	1,912	2,040	2,268	2,415	2,439
Earnings per share	2.10	2.28	2.25	2.32	2.37	2.57	2.67	2.70
Dividends per share	1.54	1.60	1.66	1.73	1.80	1.87	1.94	2.01
Cash flow per share	4.01	4.22	4.43	4.25	4.30	4.85	5.20	5.25
Price: high	37.4	39.3	40.6	33.8	38.6	46.7	48.5	48.7
low	30.5	33.2	29.8	30.8	30.8	35.7	41.8	40.0

The Southern Company
30 Ivan Allen Jr. Boulevard NW
Atlanta, GA 30308
(404) 506-5000
Website: *www.southerncompany.com*

AGGRESSIVE GROWTH

Southwest Airlines Co.

Ticker symbol: LUV (NYSE) ❑ S&P rating: BBB- ❑ Value Line financial strength rating: B+
Current yIeld: 0.7% ❑ Dividend raises, past 10 years: 3

Company Profile

Southwest Airlines provides passenger air transport mainly in the United States, all within North America. At the end of FY2013, the company served 96 cities in 41 states, and with the acquisition of AirTran it also served Mexico and the Caribbean with point-to-point, rather than hub-and-spoke, service. The company serves these markets almost exclusively with 680 Boeing 737 aircraft.

Based on the most recent data available from the U.S. Department of Transportation, as of September 30, 2013, Southwest was the largest domestic air carrier in the United States, as measured by the number of domestic originating passengers boarded. This should give an idea of their business model—low-cost, shorter flights, and maximum passenger loads. Indeed, the average trip is 693 miles and the average one-way fare is $232, substantially higher than the $142 charged in 2005 but still one of the lowest in the industry. The business model is one of simplicity—no-frills aircraft, no first-class passenger cabin, limited interchange with other carriers, no onboard meals, simple boarding and seat assignment practices, direct sales over the Internet

(80 percent of revenues are booked this way, down from 84 percent prior to AirTran, but we think this will rise with AirTran's integration), no baggage fees—all designed to provide steady and reliable transportation, with one of the best on-time performances in the industry, and to maximize asset utilization with minimal downtime, crew disruptions, and other upward influences on operating costs. The company has long used secondary airports—such as Providence, RI, and Manchester, NH, to serve Boston and the New England area; Allentown, PA, and East Islip, NY, to serve the New York/New Jersey area; and Chicago Midway to reduce delays and costs. This strategy has worked well.

Most of what we have just said reflects the business of the original Southwest Airlines. In 2012 the company completed the financial integration of AirTran Holdings, a medium-sized, Florida-based discount carrier. With 140 aircraft, again mostly 737s, AirTran brings a similar operational footprint but expands service to mainstream eastern airports, particularly Atlanta, Orlando, the D.C. area, and Mexico and the Caribbean. By the end of FY2014, AirTran will be *operationally* integrated, sharing the same passenger booking systems, website, and other Southwest operating practices.

We expect the combined carrier to continue the simple, straightforward value proposition that has been a customer favorite for years. Southwest has successfully implemented a few initiatives to squeeze out some extra revenue without alienating the core passenger group, mostly targeted to business travelers. One is Business Select, which offers priority boarding, priority security, bonus frequent flyer credit, and a free beverage for an upgrade fee. The company also sells "one-off" early boarding for a small fee. The company is also tinkering with baggage fees, raising fees for overweight or excess bags, though leaving the basic two-bag limit free for now.

Finally, Southwest is getting a bit more aggressive in adjusting its destinations served, adding not only AirTran's destinations but ten of its own while also cutting three smaller city destinations. The airline also added ten gates at New York's LaGuardia in the wake of the American/US Airways merger.

Financial Highlights, Fiscal Year 2013

With the continued economic recovery and Southwest's reputation and inherent competitive advantages, the airline enjoyed another good year from a revenue perspective, with total FY2013 revenues up 3.6 with steady load factors (at 80.1 percent), improved pricing, and new revenues from new sources as pointed out above. Capacity reductions and moderating fuel prices really helped the bottom line take off with a stellar 75 percent gain in net earnings on an almost doubling of the net profit margin to 4.3 percent. The company also sliced another 35 million shares out of its float with buybacks—5 percent of its total, helping to almost double per-share earnings. Revenue and profit gains will level off a bit in FY2014 with a modest 2.3 percent top-line increase, but again a healthy 20 percent gain in net income and per-share earnings.

Reasons to Buy

Those who have read *100 Best Stocks* over the years used to hear us claim that we'd never put an airline on the list. Why? Because airlines are extremely competitive with little to no control over prices, and with the major cost components of fuel, airport fees, and union labor, they have almost no control over their costs. In other words, the exact opposite of what you'd want to see in a business you would own yourself.

However, we took a flyer (sorry) on Southwest two years ago, and it has been one of our best performers. Why? Because it has continually proved to be the exception to the "rules" about the airline business, and after a long taxi, that success finally started to take off.

The value proposition is the envy of the industry, and we continue to be surprised that no one else has been able to emulate it (United and Delta and now Allegiant and Spirit and Frontier have tried or are trying but with mixed success at best). The airline realizes that what customers want is no-hassle transportation at best-possible prices—and yes, no bag fees—and has been able to do that better than anyone else for years. Good management, efficient operation, and excellent marketing make it possible. The value proposition and business model have been accepted by a greater portion of the flying public, and now the company is expanding coverage. Larger market share in a larger market—we like that. When that happens, not being able to control price becomes more of a problem for the competition than it does for Southwest. We thought this was a stock people had forgotten about after its glory days decades ago—and we were right. Now, with margins, earnings, and share buybacks on a strong ascent, and little in the way of competitive threats, all with the tailwind of an improving economy, it still looks like you can hop on board, and the change to Aggressive Growth from our Conservative Growth category turned out to be timed just right.

Reasons for Caution

The acquisition of AirTran and a modest de simplification of the Rapid Rewards frequent flyer program to provide international rewards and sell points to third parties gave us some pause, but both have gone well, and the core business model still seems intact. We're a bit surprised that AirTran hasn't been integrated more quickly.

Fuel prices are still a wild card, but increasing domestic supply should hold that in line for the time being. We, too, would like to see a bit more cash return; although aggressive buybacks have been a good substitute, we'd like to see more in the way of dividends. Currently the company pays out only a bit more than 5 percent of cash flow. We would also consider disembarking if Southwest got any more acquisition-happy—after AirTran we think a holding pattern is in order on that front. Finally, there is concern—growing in some circles—that as Southwest expands its footprint to cover the U.S., go international, and so forth, they'll fly away from their competitive advantages and start looking more like other airlines—with poorer cost structures, labor relations, operational difficulties, etc. We saw signs of this in early 2014 with reports of growing cancellations, baggage losses, and so forth. Such nega tives pose a risk but have also come up many times in the past and proven not to be a permanent problem.

SECTOR: **Transportation**
BETA COEFFICIENT: **1.08**
10-YEAR COMPOUND EARNINGS PER-SHARE GROWTH: **1.0%**
10-YEAR COMPOUND DIVIDENDS PER-SHARE GROWTH: **4.0%**

	2006	**2007**	**2008**	**2009**	**2010**	**2011**	**2012**	**2013**
Revenues (mil)	9,086	9,861	11,023	10,350	12,104	15,658	17,088	17,699
Net income (mil)	592	471	294	140	550	330	421	754
Earnings per share	0.72	0.81	0.40	0.19	0.73	0.42	0.58	1.05
Dividends per share	0.02	0.02	0.02	0.02	0.02	0.03	0.04	0.10
Cash flow per share	1.41	1.40	1.41	1.21	1.02	1.35	1.73	2.35
Price: high	18.2	17.0	16.8	11.8	14.3	13.9	10.6	19.0
low	14.6	12.1	7.1	4.0	10.4	7.1	7.8	10.4

Southwest Airlines Co.
P.O. Box 36611
2702 Love Field Drive
Dallas, TX 75235
(214) 792-4000
Website: ***www.southwest.com***

AGGRESSIVE GROWTH

St. Jude Medical, Inc.

Ticker symbol: STJ (NYSE) □ S&P rating: A □ Value Line financial strength rating: A □ Current yield: 1.7% □ Dividend raises, past 10 years: 3

Company Profile

St. Jude Medical, Inc. designs, manufactures, and distributes cardiovascular medical devices for cardiology and cardiovascular surgery, including pacemakers, implantable cardioverter defibrillators (ICDs), vascular closure devices, catheters, neuromodulation devices, and heart valves. The company has four main business segments:

- The Cardiac Rhythm Management (CRM) portfolio (responsible for about 52 percent of sales) includes products for treating heart rhythm disorders as well as heart failure. Its products include ICDs, pacemaker systems, and a variety of diagnostic and therapeutic electrophysiology catheters. The company also develops catheter technologies for the Cardiology/Vascular Access therapy area. Those products include hemostasis introducers, catheters, and a market-leading vascular closure device. Many products in this portfolio use RF (radio frequency) and other leading technologies for rhythm management, ablation, and other advanced cardiovascular problems.

- The Cardiovascular segment (24 percent) has been the leader in mechanical heart valve technology for more than 25 years. St. Jude Medical also develops a line of tissue valves, vascular closures, and valve repair products for various cardiac surgery procedures.

- The Neuromodulation segment (8 percent) produces implantable devices and drug delivery systems for use primarily in chronic pain management and in treatment for certain symptoms of Parkinson's disease and epilepsy.

- The Atrial Fibrillation business (16 percent) markets a series of products designed to map and treat atrial fibrillation and other heart rhythm problems.

St. Jude Medical products are sold in a highly targeted niche market in more than 100 countries. International sales account for about 53 percent of the total; R&D investment is also substantial at more than 12 percent of sales.

Financial Highlights, Fiscal Year 2013

As we pointed out last year, the cardiac care business is by nature really two businesses. The cardiac surgery business is critical and almost completely immune to economic cycles; when you need it, you need it. The largest segment, Cardiac Rhythm Management, which essentially makes pacemakers and related products, is a bit more discretionary and vulnerable to expense cuts on the part of patients and care providers and contractions in the inventory pipeline. The lingering effects of the Great Recession, currency exchange effects, and the tendency for health insurance to require greater co-payments for discretionary procedures kept the FY2013 monitor pretty much on a flat line, flatter than we expected but by no means close to death. Regardless, we almost cut this blue-chip health-care technology provider from our FY2014 list as a result, and indeed, business performance for the rest of FY2013 would have supported this decision. The good news started to appear in late FY2013 and into FY2014.

FY2013: Revenues and net profit stayed almost precisely flat for the year, while per-share earnings advanced 8 percent to $3.76, mostly on the back of a 1.4 percent share buyback.

Now, for FY2014, a stronger revenue environment, new product rollouts, and operational improvements arising from an earlier organizational realignment have stimulated a stronger financial heartbeat. The company is guiding forward for regular 4–6 percent annual gains despite continued currency headwinds; gradually improving margins and continued share buybacks are guiding a continued steady 7–9 percent annual earnings growth into the future. If the company continues its share buyback plans, it will reduce share counts some 22 percent from 2006; additionally, dividend raises are likely to continue in the 7–8 percent range annually. The company did not pay a dividend at all until 2011.

Reasons to Buy

St. Jude continues to be a market leader in the heart rhythm and vascular surgery niche, a solid position in the health-care industry. Both the Neuromodulation and Atrial Fibrillation segments have grown rapidly and seem well positioned for growth in at least the 15 percent range. The techniques employed in neuromodulation are growing quickly in the field as a preferred treatment for long-term pain management. St. Jude (and others) see this as a disruptive technology, potentially replacing drug and physical therapy regimens and offering improved lifestyle at a reduced cost. These two businesses, while small, serve as solid growth kickers, complementing the flatter CRM and cardiovascular segments.

As part of a bigger picture, St. Jude is an innovation leader, and its innovations are starting to pay off. We like the combination of innovation-led growth and willingness (and ability) to share the proceeds with investors.

Reasons for Caution

As stated, we almost jumped off the bandwagon last year due to flat performance; the company just seemed to be stuck in the mud on every front. Then a shot of adrenalin in its steadiest businesses, combined with new products and cost savings, sent the stock upward in a classic "hockey stick" pattern during all of FY2013,

almost doubling the share price during the year. The question is—will it continue? This is a solid company, but we might wait for a pullback to buy. Additionally, we should point out that the company has experienced technical and product problems in the past, and some have questioned whether some of the procedures it supports are really necessary—on the other hand, with the Affordable Care Act, more potential candidates are covered by at least some insurance. These factors all add some uncertainty to an otherwise fairly stable issue.

SECTOR: **Health Care**
BETA COEFFICIENT: **1.07**
10-YEAR COMPOUND EARNINGS PER-SHARE GROWTH: **18.5%**
10-YEAR COMPOUND DIVIDENDS PER-SHARE GROWTH: **NM**

	2006	2007	2008	2009	2010	2011	2012	2013
Revenues (mil)	3,302	3,779	4,363	4,681	5,165	5,612	5,503	5,501
Net income (mil)	548	652	807	838	995	1,074	1,095	1,094
Earnings per share	1.47	1.85	2.31	2.43	3.01	3.28	3.48	3.76
Dividends per share	—	—	—	—	—	0.84	0.92	1.00
Cash flow per share	2.05	2.48	2.92	3.24	3.70	4.35	4.50	4.75
Price: high	54.8	48.1	48.5	42.0	43.0	54.2	44.8	63.2
low	31.2	34.9	25.0	28.9	34.0	32.1	30.3	36.1

St. Jude Medical, Inc.
One St. Jude Medical Drive
St. Paul, MN 55117-9983
(651) 756-2000
Website: *www.sjm.com*

Starbucks Corporation

Ticker symbol: SBUX (NASDAQ) □ S&P rating: A- □ Value Line financial strength rating: A++
Current yield: 1.4% □ Dividend raises, past 10 years: 3

Company Profile

Starbucks Corporation, formed in 1985, is the leading retailer, roaster, and brand of specialty coffee in the world. The company sells whole-bean coffees through its retailers, its specialty sales group, and supermarkets. The company has 8,105 company-owned stores in the Americas (7,857 at the end of 2012) and 2,187 in international markets (1,548 at the end of 2012), in addition to 8,892 licensed stores worldwide (8,661 at the end of 2012). Retail coffee shop sales constitute about 88 percent of its revenue, up from 86 percent last year. Unlike many in the restaurant sector, the company does not franchise its stores—all are either company owned or operated by licensees in special venues.

The company continues to expand overseas, usually at first through partnerships and joint ventures; sometimes it buys out the partner as it did in China in 2011. The company now operates in 62 countries in total; the China and Asia Pacific segment, which now includes active stores in Vietnam and India, not surprisingly is the fastest-growing segment, growing revenues some 27 percent in FY2013. The company recently opened its 1,000th stores both in China and Japan.

The company is gradually expanding beyond its traditional coffee base, opening a new Teavana Fine Teas Bar in New York and adding Teavana tea-related items into its traditional stores as a consequence of its recent acquisition of that company. Evolution Fresh juices are now available at 8,000 locations, and the company has also recently introduced the La Boulange line of pastries and baked goods in 3,500 stores. Packaged coffee sales are very strong with advances both in single-serve Via packs and in the Keurig-compatible K-cup packages. The company recently negotiated enhanced terms with Keurig maker Green Mountain Coffee Roasters which will likely strengthen its already strong position in that market. Starbucks also has joint ventures with PepsiCo and Dreyer's to develop bottled coffee drinks and coffee-flavored ice creams. The company terminated a distribution agreement with Kraft, incurring some costs along the way, but continues to move forward with alternative channel distribution for packaged items.

The company's retail goal is to become the leading retailer and brand of coffee in each of its target markets through product quality and by providing a unique Starbucks experience, which the company defines as a third place beyond home and work. The "experience" is built upon superior customer service and a clean, well-maintained retail store that reflects the personality of the community in which it operates, with easy and free wi-fi access, all serving to build a high degree of customer loyalty.

The company also gets high marks for citizenship, continuing to offer health coverage and equity participation for its 200,000 employees ("partners") and recently making a commitment to hire 10,000 veterans and military spouses over the next five years, among a list of other community service commitments.

Financial Highlights, Fiscal Year 2013

Aside from the termination costs for the Kraft distributorship, FY2013 was a strong and robust brew for Starbucks. Revenues advanced another 12 percent to $14.9 billion, with global same-store sales advancing at a healthy 7 percent clip. The company has put special focus on maximizing operating leverage and improving margins, which really started to pay off in FY2013 with a record net profit margin of 11.6 percent as compared to 10.4 percent in FY2012 and

under 10 percent prior to FY2011. As a consequence, net profits advanced 24 percent in FY2013 with per-share earnings up 26 percent. FY2014 guidance calls for earnings per share in the $2.59–$2.67 range, the midpoint of which would be 16 percent ahead of FY2013. Net profit margin improvements are projected to continue northward through FY2015 in the 13–15 percent range, which should lead to an acceleration in earnings gains through the next few years; per-share earnings are expected to grow another 20 percent in FY2015.

Reasons to Buy

Starbucks continues to be a great story. We never thought the company's slow spot in 2009–2010 was permanent; the company's stores continue to be more than coffee shops and are really that "third place" where professionals, students, moms, and other prosperous people will meet and dole out a few bucks for quality drinks. The "third place" aura creates a lot of the brand strength and, in our view, represents the company's true strength—well beyond the quality of the coffee itself and related products. The company has a steadily (and profitably) growing presence on the world stage; it has trained its store-growth cannon on these markets rather than overbuilding in the U.S. New single-cup ventures and the new Blonde light-roast products are broadening appeal to larger customer segments, as we thought would happen; the single-cup market has huge potential. We expect margins to continue to improve as such specialty products catch on and as the company continues to learn generally how to earn more money selling high-end products. The company is well managed, has an extremely strong brand, has solid financials, and, once again, a steady growth track record, and it is carving out an ever-stronger international footprint. If this wasn't enough, new focus on cash returns for investors has brought generous dividend increases.

Reasons for Caution

There is continued fear—although little has happened to justify it—that coffee drinkers may learn to get along without the $5 latte and become just $1.50 drippers. As we saw at the end of the 2000 decade, oversaturation is also a risk. Competitors Peet's and Caribou Coffee have been acquired by deep pockets, and Dunkin' Donuts is making a strong play in the lower high-end segment as McDonald's did a few years ago with mixed success, but overall we don't see much change in the competitive landscape in the near term. Regrettably, the company has stopped buying back shares at least for the time being; we're not sure why. Coffee prices have been on the rise, too, but as experienced before, they don't really affect this story much since coffee is a small part of the company's total cost picture. Historically, coffee price surges have presented good buying opportunities. The biggest threat is that the stock price and P/E will remain historically high, but detractors have been calling that out for years with little success.

SECTOR: **Restaurants**
BETA COEFFICIENT: **1.25**
10-YEAR COMPOUND EARNINGS PER-SHARE GROWTH: **21.0%**
10-YEAR COMPOUND DIVIDENDS PER-SHARE GROWTH: **NM**

	2006	2007	2008	2009	2010	2011	2012	2013
Revenues (mil)	7,787	9,412	10,383	9,774	10,707	11,701	13,299	14,892
Net income (mil)	519	673	525	598	982	1,174	1,385	1,721
Earnings per share	0.73	0.87	0.71	0.80	1.28	1.52	1.79	2.26
Dividends per share	—	—	—	—	0.23	0.52	0.68	0.84
Cash flow per share	1.28	1.54	1.46	1.53	2.00	2.28	2.58	3.11
Price: high	40.0	36.6	21.0	24.5	31.3	46.5	62.0	82.5
low	28.7	19.9	7.1	21.3	21.3	30.8	43.0	52.5

Starbucks Corporation
2401 Utah Avenue South
Seattle, WA 98134
(206) 447-1575
Website: *www.starbucks.com*

CONSERVATIVE GROWTH

State Street Corporation

Ticker symbol: STT (NYSE) ❏ S&P rating: A+ ❏ Value Line financial strength rating: B++
Current yield: 1.5% ❏ Dividend raises, past 10 years: 8

Company Profile

Are you afraid of SPDRs? Not the eight-legged kind, but the original and one of three leading brands of exchange-traded funds (ETFs) out there rapidly gaining ground on the "traditional" fund industry? If you aren't afraid of SPDRs, and you aren't too afraid of financial stocks in general, State Street might make it onto your own personal buy list. In fact, we think State Street is, more than most, a safe and sane way to play this sector, which we continue to hold generally out of favor.

Like many financial power-houses, State Street has a number of businesses under its umbrella. But unlike many, its core products are concentrated on offering services to other financial services firms and on offering the relatively new and growing ETF investment package to investors. It is often analyzed as a bank, but it acts more like a company providing services to other financial institutions and the public, receiving a steady and growing stream of fees for those services.

The company operates with two main lines of business: Investment Servicing and Investment Management:

- Investment Servicing (88 percent of revenues) provides administrative, custody, analytic, and other value-add functions to investment companies—mainly mutual funds, hedge funds, and pension funds, including settlement and payment services, transaction management, and setting the NAV (net asset value, or price) of about 40 percent of U.S.-based mutual funds on a daily basis.

- Investment Management (about 12 percent of revenues) provides investment vehicles and products through its State Street Global Advisors (SSGA) subsidiary, including the well known SPDR ETFs and some of the analytic tools and indexes supporting these products.

About 76 percent of total State Street revenues come from non-interest-related sources; the rest from interest and related income. The company has operations in 29 countries, and about 28 percent of revenues come from overseas operations, mostly in Europe.

Financial Highlights, Fiscal Year 2013

In FY2013, the company's trajectory away from the 2008–2009 meltdown, which affected other players in the industry more than State Street, continued its steady pace, with revenues and profits up about 3 percent. The company bought back some 23 million shares, or 5 percent of its float, in an effort to recapture the shares issued to bolster capital in the wake of the financial crisis; that unwinding should be over in two to three years at the current pace. Per-share earnings, as a consequence, are rising at about a 10 percent annual rate to record levels beyond even those approached prior to the Great Recession. This figure was also helped along by some one-time tax benefits.

Global financial activity continues to rise, which helps State Street as a supplier to the industry. That said, some fee income in key ETF areas, notably the SPDR Gold ETF which has seen recent selloff, has declined; we don't see this as being a permanent change. The crosscurrents should turn out positive: FY2014 revenues and earnings are projected to grow to about $10.4 billion, or about 5.3 percent, with per-share earnings estimated to grow as much as 7 percent taking into account share buybacks, with another approximately 8 percent rise in the dividend. In early 2014 the company just announced authorization to repurchase some $1.7 billion in common stock through early FY2015, which would retire some 25 million, or almost 6 percent of its outstanding shares.

Reasons to Buy

When there's a gold rush, the people who sell picks, shovels, and maps usually win. That's sort of the case with State Street. It makes a lot of steady money on selling services to other financial services firms. It's a steadier income stream absent some of the risks facing its other financial brethren. We think that State Street has a steady business with an innovative growth path in the ETF business, and we like the SPDR brand. We also like the fact that, unlike most financials, the company's income is more heavily based on fees and services than on interest margins and investment gains—more than 75 percent of revenues arise from fees and services. That said, the prospect for increased interest rates would bode well for interest income. The company continues to focus on financial strength, with a Tier One capital ratio exceeding 15 percent (anything over 10 percent is considered good) and on investor returns, aggressively retiring shares and raising the dividend regularly.

Reasons for Caution

Like other financial firms, State Street is enormously complex and hard to understand—we almost gave up when we introduced this issue last year. If you insist on fully understanding how a business works, what it sells, how it delivers, and so forth, this one might not be for you. It's a bit murky, though it is easier to see how it makes money on the ETF business. Although the business is different than most financials, it could be swept up in another financial crisis. Likewise, a major market pullback and a decline in public interest could hurt. And the share price has finally caught up with its improved prospects. For all of these reasons, State Street is far from the least risky stock on our *100 Best Stocks* list, but it deserves a look if you like financials; there are only three others (Allstate, Visa, and Wells Fargo) on the list.

SECTOR: **Financials**

BETA COEFFICIENT: **1.67**

10-YEAR COMPOUND EARNINGS PER-SHARE GROWTH: **6.5%**

10-YEAR COMPOUND DIVIDENDS PER-SHARE GROWTH: **3.5%**

	2006	2007	2008	2009	2010	2011	2012	2013
Assets (bil)	107.3	142.5	173.6	157.9	160.5	216.8	222.6	243.3
Revenues (mil)	6,311	8,336	10,693	8,640	8,953	9,594	9,649	9,881
Net income (mil)	1,096	1,231	1,811	1,803	1,559	1,920	2,061	2,136
Earnings per share	3.26	3.45	4.30	3.46	3.09	3.79	4.20	4.62
Dividends per share	0.80	0.88	0.95	0.04	0.04	0.72	0.96	1.04
Price: high	68.6	82.5	86.6	55.9	48.8	50.3	47.3	73.6
low	54.4	59.1	28.1	14.4	32.5	29.9	38.2	47.7

State Street Corporation

One Lincoln Street

Boston, MA 02111

(617) 786-3000

Website: *www.statestreet.com*

AGGRESSIVE GROWTH

Steelcase, Incorporated

NEW FOR 2015

Ticker symbol: SCS (NYSE) ❑ S&P rating: B ❑ Value Line financial strength rating: BBB ❑ Current yield: 2.6% ❑ Dividend raises, past 10 years: 7

Company Profile

Steelcase are the guys who make all those beige-colored four-drawer file cabinets that line the walls of most traditional office spaces, right? Didn't we just cut two "paper" stocks from our list—International Paper and Iron Mountain—largely due to what we see as a permanent decline in the amount of paper produced and moved through corporate America?

Steelcase is the world's leading producer of office furniture, and more importantly, office systems. The company makes several lines of more traditional walls, chairs, desks, cabinets, etc. But in addition, in part through emerging subbrands such as Coalesse, Nurture, and Turnstone, Steelcase is bringing to market a lot of new ideas and office concepts that we'd probably all like to see and work in. Call it office *architecture* if you will.

Imagine arriving at the office, heading to a small visible conference area with two glass walls, a floor-to-ceiling white board, and display devices that connect immediately and wirelessly to your mobile device to display your work or your multimedia presentation. Imagine sitting in small, comfortable work areas, again with a display, possibly built into the table in front of you. Steelcase is really a bet on the demise of today's traditional office space. Why is that space in demise? Several factors. One, today's new mobile worker doesn't spend so much time in the office. When she or he does, it's to get together, to collaborate, with other workers and to demonstrate their work. Most don't have traditional PCs. Less paper moves around, so workers don't need as much storage. What they need is a workbench, places to stash their backpacks, meet, ways to connect and display what they're working on and work together, places to contemplate in ergonomic comfort, all the while connected to the business and to each other. "Work has been freed" is the slogan on their subbrand "Coalesse" website (*www.coalesse.com*).

Another is the desire to reduce office space—and cost. Cubes, especially empty ones, take a lot of space. Just as the traditional four-walled office went out in favor of the cubicle when PCs took over and nobody needed a secretary pool any more, we think the office is ready for another transition. Steelcase has been studying and innovating that space for quite some time, and it appears in our view to be ready to bring it to market, as a market leader. We think it could be big.

Steelcase doesn't just produce broad lines of office furnishings. It has conducted deep, customer-based studies of workplace activity, especially innovation, teamwork, and leadership, and it has studied and marketed to key vertical markets like health care, education, and hotels and hospitality—a case study for market-driven innovation. CEO Jim Hackett, in fact, is on the advisory board of the Mayo Clinic Center for Innovation, using that team as a test bed for highly creative workspaces as well as new medical workspaces. The company is also working with J.W. Marriott to develop innovative workspaces (called "Workspring") for business hotel guests.

Financial Highlights, Fiscal Year 2013

Since the boom-and-bust cycle of the mid-2000s, the Great Recession, and emergence in 2011, the company has steadied the ship if not turning in stellar growth. Top-line revenues were up just north of 4 percent in FY2014, with a slight improvement in operating margins, despite increased marketing spend, yielding an almost 9 percent gain in earnings. For FY2014, Steelcase expects another 4–5 percent in the top line, with a better mix and return on some of its new product lines leading to a 20–25 percent improvement in per-share earnings even with little in

the way of share repurchases. The company also raised its dividend a third to 40 cents per year, another solid sign. For FY2015 the company expects to gain a bit more traction with a 5–6 percent revenue increase and another 15 percent increase in earnings per share.

Reasons to Buy

With Steelcase, we think we are in the early stages of an accelerating trend. A couple of trends, really. First, traditional organizations are looking for new ways to meet the needs and reduce the stress of today's mobile worker. They are also looking to optimize floor space, which the new designs tend to use less of. Second, new companies (and there are a lot of them) cater to the new "Millennial" worker and aspire to create the perfect workspace for mobile collaboration and innovation. This trend is spreading around the world (currently, only 30 percent of sales are overseas). In short, we think today's traditional cube farm is ready for an update.

Steelcase gets this and has been investing in it for years. We like the designs, and its approach to key vertical markets like health care and education, which have their own special needs. Even as they ramp up, they've been registering decent earnings gains of late and returning healthy amounts of cash to shareholders. We think the ramp-up could accelerate as their ideas gain traction and more potential customers get on board.

Reasons for Caution

Steelcase, and the office furniture/business in general, are extremely cyclical, subject to dramatic ups and downs tied to the level of business activity. Put simply, office furniture is one of the first expenditures to cut in bad times. As the numbers below show, the company took a huge hit in the Great Recession, one from which it hasn't fully recovered. That may be a blessing in disguise, as it appears to be the wake-up call to move forward beyond selling traditional office furniture. A fine example of creative destruction at work, we think.

Still, there is considerable risk, admittedly more than with most of our picks. We're betting more on an idea, and less on a steady, proven track record than usual. It's quite possible that Steelcase's good ideas will fail to gain traction, at least as fast as necessary to reap the benefits needed to start a steady stream of significant growth.

Intense competition in the office environment industry is also an issue. Margins, at 8–10 percent for operating margin and 3–5 percent for net margins, are nothing to write home about. The company has invested a lot in development. However, we think Steelcase through their research efforts has at least something of a first mover advantage, and as the world's largest single supplier, strength in scale and in distributor relationships as well. The scenario may require some patience, but investors are getting a decent dividend while they wait—which we expect to be more stable than it has been.

SECTOR: **Industrials**
BETA COEFFICIENT: **1.14**
10-YEAR COMPOUND EARNINGS PER-SHARE GROWTH: **27.0%**
10-YEAR COMPOUND DIVIDENDS PER-SHARE GROWTH: **2.5%**

	2006	2007	2008	2009	2010	2011	2012	2013
Revenues (mil)	3,097	3,420	3,184	2,292	2,437	2,749	2,669	2,990
Net income (mil)	107	143	91	(12.2)	51	76	101	110
Earnings per share	0.71	1.00	0.68	(0.09)	0.38	0.58	0.79	0.85
Dividends per share	0.45	0.58	0.60	0.24	0.16	0.24	0.36	0.40
Cash flow per share	1.42	1.70	1.34	0.47	0.87	1.05	1.27	1.45
Price: high	19.3	20.7	16.7	7.7	10.9	12.1	13.3	17.0
low	13.2	14.0	5.0	3.0	6.2	5.4	7.3	12.2

Steelcase, Incorporated
901 44th St. SE
Grand Rapids, MI 49508
(616) 247-2710
Website: *www.steelcase.com*

AGGRESSIVE GROWTH

Stryker Corporation

Ticker symbol: SYK (NYSE) ❑ S&P rating: A+ ❑ Value Line financial strength rating: A++
Current yield: 1.5% ❑ Dividend increases, past 10 years: 9

Company Profile

Stryker Corporation was founded as the Orthopedic Frame Company in 1941 by Dr. Homer H. Stryker, a leading orthopedic surgeon and the inventor of several orthopedic products. The company now ranks as a dominant player in the global orthopedics industry with more than 59,000 products in its catalog and a strong innovation track record, with more than 5 percent of sales invested in R&D.

The Reconstructive segment, formerly known as Orthopedic Implants, comprising about 44 percent of sales, has a significant market share in such "spare parts" as artificial hips, prosthetic knees, implant products for other extremities, and trauma products.

The MediSurg unit, about 37 percent of sales, develops, manufactures, and markets worldwide powered and computer-assisted (and now, thanks to a recent acquisition, robotic) surgical instruments, endoscopic surgical systems, hospital beds, and other patient care and handling equipment.

The Neurotechnology & Spine segment, a large part of which was acquired from Boston Scientific in 2010, accounts for 19 percent of sales and sells spinal reconstructive and surgical equipment, neurovascular surgery equipment, and craniomaxillofacial products. This is the smallest but fastest-growing segment in the company.

At the end of FY2013, Stryker completed the acquisition of MAKO, a producer of robotic-assisted reconstructive surgery, a promising, innovative, and brand-building addition, which the company expects to eventually "transform orthopedic surgery." This follows the FY2012 acquisition of Trauson Holdings, giving it a strong and profitable presence in the Chinese market, as well as the rest of Asia. Stryker's revenue is split roughly 60/40 among implants and equipment and 66/34 domestic and international.

Financial Highlights, Fiscal Year 2013

Like many in the industry, Stryker experienced the effects of currency headwinds and a weak European market. Despite those pressures, the company carved out a 4.2 percent increase in total revenues and a 3.9

percent increase in continuing-basis per-share earnings. For FY2014 the company projects another 4.5–6 percent "organic" revenue growth and 6.5 percent total growth and a 5-plus percent growth rate into FY2015. Per-share earnings should grow 14 percent in FY2014 and another 8 percent in FY2015, helped along by modest buybacks and improved cost structures and operating leverage. Dividend growth should remain in the 15 percent range annually, but this is on a low base.

Reasons to Buy

Stryker's top line is driven largely by elective surgeries, and the Great Recession years turned out to be years for delaying whatever medical procedures could be delayed. Many consumers decided to wait and see how the medical care legislation would turn out, and some were simply deciding to hold on to their cash until economic conditions improved. That's all over now, and a resumed surgical calendar and international expansion bode well for the near-term future. We continue to see Stryker as an innovative healthcare products company with relatively less entrenched competition than many others and a strong presence in the orthopedic market, which should capitalize on aging and the availability of health insurance to greater numbers under the Affordable Care Act. Emerging markets, particularly China, are strong, and recent acquisitions should strengthen the portfolio and brand worldwide. We also see an acceleration in shareholder returns through dividends, although buybacks have slowed somewhat recently.

Reasons for Caution

Ongoing scrutiny of health-care costs and continued reliance on acquisitions to fuel growth bring risks to the company, but we don't think they are excessive. The company makes fairly high-tech medical products and as such is exposed to legal, regulatory, and manufacturing risks. Ongoing efforts to contain medical costs could hurt the more elective orthopedic procedures, but that should be offset by the wider availability of covered care to more people. Finally, FY2013 was a very healthy year for the company's stock price, which may attenuate price appreciation potential in the near term—this is more of a long-term holding.

SECTOR: **Health Care**
BETA COEFFICIENT: **0.86**
10-YEAR COMPOUND EARNINGS PER-SHARE GROWTH: **17.5%**
10-YEAR COMPOUND DIVIDENDS PER-SHARE GROWTH: **32.0%**

		2006	2007	2008	2009	2010	2011	2012	2013
Revenues (mil)		5,406	6,001	6,718	6,723	7,320	8,307	8,656	9,021
Net income (mil)		778	1,017	1,148	1,107	1,330	1,448	1,561	1,602
Earnings per share		1.89	2.44	2.78	2.77	3.30	3.72	4.08	4.24
Dividends per share		0.11	0.22	0.33	0.50	0.63	0.72	0.85	1.06
Cash flow per share		2.85	3.33	3.87	3.75	4.40	5.08	4.69	5.70
Price:	high	55.9	76.9	74.9	52.7	59.7	65.2	64.1	75.8
	low	39.8	54.9	35.4	30.8	42.7	43.7	49.4	55.2

Stryker Corporation
2825 Airview Blvd.
Kalamazoo, MI 49002
(269) 385-2600
Website: *www.stryker.com*

CONSERVATIVE GROWTH

Sysco Corporation

Ticker symbol: SYY (NYSE) ❑ S&P rating: A ❑ Value Line financial strength rating: A+ ❑ Current yield: 3.2% ❑ Dividend raises, past 10 years: 10

Company Profile

Sysco is the leading marketer and distributor of food, food products, and related equipment and supplies to the U.S. foodservice industry. The company distributes fresh and frozen meats, prepared entrées, vegetables, canned and dried foods, dairy products, beverages, and produce, as well as paper products, restaurant equipment and supplies, and cleaning supplies. The company might be familiar for its "institutional" number-ten-sized cans of food found in many high-volume kitchens, but the product line and customer base is much larger, including many specialty and chain restaurants, lodges, hotels, hospitals, schools, and other distribution centers across the country. Restaurants account for about 61 percent of the business; hospitals and nursing homes 9 percent, schools and colleges, and hotels and motels, each 6 percent, and "other" categories make up the rest. You see their lift-gated "bobtail" delivery trucks continuously, but you may not notice them delivering and unloading a pallet or two of goods at a time for a broad assortment of foodservice venues in your area. If you eat out at all, you've most likely consumed Sysco-distributed products, and their slogan, "Good Things Come from Sysco," is classic.

Sysco was founded in 1969 with the goal of becoming a national foodservice network. By 1977, the company had become the largest foodservice supplier in North America, a position it has retained for more than 30 years. It has over 425,000 customers and distributes over 400,000 products, including 40,000 under its own label, and conducts business in more than 100 countries.

Sysco operates 187 distribution facilities across the United States, Canada, and Ireland and distributes 1.4 billion cases of food annually. These facilities include its 95 Broadline facilities, which supply independent and chain restaurants and other food-preparation facilities with a wide variety of food and nonfood products. It has 11 hotel supply locations, 27 specialty produce facilities, 17 SYGMA distribution centers (specialized, high-volume centers supplying to chain restaurants), 27 custom-cutting meat locations, and two distributors specializing in the niche Asian foodservice market.

The company also supplies the hotel industry with guest amenities, equipment, housekeeping supplies, room accessories, and textiles.

Sysco is by far the largest company in the foodservice distribution industry. Up until recently, it grew via small "bolt-on" acquisitions in specialty food companies (such as seafood) or new geographies, but for the most part avoided the "blockbuster" acquisition. Such acquisitions in 2013 added a billion dollars in net revenues.

However, the "small" nature of these acquisitions changed dramatically in December 2013 with the announcement of a merger with its largest competitor, U.S. Foods, for some $8.2 billion. Sales for the resulting company would be about $65 billion, a 46 percent increase from today's levels, with obvious cost savings and synergies given the similar business footprint. As of mid-2014, a fair amount of opposition to the merger had emerged from restaurateurs about anticompetitive concerns, despite a reiterated commitment "to be our customers' most valued and trusted business partner." Termination of the agreement would cost Sysco some $300 million in severance plus other costs, and the FTC has requested more information, but Sysco claims that is "part of the process." We think the merger will go through, as the combined company will only own about 27 percent of the market—not a monopoly share.

The company will likely divest some assets as well. Sysco proposes to issue about $3 billion in shares (a 15 percent increase) and assume debts to complete the purchase.

Financial Highlights, Fiscal Year 2013

FY2013 was not a particularly stellar year for this business, as revenues, mostly pushed along by small acquisitions, grew almost 5 percent. The good news stopped there, as continued spottiness in the economic recovery made things tough for restaurants. Volume and mix changes were both unfavorable, shaving 0.5 percent off of operating margins (a big deal when the number starts out at 5.5 percent). Additionally, the company incurred acquisition costs and brought on several new operational improvements such as new enterprise-wide CRM software—which produced cost but no savings during that year. All together, earnings dipped almost 12 percent, although per-share cash flows managed to hold on with only a 2.3 percent drop, and the dividend was increased its typical 4 percent as has become the tradition.

Current trends were seen as continuing into FY2014, with finally a decent pickup in FY2015. Revenue increases were to continue in the 4–5 percent range, with FY2015 per-share earnings about 15 percent ahead of FY2014, with similar gains in years to come. That will all change if the U.S.

Foods merger comes off; once the dust settles the combined company would likely see low double-digit earnings growth on mid-single-digit revenue growth. But only if everything goes according to plan.

and extend the customer relationship. In sum, even with the merger, this is a steady and safe company with a pretty good track record for steady business, decent cash flow, and decent shareholder payouts.

Reasons to Buy

Sysco continues to be a dominant player—and may become more dominant—in a niche that won't go away anytime soon. While the current foodservice environment isn't great, the company has plenty to work on in the form of operational efficiencies, and the U.S. Foods merger, if that comes to pass, should eventually deliver substantial cost savings.

Sysco's recent investments in technology continue to bear fruit, and we like to see innovation in an industry not known for it. Improvements in routing and inventory management have allowed the company to increase its shipment frequency by 10 percent with 4 percent fewer people, all while using 10 percent less fuel. New supply-chain tools for customers—even a Sysco app—will expand efficiencies

Reasons for Caution

Although the trend is slowly reversing, the recession got many folks away from the habit of eating out, and many restaurants disappeared altogether during this period. Volatility in food and ingredient prices, and fuel costs too, can pressure margins; this is always a cause for concern. As mentioned above, this is a low-margin business with not a lot of room for error. Share counts will rise if the acquisition is completed, but we would expect resumption of buybacks after the acquisition period if the past pattern holds. Sysco, more than most, is a "sleep at night" kind of investment; investors seeking rapid growth might want to look somewhere outside of this steady and rather unsexy business.

SECTOR: **Consumer Staples**
BETA COEFFICIENT: **0.79**
10-YEAR COMPOUND EARNINGS PER-SHARE GROWTH: **6.0%**
10-YEAR COMPOUND DIVIDENDS PER-SHARE GROWTH: **12.0%**

	2006	2007	2008	2009	2010	2011	2012	2013
Revenues (mil)	32,628	35,042	37,522	36,853	37,243	39,323	42,381	44,411
Net income (mil)	855	1,001	1,106	1,056	1,181	1,153	1,122	892
Earnings per share	1.35	1.60	1.81	1.77	1.99	1.96	1.90	1.67
Dividends per share	0.66	0.72	0.82	0.93	0.99	1.03	1.07	1.11
Cash flow per share	1.92	2.23	2.46	2.44	2.67	2.62	2.63	2.57
Price: high	37.0	36.7	35.0	29.5	32.6	32.6	32.4	43.4
low	26.5	29.9	20.7	19.4	27.0	25.1	27.0	30.5

Sysco Corporation
1390 Enclave Parkway
Houston, TX 77077–2099
(281) 584-1390
Website: *www.sysco.com*

Target Corporation

Ticker symbol: TGT (NYSE) ❑ S&P rating: A+ ❑ Value Line financial strength rating: A
Current yield: 2.8% ❑ Dividend raises, past 10 years: 10

Company Profile

Target is the nation's second-largest general merchandise retailer and specializes in general merchandise at a discount in a large-store format. The company now operates 1,793 stores in 49 states (Vermont is the only state not represented), including 251 Super Targets, which also carry a broad line of groceries. The greatest concentration of Target stores is in California (15 percent), Texas (8 percent), and Florida (7 percent), with a combined total of about 30 percent of the stores. There is another concentration in the upper Midwest. With the sale of Marshall Field's and Mervyn's in 2004, the company has focused completely on discount retail in store locations and on the Internet.

Target positions itself against its main competitor, Walmart, as a more upscale and trend-conscious "cheap chic" alternative. The typical Target customer has a higher level of disposable income, which the company courts by offering brand-name merchandise in addition to a series of largely successful house brands such as Michael Graves and Archer Farms. The company's revenues come from retail pretty much exclusively; it sold its credit card operations to TD Bank in late 2012.

By mid-2014, Target was in the final stages of a 125-store expansion into Canada, with some 124 stores in place across the country. The company is also investing domestically in its food lines, which now account for 21 percent of total sales; up from 19 percent last year. Food is sold in about 70 percent of stores, up from 50 percent last year. The total sales breakdown: 25 percent household essentials, 21 percent food and pet supplies, 19 percent apparel and accessories, 18 percent hardlines, and 17 percent home furnishings and décor.

With this short sketch in place, we must cover the two big news items of the year, both of which in our opinion reflect significant short term adverse effects but should fade from the picture as we enter FY2015:

■ Data breach. On December 18, 2013, at the height of the holiday shopping season, the company announced a major data breach as a hacker reached into their point-of-sale credit card systems to compromise as many as 110 million customers using credit cards of all types. The breach led to the resignation of both the CEO and Chief Information Officer and more than $60 million in expenses in direct response. More crucially, and despite a best-in-class response to the hit, the company took a significant public relations setback which will hit both the top and bottom lines through FY2014. One bright spot: the company will be the first to adopt so-called "smartcards"—credit cards with embedded microprocessors containing an encrypted version of key personal data—rendering hacked data useless unless the hacker has the microprocessor chip. This technology is already widely used outside the United States.

■ Oh, no, Canada. The Canadian expansion generated less in sales and more in expenses than planned, in all costing the company a $941 million hit to the bottom line for FY2013, a loss some 35 percent larger than management expectations. Competition from Walmart Canada and other Canadian competitors hurt sales, while startup expenses exceeded expectations. The company expects both of these effects to diminish during FY2014 and into FY2015.

Despite these two major setbacks, the company reaffirmed its commitment to shareholders with constant communication and by increasing dividends at the same rich pace as before.

Financial Highlights, Fiscal Year 2013

Without the breach and the Canadian disappointment, the company would have fared well for the year, in our opinion. With these two factors, total revenues dropped about 1 percent, while total earnings, mainly hurt with the Canadian situation as the consequences of the data breach had not fully taken hold in FY2013, dropped about 29 percent. Comparable same-store sales did drop 2.5 percent in the reported fourth quarter, which ended January 31, 2014.

Target projects a decent top-line recovery in FY2014 to about $75 billion, which would be about 3.3 percent ahead of FY2013, and more significantly, 2.3 percent ahead of the "intact" year of FY2012. About half the earnings hit will be recovered in FY2014, all of it in FY2015. We expect ongoing revenue gains between 3–4 percent annually, with per-share earnings gains, helped along rather well by share buybacks, to approach the high single digits to 10 percent each year.

Reasons to Buy

We think the long-term consequences of FY2013's problems will fade rather quickly, although the departures of the CEO and CIO give us some pause. The company has handled both issues and particularly the data breach quite effectively, in fact using it as an opportunity to pioneer new technologies, which we think in the long term will not only assuage its customers' concerns but attract new customers. The company is simply too strong in its brand and position to lose in the long term over an incident like this, particularly if handled well which currently appears to be the case.

Target remains a classic positioning success story. Aside from the breach, customers understand and appreciate Target, and it has some of the highest customer satisfaction numbers in the industry. The company continues to take share away from specialty retailers in home lines, clothing, children's items, and other areas. People like the Target brand and associate it with well-managed stores and quality and good taste at a reasonable price with good locations. More recently they appear to be making more regular and frequent visits to the store because of the grocery department.

Better economic conditions and more spending on home and domestic goods should improve Target's market share. While the Canada expansion has provided some important lessons, we do feel that international expansion will work and extend Target's future potential. Share counts have dropped from 911 million in 2003 to about 650 million recently and dividend increases have run at about 15 percent annually. Bottom line: There are some risks, but we feel the story remains solid; recent headlines presented a good buying opportunity in 2014 which will probably extend some into FY2015.

Reasons for Caution

Of course, both the data breach and the Canada expansion could have long-lingering effects. We don't expect a permanent shift in customer preferences, nor a pervasive fear of shopping at Target, but more bad news could change this considerably. Changes in leadership can be difficult, too; the fact that the interim CEO goes by the name of "Mulligan" is an amusing coincidence, and we hope the current situation is just that. We hope that no more Target drives go out of bounds in 2014, or beyond for that matter; the ball could be harder to find the next time around.

Aside from that, Target is up against some very tough competitors: Walmart, Costco, and others. The success of international expansion, which has gone well for Walmart and Costco, is still an unknown for Target.

We still see some risk in the grocery business, as groceries are very low margin, and the company hasn't really figured out how to make the grocery offering complete with meats and fresh produce. Gross and operating margins may continue to see some pressure from this business, depending on how valuable the generation of more frequent store visits turns out to be.

SECTOR: **Retail**
BETA COEFFICIENT: **0.58**
10-YEAR COMPOUND EARNINGS PER-SHARE GROWTH: **10.0%**
10-YEAR COMPOUND DIVIDENDS PER-SHARE GROWTH: **17.0%**

	2006	2007	2008	2009	2010	2011	2012	2013
Revenues (mil)	59,490	63,367	64,948	63,435	67,390	69,865	73,301	72,596
Net income (mil)	2,408	2,849	2,214	2,488	2,830	2,829	2,925	2,060
Earnings per share	3.21	3.33	2.86	3.30	3.88	4.28	4.38	3.21
Dividends per share	0.42	0.56	0.60	0.66	0.84	1.10	1.32	1.56
Cash flow per share	4.98	5.51	5.37	5.90	6.98	7.46	7.82	6.77
Price: high	60.3	70.8	59.6	51.8	60.7	61.0	65.5	73.5
low	44.7	48.8	25.6	25.0	46.2	45.3	47.3	55.0

Target Corporation
1000 Nicollet Mall
Minneapolis, MN 55403
(612) 304-6073
Website: *www.target.com*

Tiffany & Co.

Ticker symbol: TIF (NYSE) □ S&P rating: NR □ Value Line financial strength rating: A+ □ Current yield: 1.6% □ Dividend raises, past 10 years: 10

Company Profile

As a variant on the old cliché goes, "If you have to ask who they are, you can't afford them." But when it comes to investing, it's perfectly okay to ask, and we're here to provide the answer, so here goes . . .

Tiffany is a jeweler and specialty retailer principally offering jewelry (accounting for 92 percent of FY2013 sales) but also timepieces, sterling silver goods (e.g., silver spoons), china, crystal, fragrances, stationery, leather goods, and other personal items. As of early 2014, the company operates some 289 retail locations worldwide, 121 of those in the Americas with a complementing online and catalog order operation.

The design of both product and packaging is distinctive, with a historic tradition and elegant simplicity that sets it apart. Ditto for the stores and catalog. Tiffany is probably the world's most recognized general jewelry brand (aside from Rolex and similar brands in the watch business).

The geographic tour of Tiffany's worldwide footprint is both interesting and insightful. First stop: Some 52 percent of FY2013 sales are from outside the Americas. There are 94

stores in the United States (up from 87 in 2012), 12 in Canada, 10 in Mexico, and 5 in Brazil. Notably, the multistory flagship store on Fifth Avenue in New York City accounts for about 10 percent of Tiffany's business alone, albeit much of it from visiting foreign tourists craving the experience (and what is still a historically weak U.S. dollar).

Now, moving on to the Asia-Pacific region, which accounts for 23 percent of sales, there are now 26 stores in China (including Hong Kong), 14 in Korea, 8 in Taiwan, 6 in Australia, 5 in Singapore, 2 in Macau, and 2 in Malaysia. Oh, yes—what about Japan? Japan is so large it is accounted for as a separate region, with 14 percent of the business and 54 stores. Do the Japanese appreciate quality and elegant simplicity? Always.

Finally, we come to Europe, which represents 12 percent of sales with 10 stores in the U.K., 7 in Germany, 4 in France, 2 in Spain, 2 in Switzerland, and 1 each in 5 other countries. Beyond Europe, the company also does business in the Middle East, Russia, and elsewhere through distributors. The Middle East and the BRIC countries (Brazil/Russia/ India/China) are the most important growth areas, although the timing of a Russia store opening in February 2014 turned out to be a bit unfortunate because of anti-Western angst and concerns arising from the situation in the Ukraine. Interestingly, the sovereign wealth fund of Qatar apparently sees Tiffany as a crown jewel, owning almost 13 percent of the company.

In addition to retailing a broad line of luxury goods, Tiffany also designs and manufactures much of its branded jewelry. The Tiffany cachet raises margins on these items without significantly diluting brand strength, while at the same time driving store visits higher. Clearly, the company is a bastion for wealthy consumers, but it also works hard to attract so-called "aspirational" consumers seeking moderately priced $100–$300 items with that Tiffany cachet and experience. Internationally, and particularly in Asia, Tiffany appeals to the very wealthy, and the average selling price of items in Asia runs 8–10 times the average price of items sold in the Americas. That said, the growing middle class in that region is good news, too.

Financial Highlights, Fiscal Year 2013

Strong 6 percent same-store comparisons and broad contributions from all regions with particular strength in Asia Pacific led to a 10 percent constant-currency revenue gain for FY2013, which was attenuated to 6.2 percent when currency was factored in. A better product mix and improved operating expenses led the way to a 15 percent gain in operating earnings, and a similar gain in per-share earnings, as share counts remained unchanged.

The company expects continued strength in the fine and fashion jewelry categories, with new product lines called Gatsby and Ziegfried and a new "Tiffany Harmony" collection. The company has also invested in a website redesign and the incorporation of more "theater" in its stores—both well executed in our opinion. For FY2014 and FY2015 the company expects revenue growth in the 7–8 percent range, with per-share earnings continuing upward in the 15 percent range. Per-share earnings will be helped along, perhaps beyond these figures, as the company also announced a new $200 million share repurchase plan over three years, which would retire about 2 percent of outstanding shares—significant as few repurchases have been done in recent years.

Reasons to Buy

"We deliver the promise of the blue box." Tiffany is a classic branding story, where brand image supports the product and the product (and packaging) supports the brand image.

People buy Tiffany because it is Tiffany and because they are attracted to the brand's distinctive cachet and elegant simplicity. While the company is working to offer more moderately priced items for the "aspirational" market, we don't expect it to lower quality and damage the brand prestige. Pricing power appears strong, and the sales mix has improved recently.

We are very strong on the company's international footprint and the ability to grow sales and leverage the brand, particularly in Asia. The company is also introducing a new smaller-footprint store format to cover moderately sized markets. Dividend raises have been steady, and renewed share repurchases add a few jewels to the story as well.

Finally—and one might not expect this in the typically sales-y jewelry industry—the company makes a notably complete and digestible presentation of its own business in its annual reports and other releases— elegant and simple. We like that and think it reflects good management overall.

Reasons for Caution

In 2012, we added this company to our list but with caution, as there was some risk in going too far to cater to the aspirational base with less expensive, and perhaps lower-quality and less "elegantly simple" items. We were worried about the possibility that Tiffany could become just another corner jeweler, especially as store counts ramped up. Early results proved us right, but since then the world economy, new offerings, and continued strong positioning have reduced this concern. Tiffany seems solid in its growing and profitable niche and not so inclined to move out of it. Still, if sales stall, this concern remains on our radar.

Naturally, the company is somewhat exposed to economic cycles, particularly economic circumstances that affect the rich, as the Great Recession clearly did. It is also exposed to the volatility of gold and silver— although this volatility actually creates some demand as buyers, particularly in Asia, look at fine jewelry and its precious metals as a store of value. Recently, lower precious metals prices have given a boost to results, but this and other factors may be reflected in the company's strong stock price. What glitters here is probably gold, but you should pick your mining spots carefully.

SECTOR: **Retail**
BETA COEFFICIENT: **1.77**
10-YEAR COMPOUND EARNINGS PER-SHARE GROWTH: **10.5%**
10-YEAR COMPOUND DIVIDENDS PER-SHARE GROWTH: **22.0%**

	2006	2007	2008	2009	2010	2011	2012	2013
Revenues (mil)	2,648	2,938	2,860	2,709	3,085	3,643	3,794	4,031
Net income (mil)	254	322	294	266	378	465	416	481
Earnings per share	1.60	2.33	2.33	2.12	2.93	3.61	3.25	3.73
Dividends per share	0.38	0.52	0.66	0.68	0.95	1.12	1.25	1.34
Cash flow per share	2.74	3.50	3.44	3.21	4.13	4.82	4.57	5.15
Price: high	41.3	57.3	50.0	44.5	65.8	84.5	74.2	93.0
low	29.6	38.2	18.8	16.7	35.6	54.6	49.7	57.1

Tiffany & Co.
727 Fifth Ave.
New York, NY 10022
(212) 755-8000
Website: *www.tiffany.com*

Time Warner Inc.

Ticker symbol: TWX (NYSE) □ S&P rating: BBB □ Value Line financial strength rating: A □ Current yield: 1.9% □ Dividend raises, past 10 years: 8

Company Profile

Time Warner is a $30 billion media and entertainment company aimed squarely at producing and distributing media in both traditional and innovative ways. Five years ago, the company undertook a well-publicized—and necessary—downsize, untying itself from America Online (AOL), and went back to working in the areas it knows best—content—and working on new ways to make more money producing and delivering that content.

A few years ago, we liked the story, and we had no entertainment stocks, so we bought a ticket for the 2013 *100 Best* list . . . and have been pleasantly surprised, to say the least. The story had an interesting epilogue, with last year's announcement to spin off Time Inc.—the print portion of the business. Altogether, we still give this movie a pretty solid "thumbs up."

With the disposal of much of the publishing operation, and an expansion in digital and cable services, the company reorganized itself into three reporting business segments during 2013, to take effect with the Time separation in mid-2014:

■ Turner (33 percent of 2013 revenues) was a big part of the old "Networks" segment, which provides content through digital and cable networks. The segment includes industry-leading properties formerly part of the Turner Broadcasting System, including CNN, TBS, TNT, Turner Classic, as well as other standards such as Cartoon Network, Adult Swim, Boomerang, and a series of digital sports networks including NBA.com, PGA.com, TMZ, and others. The unit is investing heavily in on-demand viewing and live streaming of content, which they now estimate to be available to 82 million U.S. households. The unit, in all, has 150 channels broadcast in 36 languages in 200 countries worldwide.

■ Home Box Office (16 percent of revenues) delivers premium pay-TV services in the U.S. with an estimated 43 million subscribers, and premium and basic pay services internationally with about 127 million subscribers.

■ Warner Bros. (41 percent) includes Warner Bros. Pictures

and New Line Cinema. Warner Bros. produces more than 60 TV shows and about 15–25 feature films a year and distributes hundreds of others. The studio won more Academy Awards than all other studios combined, and ranked number one in domestic and international box office gross in 2013. The unit also produces and licenses content for video games and other delivery modes, and distributes its content in more than 125 countries, many in local languages.

The remaining 10 percent of TWX's revenues originated from the Publishing unit, which were included in the numbers presented below but will be eliminated with the spinoff.

The details of these businesses and sub-businesses expand far beyond what is described here; suffice it to say TWX has a huge presence in the creation and distribution of many forms of media. The company is quite dedicated to innovation, and the use of innovations to get more content to more people in more places at more times than ever before. A new "TV Everywhere" initiative is one example, and there are many more innovations in the digital space. The company has also been actively expanding and managing its global footprint, with about 10 percent of total revenues from outside the United States.

Financial Highlights, Fiscal Year 2013

In FY2013 the company rode a cross-current of successful movie releases, mixed television and especially home video revenues, currency effects, and the complexities of reorganization into a 4 percent rise in revenues, but a happy ending on the earnings front, with an 18 percent increase in the bottom line, which translated into a smash-hit 22 percent increase in per-share earnings on the back of a 37 million share (4 percent) buyback. Clearer operating focus in the wake of the publishing spinoff, international expansion, and improved monetization of new and backlist titles is estimated to give rise to 4–5 percent revenue gains through FY2015, with per-share earnings increasing in the 10 percent range through FY2015, putting the company, at least according to projections, into our "5 and 10" club: 5 percent revenue growth, 10 percent earnings growth ongoing.

Reasons to Buy

Time Warner has taken its medicine with AOL, and we think it is unlikely to repeat past mistakes. Too, it has made the right, if emotionally difficult, decision to separate from its legacy publishing unit. As the Internet universe expands, and as people have smart devices capable of receiving anything anywhere anytime, we think the demand for content will only go up, and TWX has some of the great properties and brands, such as CNN, HBO, and TBS, to leverage as platforms to develop and deliver this content. We thought that once TWX regained focus and investors started to "get" the story, good things could happen. Apparently that wish has come true. Additionally the company is working hard on new programming, new delivery, new channels for its content library, cost structure, and profitability. This is a cash-generating business, and we like the cash returns to investors.

Reasons for Caution

The entertainment business is complex, fickle, and ever changing, which in part explains why we had no such companies on our *100 Best* list until 2013—and why we have only one today. It's a struggle to keep up with what's new and what's changing, and in particular, what's working, but we've admired this company's ability to build good brands, put good products on the market, and achieve lasting revenue streams from all of it. Others have also recognized the "new and improved" operating model that has emerged since the AOL days, so the stock price has risen considerably; investors should look for matinee pricing.

SECTOR: **Entertainment**

BETA COEFFICIENT: **1.16**

10-YEAR COMPOUND EARNINGS PER-SHARE GROWTH: **33.5%**

10-YEAR COMPOUND DIVIDENDS PER-SHARE GROWTH: **14.5%**

		2006	2007	2008	2009	2010	2011	2012	2013
Revenues (mil)		44,224	46,482	46,894	25,785	26,888	28,944	29,729	29,795
Net income (mil)		5,114	4,051	3,574	2,079	2,578	2,886	3,019	3,554
Earnings per share		3.63	2.97	2.88	1.74	2.25	2.71	3.09	3.77
Dividends per share		0.63	0.71	0.75	0.75	0.85	0.94	1.04	1.15
Cash flow per share		6.75	7.07	6.83	2.66	3.20	3.91	4.20	4.96
Price:	high	66.8	69.5	50.7	33.5	34.1	38.6	48.5	70.8
	low	47.1	45.5	21.0	17.8	26.4	27.6	33.5	48.6

Time Warner Inc.

One Time Warner Center

New York, NY 10019-8016

(212) 484-8000

Website: *www.timewarner.com*

GROWTH AND INCOME

Total S.A. (ADR)

Ticker symbol: TOT (NYSE) □ S&P rating: AA- □ Value Line financial strength rating: A++
Current yield: 4.8% □ Dividend raises, past 10 years: 7

Company Profile

Total S.A. (S.A. is short for "Société Anonyme," which is the French equivalent of "incorporated") is the fifth-largest publicly traded oil and gas company in the world. Headquartered in France and primarily traded on the French CAC stock exchange, the company has operations in more than 130 countries. Total is vertically integrated with upstream operations engaged in oil and gas exploration and downstream operations engaged in refining and distribution of petroleum products; the company also has a chemicals subsidiary.

Upstream activities are geographically well diversified, with exploration occurring in 50 countries and production happening in 30. Many of the E&P projects are done through partnerships to spread risk. The largest production regions are (in production-volume sequence) in the North Sea, North Africa, West Africa, and the Middle East, with smaller operations in Southeast Asia and North and South America. Liquids (oil) account for about 61 percent of production, while natural gas is 39 percent. The company is a leader in the emerging liquefied natural gas (LNG) market for export,

and recently strengthened an agreement to supply LNG to the China National Offshore Oil Corporation.

Downstream operations are also worldwide and centered in Europe. Operations include interests in 20 refineries worldwide, with 11 refineries and 85 percent of total refining capacity in Europe. There are also 20 petrochemical plants. Total also operates 14,725 service stations in 68 countries, mainly under the Total, Elf, and Elan names, again weighted toward Europe and North Africa. The downstream presence is also growing in Asia Pacific (including China), Latin America, and the Caribbean. The new Saudi Arabia refinery, online in 2013, will help longer-term results as the company diversifies its processing and marketing capacity into the faster-growing Middle East and Asian regions; it now has a leading market presence in those regions. Total also has ventures in alternative energy, notably solar. It owns a 66 percent interest in global solar leader Sunpower. With two major partners it brought online in 2013, it also has an interest in what is thought to be the world's largest concentrated solar power plant at 100 megawatts in Abu Dhabi.

Financial Highlights, Fiscal Year 2013

General softness in Europe, soft pricing, and softness in refining margins led to a pretty unimpressive year in FY2013. Revenues dropped 3 percent, and a decline in overall operating margin led to a more substantial 11 percent downturn in earnings. All three sources of "softness" are expected to strengthen going forward, which should put the company back on a 2–3 percent annual growth track for revenue, and a solid recovery to FY2012 levels of net profit for FY2014 and a solid 5–10 percent annual growth rate beyond that. Additionally, the company recently announced authorization to repurchase some 10 percent of its stock over an 18-month period (which doesn't mean that it has to occur, only that it is authorized). This is significant; share repurchases had been almost nonexistent since 2007.

Reasons to Buy

While the diverse international footprint, strong cash flow, and high yield have attracted us until now, Total has two more clear attractions going forward—recovery in Europe and many of the markets that Total serves at a retail and refining level, and a reserve replacement rate some 30 percent higher than depletion—if you've been reading the headlines about failure to replace outgoing reserves at Royal Dutch Shell, ExxonMobil, and other "big oils," this is pretty attractive.

Too, because of their geography, Total realizes better prices than some of the bellwether markets for their products—about $103 per barrel for its crude and $7.12 per million BTU for natural gas. Finally, with the new instability in Russia and its satellites, Total may be counted on to supply more of Europe's energy needs, but this situation remains volatile.

Total S.A. is a solid energy sector play with many of the features that make "big energy" attractive—namely, strong cash flows, high dividend yields, and demand that isn't going away any time soon. The potential for renewed share buybacks has our attention too. As for big energy stocks, Total is "plus interessant" than most.

Reasons for Caution

We remain cautious on investing in foreign companies because of differences in management style and accounting rules; they aren't necessarily bad but are difficult to understand and follow. Antiquated European pension rules and other labor practices could also be a disadvantage. There is a degree of political risk common to all international oil companies, but Total, not being an American company, may be better positioned and less of a target. Typically, we prefer U.S. companies that do a lot of business overseas, but we still feel the strengths of Total overcome these concerns. Finally, the stock has recently woken up to the improving situation; new investors should shop carefully.

SECTOR: **Energy**
BETA COEFFICIENT: **1.31**
10-YEAR COMPOUND EARNINGS PER-SHARE GROWTH: **11.5%**
10-YEAR COMPOUND DIVIDENDS PER-SHARE GROWTH: **15.5%**

	2006	2007	2008	2009	2010	2011	2012	2013
Revenues (mil)	167,188	167,149	236,087	157,014	186,131	215,849	234,224	227,887
Net income (mil)	15,463	16,718	18,205	11,626	14,006	15,910	15,884	14,270
Earnings per share	6.82	7.35	8.55	5.31	6.24	7.05	7.01	6.28
Dividends per share	2.10	2.81	3.10	3.28	2.93	3.12	2.98	3.10
Cash flow per share	9.60	10.73	12.42	9.49	11.25	11.37	12.46	11.57
Price: high	73.8	87.3	91.3	66	67.5	64.4	57.1	62.4
low	58.1	63.9	42.6	42.9	43.1	40.0	41.8	45.9

Total S.A. (ADR)
2, place Jean Millier
La Défense 6
92078 Paris La Défense Cedex France
+ 33 (0) 47 44 45 46
Website: *www.total.com*

Union Pacific Corporation

Ticker symbol: UNP (NYSE) □ S&P rating: A- □ Value Line financial strength rating: A++
Current yield: 2.0% □ Dividend raises, past 10 years: 9

Company Profile

Union Pacific has been a familiar name and logo in the railroad business since its inception during the Civil War. With about 32,000 miles of track covering 23 states in the western two-thirds of the United States, today's Union Pacific Railroad, the primary subsidiary of the Union Pacific Corporation, describes itself as "America's Premier Railroad Franchise." The route system is anchored by Gulf Coast and West Coast ports and areas in between and has coordinated schedules and gateways with other lines in the eastern U.S., Canada, and Mexico.

With 10,000 customers, a large number in today's era of trainload-sized shipments, UNP has a more diversified customer and revenue mix than the other rail companies, including the other three of the "big four" railroads: BNSF, Norfolk Southern, and CSX. Energy (mainly Powder River Basin and Colorado) accounts for 19 percent of revenues; Intermodal (trucks or containers on flatcars), 20 percent; Agricultural, 16 percent; Industrial, 18 percent; Chemicals, 15 percent; and Automotive, 10 percent of FY2013 revenues.

The company has long been an innovator in railroad technology, including motive power, communications and technology automation, physical plant, community relations, and marketing. The company functions with one of the lowest operating ratios in the industry, 65.0 percent, meaning that operating costs account for 65 percent (67.8 percent in FY2012, 70.6 percent in FY2011) of total costs. This allows a good contribution to the substantial fixed costs of owning and running a railroad. This success has translated to continued strong operating margins, which of course have helped earnings and cash flows.

The company also invests a lot in marketing and community relations. The company just began a five-year program to restore a "Big Boy" steam locomotive, the largest ever used in regular service (of course, for the UP) for a Golden Spike sesquicentennial rollout. Such public relations efforts based on a company's history may seem ordinary for a major U.S. corporation, but for the railroad industry, these well-executed activities show an extra measure of pride, an appreciation for heritage, and community relations not common in the industry (or any industry, for that matter).

Railroads have quietly been learning to use technology to improve operations and deliver better customer service. New tools can track shipments door to door using GPS-based technology, and the railroad will accept shipments and manage them door to door, even over other railroads or with other kinds of carriers. Customers can check rates and routes and track shipments online. These services, combined with high fuel prices, have led to a continuing migration from trucks back to rail and intermodal rail services.

Financial Highlights, Fiscal Year 2013

The company continues to deal with a shift in mix away from the profitable coal segment, as more power plants convert to gas, but has made up for that decline in most of its other categories, particularly agricultural, industrial, and automotive, and intermodal shipments remain strong. New export coal shipments, especially to Japan which has downsized its nuclear exposure in favor of coal, may make up for some of the U.S. decline, which has brought coal down from 22 percent to 19 percent of the traffic mix.

All that said, the good news really lies in the payoff from previous investments in physical plant and equipment, which continue to deliver operating efficiencies. The drop in operating ratio in two years from 70.6 percent to 65 percent is remarkable and probably an industry first—and most of this efficiency drops straight to the bottom line. Revenues were up 5 percent, but the real light at the end of the tunnel was in profit margins and net earnings, which rose 11 percent; and with a 2 percent share buyback, per-share earnings rose some 14 percent. Cash flow per share has almost quadrupled since 2005, and the company chipped in a 19 percent dividend increase for the year as well. No slowing down for FY2014 and FY2015; favorable trends in oil and gas exploration and shipments, intermodal, automotive, and general industrial production in the U.S. and Mexico bode well for the business, and the operational improvements are here to stay. The company projects another 15 percent rise in per-share earnings in FY2014 followed by a similar increase in FY2015, and the future direction and volume of oil shipments could propel this higher. The company is also stepping up its already healthy share buybacks, with plans to retire 60 million shares (13 percent) in the next four years, and has nearly tripled its dividend in the past four. It's not hard to see why the stock price has doubled in just a little over two years.

Reasons to Buy

Put simply —whether you enjoy watching trains or not, this company has been as exciting as any tech stock, and it is also returning plenty of cash to shareholders. UNP is an extraordinarily well-managed company and has become more efficient and at the same time more user friendly to its customers and to the general public. The company continues to make gains at the expense of the trucking industry, and new short- and long-distance intermodal services move higher-valued goods more quickly and cost-effectively; we see a steady shift toward this business. New trends in domestic energy exploration and distribution only add to the story. The company has a solid and diverse traffic base and continues to have a good brand and reputation in the industry.

Reasons for Caution

Railroads are and will always be economically sensitive because of commodity revenue and their high fixed-cost structure. They also have significant headline risk—a single event like a derailment can hurt them in the public eye or tangle them up in regulation, lawsuits, and unplanned costs. Regulation and mandates for Positive Train Control and other safety features can be expensive. Another longer-term factor may be the widening of the Panama Canal, which may shift some Asian import/export traffic to southern and eastern ports and away from the West Coast. Finally, the increase in profitability has been reflected "full throttle" in the share price, and further gains may be hard to come by, particularly if coal and agriculture remain soft or some other traffic segment runs into problems.

SECTOR: **Transportation**
BETA COEFFICIENT: **1.06**
10-YEAR COMPOUND EARNINGS PER-SHARE GROWTH: **15.0%**
10-YEAR COMPOUND DIVIDENDS PER-SHARE GROWTH: **19.5%**

		2006	2007	2008	2009	2010	2011	2012	2013
Revenues (mil)		15,578	16,283	17,970	14,143	16,965	19,557	20,926	21,953
Net income (mil)		1,606	1,856	2,338	1,826	2,780	3,292	3,943	4,388
Earnings per share		2.96	3.46	4.54	3.61	5.53	6.72	8.27	9.42
Dividends per share		0.60	0.68	0.93	1.08	1.31	1.93	2.49	2.96
Cash flow per share		5.15	6.09	7.40	6.47	8.68	10.23	12.15	13.52
Price:	high	48.7	68.8	85.8	66.7	95.8	107.0	129.3	168.2
	low	38.8	44.8	41.8	33.3	60.4	77.7	104.1	127.3

Union Pacific Corporation
1400 Douglas St.
Omaha, NE 68179
(402) 544-5000
Website: *www.up.com*

AGGRESSIVE GROWTH

UnitedHealth Group Inc.

Ticker symbol: UNH (NYSE) ❑ S&P rating: A- ❑ Value Line financial strength rating: A++
Current yield: 1.4% ❑ Dividend raises, past 10 years: 4

Company Profile

UnitedHealth Group is the parent company of a number of health insurers and service organizations. It is the second-largest publicly traded health insurance company in the United States, with more than $120 billion in revenue reported in 2013.

The company has reorganized and rebranded part of its business and now operates in two major business segments: UnitedHealthcare and Optum. UnitedHealthcare provides traditional and Medicare-based health benefit and insurance plans for individuals and employers, covering approximately 27 million Americans with about 400 national employer accounts and many other smaller employer accounts. The company estimates that it serves more than half of the *Fortune* 100 companies list. The company, mainly through this unit, has been an active acquirer of other familiar health-care and insurance brands, including Oxford Health in 2004, PacifiCare in 2005, Sierra Health Plans and Unison Health Plans in 2008, AIM Healthcare Services in 2009, and more recently an assortment of small, mostly Medicare-related providers.

The UnitedHealthcare Medicare and Retirement business, formerly known as Ovations, serves about 9 million seniors—one in five Medicare beneficiaries. Taken together, these operations generated approximately 75 percent of UNH's overall revenue in 2013 and 76 percent of profits.

The remainder of the company's revenue comes from its health services businesses, which it markets under the Optum brand umbrella. This segment, which touches some 64 million customers, is far and away big enough to be a separate company, and is an increasingly important part of the overall UNH business offering. Optum delivers service through three separate businesses. OptumHealth is an "information and technology"–based health solution, deploying mostly remote tele-support for well care, mental health, ongoing disease management, and substance abuse programs. The OptumRx business is a pharmacy benefits provider serving 25 million customers with about 350 million prescriptions annually, while OptumInsight is a management information, analytics, and process-improvement arm providing an assortment of services for health plans, physicians, hospitals, and life science research, formerly marketed under the Ingenix brand. Of the total Optum-branded business of $37 billion (25 percent ahead of FY2012), Rx accounts for the lion's share at $24 billion, while OptumHealth, which grew some 21 percent in FY2013, weighs in at $9.8 billion and OptumInsight at $3.1 billion. Although these numbers may seem small in the context of UNH's total $122.5 billion annual revenue footprint, they are sizeable businesses when looked at individually. The Optum umbrella brand is gaining in prominence, and even has its own unique web presence at *www.optum. com*. Together, the two business units serve about 85 million individuals in all 50 United States and in 125 other countries.

UnitedHealthcare has been a leader in process, delivery, and cost improvement and a recognized innovator in the industry. Currently, while not participating in all Affordable Care Act exchanges, the company is learning to adapt to the new environment and has moved aggressively to offer tools to manage and contain costs in the health-care system, mostly through the Optum business. One such venture is a new joint partnership launch with West Coast hospital operator Dignity Health called "Optum360," where tools to optimize cost management, administration, and patient transparency will be placed into the hospital infrastructure. This is an important

pilot of payer (UNH) partnering with provider (Dignity) in a joint effort to understand and contain costs while improving efficiency, experience, and outcomes; this venture may also contract to offer similar services to other providers. The company sits on top of a mountain of health-care data and is putting it to good use. For these and other reasons, the company was voted the "World's Most Admired Company" in the insurance and managed care sector for the third straight year in 2013 by *Fortune* magazine, and was also named number one in its sector for innovation for the fourth year in a row.

Financial Highlights, Fiscal Year 2013

While in a bit of a holding pattern to understand and better position itself regarding the Affordable Care Act and other industry reform, UnitedHealth posted solid FY2013 revenue results, with revenues advancing some 11 percent over FY2012. However, cutbacks in Medicare reimbursements, other reforms, and investments in the new Optum businesses attenuated growth in per-share earnings to 4 percent. This earnings flat spot may continue through FY2014 but is expected to return to an 8–9 percent growth, aided some by moderate buybacks, in FY2015, and the projection is for stronger earnings growth in FY2016 and beyond as reforms are figured out and the new growth businesses gain traction in profitability to match or exceed their strong revenue growth trajectory.

Reasons to Buy

The company is one of the most solid, diverse, and innovative enterprises in the health insurance industry. Health insurers such as Aetna, included on our *100 Best* list, seem to be getting past many of the fears of reform and other contrary public opinion; these companies by design simply pass costs through but are doing more to control and reduce costs through utilization management and other initiatives, and these efforts are paying off. Meanwhile, like Aetna, UNH brings a fair amount of innovation to the marketplace, primarily through its Optum offerings. We like its initiatives to make use of its own "big data" with analytics; the size of its database and the tools it possesses can deliver efficiency improvements, and even slight efficiency improvements can help the bottom line substantially. If price competition eventually dictates lower premiums, UNH will be in good position with cost-side improvements.

The scale of UNH's operation gives it tremendous leverage when negotiating for the services of healthcare providers. Hospitals and physicians are strongly motivated to join UNH's network, as doing so will provide assurance of steady referrals. The Optum360 venture shows a new level of partnering between payer and provider; we await the outcome.

UnitedHealth has easily scored the quintuple play, with ten-year compounded growth in revenues, earnings, cash flow, dividends, and book value well into double digits; in fact, each has grown over 15 percent. True, some of that results from acquisitions, which we don't expect (or hope) to continue at this pace going forward—but it gives an idea of the growth potential of the issue. And cash returns haven't been too bad either—through increased dividends and share buybacks, the company is growing its cash returns to shareholders.

Reasons for Caution

The outcomes of the Affordable Care Act are still not certain on both the cost and the revenue side; like others, the company is stepping through these changes at a deliberate pace while the final imprint on the business is far from clear. The company is vulnerable to shifts in public opinion and to new regulation, as well as economic downturns, which can hurt employer participation. The company also has demonstrated a fairly aggressive acquisition strategy in the past; this seems to be on the back burner as focus has shifted to the Optum offerings. That's probably a good thing.

SECTOR: **Health Care**
BETA COEFFICIENT: **0.62**
10-YEAR COMPOUND EARNINGS PER-SHARE GROWTH: **17.0%**
10-YEAR COMPOUND DIVIDENDS PER-SHARE GROWTH: **58.5%**

	2006	2007	2008	2009	2010	2011	2012	2103
Revenues (mil)	71,542	75,431	81,186	87,138	94,155	101,862	110,518	122,469
Net income (mil)	4,159	4,654	3,660	3,822	4,633	5,142	5,526	5,625
Earnings per share	2.97	3.42	2.95	3.24	4.10	4.73	5.28	5.50
Dividends per share	0.03	0.03	0.03	0.03	0.41	0.61	0.80	1.05
Cash flow per share	3.59	4.35	3.86	4.20	5.25	5.86	6.67	7.09
Price: high	62.9	59.5	57.9	33.3	38.1	53.5	60.8	75.9
low	41.4	45.8	14.5	16.2	27.1	36.4	49.8	51.4

UnitedHealth Group Inc.
9900 Bren Road East
Hopkins, MN 55343
(952) 936-1300
Website: *www.unitedhealthgroup.com*

CONSERVATIVE GROWTH

United Parcel Service, Inc.

Ticker symbol: UPS (NYSE) ❑ S&P rating: AA- ❑ Value Line financial strength rating: A ❑ Current yield: 2.8% ❑ Dividend raises, past 10 years: 10

Company Profile

Back in 2011, we removed UPS from our *100 Best* stocks list in an early effort to weed out multiple companies on our list doing the same thing. We saw FedEx and UPS converging on the same business from different directions—FedEx being an air company getting ever more into the ground business; UPS being a ground business taking to the air. That convergence is still happening. Both companies continue to build international capabilities, invest in technology to track shipments, and provide logistics services beyond basic assortments of transportation services.

Since being re-added, UPS continues to deliver, with a stock price up from the mid-60s to the high 90s and a 32 percent increase in the dividend.

With those gains in mind, and with a pondering of just where any additional growth might come from, coupled with a softness in its international business led by a moderation in China trade, we once again pondered whether UPS should remain on our list. As you can see, we decided to retain Big Brown.

There are two primary reasons. First, the time continues to be right for UPS because of the continued expansion of e-commerce and the gradual demise of the U.S. Postal Service, as well as the increased importance of the small package and document shipping business which is in turn augmented by the resurgence of U.S. manufacturing activity and the domestic economy in general. Second, UPS has put new focus on operating efficiency, with net profit margins rising steadily back into the 8–9 percent price range from the 7s—more volume times more margin equals more rapidly expanding profitability. UPS derives about 61 percent of revenues from U.S. package operations (up slightly), 22 percent from international (down slightly), and 17 percent from an assortment of bundled logistics and supply-chain services and solutions (about the same). The company operates 615 aircraft and almost 95,361 ground vehicles ("package cars"), most of the familiar brown variety. They serve more than 220 countries with an assortment of priority to deferred services, with 154,000 domestic and international entry points including 39,000 drop boxes, 1,600 customer service centers, and 4,800 independently owned "UPS Store" (formerly "Mailboxes Etc.")

storefronts. Once thought to be old-fashioned and averse to innovation, the company has invested in sophisticated package-tracking systems and links for customers to tie into them. An example is the recently introduced My Choice service, which allows a customer to control the timing of deliveries mid-service—so no more waiting half a day at home for a delivery that might come anytime (hallelujah!), a nice perk for a consumer waiting for an e-commerce shipment as well as a savings for the company, avoiding multiple delivery attempts. The company is also creating specialized logistics services for vertical markets, such as the auto industry "Autogistics" and the health-care industry, retail, high tech, and more.

Financial Highlights, Fiscal Year 2013

International volume and currency headwinds led the way to another sluggish year in FY2013. Total revenues rose a relatively modest 2.4 percent, and a slight dip in margins due to lower volumes and some price competition caused the bottom line to level off at almost breakeven from FY2012, although an aggressive 28 million share repurchase led to a 2 percent increase in per-share earnings.

That was then, this is now, as they say. Improving domestic volumes, driven by the aforementioned e-commerce and manufacturing resurgence, and an improvement in export volumes have all worked together toward a 4.6 percent projected revenue gain in FY2014 and more than 5 percent in FY2015; per-share earnings, with aforesaid margin improvements are expected to grow 13.4 percent and 8 percent respectively over the period. Dividend increases should be steady and significant through the period, although share buybacks, which have knocked out 14 percent of the float since 2006, look to be moderating.

Reasons to Buy

The "fastest ship in the shipping business" continues to also be one of the most stable; UPS continues to position itself as the standard logistics provider of the world. After a failed merger with TNT in 2012, it shows a welcome ability to focus more on the domestic e-commerce business. Improvements in U.S. export trade should also be a positive, as will be a recovery of the European economy. Focused and productive efforts to increase efficiency and margins are also appealing. We are also fans of its logistics and supply-chain management businesses and the many innovations in that space, as the push for many customers to optimize this part of their business will lead them to UPS's front door.

Reasons for Caution

Competition in this industry, particularly in lucrative Asia–U.S. lanes, is fierce. The demise of the U.S. Postal Service is a question mark and may be an opportunity, but what if Congress votes to subsidize more services, as they did with the recent resumption of funding for Saturday delivery and package delivery? Too, the Postal Service is getting more aggressive in marketing its small package and logistics services as it sees the writing on the wall for traditional mail services. Of about 400,000 employees, 62 percent are union, so labor relations and pension funding both bear watching. Of course, fuel prices and the state of the global economy are big factors in UPS's success in any short-term scenario.

SECTOR: Transportation
BETA COEFFICIENT: 0.96
10-YEAR COMPOUND EARNINGS PER-SHARE GROWTH: 6.5%
10-YEAR COMPOUND DIVIDENDS PER-SHARE GROWTH: 11.0%

	2006	2007	2008	2009	2010	2011	2012	2013
Revenues (mil)	47,547	49,692	51,466	45,297	49,545	53,105	54,127	55,438
Net income (mil)	4,202	4,369	3,581	2,318	3,570	4,213	4,389	4,372
Earnings per share	3.86	4.11	3.50	2.31	3.56	4.25	4.53	4.61
Dividends per share	1.52	1.64	1.77	1.80	1.88	2.08	2.28	2.48
Cash flow per share	5.56	5.91	5.42	4.09	5.43	6.60	6.90	6.75
Price: high	84.0	79.0	75.1	59.5	73.9	77.0	84.9	105.4
low	65.5	68.7	43.3	38.0	55.6	60.7	75.0	75.0

United Parcel Service, Inc.
55 Glenlake Parkway NE
Atlanta, GA 30328
(404) 828-6000
Website: www.ups.com

CONSERVATIVE GROWTH

United Technologies Corporation

Ticker symbol: UTX (NYSE) ❑ S&P rating: A ❑ Value Line financial strength rating: A++ ❑ Current yield: 2.0% ❑ Dividend raises, past 10 years: 10

Company Profile

United Technologies is a large and diversified provider of mostly high-technology products to the aerospace and building systems industries throughout the world, selling to an assortment of mostly commercial and public sector customers. To many, it is an aerospace company, to many others it is a producer of key pieces, parts, and systems for the building industry; to investors, it is a broadly diversified industrial conglomerate.

In 2012, the company made a significant $18.4 billion acquisition of aerospace material and system provider Goodrich Corp. The mix of businesses changed considerably with the acquisition, and as such, UTX realigned its division structure considerably. Here is how it looks now:

- UTC Propulsion & Aerospace (44 percent of FY2013 revenues) combines the former Aerospace division with the Pratt & Whitney jet engine division and most of the Goodrich assets. Aerospace, formerly known as Hamilton Sundstrand, produces aircraft electrical power generation and distribution systems;

engine and flight controls; propulsion systems; environmental controls for aircraft, spacecraft, and submarines; auxiliary power units; space life-support systems; and industrial products including mechanical power transmissions, compressors, metering devices, and fluid handling equipment. It also provides product support and maintenance and offers repair services. Pratt & Whitney produces large and small commercial and military jet engines, spare parts, rocket engines and space propulsion systems, and industrial gas turbines, and it performs product support, specialized engine maintenance and overhaul, and repair services for airlines, air forces, and corporate fleets.

- UTC Building & Industrial Systems (47 percent of revenues) also combines two former divisions, Climate Controls and Security, and Otis. Climate Controls and Security, formerly known as Carrier, produces heating, ventilating, and air conditioning (HVAC) equipment for commercial, industrial, and residential buildings; HVAC replacement parts and services; building controls; and commercial, industrial, and transport refrigeration equipment. The Climate Controls and Security group also includes the old UTC Fire and Security business, which provides security and fire protection systems; integration, installation, and servicing of intruder alarms, access control, and video surveillance and monitoring; response and security personnel services; and installation and servicing of fire detection and suppression systems. Otis is probably one of the most recognizable brands. It designs and manufactures elevators, escalators, moving walkways, and shuttle systems, and performs related installation, maintenance, and repair services; it also provides modernization products and service for elevators and escalators. Most of the Goodrich business was absorbed into this unit.

■ Sikorsky (10 percent of revenues) remains a standalone division (we're not sure for how long) and designs and manufactures military and commercial helicopters and fixed-wing reconnaissance aircraft, and it provides spare parts and maintenance services for helicopters and fixed-wing aircraft.

Financial Highlights, Fiscal Year 2013

FY2013 was a year of strength despite the uncertainties of a major acquisition. Business was strong, and the numbers reflect the accretion of a healthy Goodrich business, which seems to have been bought at a bargain price. Revenues rose 8.5 percent to almost $63 billion, while net income rose more than 17 percent, reflecting the acquisition, significant cost reductions, and higher margins overall. The company expected to have a mostly flat year without the acquisition; in fact, it turned out a bit better than that helped along by strength both in the construction and aerospace sectors.

Buybacks slowed during the year as the Goodrich acquisition was completed but should help per-share earnings in future years, which are expected to grow in the 10 percent to low double-digit range through FY2015—on sale growth in the 4–5 percent range—qualifying UTX as another "5 in 10" company: 10 percent earnings growth on 5 percent revenue growth.

Reasons to Buy

UTX is a classic conglomerate play. The separate and loosely related or unrelated businesses buffer each other in line with what's happening in the economy, both in the private and public sectors, and the economic recovery should continue to help most, if not all, of the businesses. Unlike many of its competitors, United Technologies maintains a global presence (60 percent of sales are from overseas), which benefits from global and emerging market infrastructure and other construction and even from defense spending by other countries. The company's brands, particularly Otis, are well-known and very well supported worldwide, and a return of strength in global construction should help its two largest businesses. The stock price is on a very stable upward growth track. The company is focused on shareholder returns, managing the Goodrich acquisition without increasing share count and offering a 10 percent dividend increase; more aggressive share buybacks and continued dividend raises are in the offing.

Reasons for Caution

The stability of the public sector portion of the business may diminish as Congress wrestles with the budget deficit and overseas military actions diminish, which is the case for the moment. The rest of the business is still sensitive to construction, and construction may not be out of the woods yet and there is plenty of competition in most of its construction businesses. While Goodrich was a good fit, we would hope the company doesn't get too intoxicated with acquisitions, for, like all conglomerates, UTX is a very complex business to manage. It can also be vulnerable to headline risk (like jet engine problems), hiccups in the airline industry, and public sector spending cuts.

SECTOR: **Industrials**
BETA COEFFICIENT: **1.14**
10-YEAR COMPOUND EARNINGS PER-SHARE GROWTH: **10.0%**
10-YEAR COMPOUND DIVIDENDS PER-SHARE GROWTH: **15.0%**

	2006	2007	2008	2009	2010	2011	2012	2013
Revenues (mil)	47,740	54,759	58,681	52,920	54,326	58,190	57,708	62,626
Net income (mil)	3,732	4,224	4,689	3,829	4,373	4,979	4,840	5,685
Earnings per share	3.71	4.27	4.90	4.12	4.74	5.49	5.34	6.21
Dividends per share	1.02	1.28	1.55	1.54	1.70	1.87	2.03	2.20
Cash flow per share	4.79	5.50	6.38	5.43	6.22	6.97	6.93	8.19
Price: high	67.5	82.5	77.1	70.9	79.7	91.8	87.5	113.9
low	54.2	61.8	41.8	37.4	62.9	66.9	70.7	92.1

United Technologies Corporation
One Financial Plaza
Hartford, CT 06103
(860) 728-7000
Website: *www.utc.com*

AGGRESSIVE GROWTH

Valero Energy

Ticker symbol: VLO (NYSE) ❑ S&P rating: BBB ❑ Value Line financial strength rating: B++
Current yield: 1.9% ❑ Dividend raises, past 10 years: 9

Company Profile

Valero Energy is the largest independent oil refiner in the United States. The company owns 16 refineries and distributes primarily through a network of 7,300 retail combined gasoline stations and convenience stores throughout the United States, the U.K. and Ireland, and Canada. In 2013 the company spun off 80 percent of the retail operations, mostly U.S.-based, to shareholders in the form of an independent public company called CST Brands but still maintains distribution to most of these outlets. Aside from unlocking capital and increasing focus on refining, the separation of these businesses allows more refining sales to other channels, and allows the retailers to source from their lowest cost supplier—improving the performance of both.

Most of the 16 Valero refineries are located in the United States, centered in the South and on the Texas Gulf Coast with others in Memphis, Oklahoma, and on the West Coast. Others are located in the Caribbean, Quebec, and Wales in the U.K. The refinery network was mostly assembled through a series of acquisitions from Diamond Shamrock in 2001; El Paso Corporation in the early 2000s; and, more recently, the Pembroke (Wales) refinery from Chevron in 2011. The refining operations produce the full gamut of hydrocarbon products: gasoline, jet fuel, diesel, asphalt, propane, base oils, solvents, aromatics, natural gas liquids, sulfur, hydrogen, and middle distillates. The company is strictly focused on downstream operations—now just the refining portion, not retail—and owns no oil wells or production facilities. Instead, they purchase a variety of feedstocks on the open market and can adjust those purchases to market conditions while using contracts and hedging tools to manage input prices to a degree—and rail transport to get it to the refinery. About 51 percent of feedstocks are purchased under contracts, with the remainder on the spot market. Most of these refineries are legacy operations and have been in place for many years, as far back as 1908. The company has invested heavily in upgrading these refineries to improve capacity, efficiency, and environmental compliance.

The company is increasing its activities in transportation and logistics, where it already owns key pipelines—by adding approximately 1,800 rail cars to its fleet as part of a 5,300-car expansion. With today's rapidly transformed domestic crude production activities, this logistics flexibility represents a key strategy toward optimizing input costs. Bulk sales to other retail, commercial distributors, and large-end customers like airlines and railroads are also important.

Financial Highlights, Fiscal Year 2013

FY2013 was a complex year for VLO, with the retail operation spinoff, the dynamics of domestic crude production, and a resurgence in the ethanol business. FY2013 revenues were flat with the effects of the retail spinoff. But as predicted last year, the shift in oil supply to relatively less expensive U.S. sources served to increase refining profitability considerably. That and renewed activity and profitability in ethanol (corn prices are down 40 percent since 2012) drove a 15 percent increase in net profits, even with the costs of the spinoff built in. The company used some of the proceeds of the spinoff to retire about 2.5 percent of its shares, driving per-share earnings almost 17 percent higher for the year. With the retail operations gone, focus for the next two years will be on profits, not revenues—and the company is looking at a 25 percent per-share earnings increase in FY2014 and

another 5 percent in FY2015. Share buybacks and dividend increases in the 8–10 percent range look likely, so long as the domestic crude continues to flow.

Reasons to Buy

The profitability of this business, like other refining businesses, depends on the supply and cost of feedstocks and the wholesale and retail prices of finished products. In addition, the availability of refining capacity is also a factor; when markets get tight, it is extremely difficult to put another refinery on the ground to handle demand. These two factors together work very favorably for Valero—lower input costs, no new competition—it's an oligopolistic dream and should bode well for profits for years to come. If the Keystone pipeline project or other projects come online to make cheaper domestic crude more available, the company's fortunes should improve even more. But in the meantime, rail transport provides excellent flexibility, and some say flexible methods, not fixed pipelines, are the optimal way to distribute crude from multiple sources in the future. Valero's investments in rail cars will help to capitalize on this trend.

We like Valero's leading position in the refining business, and having 18 well-distributed and largely successful operating refineries on the ground already is a good thing. We also like the branding, abundance, look, and feel of the retail presence—even though the company no longer own the stations outright.

Reasons for Caution

The refining business in particular is inherently volatile and complex, and what may appear today as an advantageous input and output pricing profile might disappear in a minute. Gross, operating, and net margins are very thin, typically in the 1–2 percent range—although Valero appears to be breaking slightly above that range at about 2.2 percent currently. Refiners also endure the headline risk of refinery mishaps, a few of which have already come Valero's way in recent years. And now we incur more risks in rail transport of crude and saw what can happen in 2013's two major mishaps (neither of which affected Valero directly). We doubt if rail shipment of crude will be shut down, but it could become more expensive as mandates for safer cars, slower speeds, track improvements, etc., come into play.

The retail spinoff seems to be working even though we were a bit skeptical—we like some brand equity in this commodity business, and there is value in having a captive retail market for your product. Valero seems to have retained most of the advantage while allowing itself more focus on the refining business.

SECTOR: **Energy**
BETA COEFFICIENT: **1.53**
10-YEAR COMPOUND EARNINGS PER-SHARE GROWTH: **9.0%**
10-YEAR COMPOUND DIVIDENDS PER-SHARE GROWTH: **13.5%**

		2006	2007	2008	2009	2010	2011	2012	2013
Revenues (bil)		91.8	94.5	118.3	87.3	81.3	125.1	138.3	138.1
Net income (mil)		5,251	4,565	(1,131)	(352)	923	2,097	2,083	2,395
Earnings per share		8.30	7.72	(2.16)	(0.65)	1.62	3.69	3.75	4.37
Dividends per share		0.30	0.48	0.57	0.60	0.20	0.30	0.65	0.85
Cash flow per share		10.81	11.04	0.67	1.91	4.10	6.52	6.60	7.65
Price:	high	70.8	75.7	71.1	26.2	23.7	31.1	34.5	50.5
	low	46.8	47.7	13.9	16.3	15.5	16.4	16.1	33.0

Valero Energy Corporation
One Valero Way
San Antonio, TX 78249
(210) 345-2000
Website: *www.valero.com*

AGGRESSIVE GROWTH

Valmont Industries, Inc.

Ticker symbol: VMI (NYSE) ❑ S&P rating: BBB ❑ Value Line financial strength rating: A+
Current yield: 0.7% ❑ Dividend raises, past 10 years: 10

Company Profile

Valmont Industries was founded in 1946 as a supplier of irrigation products and became one of the classic postwar industrial success stories, growing along with the need for increased farm output. It was an early pioneer of the center-pivot irrigation system, which enabled much of that growth and now dominates the high-yield agricultural business. These machines remain a mainstay of its product line. But the company has expanded on that core expertise in galvanized metal to make such familiar infrastructure items as light poles, cell phone towers, and those familiar high-tension electric towers that crisscross the landscape, and to provide such galvanizing services to other product manufacturers.

Valmont products and product lines now include:

- Engineered Infrastructure Products (27 percent of FY2013 revenues)—lighting poles, including decorative lighting poles, guard rails, towers, and other metal structures used in lighting, communications, traffic management, wireless phone carriers,

and other utilities. Products are available as standard designs and engineered for custom applications as needed for industrial, commercial, and residential applications. If you've ever sat at a stoplight and wondered how a single cantilevered arm could support four 400-pound traffic signals, these are the folks to ask.

- Utility Support Structures (29 percent)—This segment produces the very large concrete and steel substations and electric transmission support towers used by electric utilities. This has been Valmont's most profitable operation over the last few years, due mainly to increased volumes in a period of declining costs, and we like its prospects as utility infrastructure is replaced and modernized in the interest of grid efficiency.

- Irrigation (27 percent)—Under the Valley brand name, Valmont produces a wide range of equipment, including gravity and drip products, as well as its center-pivot designs, which can service up to 500 acres from a single machine. Valmont also sells its irrigation controllers to other manufacturers.

■ Coatings (7 percent)—Developed as an adjunct to its other metal products businesses, the coatings business now provides services such as galvanizing, electroplating, powder coating, and anodizing to industrial customers throughout the company's operating areas.

There is also an "other" segment comprising about 10 percent of the business.

Financial Highlights, Fiscal Year 2013

FY2013 was a very good year as irrigation product demand strengthened after the 2012 drought year, and as sales and margins were healthy in both the support structure and utility segments, which were a bit of a question mark as we approached this analysis last year. Revenues advanced 9 percent, and per-share earnings advanced a very healthy 18 percent even without share buybacks, which are not a hallmark of this company as the share count is already at a slim 27 million. The company is facing some headwinds in the form of lower crop prices and continued tight public sector budgets into FY2014; FY2015 is a wait-and-see. International markets are growing in importance and too, represent something of a wild card. Current forecasts call for a flat top

line in FY2014 with a breather in per-share earnings growth in the 1–2 percent range, with a resumption of sales growth in the 5 percent range and earnings growth in the 9–10 percent range in FY2015 as margins improve. (It's another in our lengthening list of "5 and 10" companies: 5 percent sales growth, 10 percent earnings growth.)

Reasons to Buy

We continue to view Valmont as a key infrastructure play. America's infrastructure needs to be replaced, as does infrastructure in much of the developed world. As for the less-developed world, that infrastructure needs to be built in the first place. We think, long term, that Valmont is in the right place to capture a decent share of this replacement business, including electric utility infrastructure. The original irrigation business should also do well in the long term as global food consumption increases and as agriculture, farmland, and farm commodity prices eventually strengthen. Valmont has retained market share and remains the leader among the four dominant U.S.-based players in the large-scale irrigation market. The company's continued emphasis on growth into new geographies should pay dividends as India and China begin to build infrastructure and adopt more modern agricultural methods. We also like the relatively simple, straightforward nature of this business and the way the company presents itself online and in shareholder documents. Frankly, as the company is headquartered in Omaha, we wonder out loud why it hasn't garnered the interest of its prosperous and acquisitive neighbor, Berkshire Hathaway. Perhaps it has.

Reasons for Caution

Many Valmont products are purchased by public sector and government agencies, and these agencies will be scrutinizing purchases to a greater degree than in the past. Escalating raw materials costs may also hurt, especially in a reduced-demand, softer-pricing environment that might ensue from contracting government purchases. Indeed, the sectors that have showed strength sell to agriculture and utility interests, not government agencies. Finally, although the stock has done well, we would like to see a little more shareholder return; while dividends are raised regularly, they remain small with respect to the share price and per-share cash flow. The low share count may be part of the high stock price as institutions have bought in—any bad news could lead to a sharp downturn in the stock price if those investors flee. That said, the current and likely future results are too strong to suggest that scenario.

SECTOR: **Industrials**
BETA COEFFICIENT: **1.27**
10-YEAR COMPOUND EARNINGS PER-SHARE GROWTH: **21.5%**
10-YEAR COMPOUND DIVIDENDS PER-SHARE GROWTH: **11.5%**

	2006	2007	2008	2009	2010	2011	2012	2013
Revenues (mil)	1,281	1,500	1,907	1,787	1,975	2,661	3,029	3,304
Net income (mil)	61.5	94.7	132.4	155.0	109.7	158.0	234.1	278.5
Earnings per share	2.38	3.63	5.04	5.70	4.15	5.97	8.75	10.35
Dividends per share	0.37	0.41	0.50	0.58	0.65	0.72	0.88	0.98
Price: high	61.2	99.0	120.5	89.3	90.3	116.0	141.2	164.9
low	32.8	50.9	37.5	37.5	65.3	73.0	90.2	129.0

Valmont Industries, Inc.
1 Valmont Plaza
Omaha, NE 68154-5215
(402) 963-1000
Website: *www.valmont.com*

GROWTH AND INCOME

Verizon Communications Inc.

Ticker symbol: VZ (NYSE) ❑ S&P rating: A- ❑ Value Line financial strength rating: A+ ❑ Current yield: 4.5% ❑ Dividend raises, past 10 years: 8

Company Profile

Verizon operates two telecommunications businesses: Domestic Wireless, which provides wireless voice and data services, and Wireline, which provides voice, broadband data and video, Internet access, long-distance, and other services, and which owns and operates a large global Internet protocol network. The wireless business represents about 67 percent of the total; Wireline is about 33 percent of the total by revenues. As we'll get to shortly, the company's data and cloud computing business is one of its more exciting prospects.

In the consumer space, the Wireline segment also supplies Verizon's fiber-to-the-home (FiOS) broadband data infrastructure. One of Verizon's largest investments, FiOS provides a very high bandwidth link to the Internet, easily surpassing DSL and even cable. Over this network, Verizon can provide hundreds of HD video streams, high-speed data, and voice all simultaneously. This service competes head-to-head with AT&T's (a *100 Best* stock) U-verse and Comcast's (another *100 Best* stock) Xfinity services, among others.

The Domestic Wireless segment is served by the now wholly owned Verizon Wireless, the remaining unowned 45 percent acquired from Vodafone in a $130 billion deal that closed in early 2014. Verizon Wireless is now the largest wireless carrier in the United States, and it operates in 19 countries outside the United States as well. The wireless side of the business has been rolling out its new LTE mobile broadband network, a leading-edge 4G network designed to be 10 times faster than the standard 3G network, and now available in some 500 U.S. markets to more than 97 percent of the U.S. population.

Adding hardware products and wireless capacity hasn't been the only growth strategy employed at Verizon—the company has a healthy appetite for acquisitions, growing its footprint in advanced networking, private networks, and cloud computing, with the 2011 acquisition of IT and cloud services provider Terremark Worldwide, and a small but interesting partnership with a company called eMeter, which markets devices that automatically read and transmit energy usage for utilities using Verizon's wireless network. The company is leveraging its investment in the 4G LTE network for corporate customers to offer secure wireless private IP networks. In mid-2012, the company acquired Hughes Telematics, expanding its offerings in vehicle telematics (more popularly known as OnStar in GM cars) and other machine-to-machine communications. In 2013, Verizon acquired upLynk, a television cloud company, and in early 2014 it acquired the Intel Media arm of Intel, which develops cloud TV products and services, and EdgeCast Networks, a fast-content delivery network originally funded by Disney. In all, you can see where these additions are going—they provide more pipe, new kinds of pipe, and some of the content that flows through the pipe.

Financial Highlights, Fiscal Year 2013

For a company its size, Verizon continues to dial in pretty strong top-line growth in revenues, up just over 4 percent for the year, led by growth in FiOS, enterprise services, and the wireless business more generally, which grew at 8 percent for the year. The company added 648,000 FiOS Internet and 536,000 FiOS video subscribers, leading to a 14.6 percent growth overall in that business. Low churn rates and reduced equipment subsidies particularly for iPhone led to a healthy increase in net profit margin from 5.2 percent to 6.6 percent, driving the total bottom line up some

32 percent for the year. An increase in share count, however, attenuated per-share earnings to a more moderate 22 percent. Free cash flow of $22 billion is significant given the high capital expenditure profile ("free" means "after capex") and is a sixth of total revenues.

The Verizon Wireless/Vodafone acquisition makes forward comparisons into FY2014 and FY2015. The company issued some 1.3 billion shares to make the payment, but reportable net profits will almost double. When the dust settles, per-share earnings are forecasted to rise 16–23 percent to $3.30–$3.50 in FY2014, and another 14 percent from the midpoint of this range in FY2015. Dividends will most likely continue to grow in the 3–4 percent range during this period.

Reasons to Buy

Verizon offers a nice combination of stability, financial strength, and income with a play in the growth of the "new economy" and supporting technology. After a few years of lean profit growth as the company invested in infrastructure and iPhones, earnings growth is now well ahead of top-line growth. We especially like the new cloud and wireless data services for the commercial market, which offer good promise and significant leverage of existing investments, and the promise of emerging services in the consumer space such as video-on-demand.

We're glad the Vodafone acquisition is finally behind the company. This cast some uncertainty for quite a while: whether or not it would happen and what the price would be. Check that box. The company has typically paid out a high portion of earnings as dividends and has increased its dividend regularly. Strong cash flows and advancing per-share earnings indicate decent future increases, but what now happens to share repurchases remains to be seen. The high payout and low beta of 0.34 make the stock a safe core holding.

like others, must spend heavily just to keep up with technology and competition. Getting a solid return on new capital investments is thus critical, and one slip-up could be costly for shareholders, especially with a high ratio of dividend payout to total earnings; a dividend cut could result. The business environment is extremely competitive, and Verizon's sheer size may hamper its flexibility to compete. Finally, on the acquisition front, Verizon has gobbled up a lot, and while we think the add-ons make sense, they add to risk and perhaps make the company a bit unwieldy to manage.

Reasons for Caution

The telecommunications business is always capital intensive, and Verizon,

SECTOR: **Telecommunications Services**
BETA COEFFICIENT: **0.34**
10-YEAR COMPOUND EARNINGS PER-SHARE GROWTH: **1.0%**
10-YEAR COMPOUND DIVIDENDS PER-SHARE GROWTH: **2.5%**

	2006	2007	2008	2009	2010	2011	2012	2013
Revenues (mil)	88,144	93,469	97,354	107,808	106,585	110,875	115,846	120,550
Net income (mil)	6,021	6,854	7,235	6,805	6,256	6,087	6,535	7,920
Earnings per share	2.54	2.36	2.54	2.40	2.21	2.15	2.32	2.84
Dividends per share	1.62	1.65	1.78	1.87	1.93	1.96	2.02	2.09
Cash flow per share	7.07	7.40	7.65	7.70	7.60	7.96	7.80	8.15
Price: high	38.9	46.2	44.3	34.8	36.0	40.3	48.8	54.3
low	30.0	35.6	23.1	26.1	26.0	32.3	36.8	41.5

Verizon Communications Inc.
140 West Street
New York, NY 10007
(212) 395-1000
Website: *www.verizon.com*

Visa Inc.

Ticker symbol: V (NYSE) □ S&P rating: A+ □ Value Line financial strength rating: A++
Current yield: 0.7% □ Dividend raises, past 10 years: 5

Company Profile

If we wrote about a company with a 42 percent net profit margin—and growing rapidly—and a global brand that was in the business of collecting small fees on every one of the billions of transactions worldwide; a company that required almost no capital expenditures, plant, equipment, or inventory; a company that brought in almost $1.4 million per employee in revenue and $515,000 per employee in net profit (the company refers to this as "people light and technology heavy"; a company growing earnings 20–30 percent a year; a company with a time-tested business model and absolutely zero long-term debt— would you believe that it existed? Not to mention a company with a share price that rose from $74 to $118 in our 2011 measurement period, to $168 in 2012, and to more than $220 in 2013?

It's all true. And the company, formed in a 2007 reorganization and taken public in 2008, is Visa. Yes, the same Visa whose emblem has traditionally appeared on a majority of the world's credit cards—and now debit cards. In fact, there are about 2.1 *billion* such cards worldwide. The company operates the world's largest retail electronic payment network, providing processing services; payment platforms; and fraud-detection services for credit, debit, and commercial payments. The company also operates one of the largest global ATM networks with its PLUS and Interlink brands. In total, the company processes about 12,000 transactions *per second* and estimates that it can process about four times that amount in a peak scenario—while being operational 99.999999 percent of the time!

For years, Visa has been synonymous with credit and credit cards, but in recent years it has become more of a digital currency company, stitching together consumers, retailers, banks, and other businesses in a giant global network. Really, Visa is a global payments technology business that not only develops and supplies the technology but also collects fees upon its use.

The shift from traditional cash and check forms of payment to debit cards and other digital forms is growing at about a 12 percent annual rate, driven by the security and convenience of these transactions as well as a shift away from consumer debt more to "paid for today" debit transactions. Debit transactions now account for more than half of the company's overall business volume, albeit at a small penalty, as average transaction sizes are smaller.

The company is also active in mobile payment and mobile wallet innovations with "V.me" and "pay-Wave" licensed products, and, not surprisingly in light of recent news events, the company is also working on new payment and card security initiatives.

More than its rivals, Visa derives a significant percentage of transaction volume, about 45 percent, from overseas. International volumes are growing faster than in the United States, about 16 percent compared to 11 percent, as cash electronic payments gradually replace cash as a payment method especially in emerging markets.

The bad news—and there hasn't been much until recently—has come from two sources: first, litigation holding the company responsible for colluding with bank issuers (its channel) to fix high transaction fees and offer unfair favor to certain players, and second, the recent security breaches at Target and other retailers, calling into question the security of the whole system. While the company did pay a settlement to a class of 19 retailers in late 2013 and now faces, in early 2014, a $5 billion lawsuit from Wal-Mart, we don't see a lot of merit in

these actions—the company has substantial competition in the form of MasterCard, AMEX, Discover, etc., and working with its bank partners is no more collusive than Apple setting the price of its products at Target or elsewhere. Still, public sentiment has sided with retailers on the fee issue, and the company has felt an urge to settle rather than fight and was able to stem any future litigation from these parties. In the long run, we feel this is the right approach and that it will all work out, and while perhaps attenuating earnings in the near term, it will secure the long-term path to success. Provisions of the Dodd-Frank Wall Street Reform and Consumer Protection Act also mandated some adjustments in debit interchange fees. As far as the security issues go, it's a problem but will not likely have any material impact in the short run; all providers and retailers experience it, not just Visa. Still, it bears watching.

Financial Highlights, Fiscal Year 2013

Helped by international expansion, increased economic activity, and e-commerce, Visa continued to deliver in FY2013 and will for the immediate future in our opinion, litigation notwithstanding. Revenues advanced another 13 percent; net profit margins improved, and net profits hence rose more than 18 percent. It didn't stop there however—$5.3 billion in share repurchases sent per-share earnings up 22 percent. Per-share earnings are expected up another 17 percent for FY2014 on another 13 percent topline increase.

Reasons to Buy

Simply, it continues to be difficult to come up with a better business model—a company that develops and sells the network and collects fees every time it's used. It would be like Microsoft collecting fees every time a file is created and saved, or an e-mail platform that charges fees for every message. Visa is in a great position to not only capitalize on overall world economic growth, as most companies should be, but also to capitalize on a shift in this growth toward electronic payments. Even as debt-conscious consumers pull back on using credit cards, debit card usage continues to advance. This reinforces one of Visa's big strengths—unlike most other financial services businesses, Visa is relatively immune to downturns, as it makes its money by processing payments, not by extending credit. On the growth side, the company is expanding its footprint in emerging markets, and there is plenty of innovation opportunity in this business. Overall, while Visa has competitors (MasterCard, American Express, and Discover), it has the strongest franchise, technology leadership, and pricing power at its back.

Reasons for Caution

The company has pricing power, but as with many companies that do, that power has come under government, merchant, and public scrutiny; the company must tread lightly or face possible consequences. Recent litigation and regulatory actions have presented some headline and profit risk and may be construed as a threat to the franchise—perhaps if it sounds too good to be true, it may be. But we think that even after some legal and regulatory bumps, Visa will emerge rock solid. In fact, in some ways it would be good to confront these issues and get past them even if they do cause some short-term stomach pain for investors. The stock has recognized a lot of this excellence and has risen sharply; proper entry points are still required and may become available as some of these legal hurdles are dealt with.

SECTOR: **Financials**
BETA COEFFICIENT: **0.76**
10-YEAR COMPOUND EARNINGS PER-SHARE GROWTH: **NM**
10-YEAR COMPOUND DIVIDENDS PER-SHARE GROWTH: **NM**

	2006	2007	2008	2009	2010	2011	2012	2013
Revenues (mil)	—	—	6,263	6,911	8,065	9,188	10,421	11,776
Net income (mil)	—	—	1,700	2,213	2,966	3,650	4,203	4,980
Earnings per share	—	—	2.25	2.92	3.91	4.99	6.20	7.69
Dividends per share	—	—	0.21	0.44	0.53	0.67	0.99	1.39
Cash flow per share	—	—	2.50	3.22	3.86	5.34	6.59	8.21
Price: high	—	—	89.6	89.7	97.2	103.4	152.5	222.7
low	—	—	43.5	41.8	64.9	67.5	98.3	153.9

Visa Inc.
900 Metro Center Blvd.
Foster City, CA 94404
(415) 932-2100
Website: *www.visa.com*

CONSERVATIVE GROWTH

W.W. Grainger, Inc.

Ticker symbol: GWW (NYSE) □ S&P rating: AA+ □ Value Line financial strength rating: A++
Current yield: 1.7% □ Dividend raises, past 10 years: 10

Company Profile

Grainger is North America's largest supplier of maintenance, repair, and operating supply (MRO) products. It sells more than a million different products from more than 4,800 suppliers through a network of 709 branches (390 in the U.S.), 33 distribution centers (18 in the U.S.), and several websites, with a catalog containing some 570,000 items (a fascinating read if you like this sort of thing). Grainger also offers repair parts, specialized product sourcing, and inventory management supplies. Grainger sells principally to industrial and commercial maintenance departments, contractors, and government customers, but the range of both customers and products is quite broad (see the 2014 Fact Book referenced). The company has nearly 2 million customers, mostly in North America, and achieves overnight delivery to approximately 95 percent of them.

Its Canadian subsidiary is Canada's largest distributor of industrial, fleet, and safety products. It serves its customers through 171 branches and six distribution centers, and offers bilingual websites and catalogs. Grainger, S.A. de C.V. is Mexico's leading facilities maintenance supplier, offering

customers more than 84,000 products. The company also has important operations, through joint ventures, in Japan, China, and India and does business in 166 countries worldwide.

Grainger's customer base includes government offices; heavy manufacturing customers (typically textile, lumber, metals, and rubber industries); light manufacturing; transportation (shipbuilding, aerospace, and automotive); hospitals; retail; hospitality; and resellers of Grainger products. Grainger owns a number of trademarks, including Dayton motors, Dem-Kote spray paints, and Westward tools.

Many of Grainger's customers are corporate, primarily *Fortune* 1000 companies that spend more than $5 million annually on facilities maintenance products. Corporate account customers typically sign multiyear contracts for facilities maintenance products or a specific category of products, such as lighting or safety equipment. The company also helps its customers, large and small, with inventory management, supplying a tool called "Keepstock" to help them manage their MRO inventories. The Grainger strategy is quintessentially multichannel and centered on being easy to do business with. Customers can interact with a direct sales force, interact with one of the 400 distribution outlets in the United States, or order through an e-commerce website. Released quietly during the dot-com boom, *www.grainger.com* handled some $2.1 billion, or about 33 percent of the company's U.S. business in FY2013, up from 30 percent the previous year, making it the fifteenth largest e-commerce site in North America. It is a solid e-commerce success story.

Financial Highlights, Fiscal Year 2013

The U.S. manufacturing sector has been strong, and about 85 percent of Grainger's sales come from it. The company has also successfully gained market share in this fragmented industry, and the turnaround in Europe is helping, too. All taken together with softness in Brazil and China and modest negative currency effects, FY2013 revenues rose 5.4 percent to $9.44 billion. Higher volumes created some operating leverage, which in turn led to a substantial gain in operating margins from the mid-14 percent range to 16 percent, in turn leading to a 19 percent gain in net profits, and, with a half million shares retired, a 21 percent gain in per-share earnings. For FY2014, Grainger is guiding sales at $10.08 billion, which would be about 7 percent ahead of FY2013, expanding to a 9 percent projected rise for FY2015. FY2014 gains would be greater save for the recent divestiture of a few direct marketing specialty brands. Per-share earnings are guided between $12.10–$12.85, the midpoint of which would represent an 8 percent gain over FY2013; for FY2015 the gain is projected at closer to 16 percent.

It's worth noting that Grainger has reduced share count 25 percent since 2004, while doubling revenues and tripling profits in that same period. The company has raised its dividend 42 years in a row, and has doubled it in the past four years $4.32 per share (if only you were receiving similar raises!). In early 2014, the company raised the dividend 16 percent and authorized repurchase of some 10 million shares, about 15 percent of the outstanding float—if this goal is achieved, per-share earnings could increase far more quickly.

Reasons to Buy

"This Is How We Win" is the title of the company's 2014 Fact Book, an appropriate title and an informative and fun read. Grainger is far and away the biggest presence in the MRO world. Its only broadline competitor is one-quarter its size, and the rest of the market is highly fragmented. The company also has the deepest catalog by far. It's estimated that 40 percent of purchases in the MRO market are unplanned, so having the broadest inventory, fastest delivery, and friendliest service is a big advantage for Grainger. If you doubt the value of a broad catalog, consider that this is primarily an industrial supplier that skated through the Great Recession practically untouched (just a 10 percent decline in sales).

Even with its size and scope, the company estimates that it still has less than 6 percent of the U.S. MRO market, leaving a large growth opportunity. The company has minimal debt and outstanding cash flow—it's starting to leverage its footholds in international locations with the purchase of existing distribution chains in Mexico, Brazil, China, Japan, and Korea. The international opportunity looks very promising for Grainger.

Every year we review this company and its stock, and every year we get a little nervous about its high and persistently rising share price. Then we look at the fundamentals and lo and behold: It ends up back on our list! Part of the reason, too, for that is the share repurchases and dividend increases reflect a better-than-average orientation to shareholder value, and shareholder value is indeed one of the stated goals of the company. To that end,

the company has produced an average annual total shareholder return of over 28 percent for each of the past five years. We find it refreshing to see it not only stated but also delivered upon.

Reasons for Caution

Grainger will always be vulnerable to economic cycles and manufacturing displacement, especially so long as it remains concentrated on U.S. soil. International expansion should help alleviate this concern. Over the past five years, the share price has reflected most of the good news, mandating either careful price shopping for the stock or reliance on incremental growth opportunities in United States and especially overseas market share. Look for price pullbacks in times of greater macroeconomic concern.

SECTOR: **Industrials**
BETA COEFFICIENT: **0.87**
10-YEAR COMPOUND EARNINGS PER-SHARE GROWTH: **15.5%**
10-YEAR COMPOUND DIVIDENDS PER-SHARE GROWTH: **15.5%**

	2006	2007	2008	2009	2010	2011	2012	2013
Revenues (mil)	5,884	6,418	6,850	6,222	7,182	8,075	8,950	9,438
Net income (mil)	383	420	479	402	502	643	690	824
Earnings per share	4.25	4.94	6.09	5.25	6.81	9.04	9.52	11.52
Dividends per share	1.16	1.40	1.55	1.78	2.08	2.52	3.06	3.59
Cash flow per share	5.79	6.95	8.28	7.60	9.40	11.33	12.22	14.51
Price: high	80.0	98.6	94.0	102.5	139.1	193.2	221.8	276.4
low	60.6	68.8	58.9	59.9	96.1	124.3	172.5	201.5

W.W. Grainger, Inc.
100 Grainger Parkway
Lake Forest, IL 60045
(847) 535-1000
Website: *www.grainger.com*

CONSERVATIVE GROWTH

Wal-Mart Stores, Inc.

Ticker symbol: WMT (NYSE) □ S&P rating: AAA □ Value Line financial strength rating: A++
Current yield: 2.4% □ Dividend raises, past 10 years: 10

Company Profile

Wal-Mart is the world's largest retailer. At 2.2 million employees, it is also the world's largest private employer, ranked overall behind only the U.S. Department of Defense and the People's Liberation Army of China. So if on your next visit to the 'Mart the greeter gives you a snappy salute, don't say we didn't warn you about the upcoming move toward world domination. Better learn to speak Arkansas.

To clear up some confusion before it occurs, the Wal-Mart company operates stores under the "Walmart" brand, so if you feel like you're seeing two spellings of the same thing in error, that's the explanation (we expect they will clear this up someday by changing the corporate name). In total, the company operates more than 10,300 retail units and 359 wholesale units in 12 countries. In the U.S., Wal-Mart operates 3,288 Walmart Supercenters (up from 3,150 last year), 632 Sam's Club stores (up from 620), 508 Walmart Discount Stores (down from 561, reflecting some conversion to Supercenters), and 407 Walmart Neighborhood Markets and other small formats (versus 286). Rest-of-world retail locations total 6,107 medium and smaller footprint stores, mostly in Latin America, Canada, Japan, China, India, and the U.K. Nearly all of the stores are owned by the company, with the exception of those in India and China, which are mainly joint ventures.

Wal-Mart operates in three business segments: the Walmart U.S. segment, the Walmart International segment, and the Sam's Club segment. In 2013, the Walmart U.S. segment (which includes the online retail presence at Walmart.com) accounted for approximately 60 percent of revenue. The Walmart International segment accounted for 29 percent of sales in 2013, while the Sam's Club segment and its own online presence accounted for approximately 12 percent of net sales. Walmart's mainline stores operate on an "everyday low price" philosophy. The idea is that customers need not wait for sale prices, as Walmart's normal price is at or near the bottom of the competitive market at all times. "Sale" prices are typically limited to seasonal and promotional goods, but there are occasional rollbacks on everyday items, typically staples.

The Sam's Club stores are membership clubs, focused on selling brand-name and private-label goods in larger quantities to individuals and businesses. They compete with Costco and other warehouse merchandisers.

The Walmart U.S. segment does business in six merchandise units, including grocery, entertainment, hardlines, health and wellness, apparel, and home. Grocery is typically available at its superstore and Neighborhood Market formats; the grocery section is quite large although oriented toward packaged and frozen goods. Other lines found in Superstores include Entertainment, which contains electronics, toys, cameras and supplies, cell phones, service plan contracts, and books; Hardlines includes stationery, automotive accessories, hardware and paint, sporting goods, fabrics and crafts, and seasonal merchandise; Health and Wellness, which includes pharmacy and optical services; Apparel includes apparel for women, girls, men, boys, and infants, and shoes, jewelry, and accessories; Home includes home furnishings, housewares and small appliances, bedding, home decor, outdoor living, and plants. The Walmart U.S. segment also offers financial services and related products, including money orders, wire transfers, check cashing, and bill payment. It has a private-label store credit card issued by a third-party provider and accepts online payments through PayPal. In addition, its pharmacy and optical departments accept payments for products and services through its customers' health-benefit plans.

The company is embracing a segment of the market less inclined to do a full, supersized "big-basket" trip and more inclined to more frequent, convenience-oriented "stock-up" trips. To that end they plan to add some 180 Neighborhood Markets, which concentrate on groceries, and as many as 120 smaller "Walmart Express" locations. E-commerce is also an expanding sector, growing some 30 percent in 2013 and accounting for some 2.7 percent of the total business. In Walmart's case, that's $10 billion a year, making it in itself one of the world's largest e-commerce businesses.

Financial Highlights, Fiscal Year 2013

The company calls it Fiscal Year 2014 because it ends on January 31, 2014. To make it more comparable to other businesses, we will refer to it as "2013" and drop the "FY."

In 2013, Wal-Mart grew revenue a modest 1.5 percent in total and close to that figure across its three sectors. That sounds small, but we must note that that figure represents some $7 billion-plus in new revenue. Still, the company was less than totally pleased at this figure. As we emerge from the Great Recession, the increasing income gap between wealthy and non-wealthy has grown. Translation:

The economic recovery has favored the wealthy, not so much the bread-and-butter Walmart customer. Constant margins and a slightly higher tax rate actually led to a small earnings shortfall compared to last year, while a substantial 2.4 percent share buyback eked out a per-share earnings gain of just under 2 percent.

The company is guiding 2014 (their FY2015) per-share earnings in the $5.15–$5.45 range, a relatively wide range for this size of business; the midpoint would represent a 4 percent gain over FY2013 and a bit lower than the markets had initially expected. For 2015, aided by ramped-up buybacks, the expected rise will likely approach 10 percent on a revenue gain between 4 and 4.5 percent, qualifying the behemoth retailer for a spot on our "5 and 10" list—10 percent earnings growth on 5 percent revenues—if the company can recover from the modest soft spot due to weak economic expansion for its big target market, and as new store footprints and international expansion take effect.

The company recently raised its dividend a full 20 percent, and continues a moderate buyback pace which has already retired about a quarter of its outstanding shares (now about 3.2 billion) in the past ten years.

Reasons to Buy

Although 2013 was less than impressive, improved domestic employment numbers and rapid growth in the International segment, and business conducted in new formats give some promise to 2014 and beyond. The company will also roll out modest operational improvements over the years, which could drive margins up as much as a half percent, with decent-sized effect on a business the size of Wal-Mart. We do think the new formats and strong international presence hold promise toward a vision of Walmart everywhere for everyone some day.

We like the growing cash returns and share buybacks (the company has returned some $68 billion to shareholders since 2010) and the dividend yield is increasingly attractive, rising 18 percent last year alone. Finally, we like the safety and low-volatility profile of both the business and the stock, as the long-term share-price chart and the beta of 0.43 would indicate.

Reasons for Caution

So far, the economic recovery has helped those at the upper end of the income ladder to a greater degree; Wal-Mart doesn't really serve there, at least yet. The company is very large, with few major growth vectors. We wouldn't want to see a major shopping spree in the acquisition market—so far, they've stayed out of that aisle. Its size may also make it difficult to manage, though today's management operates with near-military precision and does it well. Finally, despite its best efforts, and to a degree stretching the truth, the company is the butt of a lot of hyperbole and jibes about its working conditions, morale, tough terms for suppliers, and the clientele it serves—while shareholder returns are solid, the brand leaves something to be desired in the annals of favorite American brands.

SECTOR: Retail

BETA COEFFICIENT: 0.43

5-YEAR COMPOUND EARNINGS PER-SHARE GROWTH: 10.5%

10-YEAR COMPOUND DIVIDENDS PER-SHARE GROWTH: 18.0%

	2006	2007	2008	2009	2010	2011	2012	2013
Revenues (bil)	348.7	378.8	405.6	408.2	421.8	447.0	469.2	476.3
Net income (bil)	12.2	12.9	13.6	14.2	14.9	15.5	17.0	16.7
Earnings per share	2.92	3.16	3.42	3.66	4.07	4.45	5.02	5.11
Dividends per share	0.67	0.88	0.95	1.09	1.21	1.46	1.59	1.88
Cash flow per share	4.27	4.83	5.16	5.64	6.42	6.92	7.69	7.92
Price: high	52.2	51.4	63.8	57.5	56.3	60.0	77.6	81.4
low	42.3	42.1	43.1	46.3	47.8	48.3	57.2	67.7

Wal-Mart Stores, Inc.
702 S.W. 8th St.
Bentonville, AR 72716
(479) 273-4000
Website: www.Walmart.com

GROWTH AND INCOME

Waste Management, Inc.

Ticker symbol: WM (NYSE) □ S&P rating: BBB □ Value Line financial strength rating: A
Current yield: 3.6% □ Dividend raises, past 10 years: 10

Company Profile

You may refer to it as a "garbage company" if you want—we won't take offense. Waste Management is the largest and steadiest hand in the North American solid waste disposal industry. Like most large waste firms, WM has grown over time by assembling smaller, more local companies into a nationally branded and highly scaled operation with a notable amount of innovation on several fronts in the core business and especially in material recovery—translation, recycling.

The business is divided into three segments:

- Collection, which accounts for 61 percent of the business, includes the dumpster and garbage truck operations. The company has more than 600 collection operations, many of which have long-term contracts with municipalities and businesses. Innovations include a landfill-to-gas-liquefaction project that produces 13,000 gallons of fuel per day for WMI's trucks, online dumpster ordering, and the Bagster small scale disposal units now sold through retail home-improvement outlets.

For the 2,000 trucks that have been converted to compressed natural gas recovered from trash, the company estimates savings of 8,000 gallons of diesel fuel per truck per year with a 21 percent greenhouse gas reduction and reduced maintenance costs. The company perceives itself as a world-class logistics company (and why not?) and has equipped its trucks with the latest in onboard computers, centralized dispatching, and routing processes, saving some 4 percent in collections costs.

- Landfill (20 percent of revenues). The company operates 266 landfills across North America, servicing its own collection operations and other collection service providers. Among these sites, there are 137 landfill-gas-to-energy conversion projects producing fuel for electricity generation currently 1,400 megawatts of power, enough to power 1.1 million homes.
- Waste to energy, recycling and transfer (20 percent). These operations perform specialized material recovery and processing into useful commodities. There

are 345 transfer stations set up for the collection of various forms of waste, including medical, recyclables, and e-waste. A wholly owned subsidiary, Wheelabrator Technologies, operates 17 waste-to-energy plants and five electric-generating facilities producing electric power for about 1 million homes, in addition to the gasification projects at the landfills. The company has also pioneered single-stream recycling, where physical and optical sorting technologies sort out unseparated recyclable materials. Single-streaming has greatly increased recycling rates in municipalities where it is used and provides a steady revenue stream in recovered paper, glass, metals, etc., for the company. The company also further refines these materials into industrial inputs, e.g., glass or plastic feedstocks in certain colors. The company recycles 8 million tons of commodities annually and expects to grow that figure to 20 million by 2020.

Financial Highlights, Fiscal Year 2013

Results for FY2013 and into FY2014 continued to be hampered by a soft recycled material market, especially in the paper and cardboard sector, and some of its energy contracts were renewed at lower rates. Revenues posted another modest 2.5 percent gain in FY2013, while net profit rose 4 percent, which isn't so great considering it dropped 4 percent the prior year. Per-share earnings, too, rose a lackluster 3.5 percent in FY2013. FY2014 and beyond are shaping up to be a bit better, in part due to a 4 percent price increase in the disposal business, firming recycled paper and fiber business, and some restructuring savings—although this is offset somewhat by new restrictions on recycled material export to China, compliance with which will cost more. Revenues are projected to rise 2.6 percent in FY2014 and another 3.7 percent in FY2015, with per-share earnings up a more robust 10 percent in both years. Regular dividend increases should continue through this period and are well supported by cash flow.

Reasons to Buy

"Strategic" waste collection, particularly with the high-value-add material recovery operations that have become core to WM's business, will only become more important to all customers as time goes on.

WM exhibits great innovation in an industry not particularly known for it. Additionally, the 4 percent dividend and share repurchase efforts make up for a relatively unexciting stock performance over the years; we feel that WM could break out of the doldrums as material recovery becomes an even more strategic and profitable enterprise. In the past ten years, earnings have nearly doubled, while the share price is only up a third. The dividend has risen from 1 cent in 2003 to $1.50 expected in 2014 and the company has authorized $600 million in buybacks, reinvigorating a buyback program that had slowed recently but that has retired about 100 million shares, or close to 20 percent, in ten years. The company has clearly gotten the memo about shareholder returns. This among other considerations makes WM a relatively safe bet, and, with a beta of 0.62, is a "sleep at night" stock in an economic storm.

Reasons for Caution

The company does rely on acquisitions for a lot of its growth. In this business, that might not be so bad, for existing companies have captive markets and disposal facilities and can likely benefit from proven management processes and reduced overhead costs. The recycling operations, while cool and sexy, aren't always profitable, especially when competing material prices, like natural gas these days, are soft. The right combination of factors to drive improved recycling profitability may be close at hand or a ways off—you can have a clear environmental conscience (and collect your dividends) while you wait for better times. Additionally, any waste company runs the risk of going afoul of environmental regulations; WM has largely steered clear of trouble thus far, but there are no guarantees. Growth may be difficult to handle if regulations become more stringent.

SECTOR: **Business Services**
BETA COEFFICIENT: **0.62**
10-YEAR COMPOUND EARNINGS PER-SHARE GROWTH: **5.5%**
10 YEAR COMPOUND DIVIDENDS PER-SHARE GROWTH: **63.5%**

	2006	2007	2008	2009	2010	2011	2012	2013
Revenues (mil)	13,363	13,310	13,388	11,791	12,515	13,375	13,649	13,983
Net income (mil)	994	1,080	1,087	988	1,011	1,007	968	1,008
Earnings per share	1.82	2.07	2.19	2.00	2.10	2.14	2.08	2.15
Dividends per share	0.88	0.98	1.08	1.16	1.28	1.36	1.42	1.46
Cash flow per share	4.35	4.68	4.74	4.43	4.64	4.85	4.88	5.04
Price: high	35.6	41.2	39.3	34.2	37.3	36.7	36.3	46.4
low	30.1	32.4	24.5	22.1	31.1	27.8	30.8	33.7

Waste Management, Inc.
1001 Fannin, Suite 4000
Houston, TX 77002
(713) 512-6200
Website: *www.wm.com*

GROWTH AND INCOME

Wells Fargo & Company

Ticker symbol: WFC (NYSE) ▢ S&P rating: AA- ▢ Value Line financial strength rating: A ▢ Current yield: 2.4% ▢ Dividend raises, past 10 years: 7

Company Profile

Wells Fargo & Company is a diversified financial services company, providing banking, insurance, investments, mortgages, and consumer finance from more than 9,000 offices (more than any other bank) and other distribution channels, including mortgage, investment management, commercial banking, and consumer finance branches across all 50 states, Canada, the Caribbean, and Central America.

The business is divided into three segments. First and largest is Community Banking, which provides traditional banking and mortgage services in all 50 states through a combination of branches, ATMs, and online services. Wholesale Banking provides commercial banking, capital markets, leasing, and other financing services to larger corporations. Wealth, Brokerage, and Retirement provides financial advisory and investment management services to individuals.

As of 2013, Wells Fargo had $1.53 trillion in assets, loans of $811 billion, and shareholder equity of $170 billion (this latter figure is up almost 35 percent from the end of 2010, a sign of health). Based on assets, it is the third-largest bank holding company in the United States. The company expanded its footprint and market share—which is close to 10 percent of all U.S. banking services—considerably with the 2009 acquisition of Wachovia. It is currently making a big push into eastern U.S. markets, particularly the New York area. It also recently announced the opening of an Asset Management office in Paris, to add to an already sizeable international footprint with offices in some 35 countries. The company is also an innovation leader, for instance, with experiments with a new 1,000-square-foot "minibank" with personalized service and interactive technologies, and with large-screen ATMs and mobile banking which, it estimates, 11.9 million customers are using at present.

Financial Highlights, Fiscal Year 2013

Wells Fargo continues to rebound from the Great Recession more successfully than its larger brethren. Loan losses and nonperforming assets continue to drop, and the so-called "tier 1" ratio, a measure of equity to total assets, has improved from 8.3 percent in 2010 to 9.9 percent at the end of 2012 to 10.82 percent at the end of 2013, healthy by banking standards. The company also reported charge-offs for nonperforming assets of 0.47 percent compared to 1.36 percent in 2011; allowance for loan losses of 1.81 percent, down from 2.56 percent, and nonperforming assets down to 2.37 percent from 3.37 percent. In line with these numbers, the loan loss reserve has dropped from $15.7 billion at the end of 2010 to $2.3 billion at the end of 2013. These figures all deliver a picture of vastly improved financial health and asset quality, and we like the fact that the company presents these figures clearly on their "Investment Profile" page (*www.wellsfargo.com/invest_relations/investment_profile*).

These figures, while indicating health, also brought improved performance. Per-share earnings for FY2013 were $3.89, up a full 16 percent from FY2012, which was in turn up 19 percent from FY2011. The company raised its dividend substantially during the year, from 88 cents to $1.15 and expects both the financial means and the regulatory support to continue a march toward $2.00 by the end of the decade if not before. The company continues to buy back shares, retiring more than 110 million shares off of a 5.5 billion share base in FY2013—although this share count had been inflated dramatically with the 2009 Wachovia purchase. For FY2014 and beyond, it's probably right to say that the biggest steps in the recovery have already occurred, but the company does expect continued revenue and per-share earnings growth in the 4 percent range, with good cash returns to shareholders along the way.

Reasons to Buy

Wells Fargo has cleaned house with its Wachovia purchase, its mortgage lending, and other overhang from the financial crisis and has become more of a global brand and steady player in the consumer and commercial banking industry. We like its solid financial base, its growth in noninterest income (fees, etc.) that insulate it against possible interest rate hikes, and its reputation in the marketplace.

Especially as the macroeconomic environment improves, we think WFC is well positioned to take advantage. Shareholders will be rewarded with ample return in the form of share price appreciation, dividends, and buybacks as time goes on, although buybacks may attenuate in an effort to retain strong capital ratios—in this industry, that's not a bad thing.

Reasons for Caution

Headline risk continues to abound in the banking industry. Any sign of trouble on the mortgage front will obviously hurt, although recent settlements of litigation related to mortgage lending operations reduce this risk somewhat. Banking is a complex business—more complex than we like and hence our minimal inclusion of financial firms on the *100 Best Stocks* list; only the best, as they say. The changing interest rate landscape in the wake of Fed "tapering" is a bit hard to predict and may cause some short-term profitability hiccups as "wholesale" interest rates rise faster than "retail," but in the long term, the company is well positioned to handle any rise in interest rates and may even benefit from it.

SECTOR: Financials
BETA COEFFICIENT: 1.43
10-YEAR COMPOUND EARNINGS PER-SHARE GROWTH: 5.5%
10-YEAR COMPOUND DIVIDENDS PER-SHARE GROWTH: 11.5%

	2006	2007	2008	2009	2010	2011	2012	2013
Loans (bil)	306.9	344.8	843.8	758	734	750	783	811
Net income (mil)	8,480	8,060	2,655	12,275	11,632	15,025	17,999	20,889
Earnings per share	2.49	2.38	0.70	1.75	2.21	2.82	3.36	3.89
Dividends per share	1.12	1.18	1.30	0.49	0.20	0.48	0.88	1.15
Price: high	37.0	38.0	44.7	31.5	34.3	34.3	36.6	45.6
low	30.3	29.3	19.9	7.8	23.0	22.6	27.9	34.4

Wells Fargo & Company
420 Montgomery Street
San Francisco, CA 94104
(866) 878-5865
Website: *www.wellsfargo.com*

Whirlpool Corporation

Ticker symbol: WHR (NYSE) ❑ S&P rating: BBB- ❑ Value Line financial strength rating: A+
Current yield: 1.9% ❑ Dividend raises, past 10 years: 4

Company Profile

Whirlpool is the world's leading home appliance manufacturer in a $120 billion global industry. The company manufactures appliances under familiar and recognized brand names in all major home appliance categories including fabric care (laundry), cooking, refrigeration, dishwashers, water filtration, and garage organization. Familiar brand names include Whirlpool, Maytag, KitchenAid, Amana, Jenn-Air, Gladiator, and international names Bauknecht, Brastemp, and Consul. The Whirlpool brand itself is the number-one global appliance brand, and five of these brands, Whirlpool, Maytag, KitchenAid, Brastemp and Consul, generate over $1 billion in annual sales. About 46 percent of Whirlpool's sales come from overseas, a growth of 5 percent since 2008. Latin America has been the most dynamic player at 26 percent of sales, up from 19 percent in 2008.

In an industry not known for innovation, Whirlpool has striven to be an innovation leader in its industry. This has manifested itself both in new products and product platforms and in manufacturing and supply-chain efficiencies, such as a global platform design for local manufacture of washing machine products, recalling similar achievements in the auto industry. Such gains are key in this competitive, price-sensitive industry. The company also has initiatives to build lifetime brand loyalty and product quality, improve energy efficiency, and to expand in key developing markets such as Brazil (where the Brastemp brand is sold) and India. The company is the number-one appliance manufacturer in Latin America.

Financial Highlights, Fiscal Year 2013

The company rode the tailwinds of an improving economy, an improved replacement cycle for old units, improved demand for today's more efficient appliances, and operational improvements to a very successful FY2013 with a moderate 3.5 percent gain in revenues but a solid gain of 45 percent in net income. The operational improvements, higher product value add, and a gradual increase in premium brands have driven operating margins from the 6–8 percent range five years ago into the 10–12 percent range; these improvements look to be permanent.

The company expects these conditions to continue through FY2015, with an added bonus of a European recovery (the region has been a drag up until now). Revenue will stay on medium heat, up 3–5 percent annually, while per-share earnings, helped along by modest buybacks and continued steady margin improvements, are projected to stay on full boil in a predictable 15–22 percent growth range.

Reasons to Buy

Two years ago we added Whirlpool because we had a good feeling about the company, its management, its markets, and the health of the economy in general. We haven't been disappointed; the stock has almost tripled in two years—not bad.

Now we can add to the mix the fact that so many have put off basic appliance purchases for so long. What's more, if you shop for an appliance today—take washers and dryers, for example—they work better, they're more energy efficient, and more technology enabled. In short, they're better products, and guess what: They're more expensive and more profitable for the manufacturers, too. Operating margins have expanded from the 5–7 percent range to the 9–12 percent range in the past five years. We think some of their success is permanent, beyond the effects of a strong business cycle.

We like market leaders, particularly companies not content to sit on their laurels while others close in around them. Whirlpool used the recession and ensuing recovery as a wake-up call and an opportunity to streamline its businesses and to put some real strategic thought into how to drive its brand assortment and international portfolio to achieve better results.

The company continues to innovate toward better products and internal processes. We like their "Purposeful Innovation" motto. Long term, we see more opportunities to develop "smart" appliances, which can work together with smartphones and other residential management applications to deliver better, more energy-efficient results. Too, the company is building critical mass in overseas markets. Cash flows and investor returns are solid. More than most, the management team is a plus with a recognizable pragmatic and strategic approach to managing this business.

Reasons for Caution

By nature, the appliance business is highly competitive and cyclical. In addition, consumers with more disposable income have of late been opting for fancier, more expensive foreign brands, like Bosch and LG, a trend that could hurt if it continues. We believe that Whirlpool is countering this trend by adding elegance, advertising, and channel support for its top-tier brands and products; that plus a reversal of customer preferences toward American brands as seen to a degree in the auto industry should help. Commodity costs, labor issues, quality issues, and shifts in consumer preferences are perpetual risks. Finally, the share price has been on a roll and relatively less stable than others we review—you can see that in the high beta of 1.90. While there is little dirty laundry to be found in this story, the rapid rise makes this one of the more aggressive names in our *100 Best* portfolio.

SECTOR: **Consumer Durables**
BETA COEFFICIENT: **1.90**
10-YEAR COMPOUND EARNINGS PER-SHARE GROWTH: **4.0%**
10-YEAR COMPOUND DIVIDENDS PER-SHARE GROWTH: **2.5%**

	2006	2007	2008	2009	2010	2011	2012	2013
Revenues (mil)	18,080	19,408	18,907	17,099	18,366	18,666	18,143	18,768
Net income (mil)	486	647	418	328	707	699	559	810
Earnings per share	6.35	8.10	5.50	4.34	9.10	8.95	7.05	10.03
Dividends per share	1.72	1.72	1.72	1.72	1.72	1.93	2.00	2.38
Cash flow per share	13.26	16.32	13.90	11.37	16.91	16.54	14.05	17.53
Price: high	96.0	118.0	98.0	85.0	118.4	92.3	104.2	159.2
low	74.1	72.1	30.2	19.2	71.0	45.2	47.7	101.7

Whirlpool Corporation
2000 M-63
Benton Harbor, MI 49022-2692
(269) 923-5000
Website: *www.whirlpoolcorp.com*

▼ Appendix A: Performance Analysis: *100 Best Stocks* 2014

ONE YEAR GAIN/LOSS, APRIL 1, 2013–APRIL 1, 2014,

Excluding Dividends (*) = New for 2014

Company	Symbol	Price 4/1/2013	Price 4/1/2014	% change	Dollar gain/loss, $1000 invested
3M	MMM	$103.93	$136.53	31.4%	$313.67
Abbott	ABT	$34.70	$38.47	10.9%	$108.65
Aetna	AET	$50.47	$75.05	48.7%	$487.02
Allergan	AGN	$111.41	$123.74	11.1%	$110.67
Amgen	AMGN	$100.69	$126.07	25.2%	$252.06
Apple	AAPL	$431.74	$541.65	25.5%	$254.57
Aqua America (*)	WTR	$24.79	$25.14	1.4%	$14.12
Archer Daniels Midland	ADM	$33.02	$43.43	31.5%	$315.26
AT&T	T	$34.86	$35.09	0.7%	$6.60
Automatic Data Processing	ADP	$63.45	$77.50	22.1%	$221.43
Baxter	BAX	$70.69	$73.67	4.2%	$42.16
Becton, Dickinson	BDX	$93.73	$117.26	25.1%	$251.04
Bemis (*)	BMS	$39.32	$39.72	1.0%	$10.17
Campbell Soup	CPB	$44.40	$44.56	0.4%	$3.60
CarMax	KMX	$41.70	$47.50	13.9%	$139.09
Chevron	CVX	$114.91	$119.00	3.6%	$35.59
Church & Dwight	CHD	$63.47	$68.56	8.0%	$80.20
Cincinnati Financial	CINF	$45.67	$47.83	4.7%	$47.30
Clorox Company	CLX	$85.79	$87.91	2.5%	$24.71
Coca-Cola	KO	$39.28	$38.41	-2.2%	$(22.15)
Colgate-Palmolive	CL	$58.73	$64.22	9.3%	$93.48
Comcast	CMCSA	$40.59	$49.93	23.0%	$230.11
ConocoPhillips	COP	$57.66	$70.31	21.9%	$219.39
Corning (*)	GLW	$13.01	$20.97	61.2%	$611.84
Costco Wholesale	COST	$104.99	$111.86	6.5%	$65.43
CVS Caremark	CVS	$54.14	$74.29	37.2%	$372.18
Deere	DE	$83.97	$91.39	8.8%	$88.36
Dominion Resources	D	$56.06	$70.40	25.6%	$255.80
Duke Energy	DUK	$69.49	$70.67	1.7%	$16.98
DuPont	DD	$47.71	$67.76	42.0%	$420.25

Company	Symbol	Price 4/1/2013	Price 4/1/2014	% change	Dollar gain/loss, $1000 invested
Eastman Chemical	EMN	$68.70	$86.12	25.4%	$253.57
Fair Isaac	FICO	$45.62	$56.28	23.4%	$233.67
FedEx	FDX	$97.70	$134.11	37.3%	$372.67
Fluor Corporation	FLR	$65.69	$77.51	18.0%	$179.94
FMC Corporation	FMC	$56.58	$77.32	36.7%	$366.56
General Mills	GIS	$47.84	$51.78	8.2%	$82.36
Harman International	HAR	$44.01	$111.58	153.5%	$1,535.33
Health Care REIT (*)	HCN	$64.69	$59.72	-7.7%	$(76.83)
Honeywell	HON	$73.85	$93.26	26.3%	$262.83
IBM	IBM	$208.97	$194.50	-6.9%	$(69.24)
Illinois Tool Works	ITW	$59.65	$82.20	37.8%	$378.04
International Paper	IP	$45.31	$45.86	1.2%	$12.14
Iron Mountain	IRM	$34.85	$27.84	-20.1%	$(201.15)
Itron	ITRI	$46.40	$35.82	-22.8%	$(228.02)
J.M. Smucker	SJM	$97.03	$97.14	0.1%	$1.13
Johnson & Johnson	JNJ	$79.19	$97.94	23.7%	$236.77
Johnson Controls	JCI	$34.42	$48.21	40.1%	$400.64
Kellogg	K	$62.65	$62.62	0.0%	$(0.48)
Kimberly-Clark	KMB	$95.58	$109.04	14.1%	$140.82
Kroger (*)	KR	$32.59	$43.62	33.8%	$338.45
Macy's	M	$41.02	$59.51	45.1%	$450.76
McCormick & Co.	MKC	$72.07	$71.62	-0.6%	$(6.24)
McDonald's	MCD	$96.49	$97.90	1.5%	$14.61
McKesson	MCK	$107.25	$176.04	64.1%	$641.40
Medtronic	MDT	$45.95	$61.61	34.1%	$340.81
Molex	MOLX	$28.86	$38.68	34.0%	$340.26
Monsanto	MON	$104.02	$113.99	9.6%	$95.85
Mosaic	MOS	$58.48	$49.80	-14.8%	$(148.43)
NextEra Energy	NEE	$75.19	$94.86	26.2%	$261.60
Nike	NKE	$58.26	$74.39	27.7%	$276.86
Norfolk Southern	NSC	$75.15	$98.08	30.5%	$305.12
Otter Tail Corporation	OTTR	$29.91	$30.87	3.2%	$32.10

Company	Symbol	Price 4/1/2013	Price 4/1/2014	% change	Dollar gain/loss, $1000 invested
Pall Corporation	PLL	$67.41	$90.78	34.7%	$346.68
Patterson	PDCO	$37.42	$42.13	12.6%	$125.87
Paychex	PAYX	$34.18	$42.50	24.3%	$243.42
PepsiCo	PEP	$78.09	$82.88	6.1%	$61.34
Perrigo	PRGO	$119.07	$158.32	33.0%	$329.64
Praxair	PX	$109.32	$131.82	20.6%	$205.82
Procter & Gamble	PG	$74.77	$80.34	7.4%	$74.50
Quest Diagnostics (*)	DGX	$55.60	$60.65	9.1%	$90.83
Ross Stores	ROST	$60.00	$72.90	21.5%	$215.00
Schlumberger	SLB	$73.69	$97.96	32.9%	$329.35
Seagate Technology	STX	$35.25	$57.00	61.7%	$617.02
Sigma-Aldrich	SIAL	$76.87	$94.59	23.1%	$230.52
Southern Company	SO	$44.78	$43.50	-2.9%	$(28.58)
Southwest Airlines	LUV	$13.35	$23.94	79.3%	$793.26
St. Jude Medical	STJ	$39.70	$66.63	67.8%	$678.34
Starbucks	SBUX	$56.20	$74.01	31.7%	$316.90
State Street Corp (*)	STT	$58.40	$69.57	19.1%	$191.27
Stryker Corporation	SYK	$54.21	$81.88	51.0%	$510.42
Suburban Propane	SPH	$41.32	$42.01	1.7%	$16.70
Sysco	SYY	$34.03	$36.11	6.1%	$61.12
Target Corporation	TGT	$66.73	$60.57	-9.2%	$(92.31)
Tiffany	TIF	$69.42	$88.66	27.7%	$277.15
Time Warner	TWX	$56.55	$66.03	16.8%	$167.64
Total S.A.	TOT	$45.40	$66.00	45.4%	$453.74
Tractor Supply	TSCO	$53.15	$71.72	34.9%	$349.39
Union Pacific	UNP	$139.68	$188.44	34.9%	$349.08
UnitedHealth Group	UNH	$56.33	$81.84	45.3%	$452.87
United Parcel Service	UPS	$83.58	$97.34	16.5%	$164.63
United Technologies	UTX	$91.48	$117.92	28.9%	$289.02
Valero	VLO	$40.71	$55.51	36.4%	$363.55
Valmont Industries	VMI	$156.19	$150.90	-3.4%	$(33.87)
Verizon	VZ	$47.10	$47.75	1.4%	$13.80
Visa	V	$168.57	$214.70	27.4%	$273.65

Company	Symbol	Price 4/1/2013	Price 4/1/2014	% change	Dollar gain/loss, $1000 invested
W.W. Grainger	GWW	$221.68	$255.37	15.2%	$151.98
Wal-Mart (*)	WMT	$73.81	$79.77	8.1%	$80.75
Waste Management	WM	$37.86	$41.93	10.8%	$107.50
Wells Fargo	WFC	$36.95	$49.77	34.7%	$346.96
Whirlpool	WHR	$116.25	$153.30	31.9%	$318.71

▼ Appendix B: The *100 Best Stocks* 2015, Dividend and Yield, by Company (*) = New

Company	Symbol	2013 Dividend	2013 Yield %	2014 PROJECTED Dividend	2014 PROJECTED Yield %	Dividend Raises, Past 10 Years
3M Company	MMM	$2.54	1.8%	$3.44	2.5%	10
Aetna	AET	$0.80	1.4%	$0.88	1.2%	3
Allergan	AGN	$0.20	0.2%	$0.20	0.2%	1
Allstate*	ALL			$1.12	1.9%	6
Apple	AAPL	$11.65	2.6%	$13.16	2.3%	2
Aqua America	WTR	$0.60	2.2%	$0.60	2.4%	10
Archer Daniels Midland	ADM	$0.76	2.2%	$0.97	2.2%	10
AT&T	T	$1.80	4.7%	$1.84	5.2%	10
Becton, Dickinson	BDX	$1.98	2.0%	$2.20	1.9%	10
Bemis	BMS	$1.04	2.6%	$1.44	2.7%	10
Campbell Soup	CPB	$1.16	2.5%	$1.24	2.8%	9
Carmax	KMX					
Chevron	CVX	$3.76	3.2%	$4.28	3.3%	10
Clorox Company	CLX	$2.61	3.0%	$2.74	3.4%	10
Coca-Cola	KO	$1.12	2.6%	$1.24	3.0%	10
Colgate-Palmolive	CL	$2.66	2.3%	$1.44	2.2%	10
Comcast	CMCSA	$0.78	1.8%	$0.88	1.8%	4
ConocoPhillips	COP	$2.64	4.2%	$2.76	3.6%	10
Corning	GLW	$0.40	2.7%	$0.40	1.9%	4
Costco Wholesale	COST	$1.14	1.1%	$1.40	1.2%	10

▼ Appendix B: The *100 Best Stocks* 2015, Dividend and Yield, by Company (cont.)

Company	Symbol	Dividend	Yield %	Dividend	Yield %	Dividend Raises, Past 10 Years
CVS Caremark	CVS	$0.90	1.5%	$1.12	1.5%	10
Daktronics*	DAKT			$0.40	3.1%	6
Deere	DE	$1.84	2.2%	$2.40	2.3%	10
Devon Energy*	DVN			$0.96	1.3%	7
DuPont	DD	$1.76	3.3%	$1.80	2.7%	6
Eastman Chemical	EMN	$1.20	1.8%	$1.40	1.8%	5
Fair Isaac	FICO	$0.08	0.2%	$0.08	0.1%	1
FedEx	FDX	$0.56	0.6%	$0.60	0.4%	10
Fluor Corporation	FLR	$0.64	1.0%	$0.84	1.1%	3
FMC Corporation	FMC	$0.54	0.9%	$0.60	0.8%	7
General Electric*	GE			$0.88	3.3%	8
General Mills	GIS	$1.32	3.0%	$1.64	3.1%	9
Harman International	HAR	$0.60	1.2%	$1.20	1.1%	2
Health Care REIT	HCN	$3.06	4.1%	$3.20	5.4%	10
Honeywell	HON	$1.67	2.1%	$0.45	1.9%	8
IBM	IBM	$3.55	1.9%	$4.40	2.0%	10
Illinois Tool Works	ITW	$1.52	2.3%	$1.68	2.1%	10
Itron	ITRI					
J.M. Smucker	SJM	$2.08	2.0%	$2.32	2.4%	10
Johnson & Johnson	JNJ	$2.56	3.1%	$2.80	2.8%	10
Johnson Controls	JCI	$0.76	2.1%	$0.88	1.9%	9
Kellogg	K	$1.76	2.7%	$1.84	2.7%	10
Kimberly-Clark	KMB	$3.08	3.1%	$3.36	3.0%	10
Kroger	KR	$0.65	1.7%	$0.68	1.8%	7
Macy's	M	$0.85	1.7%	$1.24	1.8%	6
McCormick & Co.	MKC	$1.36	1.9%	$1.48	2.1%	10
McDonald's	MCD	$3.15	3.0%	$3.24	3.4%	10
McKesson	MCK	$0.96	0.7%	$0.96	0.5%	5
Medtronic	MDT	$1.12	2.2%	$1.12	1.9%	10
Microchip Technology*	MCHP			$1.44	3.0%	10

Company	Symbol	Dividend	Yield %	Dividend	Yield %	Dividend Raises, Past 10 Years
Monsanto	MON	$1.50	1.4%	$1.72	1.5%	9
Mosaic	MOS	$1.00	1.6%	$1.00	2.1%	3
NextEra Energy	NEE	$2.60	3.2%	$2.92	3.1%	10
Nike	NKE	$0.81	1.3%	$0.96	1.3%	10
Norfolk Southern	NSC	$2.00	2.6%	$2.16	2.3%	10
Oracle*	ORCL			$0.48	1.4%	3
Otter Tail Corporation	OTTR	$1.20	3.9%	$1.20	4.1%	5
Pall Corporation	PLL	$0.88	1.5%	$1.12	1.3%	9
Patterson	PDCO	$0.66	1.7%	$0.80	2.0%	4
Paychex	PAYX	$1.27	3.6%	$1.40	3.3%	8
PepsiCo	PEP	$2.21	2.7%	$2.60	3.6%	10
Perrigo	PRGO	$0.34	0.3%	$0.42	0.3%	10
Philips N.V.*	PHG			$0.93	3.5%	6
Praxair	PX	$2.40	2.1%	$2.60	2.0%	10
Procter & Gamble	PG	$2.29	3.1%	$2.56	3.2%	10
Public Storage*	PSA			$5.60	3.3%	8
Quest Diagnostics	DGX	$1.20	2.1%	$1.32	2.2%	5
Ralph Lauren*	RL			$1.80	1.2%	5
ResMed*	RMD			$1.00	2.0%	1
Ross Stores	ROST	$0.64	1.0%	$8.00	1.2%	10
Schlumberger	SLB	$1.25	1.6%	$1.60	1.6%	8
Schnitzer Steel*	SCHN			$0.75	2.8%	3
Scotts Miracle-Gro*	SMG			$1.75	3.0%	5
Seagate Technology	STX	$1.40	3.6%	$1.72	3.3%	8
Sigma-Aldrich	SIAL	$0.86	1.1%	$0.92	1.0%	10
Southern Company	SO	$2.02	4.3%	$2.10	4.7%	10
Southwest Airlines	LUV	$0.04	0.3%	$0.24	0.7%	3
St. Jude Medical	STJ	$1.00	2.4%	$1.08	1.7%	3
Starbucks	SBUX	$0.84	1.4%	$1.04	1.4%	3
State Street Corp	STT	$1.04	1.7%	$1.20	1.5%	8
Steelcase*	SCS			$0.42	2.6%	7
Stryker Corporation	SYK	$1.06	1.6%	$1.22	1.5%	9

▼ Appendix B: The *100 Best Stocks* 2015, Dividend and Yield, by Company (cont.)

Company	Symbol	Dividend	Yield %	Dividend	Yield %	Dividend Raises, Past 10 Years
Sysco	SYY	$1.12	3.3%	$1.16	3.2%	10
Target Corporation	TGT	$1.50	2.0%	$1.72	2.8%	10
Tiffany	TIF	$1.28	1.7%	$1.74	1.6%	10
Time Warner	TWX	$1.08	1.9%	$1.27	1.9%	8
Total S.A.	TOT	$3.15	5.5%	$3.35	4.8%	7
Union Pacific	UNP	$2.78	1.8%	$3.64	2.0%	9
UnitedHealth Group	UNH	$0.85	1.4%	$1.12	1.4%	4
United Parcel Service	UPS	$2.48	2.8%	$2.68	2.8%	10
United Technologies	UTX	$2.03	2.3%	$2.38	2.4%	10
Valero	VLO	$0.80	2.1%	$1.00	1.9%	9
Valmont Industries	VMI	$0.86	0.7%	$1.50	0.7%	10
Verizon	VZ	$2.06	3.9%	$2.12	4.5%	8
Visa	V	$1.32	0.7%	$1.60	0.7%	5
W.W. Grainger	GWW	$3.35	1.5%	$4.32	1.7%	10
Wal-Mart	WMT	$1.88	2.4%	$1.92	2.4%	10
Waste Management	WM	$1.46	3.5%	$1.92	3.6%	10
Wells Fargo	WFC	$1.00	3.1%	$1.40	2.4%	7
Whirlpool	WHR	$2.00	2.0%	$3.00	1.9%	4

▼ Appendix C: The *100 Best Stocks* 2015, Dividend and Yield, by Descending Projected 2014 Yield (*) = New

Company	Symbol	2013 Dividend	Yield %	2014 PROJECTED Dividend	Yield %	Dividend Raises, Past 10 Years
Health Care REIT	HCN	$3.06	4.1%	$3.20	5.4%	10
AT&T	T	$1.80	4.7%	$1.84	5.2%	10
Total S.A.	TOT	$3.15	5.5%	$3.35	4.8%	7
Southern Company	SO	$2.02	4.3%	$2.10	4.7%	10
Verizon	VZ	$2.06	3.9%	$2.12	4.5%	8
Otter Tail Corporation	OTTR	$1.20	3.9%	$1.20	4.1%	5
ConocoPhillips	COP	$2.64	4.2%	$2.76	3.6%	10
PepsiCo	PEP	$2.21	2.7%	$2.60	3.6%	10

Company	Symbol	Dividend	Yield %	Dividend	Yield %	Dividend Raises, Past 10 Years
Waste Management	WM	$1.46	3.5%	$1.92	3.6%	10
Philips N.V.*	PHG			$0.93	3.5%	6
Clorox Company	CLX	$2.61	3.0%	$2.74	3.4%	10
McDonald's	MCD	$3.15	3.0%	$3.24	3.4%	10
Chevron	CVX	$3.76	3.2%	$4.28	3.3%	10
General Electric*	GE			$0.88	3.3%	8
Paychex	PAYX	$1.27	3.6%	$1.40	3.3%	8
Public Storage*	PSA			$5.60	3.3%	8
Seagate Technology	STX	$1.40	3.6%	$1.72	3.3%	8
Procter & Gamble	PG	$2.29	3.1%	$2.56	3.2%	10
Sysco	SYY	$1.12	3.3%	$1.16	3.2%	10
Daktronics*	DAKT			$0.40	3.1%	6
General Mills	GIS	$1.32	3.0%	$1.64	3.1%	9
NextEra Energy	NEE	$2.60	3.2%	$2.92	3.1%	10
Coca-Cola	KO	$1.12	2.6%	$1.24	3.0%	10
Kimberly-Clark	KMB	$3.08	3.1%	$3.36	3.0%	10
Microchip Technology*	MCHP			$1.44	3.0%	10
Scotts Miracle-Gro*	SMG			$1.75	3.0%	5
Campbell Soup	CPB	$1.16	2.5%	$1.24	2.8%	9
Johnson & Johnson	JNJ	$2.56	3.1%	$2.80	2.8%	10
Schnitzer Steel*	SCHN			$0.75	2.8%	3
Target Corporation	TGT	$1.50	2.0%	$1.72	2.8%	10
United Parcel Service	UPS	$2.48	2.8%	$2.68	2.8%	10
Bemis	BMS	$1.04	2.6%	$1.44	2.7%	10
DuPont	DD	$1.76	3.3%	$1.80	2.7%	6
Kellogg	K	$1.76	2.7%	$1.84	2.7%	10
Steelcase*	SCS			$0.42	2.6%	7
3M Company	MMM	$2.54	1.8%	$3.44	2.5%	10
Aqua America	WTR	$0.60	2.2%	$0.60	2.4%	10
J.M. Smucker	SJM	$2.08	2.0%	$2.32	2.4%	10
United Technologies	UTX	$2.03	2.3%	$2.38	2.4%	10

▼ **Appendix C: The 100 Best Stocks 2015, Dividend and Yield, by Descending Projected 2014 Yield (cont.)**

Company	Symbol	Dividend	Yield %	Dividend	Yield %	Dividend Raises, Past 10 Years
Wal-Mart	WMT	$1.88	2.4%	$1.92	2.4%	10
Wells Fargo	WFC	$1.00	3.1%	$1.40	2.4%	7
Apple	AAPL	$11.65	2.6%	$13.16	2.3%	2
Deere	DE	$1.84	2.2%	$2.40	2.3%	10
Norfolk Southern	NSC	$2.00	2.6%	$2.16	2.3%	10
Archer Daniels Midland	ADM	$0.76	2.2%	$0.97	2.2%	10
Colgate-Palmolive	CL	$2.66	2.3%	$1.44	2.2%	10
Quest Diagnostics	DGX	$1.20	2.1%	$1.32	2.2%	5
Illinois Tool Works	ITW	$1.52	2.3%	$1.68	2.1%	10
McCormick & Co.	MKC	$1.36	1.9%	$1.48	2.1%	10
Mosaic	MOS	$1.00	1.6%	$1.00	2.1%	3
IBM	IBM	$3.55	1.9%	$4.40	2.0%	10
Patterson	PDCO	$0.66	1.7%	$0.80	2.0%	4
Praxair	PX	$2.40	2.1%	$2.60	2.0%	10
ResMed*	RMD			$1.00	2.0%	1
Union Pacific	UNP	$2.78	1.8%	$3.64	2.0%	9
Allstate*	ALL			$1.12	1.9%	6
Becton, Dickinson	BDX	$1.98	2.0%	$2.20	1.9%	10
Corning	GLW	$0.40	2.7%	$0.40	1.9%	4
Honeywell	HON	$1.67	2.1%	$0.45	1.9%	8
Johnson Controls	JCI	$0.76	2.1%	$0.88	1.9%	9
Medtronic	MDT	$1.12	2.2%	$1.12	1.9%	10
Time Warner	TWX	$1.08	1.9%	$1.27	1.9%	8
Valero	VLO	$0.80	2.1%	$1.00	1.9%	9
Whirlpool	WHR	$2.00	2.0%	$3.00	1.9%	4
Comcast	CMCSA	$0.78	1.8%	$0.88	1.8%	4
Eastman Chemical	EMN	$1.20	1.8%	$1.40	1.8%	5
Kroger	KR	$0.65	1.7%	$0.68	1.8%	7
Macy's	M	$0.85	1.7%	$1.24	1.8%	6
W.W. Grainger	GWW	$3.35	1.5%	$4.32	1.7%	10

Company	Symbol	Dividend	Yield %	Dividend	Yield %	Dividend Raises, Past 10 Years
St. Jude Medical	STJ	$1.00	2.4%	$1.08	1.7%	3
Schlumberger	SLB	$1.25	1.6%	$1.60	1.6%	8
Tiffany	TIF	$1.28	1.7%	$1.74	1.6%	10
CVS Caremark	CVS	$0.90	1.5%	$1.12	1.5%	10
Monsanto	MON	$1.50	1.4%	$1.72	1.5%	9
State Street Corp	STT	$1.04	1.7%	$1.20	1.5%	8
Stryker Corporation	SYK	$1.06	1.6%	$1.22	1.5%	9
Oracle*	ORCL			$0.48	1.4%	3
Starbucks	SBUX	$0.84	1.4%	$1.04	1.4%	3
UnitedHealth Group	UNH	$0.85	1.4%	$1.12	1.4%	4
Pall Corporation	PLL	$0.88	1.5%	$1.12	1.3%	9
Devon Energy*	DVN			$0.96	1.3%	7
Nike	NKE	$0.81	1.3%	$0.96	1.3%	10
Ralph Lauren*	RL			$1.80	1.2%	5
Aetna	AET	$0.80	1.4%	$0.88	1.2%	3
Costco Wholesale	COST	$1.14	1.1%	$1.40	1.2%	10
Ross Stores	ROST	$0.64	1.0%	$8.00	1.2%	10
Fluor Corporation	FLR	$0.64	1.0%	$0.84	1.1%	3
Harman International	HAR	$0.60	1.2%	$1.20	1.1%	2
Sigma-Aldrich	SIAL	$0.86	1.1%	$0.92	1.0%	10
FMC Corporation	FMC	$0.54	0.9%	$0.60	0.8%	7
Southwest Airlines	LUV	$0.04	0.3%	$0.24	0.7%	3
Valmont Industries	VMI	$0.86	0.7%	$1.50	0.7%	10
Visa	V	$1.32	0.7%	$1.60	0.7%	5
McKesson	MCK	$0.96	0.7%	$0.96	0.5%	5
FedEx	FDX	$0.56	0.6%	$0.60	0.4%	10
Perrigo	PRGO	$0.34	0.3%	$0.42	0.3%	10
Allergan	AGN	$0.20	0.2%	$0.20	0.2%	1
Fair Isaac	FICO	$0.08	0.2%	$0.08	0.1%	1
Carmax	KMX					0
Itron	ITRI					0

About the Authors

Peter Sander (Granite Bay, CA) is an author, researcher, and consultant in the fields of personal finance, business, and location reference. He has written forty-one books, including *All About Low Volatility Investing*, *Value Investing for Dummies*, *The 100 Best Exchange-Traded Funds You Can Buy 2012*, *The 25 Habits of Highly Successful Investors*, *What Would Steve Jobs Do?*, *101 Things Everyone Should Know about Economics*, and *Cities Ranked & Rated*. He is also the author of numerous articles and columns on investment strategies. He has an MBA from Indiana University and has completed Certified Financial Planner (CFP®) education and examination requirements.

Scott Bobo (San Jose, CA) has an engineering degree from Miami University. After beginning his career in the defense electronics industry and teaching at the University of Cincinnati, he moved on to the computer and semiconductor industries in California, later specializing in audio and applications engineering in a twenty-plus year career. He is now a Tax Director for one of the world's largest software companies and continues to teach, write, and consult on technology issues for private and corporate clients.

Currently available from Value Line for individual investors

The Value Line Investment Survey

Value Line's signature publication is one of the most highly regarded comprehensive investment research resources. Published weekly, it tracks approximately 1,700 stocks in more than 90 industries and ranks stocks on Timeliness™ and Safety™.

The Value Line Investment Survey—Small & Mid-Cap

The Small and Mid Cap Survey applies Value Line's data and analysis protocols to a universe of 1,800-plus companies with market values from less than $1 billion up to $5 billion.

Value Line Savvy Investor

The Internet counterpart of the preceding two Surveys, Savvy Investor includes every one of our 3,500 reports plus constant updates during Stock Exchange hours.

The Value Line 600

Provides Value Line Investment Survey reports on 600 large, actively traded, and widely held U.S. exchange-listed corporations, including many foreign firms, spanning over 90 industries.

Value Line Select

Once a month, subscribers receive a detailed report by Value Line senior analysts, recommending the one stock that has the best upside and risk/reward ratio.

Value Line Dividend Select

A monthly, in-depth report recommending one dividend paying stock, providing extensive information about the company's finances, prospects, and projected earnings, along with follow-up on numerous alternate selections.

The Value Line Special Situations Service

The Value Line Special Situations Service is designed for those seeking investment ideas in the small-cap arena, with both aggressive and conservative selections.

A special 30-day trial of Value Line's Savvy Investor is available to individual investors with the code "100STOCKS" at *www.valueline.com/100STOCKS*.

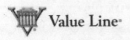 Value Line®

485 Lexington Avenue, 9th FL, New York, NY 10017
www.valueline.com

1-800-VALUELINE